*Gay American Novels,
1870–1970*

ALSO BY DREWEY WAYNE GUNN

*Gay Novels of Britain, Ireland and the Commonwealth,
1881–1981: A Reader's Guide* (McFarland, 2014)

Gay American Novels, 1870–1970
A Reader's Guide

Drewey Wayne Gunn

McFarland & Company, Inc., Publishers
Jefferson, North Carolina

All royalties from the sale of this volume
will go to purchasing books
for the Drewey Wayne Gunn Donation of Lesbian Literature
at the James C. Jernigan Library,
Texas A&M University–Kingsville.

LIBRARY OF CONGRESS CATALOGUING-IN-PUBLICATION DATA

Names: Gunn, Drewey Wayne, 1939– author.
Title: Gay American novels, 1870–1970 : a reader's guide /
Drewey Wayne Gunn.
Description: Jefferson, North Carolina : McFarland & Company, Inc.,
Publishers, 2016. | Includes bibliographical references and index.
Identifiers: LCCN 2015050180 | ISBN 9780786499052
(softcover : acid free paper) ∞
Subjects: LCSH: Gays' writings, American—History and criticism. |
American fiction—19th century—History and criticism. | American
fiction—20th—History and criticism. | American fiction—19th
century—Stories, plots, etc. | American fiction—20th century—
Stories, plots, etc. | Gay men in literature. | Bisexuality in literature.
Classification: LCC PS153.G38 G86 2016 | DDC 810.9/920664—dc23
LC record available at http://lccn.loc.gov/2015050180

BRITISH LIBRARY CATALOGUING DATA ARE AVAILABLE

ISBN (print) 978-0-7864-9905-2
ISBN (ebook) 978-1-4766-2522-5

© 2016 Drewey Wayne Gunn. All rights reserved

*No part of this book may be reproduced or transmitted in any form
or by any means, electronic or mechanical, including photocopying
or recording, or by any information storage and retrieval system,
without permission in writing from the publisher.*

Front cover image © 2016 iStock

Manufactured in the United States of America

*McFarland & Company, Inc., Publishers
Box 611, Jefferson, North Carolina 28640
www.mcfarlandpub.com*

Contents

Authors by Entry Number
vii

Introduction
1

The Novels
5

Postscript: Novels 1971–1981
183

General Bibliography
187

Index
189

Authors by Entry Number

1. Bayard Taylor; Frederick Loring
2. Alan Dale (Alfred J. Cohen)
3. Charles Warren Stoddard
4. Edward Prime Stevenson (as Xavier Mayne)
5. George Sylvester Viereck
6. Henry Blake Fuller; Sherwood Anderson
7. Carl Van Vechten; Joseph Moncure March
8. Clarkson Crane
9. Robert McAlmon; Robert Sculley
10. Benjamin Musser
11. Claude McKay; Wallace Thurman
12. Charles Brackett
13. Myron Brinig
14. Dashiell Hammett; Raymond Chandler
15. John Dos Passos
16. Blair Niles
17. Andre Tellier
18. Bradford Ropes; Fitzroy Davis
19. Forman Brown (as Richard Meeker)
20. Rex Stout
21. Kennilworth Bruce
22. Charles Henri Ford and Parker Tyler; Djuna Barnes
23. Edgar Calmer
24. Lew Levenson; Daphne Greenwood
25. Harold S. Kahm (aka Jerry Cole)
26. Alan Campbell (as Arion)
27. Elliot Paul
28. Carson McCullers
29. Harlan McIntosh
30. Charles Jackson
31. Ross Macdonald (Kenneth Millar); Margaret Millar
32. William Maxwell
33. Kenneth Fearing; Carley Mills
34. Alfred Hayes; Calder Willingham
35. Willard Motley
36. Gordon Merrick
37. John Horne Burns; Vance Bourjaily; A. M. P. Statton
38. Gore Vidal; Hugh Wheeler
39. Norman Mailer
40. Truman Capote; Speed Lamkin
41. Hubert Creekmore; Thomas Hal Phillips; William Faulkner
42. Klaus Mann; Marguerite Yourcenar
43. Nial Kent
44. Ward Thomas (Edward T. McNamara)
45. Michael de Forrest; Harrison Dowd
46. Isabel Bolton; Grace Zaring Stone
47. Eugene MacCown
48. James Barr (James Barr Fugaté)
49. Loren Wahl (Lorenzo Magdalena); Martin Dibner; Dennis Murphy
50. Edward Ronns (Edward S. Aarons); David Karp; Gerald Sykes; Allen Drury
51. Theodora Keogh; Vin Packer (Marijane Meaker); Patricia Highsmith
52. George Sklar
53. Paul Goodman
54. Fritz Peters; Gerald Tesch
55. Russell Thacher; Ralph Leveridge; Jim Barbee; Marc Rivette
56. Jay Little
57. Chester Himes; Christopher Teale
58. Mary MacLaren; Alexander Randolph; Deborah Deutsch
59. John Goodwin; John Cromwell
60. John Lee Weldon; Flannery O'Connor
61. John Selby
62. Christopher Isherwood
63. Edmund Schiddel
64. Richard McKaye (Richard K. Brunner); Marietta Wolff; Pamela Moore; Walter Ross; Ronn Marvin; Richard Sale; Gavin Lambert
65. Lonnie Coleman

66. Patrick Dennis
67. James Baldwin
68. Mary Orr; Roy Doliner; Basil Burwell; Russell O'Neil
69. Milton Rebow
70. David Stacton; Robert B. Asprey
71. William Talsman
72. Herbert D. Kastle
73. Reginald Harvey
74. Ben Travis
75. Martin Mayer
76. William S. Burroughs; Alexander Trocchi; Irving Rosenthal
77. Alexander Fedoroff
78. Donald Windham
79. Julian Green
80. Thomas Doremus
81. Lou Rand Hogan (as Lou Rand); William Gingerich
82. David Loovis; Susan Sontag
83. Roger Davis; Charles Wright; Joe Leon Houston; Alexander Goodman (George Haimsohn); Seth Young
84. Vladimir Nabokov
85. Paul Mandel; Roderick Thorp
86. Thomas Baird
87. John Rechy
88. Burt Blechmann
89. Hubert Selby, Jr.
90. Edwin Fey
91. William Goldman
92. R. V. Cassill
93. K. B. Raul
94. R. McCoy
95. James H. Ramp
96. Joseph Hansen
97. James Leo Herlihy; Richard Miles; Dotson Rader
98. Sanford Friedman; Bernard Malamud
99. Casimir Dukahz
100. Tennessee Williams
101. Tom Lockwood
102. Frederic Prokosch
103. Samuel R. Delany
104. George Baxt
105. Victor J. Banis; A. Jay
106. Richard Amory; Ricardo Armory
107. Kyle Onstott and Lance Horner; Frank Yerby
108. Don Carpenter; Malcolm Braly
109. James Purdy
110. Alfred Chester
111. Robert Somerlott
112. Bruce King (Avery Willard)
113. Nathaniel Burt
114. John Coriolan
115. James Kirkwood
116. Ursula Zilinsky
117. Ronald Tavel
118. Peter Menegas
119. Samuel M. Steward (as Phil Andros)
120. Frank Newman (Sam Abrams); Angelo d'Arcangelo (Josef Bush)
121. William Carney; Dirk Vanden; Larry Townsend
122. Stephen Koch
123. John Donovan
124. Hunce Voelcker
125. Hadrian Keene
126. Dennis Selby
127. Jeff Lawton
128. Bruce Benderson
129. David Plante
130. Andrew Blumley
131. John Weitz
132. William Harrington
133. Gerald Walker; Donald E. Westlake (as Tucker Coe)

INTRODUCTION

There have been three previous surveys of the territory covered in this guide: by Georges-Michel Sarotte, Roger Austen, and James Levin. Why do we need another? For starters, 78 of the 257 novels here appear in none of them. Some of the omissions startle (Dashiell Hammett, Wallace Thurman, Samuel Delany, Ursula Zilinsky, David Plante); others are understandable but no less regrettable (Alan Campbell, Hugh Wheeler, David Stacton, Julian Green, Stephen Koch). Even for those 179 works in common, my readings sometimes differ markedly from theirs. It is not a question of our ages: the four of us were born within five years of each other. Rather it stems, I think, from having passed from the politics of liberation to a post-gay nostalgia. I am not interested in distinguishing between "high" and "low" literature, and I seem to enjoy satire and erotica, metafictional games and comedy, more than they. Whenever possible, I have put the work into a biographical as well as a social context. Above all, when I reflect how my memory of my first encounter with a novel differs from the way I now read it, I am struck forcefully that ever so often a totally new survey is called for; there cannot be, and never should be, a definitive guide.

That does not mean that the earlier guides do not continue to hold interest, for both their differing viewpoints and as historical documents of readings made in the flush of excitement after the Stonewall Inn uprising. Sarotte finished his doctoral dissertation *Comme un frère, comme un amant* in 1974 for the Sorbonne; it was published in 1976 and translated into English in 1978. Not surprisingly, it worked within the accepted canon, from Herman Melville to James Baldwin. In this way he headed a line of gay American academics, who, unlike their lesbian counterparts, seem more interested in outing established figures than in recovering forgotten works. Austen's *Playing the Game*, 1977, is more enterprising and still provokes thought. Levin's *The Gay Novel*, 1983 (revised and expanded as *The Gay Novel in America*, 1991), is the most comprehensive. I owe many a debt to it. But it is also exasperating in its errors and its dogged determination to submit every book to a scrutiny of the way it answers four psychological questions. James Gifford's survey *Dayneford's Library*, 1995, and his anthology *Glances Backward*, 2007, and Axel Nissen's survey *Manly Love*, 2009, and his anthology *The Romantic Friendship Reader*, 2003, are of great value for exploring the nineteenth century.

Once I decided to remap the territory, I was faced with the question of where to begin. Alan Dale's 1889 novel *A Marriage below Zero* was the obvious answer. But the very silence of the love that did not even know its name at the time permits readers to discern evidence of homosexual desire decades earlier. In his introduction to his anthology, Nissen reminds us (4–5): "American men during most of the nineteenth century could feel and openly express an unashamed, unselfconscious, all-consuming love for members of their own sex. In this period, the passionate love between men did not lead to a sense of abnormality or fundamental difference from other men, nor did it exclude a concurrent sexual or romantic interest in one or more women. In other words, a man could have a strong emotional investment in another man without being considered effeminate, unnatural, or perverse." He goes on to point out, "In Victorian society, the primary identity category is *gender*, not sexuality." Therefore, "the major sexual debates focused on relations to the self or between the sexes—that is, debates about masturbation, prostitution, free love, miscegenation, and polygamy."

Gay or queer readings exist of works by Charles Brockden Brown (*Arthur Mervyn*, 1799–1800; *Edgar Huntley*, 1799), James Fenimore Cooper (*The Deerslayer*, 1841; *Jack Tier*, 1848), Melville (particularly *Moby-Dick*, 1851; *Pierre*, 1852; *Billy Budd*, 1924), Nathaniel Hawthorne (*The Blithedale Romance*, 1852), Theodore Winthrop (*Cecil Dreeme*, 1861; *John Brent*, 1862), Henry James (*Roderick Hudson*, 1875; *The Ambassadors*, 1903), William Dean Howells (*Private Theatricals*, 1876; *The Shadow of a Dream*, 1890), Mark Twain (*Adventures of Huckleberry Finn*, 1884), Owen Wister (*The Virginian*, 1902), and Jack London (*The Sea-Wolf*, 1904). (Though it was drafted in the late 1840s, Julia Ward Howe's *The Hermaphrodite* was not published until 2004.) Even antagonistic relationships have been read as manifestations of frustrated desire. (What were Chillingworth's *real* feelings about Dimmesdale?) Leslie Fiedler's notorious assertion, made in his 1948 essay "Come Back to the Raft Ag'in, Huck Honey!" (collected in *An End to Innocence*, 1955), that the basic American mythos is the story of a white boy in love with a black man brought howls of protest at the time, but has since moved into scholarly respectability. However, what Gregory Woods has to say about *Roderick Hudson* seems to apply to all these novels: they are "not yet about homosexuality as such" but rather they occupy "a curious position which largely coincides with the space where the fiction of homosexuality was starting to take shape."

The first attempt to catalog gay American writing was in 1908. Xavier Mayne (Edward Prime-Stevenson) in his important treatise *The Intersexes* wrote (376) that "similisexualism is far from being an unknown note in American belles-lettres and has even achieved its classics." For prose writers he listed Charles Warren Stoddard (*South-Sea Idyls*, 1873), Dale, and himself (*Imre*, 1906, and two short stories). Donald Webster Cory (Edward Sagarin) appended a list of gay titles to his equally important work *The Homosexual in America*, 1951, and then greatly expanded it with the help of members of the Mattachine Society in 1960. Noel I. Garde (Edgar Hugh Leoni) compiled a 1959 bibliography *The Homosexual in Literature*. Although Cory admired James's novella *The Pupil*, 1888 (which he had included in the first American anthology of gay fiction: *21 Variations on a Theme*, 1953), for both him and Garde, Dale's novel was the defining moment. Ian Young brought out the last comprehensive bibliography, *The Male Homosexual in Literature*, in 1975 and greatly expanded it in 1982. Showing the influence American academia was already having, he added Cooper, Howells, Melville, Taylor, and Winthrop. All three bibliographers used notations to distinguish between novels with major gay content and those with only minor. Only Stoddard and Dale received a star from Young.

As I continued to check out nineteenth century candidates, I began to separate the homosocial and the homoerotic from the homosexual. Though *gay* can encompass all three, I am more interested in novels in which sexual desire is unmistakably a key component. I am here trying to trace the development of *gay* identity in fiction, not *queer* identity (nor, for that matter, proto-gay identity). I am not trying to identify a "gay sensibility." Nor am I interested in examining nonsexual gender-bending games such as *Jack Tier* or *Cecil Dreeme*. (I similarly eliminated twentieth century works about transwomen, such as Stuart Engstrand's *The Sling and the Arrow*, 1947, and Gore Vidal's *Myra Breckinridge*, 1968.) By these criteria, Dale's *Marriage below Zero* is the first published novel by an American to make overt homosexuality its major theme. But given how long I wrestled with whether to include Taylor's *Joseph and His Friend* or not, I decided to open with it. It seems to be lacking only a vocabulary; its plot inverts Dale's, so that the two together presage a whole series of novels in which a gay male struggles with the question of a straight marriage. I also include Loring's *Two College Friends*, which sets the pattern for gay bonding in a school setting.

As for a stopping point, consistency would demand taking the survey to the same point as its companion volume, *Gay Novels of Britain, Ireland, and the Commonwealth, 1881–1981*. But gay American writing had already radically shifted in substance before AIDS came to dominate our conscious. Many surveys of gay and lesbian history and literature have chosen Stonewall as their *terminus ad quem*. Stonewall, however, was not that well known outside New York at the time of the riots (and maybe not even in New York: the moon landing is mentioned in Angelo d'Arcangelo's *Sookey*, but not Stonewall). Perhaps I am overly fond of symmetry, but I choose 1970 as more significant than 1969. In that year the first Gay Pride march occurred. Media coverage of the event (for which the slogan was actually "Gay Power") brought it to national attention and led to its becoming an annual happening. Linda Hirshman (*Victory*, 123–24) points out that there had been earlier riots in San Francisco and Los Angeles: "Yet none of these salient events marked the so-called birth of the gay rights movement. Only Stonewall did. Because only Stonewall was followed by a parade a year later." I do address the omitted decade in a postscript.

Gay American fiction during this hundred year period has a distinctive flavor, different from gay British and Commonwealth writing, even Canadian. The U.S. is more insular, yet richer in ethnic and religious diversity. Its fiction seems freer and simultaneously more guarded than British fiction at each stage of development. It is more democratic, less elite and class conscious. Religion played an increasing role after World War II. Family tensions, created by hostile fathers and misguided mothers, were always a staple. Gay American writers themselves interconnected in all sorts of ways, sometimes unexpected. But those friendships grew out of encounters and friends in common, not a shared class system. Most were college graduates, but their alma maters were scattered across the states; Harvard and Columbia were only two among a score. Instead of one city, there were multiple magnets for gay writers. New York exerted the greatest pull, but even there Greenwich Village and Harlem offered alternative centers. San Francisco and Los Angeles and, to a lesser extent, New Orleans and Chicago had their appeal. Provincetown, Key West, Riis Beach, and Fire Island were popular getaway spots. Other countries, other cultures attracted American gays feeling stifled by puritanism. The South Seas, the Caribbean, Tangier, Paris, and Berlin promised greater sexual freedom. The American gay literary scene, as a result, was not nearly as inbred as the English and, to a corresponding degree, not nearly as supportive. Still, tight friendships grew up among coteries of gay writers. Six degrees ruled at the publisher and in bed.

Gay school novels are comparatively rare in comparison with the English schoolboy tradition. The military as a profession was never an attraction, so we have almost exclusively combat novels. World War II had an enormous impact on gay letters. The one all-male milieu to form the setting for a significant number of novels was the prison. Novels about hustling are an integral part of gay American writing. Under Hammett's pushing, mystery fiction began to admit transgressive sexualities early on, and the genre has remained one of the richest for exploring gay and lesbian themes. Since it was assumed that the ideal science fiction reader was a teenage boy, sex was pretty much taboo throughout this period, despite attempts by Theodore Sturgeon in the 1950s and Delany in the 1960s to admit forbidden subjects. The incredible blank is the gay western, given that the genre is an American invention and that trappers, miners, and cowboys, living in an all-male environment, must have occasionally done something other than strum on a guitar or play their harmonica.

Publishing posed problems for gay writers. Censorship, legal prosecution, lack of advertising, and distribution setbacks, particularly those caused by the U.S. postal service, could kill a novel. These problems continued to plague writers even when the mass-market paperback came of age during World War II. These books were reprints of hardcover books and were normally issued in a uniform 7 inches × 4¼ inches format. They were found everywhere, generally on revolving racks specially designed to hold them: at newsstands and in tobacco shops, in train and bus stations, at airline terminals, in drugstores and five-and-dime stores, in supermarkets—everywhere save regular bookstores. Fawcett Publications served as a distributor of these books. In negotiating a contract for the various imprints of the New American Library, it agreed not to reprint any books itself. But when it became clear what a market there was for paperbacks, an executive came up with the idea of publishing paperback originals under the Gold Medal imprint. The first books appeared on the racks in 1950 and were successful enough to establish Gold Medal Books as an important new force in publishing. Since the gestation period for writing and publishing paperback originals was considerably shorter than that for hard cover books, they could incorporate current events rapidly into their pages. Perhaps because these books did not depend on the postal service, from the beginning the Gold Medal line proved receptive to works with homosexual content, especially lesbian fiction.

An erotic gay pulp explosion began in the mid–1960s. Centered largely on west coast publishing houses catering until then to straight males' tastes, they became venues for gay writers willing to introduce sex, preferably of all varieties, into the plot structure. In the last five years of the 1960s over 575 gay erotic novels were published. They explored an enormous range of genres, to the point that in many cases a pulp novel represents the first appearance of a genre in the history of gay literature. Their contents have yet to be fully explored. The publishers' demands for more and more sex posed problems for writers, who felt they were selling out, but they were almost the only sure outlet for a decade. And they provided readers hungry for a happy ending to gay stories a dependable supply. Vanity presses offered another possibility for gay subject matter. The better vanity novels were often picked up by paperback houses. It is easy enough to sneer at these works from a distance, but readers who came of age at the time remember them as life rafts in perilous heterosexual seas.

Misogyny is an attack often launched, unjustly for the most part, against American gay writing. For decades American boys grew up being told by their parents not to be sissies. Of course, such injunctions reinforced perceptions of women as inferior. At the same time, homosexuals were seen as an abnormal mixture of the sexes: male homosexuals were thought to be naturally effeminate; female homosexuals to be naturally masculine. Some embraced the stereotypes, producing the nellies or fairies and the bulldykes. Confusing the issue further, many assumed that heterosexual norms must somehow apply to any relationship, with the results that even now some straights seem to think a gay couple must play roles, one taking the "feminine" part, the other the "masculine" (the perpetual question of who does what to whom). Those gay males who did not feel any less masculine because of their sexual orientation reacted, even overreacted, feeling scorn for those who went along with current psychological interpretations. Effeminate gays were also feared because their easy visibility had the unwanted consequences of attracting police to gay hangouts. Steadily from World War II onward, what eventually was labeled the clone look evolved, even though paradoxically it was as much a masculine drag act as the feminine drag act adopted by cross-dressers.

There follow those novels that seem most significant to the evolution of gay American letters in this one-hundred-year span. Their number does not include works in which gays play only minor roles, no matter how famous their authors may be: thus, the omission of Hemingway, Fitzgerald, Steinbeck, et al. Similarly, I omit such works as Richard Brooks's *The Brick Foxhole*; even though a gay man's murder is pivotal to the plot, we see almost nothing of the victim. To give some sense of development, I have listed the works in chronological order, though I sometimes diverge from strict chronology by listing an individual author's work together and by grouping novels of a similar kind. Working with the World Catalog, I have listed the first edition, plus any contemporary British edition, though I sometimes used later reprints. I indicate which text I read with an asterisk (*). In quotations, all ellipses not in brackets are in the original. As for nomenclature, I let context dictate what seemed appropriate—*gay, homosexual, queer*—without worrying unduly about historical accuracy. That does not mean that I am indifferent to the debate on the subject; I found Frank Yerby's use of *homosexual* in a novel about ancient Greece jarring.

I again thank Rob McDonald, Stephen Delaney, and Aggie Gonzalez for their help. John Sherlock and Simon Stern were invaluable. Also helpful were Michael Bronski, Cathy Downs, Curt Evans, Ron Hamm, Bailey Killian, Richard Lipez, Joseph Ortiz, Will Parish, and Susan Roberson. These librarians helped solve problems: Siri Alderson, Seattle Public Library; Traci Barber, Okmulgee (Okla.) Public Library; Jenny Hodge, Shields Library, University of California, Davis; Richard C. Leab, Pittsfield (Mass.) Local History Department; Christopher Lopez, Fondren Library, Southern Methodist University; John O'Donnell, Danbury (Conn.) Library; Kathy Robbins, Quatrefoil Library; Philip Sutton, New York Public Library; and Lisa Vecoli, Andersen Library, University of Minnesota. Texas A&M University–Kingsville's Jernigan Library now houses the Drewey Wayne Gunn Collection of Gay Literature, while Duke University's Sallie Bingham Center houses the Drewey Wayne Gunn Collection of Gay Male Mysteries and Police Stories and the Drewey Wayne Gunn and Jacques Murat Collection of Gay American Pulps. I thank Bruce Schunemann at TAMUK and Laura Micham at Duke for bringing the collections into their catalogs.

THE NOVELS

1 Bayard Taylor: *Joseph and His Friend*, 1870. Frederick W. Loring: *Two College Friends*, 1871.

Neither Joseph Asten nor his friend, Philip Held, just as neither Ned nor Tom, the two Harvard friends, would self-identify as a sodomite or as a follower of adhesiveness, the term being pushed by Walt Whitman. (More familiar terms would not become available for more than twenty years.) Nor would readers of the novels at the time, steeped as they were in the conventions of sentimentalized male friendship, have seen anything unusual in the passion expressed between the pairs of men. For readers today, however, the possible sexual implications of the stories, particularly Taylor's, seem blatant. Joseph, a twenty-two-year-old Pennsylvania farmer, recognizes, "I am lonely, but I know not how to cry for companionship; my words would not be understood, or, if they were, would not be answered." Implying there are many gates to choose from, he accepts social strictures: "Only one gate is free to me,—that leading to the love of woman" (51). At a neighborhood party, he meets a city visitor, the ironically named Julia Blessing. Aged thirty, the daughter of a ne'er-do-well father, she is seeking a well-to-do husband whom she can manipulate. Joseph fits the bill admirably, and she quickly ensnares him. Then on the train carrying him home from his call on the Blessing family, he espies the twenty-eight-year-old Philip. The attraction is instantaneous: "towards Philip his heart sprang with an instinct beyond his control." A train wreck speeds up their intimacy, and we are told of Joseph, "If he had not been so innocent,—if he had not been quite as unconscious of his inner nature as he was overconscious of his external self,—he would have perceived that his thoughts dwelt much more on Philip Held than on Julia Blessing" (96). On the eve of the wedding, Philip declares himself, "Joseph! I can be nearer than a brother. I know I am in your heart as you are in mine. There is no faith between us that need be limited, there is no truth too secret to be veiled. A man's perfect friendship is rarer than a woman's love, and most hearts are content with one or the other: not so with yours and mine!" (112), with the result "there was not much of the happy bridegoom [sic] to be seen in Joseph's face when he arose the next morning" (113).

The Blessings quickly control Joseph. The father leads him to invest in an oil scam. The daughter lavishly refurbishes his farmhouse. Joseph falls out of love more slowly than he fell in, but Julia's mask no longer conceals her true nature from him. "Philip's earnest, dark gray eyes, warm with more than brotherly love, haunted his memory" (122), and he turns to him for support. As Joseph's debts mount and his disdain for his wife grows, he contemplates suicide. Philip saves him. In comforting Joseph, Philip describes a valley he came upon in the west: a vision of Eden or perhaps Arcadia. This valley offers "freedom from the distorted laws of men, for none are near enough to enforce them!" Philip proposes to accompany him there and begs Joseph: "Say we should be outlaws there, in our freedom!—here we are fettered outlaws" (216). Joseph cannot bring himself to accept such a radical position. But the scene ends tenderly: "Each gave way to the impulse of his manly love, rarer, alas! but as tender and true as the love of woman, and they drew nearer and kissed each other" (217). Taylor has gone further than any American writer, save Whitman, had dared venture. As if skittish, he now pulls his narrative back; of Joseph, he writes: "The tempting vision of Philip's valley, which had haunted him from time to time, faded away" (260–61). The plot takes a melodramatic turn. Confronted by her inability to delude her husband longer, Julia, who has secretly been using arsenic as a cosmetic agent, overdoses. Joseph is suspected of murder. Philip dedicates himself to proving his innocence, even hiring Allan Pinkerton. Cleared, during the celebration party Joseph "drew his chair near to Philip's, their hands closed upon each other, and they were entirely happy in the tender and perfect manly love which united them" (340). Liam Corley records (137) that in its serialization in *Atlantic Monthly*, the November 1870 installment ends here, with "no indication that the story continues in the next issue"; thus for a month "Taylor leaves his readers with the possibility that the male lovers will remain satisfied together." However, the story continues. It is deemed wise for Joseph to quit the parts for a while. He heads west and visits Philip's valley. But he turns his back on it, thus implicitly rejecting outlawed same-sex desire and accepting socially approved heterosexuality (another word, by the way, that he would not have known). In the classical ploy followed when a same-sex attraction grows too dangerous, he returns to propose marriage to Philip's sister, who has been taking care of her brother's home. Philip wonders whether the union will "take Joseph further from my heart, or bring him nearer? It ought to fill me with perfect joy, yet there is a little sting of pain somewhere" (360). His household routine thus upset, he determines to seek marriage too.

There has been much discussion about present-day difficulties understanding degrees of intimacy in nineteenth-century America. But it seems possible Taylor understood the import of what he was writing in terms close to our own. Byrne Fone points out in his introduction to Taylor's verse (*Columbia Anthology*, 568) that when the poet depicts Hylas's disrobing preparatory to his bath, "the florid diction does not conceal the erotic nature of the portrait. It is daring, desirous, and specifically sexual. No euphemism is present when Taylor looks hard at that intimated point where 'downward the supple lines have less of softness.' Taylor's gaze is as obsessively fixed upon Hylas' loins and thighs and upon the rising 'pulse of power' that awakens to 'springy fulness' and soon becomes 'outswerving.'" John Hallock maintains that the novel was inspired by the love Taylor's friend, the poet Fitz-Greene Halleck (1790–1867), held for fellow poet Joseph Rodman Drake (1795–1820). He devotes a chapter of his biography of Halleck to tracing the correspondences, arguing that Philip represents Fitz and Joseph represents Joseph. He sums up (151): "Taylor had remarkable insight into both expression and oppression of homosexuality in nineteenth-century America." James Bayard Taylor (1825–1878) was born in Kennett Square, Pennsylvania. He was a journalist, travel writer, poet, and translator of Goethe. He served in the diplomatic corps in Russia and in Germany. He was twice married, but had strong male attachments all his life. Particularly important was a German businessman, August Bufleb (1807–1874), whom he met in Egypt (Taylor wrote his mother that Bufleb "clung to me with a love like that of a woman") and whose niece he married. Taylor died in Berlin.

Despite its charged emotional language, Loring's novella is little about desire and much about honor. It opens in 1861 at Harvard, where the freshman protagonist, Ned, is roommates with Tom, a junior. Ned wonders "if I shall ever care for any woman as much as I do for Tom" (47). He wears a locket with Tom's initials engraved on it and is intensely jealous of one of Tom's friends. Using President Lincoln's call for troops to escape the muddle, Ned makes the grand gesture and enlists. Tom instantly declares his intention to join him. When Ned comes down with a fever, Tom remains by his side until he rallies. Tom himself subsequently becomes feverish, leading to his capture, along with Ned's, by Stonewall Jackson's troops. Finding Tom has been mistreated by his soldiers, the general gives Ned permission to remain with him upon his honor not to escape. Observing how Ned takes care of Tom, one of the Confederate soldiers remarks, "You care for him about as you would for a gal, don't you? [...] Well, he's pootier than any gal I ever see anywhar" (120). He tells Ned how he can spirit Tom away. In order to save him, Ned reneges on his word. Once Tom is safely in a Union camp, he delivers a long goodbye to the sedated Tom, preparatory to returning to Confederate territory to reclaim his honor and meet death: "O my darling, my darling, my darling! please hear me. The only one I have ever loved at all, the only one who has ever loved me. [...] If you knew how I love you, how I have loved you in all my jealous, morbid moods, in all my exacting selfishness,—O Tom! my darling, my darling! [...] You won't forget Ned, darling; he was something to you; and you were all the world to him" (127–30). At one point Ned has thought, "When this war is over, I suppose Tom will marry and forget me. I never will go near his wife—I shall hate her" (84). Tom does marry, and has a son. In time-honored fashion he proclaims, "We must call him 'Ned'; we couldn't call him by any other name" (157). The novel was originally serialized in the journal *Old and New.* Loring dedicated the book to his classmate William W. Chamberlain (1850–1910). Though neither man served in the Civil War, J. N. Katz (*Love Stories,* 368) correlates Ned to Loring and Tom to Chamberlain. Frederick Wadsworth Loring (1848–1871) was born in Boston and attended Harvard. Hired as a journalist to cover an exploratory expedition in the Arizona Territory, he was killed in a battle with Apaches. According to Douglass Shand-Tucci (*Crimson Letter,* 35), Chamberlain married and had a son, "who was not named after Loring."

As an indication of how much has changed in allowable discourse between males, consider the following from a 1912 novel. One male is addressing another: "Somewhere in the Cumberland there is a little island, made all for lovers, and beautiful things, and hid away snugly dreamful on the bosom of the river. But it is a secret. The way to it is a zigzag way, through shadow and shine and hard pulling. And it takes heaps of love to find it, for only love can find it—this Island of Beautiful Things. But if the skiff of ours hold out, and hold in it two people dead in love with one another, and who do not flinch for a little bit of rough rowing, I was thinking that we two old lovers might make the trip, and maybe find the Island" (131). There's much more in the same vein. The thing is: the speaker is a thirty-two-year-old man; his listener is his neighbor's six-year-old boy. The novel is the justly forgotten *The Island of Beautiful Things* by Will Allen Dromgoole (1860–1934). It is uncomfortably sticky for a present-day reader. The boy repeatedly tells the man, "you are *my Mans*" (95). The man recalls his days with fellow males in the West and tells the boy that women "are always 'beasts'" (20). We have scenes such as "a long stay behind the closed door of the bathroom, a stay enlivened by the splashing to water and the sound of laughter" (18), and the information that the boy is going to share the man's bed the night before a planned expedition: "decidedly a new turn to the affair. But then—why not?" (95). Yet presumably neither its female author nor its contemporary readers, even in that post–Wilde period, saw anything suspicious about the relationship.

Corley, Liam. *Bayard Taylor: Determined Dreamer of America's Rise, 1825–1878.* Lewisburg, Penn.: Bucknell University Press, 2014.

Dromgoole, Will Allen. *The Island of Beautiful Things: A Romance of the South.* Boston: Page, 1912 (*Wildside facsimile). London: Pitman, 1913.

Hallock, John W. M. *The American Byron: Homosexuality and the Fall of Fitz-Greene Halleck.* Madison: University of Wisconsin Press, 2000. 151–74. On Taylor.

Loring, Fred. W. *Two College Friends.* Boston: Loring, 1871 (*Hardpress facsimile).

Taylor, Bayard. *Joseph and His Friend: A Story of Pennsylvania.* New York: Putnam's, 1870 (*Hardpress facsimile).

2   Alan Dale (Alfred J. Cohen): *A Marriage below Zero,* 1889.

The earliest unmistakable appearance of sodomites (to use the language of the time) in American fiction occurs in a pulp novel, *City Crimes: or Life in New York and Boston,* published in 1849 by George Thompson (1823–1858/73) under the pseudonym "Greenhorn." A young woman goes to a masquerade ball disguised as a boy. She encounters the Spanish ambassador, Don Jose Velasquez, who is enamored of "him" and demands a kiss. When she responds that he "must be joking," the ambassador explains, "you may pronounce my passion strange, unaccountable, and absurd if you will—but 'tis none the less violent or sincere." In his country, he explains, "ardent souls confine not their affections to the fairest portion of the human race alone" (169). He departs in anger when she reveals the truth about her gender. Later, another foreigner—"one of those beasts in human shape whose perverted appetites prompts them to the commission of a crime against nature"—attempts to seduce a "handsome lad" of "twelve or fourteen" aboard a coastal steamer. The boy reports the man's advances to an officer, and the offender is "set ashore at a place destitute of everything but rocks." The authorial voice comments, "The miserable sodomite should have been more harshly dealt with." Mention is made of the number of New York boys who prostitute themselves, "liberally patronized by the tribe of genteel foreign vagabonds who infest the city" (246–47). J. N. Katz's examination of an 1842 series of articles in New York tabloids (223) uncovered the same stress on such "horrible offences" being "foreign to our shores." Katz sums up: "Attributing sodomy to foreigners simultaneously affirmed the purity of Americans and the young American nation's need to guard against foreign sources of moral corruption."

Also in 1849, *Redburn: His First Voyage*, a tale of the sea by Herman Melville (1819–1891), describes a male brothel in London in more guarded terms. Wellingborough Redburn, one of Melville's innocent Americans, encounters Harry Bolton, an English youth with the marks of a rentboy, while docked in Liverpool. One of Harry's cohorts reminds Redburn of men he has seen loitering "in sentimental attitudes" outside Palmo's on Broadway (38), a concert hall that figured in one of the sodomy cases Katz found. Harry and Redburn spend "A Mysterious Night in London" at an establishment whose entrance is lit by a "purple light." The chambers are decorated with pornographic paintings, and only males are seen within. For Redburn, "the whole place seemed infected"; he is "mysteriously alive to a dreadful feeling" that leaves him "faint with excitement." He admonishes himself to remember, "though gilded and golden, the serpent of vice is a serpent still" (46–47).

These scenes, however, are minor incidents. The first American novel in which homosexuality is the driving force for the plot does not appear for another forty years. True, Dale's novel is American by virtue of its publisher and its author's home at the time. For he was a British citizen, and his book is largely set in contemporary London. Alfred J. Cohen (1861–1928) was born in Birmingham and attended Oxford. Emigrating to the U.S. in the early 1880s, he became the music and drama critic for two New York newspapers. He wrote other novels under the Dale pseudonym, a detective story as Allen Dale, and used either the latter or Allan Dale for his work as a Hollywood silent film director and actor. His pseudonym comes from the name of one of Robin Hood's companions. (Howard Pyle's homoerotic retelling of *The Merry Adventures of Robin Hood*, 1883, had rekindled interest in the legends.) Cohen died while on vacation on a train going from Plymouth to Birmingham.

Seventeen-year-old Elsie Bouverie is naive, impulsive, educated but unworldly, the daughter of an indifferent mother. Professing to despise the usual kinds of feminine flirtations, she is drawn to twenty-five-year-old Arthur Ravener, an "extremely pretty" man (18) who, she feels, takes her seriously and is willing to converse sensibly with her. She is aware of his friendship with the older Captain Jack Dillington, whom she instinctively dislikes (he looks like the villain in melodramas) and has been told that the pair "are known in society as Damon and Pythias" (14). But the meaning of the allusion escapes her, as do the nuances of her friends' warnings about him. In her ignorance she misleads Arthur about the kind of husband she is seeking and answers affirmatively when he asks her if she would "be satisfied to marry a man who absolutely declined to be the conventional lover" (35). Thus she enters into wedlock with a man who declines to have sex with her, actually deserting her on their wedding night to be with Jack; who insists on separate bedrooms, refusing her admission to his and carefully locking its door against intrusion; and who invites Jack for long stays in their home and, unbeknownst to her, in his bed. She hires a detective, but our obtuse heroine believes that Arthur must be involved with another woman. Even when she finds Jack in the London flat that Arthur has rented for their rendezvouses, she seems incapable of imagining that anything sexual could be passing between two men.

After their confrontation, Elsie insists that he see a doctor. This man is more worldly. Anticipating the later meaning of *gay*, he tells Arthur, "All your gay doings must be renounced" (125) and prescribes a change of scenery. The couple departs for New York. Later she realizes that Arthur has spent his last night with Jack. Once away from his influence, matters between husband and wife go better, though she remains a virgin. Hearing of a preacher whose sermons have created a sensation, the two attend a service. The text is Genesis 19, the destruction of Sodom and Gomorrah. Arthur goes "white as death" (141). That evening he makes his first sexual overtures to Elsie, but she acts like the ninny she is and flees his unexpected ardor. Too bad for her, since the next day Arthur spots Jack outside a hotel. He has followed the couple to New York and reclaims Arthur. Reading Arthur's apologetic farewell note, Elsie ponders, "I wonder how I could have been so dense. It appears to me now that the veriest blockhead could have grasped the situation" (159). At novel's end we learn that a scandal, presumably homosexual in nature, has ruffled Parisian society. Jack is implicated as a principal offender and arrested. Feeling guilty for having rejected her husband at the crucial moment and thinking to save him now, Elsie rushes to the hotel where he is staying. She finds him dead from an overdose of opium. Above his head hangs his and Jack's twin portraits. Elsie angrily destroys them—"and without another look at the dead form in the chair, I left the room and the hotel" (170).

The novel's sensational plot seems all the more extraordinary when one considers that Richard von Krafft-Ebing's 1886 treatise *Psychopathia Sexualis* was not translated until 1892, that Havelock Ellis's *Sexual Inversion* did not appear until 1897, and that Wilde's arrest and trial were in 1895. Cohen's purpose in writing the book is not clear. Was he merely trying to make money from a lurid subject? Or was he indirectly pleading that young girls be better educated? Since Elsie narrates the story, it is impossible to know what Cohen's exact attitude towards homosexuality was. Matthew Kaiser praises him (xii) for having "the audacity to declare the obvious: heterosexuality is not for everyone." The ending has been read as the author's punishment of deviant behavior, but a sympathetic reading is equally possible. Arthur's suicide could grow out of fear of his own arrest. Or it could stem from despair at being separated from his beloved Jack. Kaiser continues (xii), "One of the historically noteworthy aspects of Dale's ground-breaking representation of male homosexuality, an aspect that flies in the face of homophobic stereotypes that persist to this day, is his depiction of gay men as intrinsically—obsessively—relationship-oriented, as bound by a masculine intimacy, a Hellenistic friendship, that no proselytizing maiden can break, no gaggle of disapproving dandies can sever."

Dale, Alan. *A Marriage below Zero*. New York: Dillingham, 1889. *Ed. Matthew Kaiser. San Diego, Calif.: Cognella, 2011.
Katz, Jonathan Ned. "Coming to Terms: Conceptualizing Men's Erotic and Affectional Relations with Men in the United States, 1820–1892." *A Queer World: The Center for Lesbian and Gay Studies Reader*. Ed. Martin Duberman. New York: New York University Press, 1997. 216–35.
Melville, Herman. *The Gay Herman Melville Reader*. Ed. Ken Schellenberg. Arlington, Va.: Gival, 2002.
Thompson, George. *Venus in Boston and Other Tales of Nineteenth-Century City Life*. Ed. David S. Reynolds and Kimberly R. Gladman. Amherst: University of Massachusetts Press, 2002.

3   Charles Warren Stoddard: *For the Pleasure of His Company*, **1903; also** *South-Sea Idyls*, **1873;** *The Island of Tranquil Delights*, **1904.**

Stoddard's only true novel is an early and unexpected example of modernism. It is divided into three parts that circle back upon one another so that the reader is forced to construct the chronology of events. Paul Clitheroe is a twenty-five-year-old "Misty City" (i.e., San Francisco) newspaper columnist. He is somewhat effeminate: "some of his friends thought he had narrowly escaped" being a woman "and did not hesitate to say so" (88). He becomes infatuated with the mysterious Foxlair—when he invites Paul to accompany him to his lodgings, "without a moment's hesitation, the lad did so, and for a week following they were inseparable" (33)—only to discover that he is not only a fraud but a thief. Yet he clings to hope "that Foxlair had not heartlessly betrayed him, and that he would anon return and make all square." However, "Foxlair was never again seen of men in those parts" (43). Among his many true friends, Paul has long conversations with a masculine woman, nicknamed Jack, in one of which he avows that women "are nothing to me, and I'm nothing to them" (93). In a passage in which the author is clearly working towards a language of homosexual identity, the two of them discuss "tom-boys" and "girl-boys." Jack explains why "girl-boys are so unpleasant while tom-boys are delightful" thus: "the girl-boy has lost the charm of his sex, that is manliness; and the tom-boy has lost the defect of hers—a kind of selfish dependence" (98).

Later Paul meets the actor Grattan Field: "Something in Grattan's manner; something in the warm, manly pressure of the arms that encircled Paul, something in the deep distress of his friend, won Clitheroe in a moment: All at once he began to love that wildly impulsive, strangely contradictory, utterly ungoverned and ungovernable nature." Their intimacy deepens: Paul "was to pass the remainder of the night" with him (143). The two split because of Grattan's suspicious nature (171), but not until Paul has been introduced to the Order of Young Knighthood, to which "only the elect are admitted to its privileges. Its novitiate is a secret test of all the manly virtues" (150). Failing to earn enough by his pen, Paul turns to the stage and picks up a "devotee" who makes Paul "his idol" (58). Though Paul has mixed feelings about their friendship, the young man becomes "his almost constant companion" (72). Still unable to make a living, he has a momentary interlude in a Franciscan monastery, leading to the rumor that he has decamped to Venice to join the order (114). In actuality he has headed in the opposite direction, aboard a yacht owned by rich gentleman. Somewhere in the South Pacific he discerns "the dusky forms of three naked islanders" in a canoe and recognizes them as "pals in the past." With "sudden resolve" Paul joins them (188). In his introduction, Austen notes (10) that by the novel's end Stoddard has touched on four cherished themes: "his love for other males; his blasted hopes of finding a lasting refuge in the church; his dream of escaping into some kind of secular, all-male utopia; and the fantasy of returning to the South Seas, where he might be 'natural' in a way that was proscribed in America."

The novel was not Stoddard's first exploration of gay themes. Exactly thirty years earlier, following Melville's more cautious lead in *Typee: A Peep at Polynesian Life*, 1846, and *Omoo: A Narrative of Adventures in the South Seas*, 1847, Stoddard had published a story cycle, the *Idyls*. Though the narrator often comments on the "naked and superbly built fellows" he encounters (86), only a few of the stories are homoerotic. The guarded frankness of those few, however, surprises. In "Chumming with a Savage," the narrator describes his encounter with a Hawaiian teenager, Kána-aná. He reveals that they share a bed, the teenager sleeping in the nude and "hugging" the narrator "like a young bear" (24). In a passage filled with double-entendres, he writes of the boy: "Again and again he would come with a delicious banana to the bed where I was lying, and insist upon my gorging myself." And "he would mesmerize me into a most refreshing sleep with a prolonged and pleasing manipulation" (32). In the following story, "Taboo—A Fête Day in Tahiti," he speaks again of the phallic banana: "Here was a repast of singularly appropriate mould [sic], being about the size of a respectable mouth, and containing just enough mouthfuls to satisfy temporarily the appetite. Not a morsel of it but was full of mellowness and sweet flavor and fragrance" (84–85). The penultimate story finds the narrator onboard a French ship. Its title, "In a Transport," quickly takes on several meanings. The narrator is at once embraced by a young sailor named Thanaron. Under his tutelage, "by the time we sighted the green summits of Tahiti, my range of experience was so great that nothing could touch me further" (297). The first officer, B—, is "the happy possessor of a tight little African, known as Nero," whom he "kissed [...] passionately upon his sooty cheek" and "fondled [...] to his heart's content" (303–04). The story ends, "O Thanaron, my Thanaron, with your arms about my neck, and B—'s arms about you, and Nero clinging to his master's knees—in fact, with everybody felicitating every other body, because it was such an evening as descends only upon the chosen places of the earth, and because, having completed our voyage in safety, we were all literally in a transport!" (310).

The book was reissued in 1892, dropping a Captain Cook story and adding two new ones. Its sequel, the *Island*, added eleven sketches. The title story recounts the narrator's unpleasant encounter with a snotty American consul in Tahiti when he seeks help to return home. Rebuffed by him, he continues his sexual adventures: "Was I not seized bodily one night, one glorious night and borne out of a mountain fastness whither I had fled to escape the sight of my own race? Was I not borne down the ravine by a young giant, sleek and supple as a bronzed Greek god, who held me captive in his Indian lodge till I surfeited on bread-fruits and plantain and cocoanut milk?" (20). With echoes of the Bible, he asserts, "There were those who would restore my soul with gentle dalliance; who with deft fingers manipulated my body the while they passed pleasantries from lip to lip on the unlovely whiteness of skin" (27). The narrator apparently gains an unsavory reputation, to the point the consul decides to advance him the funds for his passage home. He ends up on the same ship. There, "we unmasked the mystery of my nature," with the result "he embraced me madly." But the narrator spurns his overtures: "You were a slow match for me and struck fire when your hour was past" (34–36). Gay Sunshine Press published a selection of eleven sketches taken from the two works, *Cruising the South Seas*; its headnotes often reveal a gay biographical connection that would not otherwise be apparent.

Charles Warren Stoddard (1843–1909), though born in Rochester, New York, grew up in New York and San Francisco. In 1864 he took the first of four trips to the Polynesian islands. While in San Francisco, he was a part of its Bohemian circle and met

Bayard Taylor on his visit. Stoddard left for Europe in 1873, working briefly as Mark Twain's secretary. He had a liaison with the artist Francis D. Millet (1848–1912). Always in love wherever he was, there followed a succession of "Kids": younger men whom he befriended and bedded. Having converted to Catholicism, he was invited to teach at Notre Dame in 1885, where he promptly fell in love with various students. He soon left, upset by the university's official stance on homosexuality, but then joined Catholic University in Washington, D.C., as chair of English literature. During the 1890s he had a long affair with teenager Kenneth O'Connor. Renewing his friendship with the Bostonian Theodore F. Dwight, with whom he shared an interest in nude male photography, through him he met gay writers Thomas Russell Sullivan and Meredith Nicholson. Rudyard Kipling provided the title for the novel. He died of a heart attack in Monterey, California.

Austen, Roger. *Genteel Pagan: The Double Life of Charles Warren Stoddard*. Ed. John W. Crowley. Amherst: University of Massachusetts Press, 1991.
Stoddard, Charles Warren. *For the Pleasure of His Company: An Affair of the Misty City, Thrice Told*. San Francisco: Robertson, 1903. *San Francisco: Gay Sunshine, 1987.
———. *The Island of Tranquil Delights, a South Sea Idyl, and Others*. Boston: Turner, 1904 (*Fredonia facsimile). London: Chatto & Windus, 1905.
———. *South-Sea Idyls*. Boston: Osgood, 1873. *Summer Cruising in the South Seas*. London: Chatto & Windus, 1874. Revised: *South-Sea Idyls*. New York: Scribner's, 1892 (*Fredonia facsimile).

4 Xavier Mayne (Edward I. Prime-Stevenson): *Imre*, 1906.

In *Imre* the lovers are allowed to pledge their lives to each other: "I love thee, as thou lovest me. I have found, as thou hast found, 'the friendship which is love, the love which is friendship'" (127). Basically a novel of ideas, very little in the way of action occurs. Oswald, an Englishman in his thirties on business in Hungary, feels a deep attraction to twenty-five-year-old Lieutenant Imre von N. It is apparently reciprocated, but the two remain formal in each other's presence. Finally, Oswald discloses that since childhood he has been "homosexual" and that as an adult he has been "seeking as in a vain dream to realize again that passion of friendship which could so far transcend the cold modern idea of the tie: the Over-Friendship, the Love-Friendship of Hellas, which meant that between man and man could exist the sexual-psychic love" (84). Oswald enumerates the great figures who have belonged to "the Race-Homosexual" (86), acknowledging Heliogabalus and Hadrian, Sade and Whitman. He deplores the American doctor who advised him to marry, seeing his desires as innate: "Could one really believe in God as making man to live at all, and yet at the same time believe that *this* love is not created, too, by God? is not of God's own divinest Nature, rightfully, eternally—in millions of hearts?" (89). He regrets the mask that society forces gays to wear.

Imre, repressed by culture, family, and profession, cannot respond easily. Only after his return from summer camp, having had time to reflect upon the gift Oswald proffers, can he confess, "I am a Uranian, as thou art. From my birth I have been one. Wholly, wholly homosexual" (117). Whereas Oswald exalts in his total masculinity, to the point of looking down on anything effeminate, Imre fears, "I am more feminine in impulse—of weaker stuff." He begs Oswald for his help, and the latter, echoing the book of Ruth, pledges, "I will never go away from thee" (125–26). At the end of the novel, they are apparently ready for their first physical encounter. For all Oswald's talk of sexual-psychic love, the novel is curiously sexless. Only once does he admit that, as the result of Imre's embracing him, "the Sex-Demon brought his storm upon my traitorous nature, in fire and lava! I struggled in shame and despair to keep down the hateful physical passion which was making nothing of all my psychic loyalty, asserting itself against my angriest will. In vain!" (115). The reaction seems strange, but perhaps he does not want Imre to mistake his love as mere lust. The work is heavy-going for readers, but its historical importance makes it an integral part of any gay's library.

The novel presents itself in the guise of an autobiography sent to Xavier Mayne to edit. It was originally published in a limited edition in Naples and did not appear in the U.S. until 1975 as part of Arno Press's Homosexuality series. A corrupted 1992 Masquerade Books edition inserted globs of explicit sexuality to increase sales. In 2003 James Gifford brought out a scholarly edition. Edward Irenaeus Stevenson (1858–1942) was born in Madison, New Jersey. A journalist and music critic for *Harper's Weekly* and the New York *Independent*, his first two books, *White Cockades*, 1887, and *Left to*

Themselves, 1891, were aimed at boys. His other important book was his treatise *The Intersexes*, 1908. He fell in love with Harry Harkness Flagler (1870–1952), but Flagler ended the relationship preparatory to marriage. Stevenson fled to Europe, where he lived the rest of his life. When he took the name Edward I. Prime-Stevenson, he lopped ten years off his life. He died of a heart attack in Lausanne.

[Prime-Stevenson, Edward.] *Imre: A Memorandum*. By Xavier Mayne. Naples: Rispoli, 1906. *Ed. James J. Gifford. Peterborough, Ont.: Broadview, 2003.

5 George Sylvester Viereck: *The House of the Vampire*, 1907.

A world away from Dracula, Viereck's villain is a psychic vampire who sucks dry the creative ideas of both women and men to present as his own work. Ernest Fielding is Reginald Clarke's latest victim. The youth cannot resist the famed writer's invitation to lodge in his home. He remains under his spell even when he realizes that Clarke has lifted his half-written play complete from his mind and passed it off as his own. Though encouraged by Ethel Brandenbourgh, an earlier victim, to quit the house, Ernest cannot leave, even as Clarke now pilfers his unwritten novel inspired by Ethel. He finds himself alienated from "his dearest friend," Jack, to whom he was drawn because he "was subtler, more sympathetic, more feminine, perhaps, than the rest of my college-mates" (9, 21). At the end, when Ernest's mind has been completely drained, it is clear that Jack will take his place as Clarke's next victim. There is never anything overtly homosexual in the novella, only hints: a statue of Antinous (12), an allusion to "the mysterious loveliness of Mr. W.H." (14), Ernest's dream of "a young sea-god [...] peering amorously at the boy's red mouth" (42), "an orchid of an indefinable purple tint" in Clarke's lapel as he psychically rapes the sleeping Earnest (74). Without ever an outright reference to Wilde, his presence hovers over the entire piece. Uncannily, an argument that Clarke puts forth to Ernest to explain his actions could be used as a defense of homosexuality: "I always hoped, until it was too late, that I might yet check the mysterious power within me. Soon, however, I became aware that it was beyond my control. The unknown god, whose instrument I am, had wisely made it stronger than me" (71).

George Sylvester Viereck (1884–1962) was born in Munich, Germany, to an American mother and a German father who may have been the illegitimate son of Kaiser Wilhelm I. The family immigrated to the U.S. in 1897. Already a poet, often writing Uranian verse, he graduated from CCNY in 1906. He married in 1915 and had two sons. He supported Germany during World War I, leading to an attack on his home. His later support of the Nazis led to his federal imprisonment, 1942–47. Two works with strong homosexual elements grew out of his incarceration: the novel *All Things Human*, 1949, published under the pseudonym Stuart Benton, and the memoir *Men into Beasts*, 1952. He died of a cerebral hemorrhage in Hadley, Massachusetts. Niel M. Johnson's 1972 biography focuses almost entirely on Viereck's politics.

Viereck, George Sylvester. *The House of the Vampire*. New York: Moffat, Yard, 1907. *Las Vegas, Nev.: IAP, 2010.

6 Henry Blake Fuller: *Bertram Cope's Year*, 1919. Sherwood Anderson: *Winesburg, Ohio*, 1919.

Set before the first world war in the imaginary town of Churchton (i.e., Evanston, Illinois, where Northwestern University is located), Fuller's novel describes the effect a new English instructor has on Medora Phillips's household. Twenty-four-year-old Bertram Cope is obviously gay. Two middle-aged men sense that at once, but the fact escapes the women. Medora has three female charges that she fancies to marry off: the musician Amy, the painter Hortense, and the poet Carolyn. Amy traps Cope into an engagement, but recognizes her mistake. Cope has courage enough to reject Hortense and does nothing to encourage Carolyn: "he was conscious of a fundamental repugnance to any such scheme in life and was acutely aware that— for awhile, at least, and perhaps for always—he wanted to live in quite a different mode" (150). As for the men—both of whom come across as old queens—the wheelchair-bound Joseph Foster watches the unfolding of events with cynical scorn, while Basil Randolph sets out to captivate Cope. They share a nude swim, which Cope recalls with pleasure, but nothing untoward happens: "He had had a good swim, if but a brief one, with a companion who had been willing, even if not bold" (103). He is aware that Randolph wants more, but another has "first claim" on him (129).

This is a twenty-seven-year-old Wisconsin

friend, Arthur Lemoyne. It would seem they parted for economic reasons. Cope writes: "I miss you—even more than I thought I should" (59). He is jealous when he learns via one of Arthur's letters that he has taken a spin in some fellow's "little roadster" (105) and urges him to come to Churchton. Arthur arrives in time to enroll as a student at the start of the spring semester, joining Cope in his new quarters with a new bed for the two of them. His over-familiarity with Cope's person hastens the end of the engagement with Amy, "and Urania, through the whole width of her starry firmament, looked down kindly upon a happier household" (174–75). Scandal awaits, however. Arthur takes the role of a girl in the spring play, and it becomes his "fortune—or misfortune—to do his work all too well." At the end of the evening, "he continued to act off-stage; and in his general state of ebulliency he endeavored to bestow a measure of up-welling femininity upon another performer who was in the dress of his own sex" (208, 210). The immediate result is a bruise on his forehead; the ultimate outcome is his dismissal from school. Arthur leaves Churchton shortly afterwards. Cope joins him during the summer, a fact he discloses, for some reason, in a letter to Carolyn, letting drop the fact that he has secured a post in an eastern university. In a final exchange, Medora predicts Cope will return to marry Carolyn; Randolph more realistically predicts that they will hear that Arthur has joined Cope and the two "are keeping house together" (220).

Anderson, another resident of Chicago at the time, published his *Winesburg* story cycle the same year. The first portrait, "Hands," recounts how a schoolteacher, Wing Biddlebaum, was hounded out of a town in Pennsylvania after a "half-witted boy of the school became enamored of the young master" and "imagined unspeakable things" that he recounted "as facts" (13). Now he lives in Winesburg, where the principal character in the cycle, young George Willard, has come to know him. Wing lives in perpetual fear of his hands, knowing they are somehow connected to the hatred he experienced. One of those men "meant by nature to be a teacher of youth" (12), his wont to gently caress his students' heads and shoulders was misunderstood by the community. Originally published in *Masses* in 1916, the story has often been anthologized in collections of gay fiction; if it belongs there, it would be for the presence of the half-witted boy, not for Wing. The story is, more accurately, in the narrow view, a study of a small town's hysterical fear of pederasty; in the larger view, another indictment of American intolerance of difference.

Henry Blake Fuller (1857–1929) was born in Chicago. A private person, though active in the city's aesthetic life, he wrote romances, satires, and symbolist plays, including "At Saint Judas's," 1896, "the first play on a homosexual theme published in America" (Baim, *Out and Proud*, 24). He made several trips to Europe. On one, in 1897, he met Harold W. Curtis, with whom he had a brief correspondence. He took the young university student William Emery Shepherd on another European tour in 1924. But there is no record of any lasting relationship. He died in Chicago after suffering a stroke. Sherwood Berton Anderson (1876–1941) was born in Camden, Ohio. He resided in small towns throughout the state before moving, for the first time, to Chicago in 1897. Other works of his have relevance for gay readers. He was married four times and had three children. He died in Colón, Panama, of peritonitis.

Anderson, Sherwood. *Winesburg, Ohio: A Group of Tales of Ohio Small Town Life*. New York: Huebsch, 1919. London: Cape, 1922. *Collected Stories. New York: Library of America, 2012. 1–180.
Fuller, Henry Blake. *Bertram Cope's Year*. Chicago: Seymour, 1919. *Ed. Joseph A. Dimuro. Peterborough, Ont.: Broadview, 2010.
Scambray, Kenneth. *A Varied Harvest: The Life and Works of Henry Blake Fuller*. Pittsburgh, Penn.: University of Pittsburgh Press, 1987.

7 Carl Van Vechten: *The Blind Bow-Boy*, 1923; *Parties*, 1930. Joseph Moncure March: *The Wild Party*, 1928.

At age twenty-one Harold Prewett, the hero of Van Vechten's first novel, discovers that he has a father—indeed a very rich father who proposes to set up his unwanted son, the cause of his wife's death, in style in New York for a year and to hire a tutor to introduce him to the ways of the world so that he may choose freely what kind of life he wants to lead. The father rather skews the possibilities, however, by advertising for "young man of good character but no moral sense" (16). His choice falls on Paul Moody, a youth whose profile reminds one of Rupert Brooke (57). The father also hires, as valet for his son, a man who previously served the Duke of Middlebottom, a person "not unknown in London [...], especially in certain circles" (47). Harold falls in love at first sight with Alice Blake, a woman involved in a traffic accident whom he helps out. He pursues her even as he is being taken over by Paul's entourage, "a more motley crew than he had imagined could exist outside of literature" (106). They introduce him to thoughts and experiences far beyond what he has known in the sheltered world of the aunts who have taken care of him until now. Although everyone thinks he is on Capri, that mecca for gays, the Duke of Middlebottom shows up in New York. The Duke's stationary carries the motto "A thing of beauty is a boy for ever" (117), and he always takes with him "a hand-illuminated quotation from Goethe" that can be roughly translated as "If God had wished me different, Then he would have made me so" (126). He "immediately manifested an interest in Harold which appeared to be sincere. As for Harold, the Duke appealed to him from the beginning" (116). The Duke decides to put on a play, Fernand Nozière's libertine drama in one act, *L'après-midi Byzantine*. In order to gain a large enough audience, it is suggested that the Duke invite his friends: "I have no f-f-f-friends, retorted the Duke, only people that amuse me, and people I sleep with. [...] The people that amuse me are all in the p-p-p-play.... The theatre isn't b-b-b-b-b-big enough to hold the others" (139). Harold marries Alice, to discover on their honeymoon in Provincetown that he really does not love her after all. The novel ends aboard a ship headed for Europe. Among the passengers seen standing side by side at the rail are "Harold Prewett and Ronald, Duke of Middlebottom" (261). The novel is heavily indebted to Wilde and Ronald Firbank. Allusions to gays pepper the work, although only gay readers, for the most part, would have recognized them at the time as code.

Parties, Van Vechten's final novel, set at the height of Prohibition, depicts a set of perpetually drunken partygoers, several of whom are sexually ambiguous. Of New York life, one character says: "Nothing goes on at all. [...] Just parties, that's all. The only happy people left in New York are the Lesbians and pederasts, and they are so happy they are miserable. Nobody else has anything" (70). Of the charismatic David Westlake, his friend Hamish Wilding muses: "What was the attraction that David exerted to such a marked degree? Why did everybody who knew him talk and think so much about him? [...] A wave of softness, a melting mood of deep love for David possessed him and answered his question. Hamish *knew* why every one was attracted towards David. Who was more attracted than himself?" (159). When David mourns the unfortunate death of Roy Fern, who dies in his drunken defense in a Harlem club, he says, "He loved me." His wife responds, "David, that's just the trouble. Everybody loves you" (199). The bootlegger Donald Bliss is more obvious: "men also liked Donald, more particularly men without wives or sweethearts or sisters, or men who did not care for women at all" (28). He hires "boys who had no immediate means of support" to serve at his parties: "modern Ganymedes that they were, to one Jove after another. Sometimes this led to something" (29). Yet the novel seems more guarded, more closeted if you will, than *Bow-Boy*. Carl Van Vechten (1880–1964) was born in Cedar Rapids, Iowa. He graduated from the University of Chicago and moved to New York. His professional career divides into three overlapping parts. He began as a music and art critic for various newspapers, becoming a champion of the avant-garde and of Harlem. In these capacities he was instrumental in the rediscovery of Melville, he introduced Firbank to the U.S., and he helped Stein, Langston Hughes, Wallace Stevens, and later Chester Himes get published. During the 1920s he was a novelist. His third career, lasting until his peaceful death in New York, was as a photographer. Many of the iconic portraits of celebrities are his work. He was twice married, but was always involved in a string of relationships with various men.

March's narrative poem presents a bawdier version of the same era. Queenie, a dancer in vaudeville, decides to throw a party. Before the evening is over the room will "reek of sex" (114) and a murder fueled by two rivals' claim to the hostess's affections will occur. Pianists Oscar and Phil, the incestuous d'Armano brothers, provide the music. They end up slapping each other and pulling hair until "their faces grew smeared/With tears and mascara" (105) after Phil permits the "ambisextrous" Jackie—"a soft-shoe dancer with a special act," once sentenced to prison for being a "public nuisance" (83–84)—to kiss him. The evening closes with all three passed out. There is also a lesbian couple present, "locked as one" (114). The authorial voice comments, "Some love is fire: some love is rust:/But the fiercest, cleanest love is lust" (136). By no stretch can the poem be called even a gay novella, but its caricatures of the three gays remain etched in the memories of readers. According to the artist Art Spiegelman (in the introduction to his 1994 edition), William Burroughs claimed the narrative was "the book that made me want to become a writer." It has been loosely adapted as a movie and has become the basis for two separate musicals. Joseph Moncure March (1899–1977) was born in New York. After serving in World War I, he graduated from Amherst. He joined the staff of the *New Yorker*, then moved to Hollywood to work as a screen writer. He was married three times. He died in Los Angeles.

March, Joseph Moncure. *The Wild Party*. Chicago: Covici, 1928. London: Secker, 1928. **The Wild Party, The Set-Up, A Certain Wildness*. Freeport, Me.: Wheelwright, 1968. 61–147.
Smalls, James. *The Homoerotic Photography of Carl Van Vechten: Public Face, Private Thoughts*. Philadelphia: Temple University Press, 2006.
Van Vechten, Carl. *The Blind Bow-Boy*. *New York: Knopf, 1923. London: Richards, 1923.
———. *Parties: Scenes from Contemporary New York Life*. New York: Knopf, 1930.
White, Edward. *The Tastemaker: Carl Van Vechten and the Birth of Modern America*. New York: Farrar, Straus & Giroux, 2014.

8 Clarkson Crane: *The Western Shore,* 1925.

Set during the academic year 1919–20, the novel traces the intertwined lives of three male students and a thirty-year-old English instructor at the University of California in Berkeley. Burton has been indiscreet enough that gossip is afloat "concerning his tendencies in love (it was whispered that he had made advances to a freshman whom he had invited to his rooms)" (103). Someone spots him with "a young soldier" in San Francisco (245). We witness his trying to pick up Milton Granger. Whenever he is at the swimming pool, his eyes are always on the tanned males. One of his women students remarks, "They say he never looks at a woman" (118). Another muses how "she found herself talking to him without restraint, as if he were a friend of her own sex" (233). Still, his nonconformity to stereotypes—"Burton was not effeminate"—convinces George Towne that he cannot be "that way," that "he's not queer. All that stuff's the bunk" (106). He easily accepts Burton's lie that he "may get married next year" (113). The novel begins with George's return to Berkeley, his having previously flunked out, and ends with his going home to Wyoming. He is the type who drifts through life, lacking true ambition, allowing himself to be swayed by others. Strikingly good looking, he draws Milton's attention and is pursued by Burton. The latter offers George the rent-free use of a room in his home. George "feared the smiles of his companions when Burton appeared" (103), but he decides that, if they make fun of him, "he could tell them that he knew damn well what he was doing, and that he was willing to try anything once, especially when he could get a room for nothing" (112). He observes that two of Burton's San Francisco friends "were queer" (196). Whenever Burton shows up in his room, "he wondered if Burton were going to start something, for the suspicions he had entertained reawoke from time to time." He decides, "If Burton wanted anything, he would not refuse: a surrender of that sort would free him from any monetary obligation" (191). When he senses that he has lost Burton's interest, he seems jealous of the newcomer.

That is Milton. Still under the influence of his all-female family, a virgin, showing no interest in women, yet incapable of acting on same-sex desire, if indeed he feels such, he is the true cipher in the novel. Yes, at one point, when a fraternity brother has been hazed unmercifully, we are told that "he knew that he loved him," that "he felt a need of exile in common with Bert Hudson so that their friendship might grow stronger in suffering" (140). He becomes tight with Aaron Berg, another student writer, and invites him out for what is basically a date: "Just the two of us" (142). But when he meets Burton while on a walking trip along the Bay, he cannot respond to the older man's overtures. It is a classic cruising scene. Both lie about who they are. Both are nervous. Burton throws himself down beside the seated teenager. He reaches out and fondles his arm, admiring Milton's tan. The gesture reminds the boy of a high school teacher who "had had the same caressing habits" (226), and he escapes before anything can develop. Later, when he thinks about the man's obvious interest in him, he has "a feeling of uneasiness, as if something yet hidden in himself might emerge in answer" (275). When the two meet on campus, Aaron bringing them together, they conceal their earlier encounter. Again something passes between the two: "The sediment of innumerable jokes heard at school or in the fraternity house and long forgotten rose now from the bottom of his mind into memory, and [Milton] waited, a bit nervous, half pleased, almost understanding, for Burton to say more." He has not decided whether he will return to Berkeley after spending a summer in Europe, but he thinks that if he does, "the instructor would be an interesting person to know" (281–82). Meanwhile, it is clear that Aaron will be Burton's next chosen boy. He casually tells Milton, "Once Phil asked me to spend the night, but the folks expected me home and I couldn't" (183). They have taken walking trips together, and now that Milton, has departed, the two plan a longer one.

Harold Clarkson Crane (1894–1971) was born in Chicago. In 1911 the family moved to the Sacramento Valley. He attended the University of California and began publishing his first stories and sketches. He served with the ambulance corps in World War I. Settling in Carmel after the war, he became part of its literary coterie. He spent 1924–26 in France, writing his first novel in a small hotel in Paris. On his return he met Clyde Evans (1906–2003), and the two remained partners for the rest of his life. Financially secure, he held only intermittent jobs: teaching, working as a reference librarian, doing little writing. After World War II he published gay short stories in *Mattacine Review*, *ONE*, the Swiss-based *Der Kreis*, and the French journal *Arcadie*.

Crane, Clarkson. *The Western Shore.* New York: Harcourt, Brace, 1925. *Salt Lake City: Peregrine Smith, 1985.

9 Robert McAlmon: *Distinguished Air*, 1925. Robert Scully: *A Scarlet Pansy*, 1933.

Distinguished Air is a story cycle united by a common setting—Berlin—and a common theme—glimpses of gay and lesbian Americans taking advantage of the city's greater sexual freedom. It consists of three virtually plotless stories. In the opening one, "Distinguished Air," the unnamed narrator recounts his meeting with two men: Foster Graham, a campy type whose "manner, copied from stage fairies in America, sat strangely upon him" (24), and Carrol Timmons, exulting, "after New England, and that absurd moral bugaboo pursuing me for so many years," in a "feeling of release within myself" (34). Carrol admits "that my nostrils and my mental will rebel against my own carnal desires, but one can't be so cowardly as never to seek release" (38). He mistrusts Foster, who he thinks is showing too much attention to the German youth Carrol is with. Rudge Kepler also turns up. Supposedly both Kepler and the narrator are straight, but neither protests when men approach them in the bar. Fragments of a sexual philosophy emerge: "people's habits about certain things are only a matter of geography" (36). "Any kind of expression is cleaner than pent-up repression" (37). "We all do what we do and will do, so it might as well be flagrant" (38).

"Miss Knight" is the best known of the three. It is an extended portrait of Charlie Knight, who enjoys camping it up, referring to himself with feminine pronouns, sometimes dressing in drag, but with no hint that he wishes to be a woman, even exclaiming at one point, "I'm so glad that I'm a real man" (18). Charlie's hopes of finding love are continually smashed. He picks up a blond policeman "who was real rough trade." Charlie "would sit with his right hand in the left pocket of his policeman when they were in queer cafés, and would babble, 'My god, Mary, I've got my hand on a real piece of meat at last, O Mary.' He was additionally happy because Kate Matthews assured him that she, who could spot a queer man a mile off, knew that the policeman was just a war-made queer one." But when the policeman is spotted "getting amorous" with Kate, Charlie becomes despondent: "Everything was turning bad on her. No money; no luck with her lovers; no friends, only people who thought she was a clown, but didn't want her around at decent places with them" (11–12). An Austrian duke even informs Charlie after sex that *he* expects to receive money. Yet Charlie always bounces back. The last we hear of him is a letter from New York looking forward to his return to Europe. Foster Morris (clearly Foster Graham under a slightly different alias) appears with "a new soldier lover he had picked up on the street in the afternoon" (10). And a lesbian comes into the bar to lose herself in drink and drugs after her lover leaves for Paris to marry.

In "The Lodging House" Harold Files encounters two lesbians who live at the same place he does, out in the street, drunkenly mistaking another house as theirs. One of them is the American Steve (Stephanie) Rath; she does not seem to know the name of her Russian lover. Jerry Anderson, who makes Files "uncomfortable because of the older man's too obvious auntie-like manner," also lives there, leading Files to ask: "Are all the roomers at this place queer women, or buggers and fairies?" (69). Jerry is having problems both with a former Italian boyfriend, who threatens to pursue him to Berlin, and with his own son, who is running up debts and has got a girl pregnant, "after all the preventative training I've given him. And to think that I broke him in myself when he was twelve years old" (70–71). Another roomer, Hilda Gay, pursues Files, to his discomfort. Steve and Hilda decide independently to return to Paris; after making vague promises to join them, Files starts thinking about where he wishes to go—"it would not be Paris" (85).

The book was self-published in Paris; it did not appear in the U.S. until a posthumous edition in 1963 under the title *There Was a Rustle of Black Silk Stockings*, with an added story. It was reprinted in 1992, again with an added, though different, story. The editor of this edition records that Charlie Knight was based on the real-life figure of Dan Mahoney, who also served as the basis for Djuna Barnes's character Dr. O'Connor in *Nightwood*. The editor also notes that Carrol Timmons is McAlmon's second fictionalized depiction of the painter Marsden Hartley (1877–1943), the first being Brander Ogden in his short novel *Post-Adolescence*, 1923. Robert Menzies McAlmon (1895–1956) was born in Clifton, Kansas, but grew up in Madison, South Dakota (where he fell in love with Gore Vidal's father), and in various towns in Minnesota. He enlisted in the Army Air Corps during World War I. He attended the University of Southern California for a while before leaving for New York. There he worked as an artists' model and became friends with Hartley. With William Carlos Williams he brought out the short-lived *Contact Review*. In 1921 he met the wealthy English heiress Winifred Ellerman (Bryher). They wed in a marriage of convenience, and McAlmon moved alone to Paris; they divorced in 1926. He founded the Contact Publishing Company (publisher of Hemingway's first book) and became an important member of the expatriate colony. Among his friends was Kay Boyle, who republished his 1938 autobiography interleaved with her own: *Being Geniuses Together*, 1968. (Boyle also wrote a novel that usually appears on gay fiction lists: *Gentlemen, I Address You Privately*, 1933, revised 1991, but it is of interest mostly to lovers of her fiction.) From 1926 until 1940 McAlmon alternated between the American Southwest and Europe. Edwin Lanham based the "somewhat homosexual" poet, Guy Hart, in *Banner at Daybreak*, 1937, on McAlmon. He died of tuberculosis in Desert Hot Springs, California, leaving unpublished a *roman à clef* about the Canadian writer John Glassco, *The Nightinghouls of Paris*, 2007.

While back in the U.S., did McAlmon publish a novel under the name Robert Sculley? Several readers of *A Scarlet Pansy* have amassed evidence to support a case. There are campy similarities between it and "Miss Knight." Is the main character, Dr. Fay Etrange, a composite figure based on Hartley and Williams? (It's curious that no one has suggested Dr. Mahoney.) Is Dr. Mason Linberg a self-portrait? If so, that would suggest that Marjorie Bull Dike must be Bryher, but those seeking correspondences claim she is based on Radclyffe Hall. Turning the novel thus into a *roman à clef* obscures what a delightfully original work it is. It was published by Samuel Roth with a 1932 copyright date. Its subsequent textual history is complicated. The authentic revision most often available is a 1952 printing with the original title on the spine and a revised title, *The Scarlet Pansy*, on the title page. The 1992 Badboy revision is a travesty of the original text, to be avoided.

The novel follows Fay's life from the time he is sixteen, soon after the turn of the century, until his death on a French battlefield at age thirty-three. One forgets that *Fay* is a unisex name, obviously chosen for that reason as well as being a homophone of *fey*. Throughout the novel, without exception, feminine names and pronouns are used to describe him. A reader is several pages into the story before it becomes obvious that *she* is *he*. Yet there is no hint that Fay suffers gender diaspora. His attitudes fit the current paradigm of masculinity. He is a strong, even muscular youth, only his voice and sometimes his mannerisms suggesting the feminine, and he can be quite assertive. The novel is only intermittently interested in gender issues; when it becomes philosophical, it focuses on social and especially religious oppression: "This is a hell of a civilization which does not permit each type to live its life as it sees fit" (151). "What right has any individual to be interested in my conduct, be that what it may, so long as I do no harm to him and do not interfere with another's right to life, liberty and the pursuit of happiness?" (177). "The only recourse is to see that every ecclesiastical student is properly seduced, and thus liberalized. The pulpit, after all, makes the laws of this country" (266). "Americans do so love to manage everybody's business but their own. Religious people won't permit anybody to be happy if they can help it. To them anything this is enjoyable is a sin. Not content with being miserable themselves, they wish to make everybody else miserable, too" (308). But the novel is most serious about celebrating the joys of double entendres, camping, and drag, of open cruising and promiscuity, of making love for the sheer pleasure of the act. It is the first novel to unabashedly proclaim how much fun it can be to be gay: "Were you ever in the Navy?" Mason asks. "Quite the contrary," Fay responds (231). And though Fay suffers the conventional fate of the homosexual in the end, he is shot in wartime and gives up his life to save the man he loves.

The novel begins with his death, then instantly flashes back to his childhood growing up on a farm in Kuntzville, Pennsylvania (changed to the more decorous Huntsville in the revised text). As soon as possible he flees to Baltimore, discovering on the train that his looks attract the attention of men. There he performs menial labor in a coalyard. He is saved, in good Horatio Alger fashion, by richer men. Soon he is bound for New York. By now he has shed his religious beliefs, saving him "from the frightful and hopeless remorse from which so many of her kind forever suffer" (75). There he meets others who hold "that what people do with each other is only their own personal concern" (91). As a child Fay was interested in science. Gifted with photographic memory, he now enrolls in a Philadelphia medical school. There he becomes friends with Mason. There is a long visit to the gay community in San Francisco. Then, medical degrees in hand, they journey to Europe to continue their medical and sexual studies. Mason enters into "a marriage of convenience" with a lesbian (291). The two men are caught by the declaration of war. Fay flees to Paris and joins the Red Cross, but then resigns to become a journalist. He meets and falls in love with an American lieutenant, Frank. Fay follows him onto the battlefield: "Relations of all sorts, so close to the front, were accepted in those times without comment and without the urge to pry into other's lives and reform every and all things" (363). And there a bullet ensures that, their love tested, it is not found wanting.

Beachy, Robert. *Gay Berlin: Birthplace of a Modern Identity*. New York: Knopf, 2014.
McAlmon, Robert. *Distinguished Air (Grim Fairy Tales)*. Paris: Contact, 1925. **Miss Knight and Others*. Ed. Edward N. S. Lorusso. Albuquerque: University of New Mexico Press, 1992. 1–85.
Scully, Robert. *A Scarlet Pansy*. *New York: William Faro, 1933. Revised: *The Scarlet Pansy*. New York: Royal, 1952.
Smoller, Sanford J. "Introduction." *The Nightinghouls of Paris*. By Robert McAlmon. Urbana: University of Illinois Press, 2007. xi–liii.
Sussman, Matt. "My Strange Affair with Fay Etrange." Ed. Andrew Belonksy. *Queerty*, Oct. 11, 2006. Online.

10 Anonymous (Benjamin Musser): *The Strange Confession of Monsieur Mountcairn*, 1928.

One could call *Confession* a novel of ideas, but they are muddled ideas. At one point the protagonist says, "My head grows dizzy" (183); he could be speaking for the reader. This is the kind of book that would be forgotten were it not for its subject matter. It is the third American novel (and the first to be published in the U.S.) with a protagonist who openly and explicitly declares that he is homosexual. The plot is negligible. In the first part Baldwin P— becomes infatuated with a violinist, Paul Boyer. He fights the attraction. There is not only the social disapprobation of homosexuality, there is also the public's "general suspicion with which anyone who followed the arts was regarded" (133). He fears "that the natural fascination which man held for me, would be translated into unpardonable acts themselves" (136). But when Paul kisses him, he acknowledges that "two universes had met in me: one that represented all inherited and traditional; and the other that [represented] all the inhibited emotions I had felt all my life as to the beauty of man, which suddenly became crystalized in this magnetic Austrian-Russian-Gentile-Jew" (137). But after they consummate their love sexually, both recoil, and they separate. Baldwin holds, "The love of one man for another is foreordained to be short-lived. To begin with it has no safeguards. It depends first and last upon the degree that the one is capable of constancy to the other; and it is shipwrecked in the end by one of two alternatives: satiation and boredom; or jealousy culminating in either hate or contempt" (143). Yet he regrets "that society is so slow to recognize that so-called perversion is not a matter of election, but a driving, inward command; and that in its finest manifestations, it has never produced anything but what is awesome and honoring to the human race" (144). Still, sex bothers him, and the idea of promiscuity "unsettled and unnerved" him (146). Paul says the whole problem stems from the fact that puritanism "implanted in your mind that anything Wildean was to be crushed" (149). Paul himself marries, and two years later dies.

Baldwin's second affair is with a new hire in his office, the young Benjamin Graham. At first they warily circle each other. The physical aspects of love come no easier to Baldwin. He starts worrying, "All my life I have been seeking in others the perfect man; and I don't know whether I was actually seeking him; or whether I was trying to fill up cavities in myself" (164). In a dream, the angel Gabriel concurs with his premise that "the love of man for woman is something man has invented; and is not in the [divine] plans and specifications; while the love of man for man, or more properly for himself as he apprehends himself in others, is in the plans and specifications" (166). The two men decide to share a home and bed, but when Graham tries to get Baldwin to perform oral sex, Baldwin refuses. Graham insists that "he was of normal yearnings and I of decadence. The vague world I had sought to create for ourselves, he disclaimed, as a madness. This platonic satisfaction without completion in organic stimulation and slumping, was inconceivable" (177). Baldwin resigns from the business and escapes the city by train—debating whether, though "scarcely credible, that such a mutuality might have also found expansion in an ever broadening sphere of love; and that out of the apparent degradation, the descent into the flesh, two souls in conflict with society might have found compensation in peace with themselves" (179). He continues wrestling with the problem for many pages more.

Roger Austen and later Justin Spring identify the author as Benjamin Francis Musser (1889–1951), born in Lancaster, Pennsylvania. Musser was editor of two poetry magazines. He was involved with Charles Henri Ford and Parker Tyler, and he financed Samuel Steward's first book, apparently through money he had married into. He underwent a religious conversion and thereafter wrote Catholic poetry. He lived in Atlantic City, New Jersey. The original limited edition was published by Samuel Roth (1893–1974), a champion of writers' freedom of expression, and reprinted in Roth's hardback quarterly *American Aphrodite*. Roth's publishing house also brought out *A Scarlet Pansy*. He fought for Joyce's *Ulysses* and Lawrence's *Lady Chatterley's Lover*; Roth v. United States, 1957, began the process of applying the first amendment to literature and disarming the U.S. postal service, which until then could declare that any book concerning homosexuality was obscene and thereby subject to prosecution.

The Strange Confession of Monsieur Mountcairn. N.P.: Privately printed, 1928. **American Aphrodite: A Quarterly for the Fancy-Free*. Ed. Samuel Roth. Vol. 3, no. 11. 127–86.

11 Claude McKay: *Home to Harlem*, 1928. Wallace Thurman: *Infants of the Spring*, 1932.

Halfway through McKay's novel, the story begins to center on the friendship between Jake Brown, a veteran of the great war, and Ray, a Haitian intellectual. The two meet while working as waiters in a train's dining car and bond: "Like a black Pan out of the woods Jake looked into Ray's eyes with frank savage affection" (272). There is no indication, however, that Ray is gay. When Jake says to him, "Youse awful queer, chappie," *queer* seems to mean "simply strange," even though the comment has been occasioned by Ray's that one of the women at a house "had some nasty perfume on her that turned mah stomach" (200). On the other hand, another of Jake's friends indeed "swerved off at a different angle" (237). Billy Biasse "boasted frankly that he had no time for women" (87–88). His nickname is Wolf, "'Causen he eats his own kind" (92): "'Ise a wolf, all right, but I ain't a lone one,' Billy grinned. 'I guess Ise the happiest, well-feddest wolf in Harlem. Oh, boy!'" (88). He is first glimpsed in a nightclub with a "straw-colored boy who [...] was made up" (91), one of a dance duo who holds his own with his female partner on stage and enjoys "iced creme-de-menthe through a straw" at Billy's table (94). He is one of the stronger individuals in the book. When Jake has a medical emergency, Billy takes charge of the situation. The last chapter is entitled "The Gift That Billy Gave." In it Jake credits him with saving his life. What is remarkable is how little any of the other characters remark on Billy's way of life. Cultural historian Eric Garber provides Billy's context (318): "At the beginning of the twentieth century, a homosexual subculture, uniquely Afro-American in substance, began to take shape in New York's Harlem. Throughout the so-called Harlem Renaissance period, roughly 1920 to 1935, black lesbians and gay men were meeting each other on street corners, socializing in cabarets and rent parties, and worshiping in church on Sundays, creating a language, a social structure, and a complex network of institutions."

Garber lists the most prominent gay and bisexual writers as Howard professor Alan Locke and poets McKay, Thurman, Langston Hughes, Countee Cullen, and Richard Bruce Nugent. All of them appear under aliases and slightly redesigned biographies in Thurman's *roman à clef*, along with Leland B. Petit, the gay white church organist who was friends with Blair Niles. Thurman's novel is a meditation on and extended critique of this renaissance. It recounts the goings-on in Niggeratti Manor, a rooming house whose landlady aspires to be a patron of Harlem artists and intellectuals. The main character is Raymond Taylor (Thurman's guarded self-portrait). Clearly there is an emotional attraction between him and Stephen Jorgenson, a Danish Canadian studying at Columbia (Harold Stefansson, Thurman's lover); they share a room and a bed. But it is defined as "something delightfully naïve and childlike" (34), and Stephen is always seen sexually with women. Also prominent in the house is Paul Arbian (Nugent), who is openly homosexual, or at least bisexual. We first meet him via his paintings: "nothing but highly colored phalli" (12). As soon as he appears in person, he announces to Steve: "I think that Oscar Wilde is the greatest man that ever lived. Huysmans' Des Esseintes is the greatest character in literature, and Baudelaire is the greatest poet. I also like Blake, Dowson, Verlaine, Rimbaud, Poe and Whitman" (24). When asked, he admits to sexual liaisons with both men and women; when pushed to tell which he prefers, he equivocates, "I really don't know. After all there are no sexes, only sex majorities, and the primary function of the sex act is enjoyment. Therefore, I enjoyed one experience as much as the other" (47). Paul, however, is always in the company of men. When the Manor decides to host a salon, he shows up with a bootblack who, he says, "has the most beautiful body I've ever seen. I'll get him to strip for the gang" (175). Shortly afterwards we hear of "the fanciful aggregation of Greenwich Village uranians Paul had gathered in Raymond's studio to admire his bootblack's touted body" (184). The Manor collapses when one of its members is arrested for statutory rape of a girl. Steve leaves Ray; Paul moves to the Village. There he commits suicide. His final act has nothing to do with his being gay. Ray assumes it either stemmed from his facing reality or was the final act "in his drama of beautiful gestures" (280). Nurgent said that it "was the only way Wallie could think of to end the book" (Wirth, 15).

Nurgent was writing his own version of the same events, but his novel, *Gentleman Jigger*, did not appear until after his death. Excepts were published in 2002 and the full novel in 2008. Wirth wrote in 2002 (163): "The fact that Thurman's novel was published, while Nugent's was not, does not mean that Nugent imitated Thurman. Indeed, [...] Nugent alleged the opposite: that Thurman copied from him." However, Wirth noted that only one scene is identical in both texts. It is interesting to see how close yet how different the two works correspond. For example, in Nugent's novel, when the character corresponding to Paul is asked about his sexual experiences, the response is very close, but when pushed to declare which sex he prefers, Nugent's alter ego answers (183), "I don't quite know. I enjoyed both immensely. But then, I've never been in love myself."

Festus Claudius McKay (1889–1948) was born in Jamaica but came to the U.S. in 1912 to study. Already a poet of importance, he abandoned college to move to New York. He became an activist, was attracted to Communism, and left for England and then Russia. In 1940 he became an American citizen. Though gay, he was married. He died in Chicago of a heart attack. Wallace Henry Thurman (1902–1934) was born in Salt Lake. He attended the Universities of Utah and Southern California but took no degree. He moved to New York in 1925 and was shortly arrested for solicitation in a subway toilet. He married in 1928; the couple separated but never divorced. He collaborated on a Broadway play, *Harlem*, 1929. The same year his first novel, *The Blacker the Berry*, drew mixed reviews. In 1934 he spent several months in Hollywood writing screenplays. Back in New York, he was diagnosed with tuberculosis and died at the end of the year. Richard Bruce Nugent (1906–1987) was born in Washington, D.C., but spent most of his life in New York. He published the first gay African American short story: "Smoke, Lilies and Jade" appeared in the only issue of *Fire!!*, a journal edited by Thurman, in November 1926. Besides being a writer and a painter, he was an actor. He appears in the 1985 film documentary *Before Stonewall*. He was married, but was always open about his sexuality. He died in Hoboken, New Jersey, of congestive heart failure.

Garber, Eric. "A Spectacle in Color: The Lesbian and Gay Subculture of Jazz Age Harlem." *Hidden from History: Reclaiming the Gay and Lesbian Past*. Ed. Martin Duberman et al. New York: Meridian, 1990. 318–31.
McKay, Claude. *Home to Harlem*. New York: Harper, 1928. *Ed. Richard Yarborough. Boston: Northeastern University Press, 1987.
Nugent, Richard Bruce. *Gay Rebel of the Harlem Renaissance: Selections from the Work of Richard Bruce Nugent*. Ed. Thomas H. Wirth. Durham, N.C.: Duke University Press, 2002.
Thurman, Wallace. *Infants of the Spring*. New York: Macaulay, 1932. *Ed. Richard Yarborough. Boston: Northeastern University Press, 1992.

12   Charles Brackett: *American Colony*, 1929.

Brackett's novel depicts one day in the life of Jack and Eve Sidgwick, an American couple who have rented a villa on the Côte d'Azur. It opens with Jack and his best friend performing a strange parody of a homosexual couple on Ted's yawl. The scene shifts to the beach. The Sidgwicks' guest is Sydney Gibbs, a gay who has sought refuge with them when he became fed up with the homosexual crowd in Paris. All is tranquil until the beautiful Cliff Smith—"the one who went to the Quat'z Arts ball as Antinoüs" (51)—joins them. He is a self-centered hustler, on the make with women and men. He is also a realist. He recognizes that for people like him, "we don't go so big with all the women. Just the awful young ones, and the ones that are getting along, and the whores. That's all that can't be happy without us. Them and the fags" (146). He's not at all ashamed that he blackmailed a sculptor who rescued him from his miserable home: "I knew how to attend to that baby though. I still get checks from him now and then, he's so grateful I didn't call a cop" (99). He has come down to be with Nancy Scott, the teenaged daughter of the Sidgwicks' neighbors, with whom he is having an affair, his eyes firmly set on her father's wealth. When he finds out she is pregnant, he agrees to marry her only if her father consents. The last we see of him he has picked up an ugly woman. He does not know that Nancy meanwhile has suffered a miscarriage, but it is clear that he would not care.

On Cliff's first entrance on the beach, Sydney cannot resist making a move on him. He offers to apply lotion to his back and starts dropping the names of gay Americans he knows in Paris, to be brought up short when Cliff responds, "Yep. I guess I know every fag in Paris" (59). Feeling insulted, Sydney stalks off to sulk. Jack goes in pursuit to calm him: "I should think it would mean something to you that your friends don't mind." Sydney responds, "Mind? Why should they mind? It's a good fashionable vice, so long as it isn't found out. Just let me get clapped in the Black Maria, though, and how many of you do you think will jump on the step to wish me a good journey?" Then, having delivered his grand speech, he tells Jack, "Run along. [...] There are some rather interesting things that come swimming here just about lunch time" (86–87). Later in town Jack finds him positively radiating happiness as he is being whipped off to Nice: "Some French sailor or local gangster probably," Jack thinks (123). When Sydney returns, the two quarrel, and Jack declares that "if he ever saw the God-damned pervert after that he'd knock him down" (181). It is undoubtedly a passing ire. The very last Jack sees of Sydney on this long day, he is entering a *hôtel de passe* with his companion for the night. Other things happen. Jack and Eve bicker about her dependency on sleeping pills. A child almost drowns. In rescuing him, Nancy suffers her miscarriage. Jack picks up a prostitute, thinking how the use of a condom equates to "Fidelity new style" (153). Ted falls out of and then back into love with a fabled heartbreaker, to be publicly humiliated and cast aside at a party she gives. Other reputations are shredded at the same party, including that of "that old fairy Nat Washburn," who apparently has been beaten up by his boyfriend (175). A mistral is blowing the entire time, leaving everyone's nerves on edge. In the end, Jack and Eve reconcile, at least for this day.

Charles William Brackett (1892–1969) was born in Saratoga Springs, New York. He graduated from Williams and Harvard Law School. After serving in World War I, he married and had two daughters.

He served as drama critic for *The New Yorker*, 1925–29; *American Colony* is dedicated to fellow columnist Alexander Woollcott, also gay. In 1932 he became a Hollywood screenwriter, frequently working with Billy Wilder, winning three Oscars. He served as president of the Academy, 1949–55. Upon the death of his first wife, in 1948, he married her sister. But his long-time lover was his son-in-law, actor James Larmore (1910–1965). He died in Beverley Hills of a stroke.

Brackett, Charles. *American Colony*. New York: Liveright, 1929.
Mann, William J. *Behind the Screen: How Gays and Lesbians Shaped Hollywood, 1910–1969*. New York: Viking, 2001. 204–06.

13 Myron Brinig: *Singermann*, 1929; *Anthony in the Nude*, 1930; *This Man Is My Brother*, 1932; *The Flutter of an Eyelid*, 1933; *Footsteps on the Stair*, 1950.

Harry Singermann's story is only a small part of a two-volume family saga, but it captures the loneliness of the gay male in a rural setting. He is introduced in *Singermann* as the next to last of seven children of a Romanian immigrant to the United States who ultimately settles in "Silver Bow," Montana. As a teenager, "he was too pretty to be really handsome, too paltry in his gestures and attitudes to be manly." He feels alone: "The rawness of Silver Bow was not a proper background for him and threw him in upon himself" (327–28). He is both flattered and frightened when Mr. Jordan, his high school history teacher, takes a special interest in him: "in his realization of the teacher's peculiar weakness, [he] began to feel the proportions of his own" (349). He feels he must fight "the poison." As he flees the teacher to escape temptation, he questions: "Why had these things been twisted in him and Mr. Jordan? What was the reason for these things, these ludicrous and tragic things?" He has a vision of "Mr. Jordan going from school to school, hiding his weakness and yet coddling it within him. [...] And always he must go about wearing a mask, lest someone find him out and laugh" (351–52). In the sequel, *This Man Is My Brother*, Harry imagines how "Mr. Jordan must have turned into a shabbier Charlus than M. Proust's" (78). When we meet Harry in the second novel, he is forty-four, but "there was about him a flush of extended youthfulness, youth that is drawn out and prolonged through inverted physical desires" (7). He is still effeminate, with "the mannerisms of a 'queer'" (36). Though he has traveled abroad, he is incapable of escaping the narrowness of his environment: "Harry suffered bad nights; they are usually bad for men of his peculiar, inverted type. He lay awake in fear of those who might reveal and expose his weakness. Shy and backward as he was, there had been certain adventures here and there, in New York, in London. Supposing someone should arise to blackmail him?" (77). Indeed, rumors about him are afloat in Silver Bow, but no one seems to care: "what's the difference?" (81). His brother David has adopted an orphaned Gentile boy, Richard. Harry becomes smitten with him, keeping his photograph on his desk at the family business. He almost parodies Mr. Jordan the way he caresses the youth: "Harry began to feel that he might be showing his affection too plainly. That affection had little to do with the fact that between them there existed a legal relationship, though not one of blood ties" (294). With a growing sense of fatality, while on vacation with Richard and some of his college classmates in Florida, he embraces the boy as if to kiss him. The boy "pushed him away. Richard stared at him with angry eyes that turned to disgust" (301). When the next day the uncle pursues him into the ocean to try to explain his action, he is again harshly rejected. Intent on pursuing the boy as he swims away from the shore, Harry follows and drowns. "Two days later, the body was washed up on the shore and identified by a fiercely weeping Richard" (307).

Michael, the youngest brother—a novelist who has "not yet written an important novel" yet seems "a very promising young man" (311)—functions as the author's alter ego. His sexuality remains an enigma. *Singermann* describes his youthful infatuation with a classmate: "Michael felt the first pangs of love, the fevers, the restlessness, the sweet loneliness of love" (280). Later, on a clandestine visit to a local bar when he is still underage, he feels overpowered by the masculinity in the room: "He wanted to rub against [the men], to feel their heavy, damp hands on his body, to smell them, to roll with them in curses, to explore dark, subterranean passageways of life" (293). In the sequel, he is still unmarried at thirty-seven. Questioned by Harry about his single state, he brushes the matter aside (36). Nothing occurs further to hint at his sexuality, but we are informed that his and

Harry's "temperaments" are "similar" (38). Both books' curious mixture of the explicit and the evasive, of approval and extreme disapproval of homosexuality, limits their appeal for present-day gay readers.

Footsteps returns readers to, this time, "Silver Peak," Montana, for a saga about the intertwined Benjamin and Joyce families, the one Jewish and the other Catholic. Closeted Jimmie Joyce leads as miserable an existence as Harry Singermann: perhaps worse since, after his one momentary release, he voluntarily shuts himself up again. While growing up, Jimmie "became more and more frightened of his emotional propensities and feigned a lack of interest in other men, a purely defensive measure to save himself from unhappiness and ridicule. Unhappily out of focus with himself, he was not so much a hypocrite as a coward" (173). He becomes an alcoholic. He frequently visits one of the town's prostitutes—to talk. He accompanies his sister to San Francisco, where she has gone to seek her estranged husband (an actor Jimmie finds attractive). There, in a bar, he meets Abel Birmingham, whom he drunkenly asserts is his double. For a moment alone in the fog-covered city, he gains alcoholic courage enough to say, "You're what I've always wanted to do and never had the courage to try" (282). Morning brings "a feeling of mixed horror and revulsion" (284). He flees the room before Abel can awake. At the hotel he finds a note from his sister; she has "gone back" to her husband, and Jimmie accepts, "I have gone back to me" (286). He returns to Silver Peak: "There had been a time when Jimmie could have gone away to some other place and made something of his life. He had delayed and hesitated and now it was too late" (305). Defending his failure to the bartender at his favorite drinking place, he blames God for having given him the "wrong ingredients" to make him a man. The bartender ripostes, "Brother, don't kid yourself. He didn't give them things to you. You picked 'em up yourself" (309).

More positive gay characters appear in two satires. A gay couple appears in *Flutter*, a Southern California experimental extravaganza. Antonio has been plucked from a garage to serve as Mrs. Forgate's consort. Having already dispatched a number of unsatisfactory lovers, she seems ready to strike again when she realizes he is smitten with the poet Hubert Daché. Instead of Antonio, she chooses to poison Daché. Antonio proves her guilt and turns her over to the police. Since the novel we are reading is the creation of one of the characters in it, a semblance of a happy ending is obtained. The whole of California slides into the Pacific as the result of a massive earthquake. In death by water, Antonio, "olive and naked, an incomparable young prince of the sea," sees Daché "smiling and beckoning to him [...] Antonio laughed and clung happily to the hand of his friend that reached out to him; and they floated together down the many crystal corridors of the oceanic palace" (308). Another character regrets that he is not bisexual: "In the bi-sexual world, when you tire of one sex you can turn to another and obtain an equal amount of pleasure. Certainly, a bi-sexual person has a great advantage over the normal, for he can go back and forth, weaving his senses into a complete pattern of gratification." He mentions that he has heard "Hollywood is swarming with bi-sexuals" (106). The composer Jack Frear is an early fictional depiction of a heterosexual transmale (perceived here, of course, as an example of a masculine lesbian).

Anthony is a study of shallowness. Paul, the gay character, serves as a foil to the title character, a gigolo who hunts out rich women. A "tall, fair youth with wrists that hung limply, and long, sad fingers" (8–9), Paul is a chorus boy in a Broadway musical. He offers to share his apartment with the penniless Anthony upon his arrival in New York on the basis of their common Oregon origins. Anthony freely uses it for sexual trysts with married women. But when Paul asks him to give up the apartment for the night so that he can entertain a friend, Anthony reacts angrily to Paul's using it "for obscene purposes." Paul gives in at once. Anthony returns unexpected one evening to discover Paul in bed with another young man (wearing "lavendar colored pyjamas"). He punches him in the face and announces that he is moving out (his having safely secured his next provider, so he won't have to sponge off Paul anymore). With no sense of irony, he announces lordly to Paul that "you're getting too old for adolescent vices" (115–16). The next time they meet, Paul seems to have picked up something of Anthony's *modus operandi*: he is riding in a "large, ornate limousine that shone and shimmered with a prodigal resplendence" (180), having become the secretary to a theatrical producer. For a fleeting moment, Anthony sees their similarities but draws no conclusions. Even if Paul lives more openly than Singermann or Joyce, the author remains uneasy about the subject of homosexuality, whether from publishing constraints or personal feelings, even as he seems compelled to introduce gay characters into his works. A comment, however, reminds us how daring it was to admit that gays lived in rural Montana: "As for Paul, he would not be at home in any place that was very far removed from an artificial city background, a theater, for instance, a city street for a bedroom. This did not mean that the Pauls of the world were not to be found in rural communities; but in a less urban background, they were inclined to be so repressed, so different in appearance and manner that you did not recognize them for what they were" (41).

The author has been largely forgotten despite his status as a pioneer on several fronts. Myron Brinig (1896–1991) was born in Minneapolis to Romanian-born parents but grew up in Butte, Montana. He studied at NYU and Columbia. After serving in World War I, he took a job with Zanuck Film Studio in Fort Lee, New Jersey. His publishing career stretched from 1929 to 1958; many of his novels were about Jewish-American life. I would not be surprised to discover gay characters in his other works. In 1933, on a visit to Taos, New Mexico, he met painter Cady Wells (1904–1954). Their year-long affair is the basis for Earl Ganz's fictionalized account, *The Taos Truth Game*, 2006. After a long period in San Francisco, Brinig returned to New York in 1955. He and Stephen J. Morello (1918–) shared a home for the last thirty-five years of his life. He died in New York of a gastrointestinal hemorrhage.

Brinig, Myron. *Anthony in the Nude*. New York: Farrar & Rinehart, 1930.
_____. *The Flutter of an Eyelid*. New York: Farrar & Rinehart, 1933.
_____. *Footsteps on the Stair*. New York: Rinehart, 1950.
_____. *Singermann*. New York: Farrar & Rinehart, 1929 (*Arno facsimile, 1975). London: Cobden-Sanderson, 1932.
_____. *This Man Is My Brother*. *New York: Farrar & Rinehart, 1932. *Sons of Singermann*. London: Cobden-Sanderson, 1932.

14 Dashiell Hammett: *The Maltese Falcon*, 1929–30. Raymond Chandler: *The Big Sleep*, 1939.

Hammett's novel introduces homosexual criminals. Even before the reader actually sees Joel Cairo, we are informed that he is "queer." When he appears, his physique, his attire, his demeanor, even his scent serve as code: "His black coat, cut tight to narrow shoulders, flared a little over slightly plump hips. His trousers fitted his round legs more snugly than was the current fashion." He uses "a lavender-barred silk handkerchief." He walks "with short, mincing, bobbing steps. The fragrance of *chypre* came with him." He seats himself "primly, crossing his ankles." "His hands were soft and well cared for." When he speaks, it is in "a high-pitched thin voice" (425–26, 454). In case the reader misses these clues, private investigator Sam Spade pointedly labels him a "fairy" (471). There is nothing particularly sinister about Cairo, however; the homosexual has not yet evolved into the villain, the way he will in later detective stories. Young Wilmer Cook is his sidekick, his boyfriend. Spade calls him a gunsel, a punk—terms that signify a gun-toting hoodlum, but also a passive homosexual. In a novel in which we see only the outward appearances of people, the visual clue to Wilmer's sexuality is his "curling lashes" (435), which are referred to constantly. When Spade slugs Wilmer, Cairo jumps to defend him: "Tears were in Cairo's eyes and his red lips worked angrily [...] Cairo cried, 'Oh, you big coward!'" (555). But later the two of them have a spat while the gang head ponders whether to follow Spade's suggestion that Wilmer become a fall guy. Spade grins: "The course of true love" (568).

Cairo wants Spade to retrieve the title statue. Brigid O'Shaughnessy is also after it. No love is lost between the two. She taunts Cairo about a boy he had in Constantinople; he retorts, "The one you couldn't make?" (449). But Cairo, Wilmer, and Brigid are all under the control of Casper Gutman, a fat, larger than life megalomaniac. He has a daughter and says he feels "towards Wilmer just exactly as if he were my own son" (549), but some readers identify him as likewise homosexual. Tennessee Williams resurrected him as essentially an asexual character in his play *Camino Real* (though the character was probably based on the 1941 John Huston movie rather than the novel). It is also worth noting the suggestions that Spade's secretary, Effie Perine, is lesbian. She is repeatedly defined by her "boyish face," and she concerns herself with Brigid more than seems called for. And Spade? He is a heterosexual opportunist, ready to lead his partner's wife into adultery and to be seduced by his client. The novel, Hammett's third of five, was serialized 1929–30 in *Black Mask*. In response to his Knopf editor's request to make changes to the sexual content, Hammett defended its inclusion: "It seems to me that the only thing that can be said against their use in a detective novel is that nobody has tried it yet. I'd like to try it" (961). The novel was filmed twice before Huston got it right, in the process retaining much of the sexuality.

Samuel Dashiell Hammett (1894–1961) was born on a farm in Maryland and grew up in Baltimore. He worked briefly as a Pinkerton agent before enlisting in World War I. After being treated for tuberculosis, he returned to the Pinkerton agency in San Francisco. He married and had two daughters. In 1930 he began his relationship with playwright Lillian Hellman. He pushed her throughout the process of writing *The Children's Hour*, 1934, about two teachers accused of having a lesbian relationship. He rejoined the army for World War II. In 1951 he was sentenced to prison for refusing to answer questions about his knowledge of Communist party supporters. He died in New York of lung cancer and was buried at Arlington National Cemetery.

Curiously, Hammett's novel does not show up on lists of gay fiction, while several by Chandler do regularly. The gay lovers in *Big Sleep*, however, have a far less significant role than Joel and Wilmer. We see Arthur Gwynn Geiger, who was engaged in blackmail and the pornography trade, only as a corpse. We meet his lover, Carol Lundgren— whom Philip Marlowe has earlier called a "punk kid" (651)—just after he shoots the man he mistakenly thinks killed Geiger. Marlowe comments, "You must have thought a lot of that queen." Carol perhaps speaks for the gay reader: "Go — yourself." After being further browbeaten by the P.I., the youth takes a swing at him. Marlowe laconically comments, "It was meant to be a hard one, but a pansy has no iron in his bones, whatever he looks like" (662– 63). It is the kind of comment one would expect from an investigator who describes Proust as "a connoisseur in degenerates" (629). Chandler may be a better writer than Hammett, but Marlowe's homophobic comments are more annoying than Spade's. For one thing, Chandler wants Marlowe to come across as a slightly tarnished knight, more admirable than the amoral Sam Spade. For another, there lingers the suspicion that Marlowe (and by extension Chandler) is a closet case. What else is one to make of a series of double entendres in a small scene between Marlowe and a cab driver? Marlowe "leaned in and showed him a dollar: 'Tail job?' He looked me over. 'Cop?' 'Private.' He grinned. 'My meat, Jack.'" The case over, "I gave the fresh-faced kid too much money and he gave me a dog-eared business card which for once I didn't drop into the majolica jar of sand beside the elevator bank" (627–28). This small scene was altered in William Faulkner's screenplay to remove any suspicion of a homosexual exchange; the very fact he felt it had to be changed buttresses a gay interpretation. (The movie was directed by Howard Hawks.)

Chandler's biographer Tom Williams writes (157) that his second novel, *Farewell, My Lovely*, 1940, has "been pored over by critics looking for evidence that [Chandler] was gay. Certainly the novel manifests some of the most homoerotic language that he ever deployed" in his depiction of Marlowe's relationships with the criminal Moose Malloy and ex-cop Red Norgaard. It is possible to read *The Long Goodbye*, 1953, as a covert gay novel. Marlowe has a strong emotional bond with Terry Lennox. Again, in Williams's words (80): "Marlowe seems to constantly hanker after a real connection with another man and regrets that such a thing seems impossible to achieve. In Marlowe's experience, male friends always leave or betray him, as is made most clear in *The Long Goodbye*." It is also worth looking at the relationship between Walter Gage, the detective, and Henry Eichelberger, the thief, in the 1939 story "Pearls Are a Nuisance," which at the least depicts strong male bonding.

Raymond Thornton Chandler (1888–1959) was born in Chicago, but grew up in Nebraska and England. He became a British subject in 1907, served with the Canadian army in World War I; though he returned to the States, living mostly in the Los Angeles area, he did not regain his American citizenship until 1956. In 1924 he married a woman eighteen years older than he. She died in 1954. He was one of the writers on the screenplay for Patricia Highsmith's *Strangers on a Train*. After his wife's death he was briefly involved with Natasha Spender, wife to Stephen Spender; she later remarked that she just assumed Chandler was a closet case. Chandler died in La Jolla, California, of pneumonia aggravated by alcoholism.

Chandler, Raymond. *The Big Sleep*. New York: Knopf, 1939. London: Hamilton, 1939. **Stories and Early Novels*. New York: Library of America, 1995. 587–764.

Hammett, Dashiell. *The Maltese Falcon*. New York & London: Knopf, 1930. *Complete Novels. New York: Library of America, 1999. 387–585.

Williams, Tom. *A Mysterious Something in the Light: The Life of Raymond Chandler*. 2012. Chicago: Chicago Review, 2013.

15 John Dos Passos: *U.S.A.*, 1930–38.

A trilogy, one of the landmarks of the modernist movement, gays appear in both minor and major roles across its length. Published as a whole in 1938, *U.S.A.* presents in cubist fashion a massive collage made up of sixty-eight Newsreels (headlines and brief excerpts from newspapers), fifty-one autobiographical Camera Eyes, twenty-eight impressionistic biographies of famous American figures, and twelve short stories and novellas each named after a principal character. These last are split into fifty-two chapters. Characters from one story appear in another, to create a complex set of relationships. The novel's innovative structure had a tremendous impact on later novelists. The first volume, *The 42nd Parallel*, appeared in 1930. In the story of Eleanor Stoddard two gay artists are introduced. Eric Egstrom works for the interior decorating department of a major Chicago store. With the money he earns he rents a studio. His roommate is a Frenchman, Maurice Millet. They seem "to be thoroughly happy. They slept in the same bed and were always together," to the point that Eleanor "used to wonder about them." We are told that "Maurice painted the loveliest pictures in pale buffs and violets of longfaced boys with big luminous eyes and long lashes, and longfaced girls that looked like boys" (195). Eric loses his job. To Eleanor's dismay, the two men start "drinking a great deal and going around with questionable companions" (199). Maurice shows up again in the second volume, *1919*, in the story of Eleanor's friend, Eveline Hutchins. He has returned to France to serve in the war as a stretcher-bearer for a military hospital in Nancy: he now looks "middleaged and pasty and oldmaidish in his stained blue uniform" (545). Maurice returns another day with a young French writer, Raoul Lemonnier. The latter briefly courts Eveline, obviously for some ulterior motive, for all the signs are that he too is gay.

1919 was published in 1932. In its opening chapter an enlisted sailor, Joe Williams, is introduced in the act of desertion. No sooner has he jumped ship than "a man who had come up behind him said something to Joe in Spanish. [...] for some reason he made Joe feel panicky" (365). Joining the merchant marine, he sails on a steamer that calls at Port of Spain. Once again he is cruised, this time by Warner Jones, "a youngish man in a white suit and a panama hat," who stutters when he speaks. He turns out to be on a West Indies cruise with his mother and a boat full of women. "The man's palm was soft when he shook his hand. Joe didn't like the way his handshake felt" (376). Still, Joe allows himself to be picked up by "the man who said his name was Jones," and the two hire a tourist car to see the island. Jones admires Joe's muscles and complains that his mother does not like his having "intimate friends," while he wants a companion, "a fellow like Joe in fact" (378). He takes the opportunity to stand close to Joe when they stop to urinate. Caught in the rain, they return to Jones's hotel room, where he urges Joe "to take your clothes off and take it easy." Joe attempts to leave, but Jones protests, "You can't go away like this, now that you've got me feeling all sort of chummy and you know amorous." He offers him fifty dollars. Joe runs. When he recounts the story to a shipmate, the listener laughs: "Fifty dollars, that's ten quid. I'd a 'ad 'arf a mind to let the toff 'ave a go at me for ten quid" (382–83).

We also meet Richard Ellsworth Savage in *1919*. As a youth he hates "the smell of girls" (426) and has an adolescent "crush" on "the yellowhaired captain of his school ballteam" (428). He becomes the protégé of Hiram Halsey Cooper, who "showed him first editions of Beardsley and Huysmans" (431) and pays for his Harvard education. In Cambridge he becomes thick with Ned Wigglesworth: "They had quite a bunch of friends who were interested in English and Fine Arts and things like that" (437). Ned spends an evening with "a thuggy-looking individual," ending up "in a Turkish Bath ... a most curious place." Dick has to fight "to keep from crying" about Ned's betrayal (439–40). The two men end up in France during the war, and both confess that they "got into hot water" (539). *The Big Money*, 1936, continues Dick's life. Stories follow him in his career in public relations (948). He sets off gays' gaydar. The Archimandrite O'Donnell looks him over with "an impudent rolling eye" and pinches his buttock with "a slow vigorous wink" (1179). As part of his job, he meets Senator Bowie C. Planet, who first shows up in *Parallel*. The senator "is very susceptible"; he "never has women to dinner" and has "a funny reputation" (948). Dick is one of the men who goes to the dinners (1195). One drunken evening Dick ends up in a Harlem nightclub. While his date dances with "a pale pretty mulatto girl [...] Dick was dancing with a softhanded brown boy in a tightfitting suit the color of his skin," who tells Dick that his name is "Gloria Swanson." After dropping off his date, Dick returns. He invites Gloria and "a strapping black buck he said was his girlfriend Florence" home with him. There he is mugged. He worries about the possibility of "being blackmailed" since they now know "his name his address his phonenumber" (1202–03), but back in his office he seems untouched by the episode.

The Cuban Tony Garrido is another important character in *Money*. He appears throughout the actress Margo Dowling's story. They first meet at a New York apartment house where they live. Because he respects her, unlike the other men in the house, the teenage Margo falls in love. She convinces him to marry her even though "Tony didn't seem to like the idea" (922), and the two embark for Havana. Matters do not go well there. Her in-laws expect Margo to conduct herself with propriety, but "Tony was always around with a middleaged babyfaced fat man in a white suit," whom Margo feels "there was something funny about." He is "a sugarbroker," who is "going to send Tony to Paris to study music" (974). She desserts him and returns to New York. Later she and a girl friend are invited on a yacht trip to Florida. In Jacksonville she runs into Tony: "He looked awful. He wore a rumpled white suit frayed at the cuffs of the trousers and he wiggled his hips like a woman as he talked. The first thing Margo thought was how on earth she could ever have liked that fagot" (997). Still legally married to him, they share a hotel room. But Tony has not changed: he hooks up with a bellhop, steals everything valuable she has, and takes off. Back in New York Margo makes the most of her looks to get jobs in fashion and photography. Then Tony shows up, "suffering from dope and exposure" (1051). She gets him into a sanatorium for a cure. After he is out, Margo decides to try her luck in Hollywood. Tony poses as her chauffeur: "He turned morose and peevish and took to driving the car around filled up with simpering young men he'd picked up, until Margo put her foot down" (1100). Soon he leaves again, this time for an Austrian count. When the count turns out to be impoverished, Tony tries to blackmail Margo into supporting the two of them. Finally, Tony provides a headline that could fit into a Newsreel section of the novel: "Hollywood Extra Slain at Party" (1124).

Tony is such an unsavory character that readers have generally assumed Dos Passos was putting down fags. In an alternate reading, Rebecca Blauvelt argues that Dos Passos actually used Tony to dramatize the dissent of the homosexual from social conventions and the repression of that dissent to the point of being silenced. Certainly, the cosmopolitan author was more sensitive than many of his peers to the gay presence on the American scene even if he did not entirely grasp the implications. Earlier, in his novel *Manhattan Transfer*, 1925, he briefly introduced the gay actor Tony Hunter. John Roderigo Madison (1896–1970) was born in Chicago. He spent much of his childhood in Europe. His parents married in 1910, and he began using Dos Passos as his surname. He graduated from Harvard. During the war he served with the volunteer ambulance corps. A painter as well as a writer of both novels and travel books, he was married twice and had a daughter. He died in Baltimore of congestive heart failure.

Blauvelt, Rebecca. "Main Character in the Margins: Homosexual Voice in *The Big Money* by John Dos Passos." *Forced Perspective*, Dec. 20, 2009. Online.

Dos Passos, John. *U.S.A.* New York: Harcourt, Brace, 1938. London: Constable, 1938. *New York: Library of America, 1996.

16 Blair Niles: *Strange Brother*, 1931.

Niles's novel is an anthropological expose of the hidden world of gay Harlem as seen by the white protagonist and her newfound gay friend, also white. It is a problem novel, with the novelty that the problem is not homosexuality but society's misunderstanding and mistreatment of homosexuals. It is a novel of ideas in which scientifically educated people discuss theories of sexuality and call upon the latest theorists in the field of sexology. In some ways it is a handbook, detailing cruising areas and drag balls, describing what we would now call gaydar, warning about the dangers of vice cops, blackmail, and gay self-hatred, and explaining the uses and the damages of what we now label the closet. It is melodrama, concluding with another gay suicide. And for straight readers it is romance, since the heroine finds new courage in the failures of the men who surround her. Historically, it is important. As literature, it is strained.

June Westbrook, with two male friends, is in a Harlem nightclub that caters to whites. She becomes fascinated by a white man in company of two black males: Mark Thornton. They meet up again at a spot frequented more exclusively by blacks, including "fairies" dressed like women. One of them is arrested by a vice squad officer upon leaving. Identifying with the plight of "Nellie," Mark makes a point to attend the trial, at which the youth is sentenced to six months in prison for solicitation. The clearly unjust sentence sends Mark to the library to investigate the legal code on Crime against Nature. He concludes that "it's love that [the Law] specially degrades. When you're read what it has to say about love—even about what they call normal love—you feel foul. It's loathsome. And when it comes to people who are different ... then it's sickening" (130). He calls upon June to report what has happened to Nellie and outs himself, thus beginning her education about homosexuality. This takes her into various byways, including attending a drag ball in Harlem. There she sees her ex-husband dancing with another man: "for the first time, June saw him for what he was" (219). Later she muses, "Perhaps when Palmer had married her he hadn't known. Understanding of himself might have come later" (224).

Mark has escaped the small Midwestern town in which he grew up, come to New York on the advice of his friend Tom Burden to find "a place big enough for a man to be different safely" (74). Tom himself has left on a pilgrimage to India, though the two remain in touch. Mark begins his education by reading Whitman and Edward Carpenter, Plato's *Dialogues* and Havelock Ellis. He conceives the idea of assembling a book on "Manly Love" with excerpts taken from the Bible onward dealing with same-sex attractions. As George Chauncey (*Gay New York*, 283) has written, "Having no access to a formal body of scholarship, gay men needed to invent—and constantly reinvent—a tradition on the basis of innumerable individual and idiosyncratic readings of texts. They also had to embed its transmission in the day-to-day social organization of their world. The folklore was typically passed on in bars and at cocktail parties, from friend to friend, from lover to lover, and from older men serving as mentors to younger men just beginning to identify themselves as gay." Mark has the courage to tell a young woman who has fallen in love with him forthrightly, "I'm the riddle that modern science hasn't solved. [...] I'm the sort of man who can never love a woman. I'm doomed to love a man" (244). He feels angry and speaks out when he discovers that the man for whom he works at a Settlement House has put pressure on the barber at a nearby shop to fire his helper because "he was a boy-lover." Mark speculates on projection, on how "it's odd how people do give themselves away [...]. When a man is as vicious as all that about a thing, you can't help wondering" (291–92). He befriends a young gay, "Lilly-Marie," who fell prey to drugs and was sentenced to the same prison in which Nellie was placed. In being kind he discovers that New York is not safe either. The young vendor whose fruit stand is just outside his apartment sees him with Lilly and, apparently motivated to some extent by jealousy, threatens to tell Mark's boss unless he pays up: "Blackmail! Mark vowed that he would never begin that. Blackmail was a long horror. It destroyed you in the end always" (317). And so he kills himself.

Why? The authorial voice provides one answer: "What was there to live for? He could never have the thing he desired. There had never been any possibility of that, never from the beginning" (318). (The "thing" is never specified. Is it June's cousin, the straight man he falls in love with? Or respectability and social acceptance?) June comes up with another answer: that despite his candor Mark has lacked true courage. Given what we have seen of his character, neither of these explanations seems plausible. For some readers it might be some kind of punishment; if so, the punishment is society's, not God's. Perhaps it is the author's attempt to arouse pity for gays. On the most elementary level, it may simply be the author's way to end the novel. Mary Blair Rice (1880–1959) was born on a tobacco plantation in Virginia. She married the marine biologist William Beebee in 1902. They were divorced in 1913, and she married the architect Robert L. Niles. In both marriages she showed her passion for exploration and writing about exotic places. Her white friend Leland B. Pettit, the organist at Grace Church, provided her an introduction to gay Harlem. She died in New York of a cerebral hemorrhage.

Niles, Blair. *Strange Brother*. New York: Liveright, 1931. London: Laurie, 1932. *London: GMP, 1991.

17 Andre Tellier: *Twilight Men*, 1931.

Armand Bironge is the natural son of the Comte de Rasbon. Distressed at the early death of the mother, his mistress, the comte has sent the child to be reared by her brother. When father and son finally meet on the boy's eighteenth birthday, the father is disgusted to learn he has sired an effeminate boy, undoubtedly a homosexual, who aspires only to be a writer, and refuses to acknowledge him as he had originally planned to do: "Wildness I could have excused, that at least would have been strength. But this! He might as well be a cripple—" (2). He arranges to have a woman of the world seduce Armand, never thinking that she might fall in love with the youth. She searches for reasons why her emotions are not reciprocated and reads Havelock Ellis. Poor Armand seeks love, but he loses all the men he feels affection for. He is whisked off to London, away from his beloved gardener Henri. There his uncle dies, his new friend Lucien, the comte's nephew, succumbs to tuberculosis, and his tutor kills himself rather than give in to desire. So much for the tutor's insight that people were wrong when they "denied the holiness and saw shame and degradation in one aspect of love—honor and nobility in another. In spite of them the unknown law attracted and held and drew" (98).

Armand flees to New York, to be taken up by another woman, provoking jealousy on her husband's part. By chance he meets Stephen Kent, a writer living in Greenwich Village. They move in together, and Armand becomes a poet. Young Armand, now in his twenties, becomes bored and wants to party. Another Villager, the bisexual Don Martin, introduces him to the gay gatherings hosted by the well-to-do roué John Wright. Under these new influences Armand flounders: "Sex, liquor, and narcotics, three factors that had done for stronger characters than Armand's" (162). On a dare, Armand goes out in the streets dressed in drag and is arrested. Stephen calls Judge Adrian Ware, also homosexual, for help, only to have Ware take Armand up. Despite the "carnal pleasure" of their relationship (196), the judge "had given up all hope of ever meeting a monogamous homosexual, and had learned years before that therein lay the tragedy of the inverted" (201). In a final burst of melodrama the Comte comes to New York. He informs Armand that he plans to have him institutionalized as a drug addict and while thus incarcerated to have him cured of his abnormality. Enraged, Armand strikes him dead with a heavy candelabra. Fleeing, he take a cheap room and there accidentally overdoses on morphine. Though it is hard to imagine who was reading the novel, it went through a second hardback and two paperback editions after World War II. No biographical data seems available about André Tellier (1902–?). Two other novels and a collection of poems are ascribed to him in the World Catalog.

Tellier, Andre. *Twilight Men*. New York: Greenberg,1931. London: Laurie, 1933. *New York: Greenberg, 1948.

18 Bradford Ropes: *42nd Street*, 1932. Fitzroy Davis: *Quicksilver*, 1942.

Set at the beginning of the 1930s, Ropes's novel follows the history of a Broadway musical from its casting to its opening night. It offers some insight into the technical problems involved, but the focus is on the "sharp clash of personalities" that comes with the setting. The director, Julian Marsh, is gay. His lover is the blond-haired juvenile lead, Billy Lawler. They are discreet, but they share adjacent hotel bedrooms with a connecting door (273). Julian is pretty universally respected for his knack to pull off a hit. One of his actors muses how "these artistic fellers gotta be queer. They's why they're artistic, I guess!" (86). "Miss Lawler" (263) is, to the same degree, "disliked by principals and chorus alike" (244). The same actor says of him, "Thinks he runs the show. I'd just as leave tell him he can't boss me just because he's Julian Marsh's mistress" (86). Billy is suspected of being responsible for the firing of good-looking blond chorus boys who might compete with him in the looks department (293, 328). Young, innocent Peggy Sawyers is the only one who stands up for him and continues to speak to Billy naturally. Her philosophy is simple: "what business is it of ours?" (108). Her kindness serves her well. The drunken star trips and suffers a concussion the evening before opening night. With no understudy, it appears the show will have to be canceled. But Billy saves the production with his unexpected perspicacity. He persuades Julian that he should look to the chorus for a replacement and pushes Peggy forward, arguing that she can step into the role with just a day's intensive rehearsal. He also uses the opportunity to push for his own exposure on stage to be amplified, a move blocked until then by the self-centered star. The day of the opening, he takes Peggy out. The gesture is basically a kind one, his acknowledgment that she has been "the one human being who seemed to respect him." At the same time he is aware that if she succeeds, she can help his career and provide a perfect "smoke screen for his relations with Julian Marsh" (332–33).

They are not the only gay presence in the novel. Jack Winslow is one of the chorus boys. The others level all kinds of sneers at him too. Two fellow dancers hard up for money ponder asking "that fagot" for a loan, but "with a sense of outraged virility," one says, "Lissen! I ain't puttin' myself under obligation to no fag. He won't keep his hands offa me now. Someday, I'm gonna sock that guy!" (52). The last we see of Jack, he is being accosted by two "hoodlums," as Billy and Peggy watch. One of the tough guys calls out, "Whoops, dearie, mind all the bad men or they'll change your name to Brown." Jack dismisses them with a putdown of their manliness. Billy tells Peggy that Winslow is the type she wants to steer clear of, but Peggy defends him (334–35). Names of other gay dancers are dropped. On opening night, when Billy first appears on stage, "There was a smattering of applause from a few oversexed matrons and three or four Park Avenue homosexuals. 'The belles stick together on a night like this,'" the producer thinks (341). But Billy and Julian's relationship is the only one developed. It seems to be based equally on genuine affection and opportunism. As Billy somewhat cynically says, "There's no such thing as sentiment in our business. It's dollars and sex!" (331). *42nd Street* is not a very good novel, but it is a kind of milestone.

Bradford Ropes (1905–1966) was born in Boston. According to Richard Barrios (107), in the novel he "evened the score with everyone who crossed him during his years as a Broadway chorus boy." The novel took him to Hollywood, where it was turned into the first of the Busby Berkeley film musicals and where he became a screen writer. The movie, which eliminated any hint of homosexuality, was a hit. Despite that, the novel was never reissued. Curiously, again according to Barrios (107–08), when Hollywood snatched up his second novel, *Stage Mother*, the studio "proceeded to expand on what little gay content it had." Ropes died in Wollaston, Massachusetts. In 1980 the movie of *42nd Street* was transformed into a stage musical, one of the longest running hits in Broadway history.

Quicksilver is the next theater novel with a number of gay characters. It describes the travails of a road company playing *Romeo and Juliet*. Set in 1935–36, the sprawling *roman à clef* was based on the author's experience with Katharine Cornell's company. The asexual assistant stage manager, Carl Talmadge, and straight actor Henry Carmichael form emotional bonds with other men. Henry is particularly tolerant of others' sexuality. Almost everyone else disdains Roger Winston, the lover of one of the stars, Anthony English. We see very little of their relationship, nor do we see much of the star's lesbian relationship with her longtime companion. More is made of teenager Arthur Fletcher's blundering attempts to find a boyfriend. His infatuation with a straight actor earns him a blow to the chin; his appeal to Douglas Grey results in their sharing a bed and his being tutored on how to survive in a homophobic world. Despite the fact that its author was gay, the novel contributes little to our understanding of a gay presence in the theater between the world wars. Fitzroy Davis (1912–1980) was born in Evanston, Illinois. He attended Williams and Columbia. He was by turns an actor, a singer, a painter, and a scriptwriter. During the late 1950s and early 1960s, he sent off a series of eleven articles to the gay Swiss magazine *Der Kreis* under the pseudonym "Hadrian." He died in Putnam, Connecticut, of cancer.

Barrios, Richard. *Screened Out: Playing Gay in Hollywood from Edison to Stonewall*. New York: Routledge, 2003. 107–09. On Ropes.

Davis, Fitzroy. *Quicksilver*. New York: Harcourt, Brace, 1942.

Ferris, Lesley. "Kit and Guth: A Lavender Marriage on Broadway." *Passing Performances: Queer Readings of Leading Players in American Theater History*. Ed. Robert A. Schanke and Kim Marra. Ann Arbor: University of Michigan Press, 1998. 197–220. On Davis.

Fumento, Rocco. "Introduction: From Bastards and Bitches to Heroes and Heroines." *42nd Street*. Wisconsin/Warner Bros. Screenplay Series. Madison: University of Wisconsin Press, 1980. 9–38.

Kennedy, Hubert. "A Latter-Day Hadrian: Fitzroy Davis and *Der Kreis*." *San Francisco Bay Area Gay & Lesbian Historical Society Newsletter*, 5.2 (Winter 1989): 1, 6. Online.

Ropes, Bradford. *42nd Street*. New York: Grosset & Dunlap, 1932.

19   Richard Meeker (Forman Brown): *Better Angel*, 1933.

The novel is a *Künstlerroman* that details the development of Kurt Gray as a composer and librettist. It is a coming out story that records his relationships with three men and a woman. And it becomes a manifesto adumbrating future calls for gay liberation. It opens in Kurt's hometown in Michigan, where his mother instills in him "pride in difference" (17) and where he suffers through the agonies of masturbation and wet dreams until another boy assures him that it all is perfectly natural. The novel jumps to his years at Ann Arbor. There he becomes friends with the siblings Derry and Chloe Grayling and falls in love with the former, not without misgivings. But he begins to understand himself better: "He had read for the first time the new psychology—Brill, Jung, Freud, Ellis, Carpenter; he had discovered Wedekind. From them he learned that his sin and Derry's was not the unique sport he had believed it to be. There were others, it seemed (at least in Europe there were) of his sort. Plato he reread with a new interest." He discovers Lord Douglas's famous poem and feels a kindred spirit with Cellini, Michelangelo, Shakespeare, and, "he felt almost certain, Shelley." He concludes, "Nothing so rich, so filling, so troubling, so goading, could be evil. The world might say what it chose" (68–69). Derry does not respond to Kurt's overtures in kind; instead he introduces him to David Perrier. Now he faces an added problem: "Was it possible to love two people at the same time?" (79). Complicating the muddle, Chloe falls in love with him. He has his first fumbling experience with a woman and concludes that he must be honest with her: "It's such a strange mix-up, such a queer lopsided triangle, yet the lines are all straight and perfect in their way. I've loved Derry for years. He doesn't love me much, if at all. You love me. Three relations, different, right, wrong, who knows?" And in a twinkle, another triangle comes into existence: David, Derry, and Kurt—"three human beings bound by one desire, by one splendid ideal" (111–12).

Kurt, however, departs to France alone to work. Chloe writes a spiteful letter telling him that David and Derry have gone in for the gay scene in Greenwich Village in a big way. Tony McGauran, whom he has met on the boat, shows up. Passionately bisexual, the actor seduces Kurt, and for the first time "Tony's vivacity, his scoffing intolerance of the sentimental, made introspective probings and questionings and self-pityings seem puerile, and strangely—for Kurt—out of place." He feels "utter content." He accepts, "To worry, to question, to submerge oneself in a sticky swamp of conjectures about things one couldn't hope to change, was stupid, undeniably" (145–47). The time with Tony becomes "a sort of golden interlude" (149). Under his tutelage Kurt grows. In a final discussion on the terrace of a Nice café, Kurt holds forth: "You said [one night] that love was all alike. You were right about that. So is lust. Each kind of passion—man-and-woman passion, man-and-man passion—has all degrees of love; from love that is pure and high and fine, down the scale to lust that is ugly and despicable and beastly. Each kind has its prostitutes, its procurers and pimps and 'houses,' and each kind has its ideal lovers. Its Paola and Francesca, and Dante and Beatrice, on the one hand; and its David and Jonathan, and its Shakespeare and Willy, on the other. The only difference is—the only damned difference is that for us there's no way of getting social sanction—so we go around the world like a lot of sorry ghosts, being forever ashamed of a thing we've no reason to be ashamed of" (154). In Paris he tries to penetrate the mystery of women's sexual attraction once more before rejecting such knowledge as unimportant to his development.

He returns to America and David, knowing now "that he loved David as he never could have loved Derry, loved him more deeply because his love was requited and understood" (171). They have mixed feelings about the gay world: "It's like some great and terribly secret society, with its own life, its own passwords and signs; and once you're in it, it's the very devil to break out" (168). David determines to write the novel that will serve as a "vindication of our kind of loving," "to show people we're not monsters any more than Shakespeare was." He says, "Oh, I know the continentals have had a hand in it—Proust, and Mann, and Gide, and Wedekind; but it's America I want in my book" (170). Chloe tries to interfere; Kurt rejects her arguments and her. He accepts that by necessity his life has a dual quality: the face he must present to the straight world and the secret fullness of his life with David. His newly acquired equilibrium is tested when Derry is entrapped by a vice detective. Further tests follow. But the novel ends on an affirmative note. The title comes from Shakespeare's Sonnet 144. An abridged paperback edition was published in 1951 under the misleading title *Torment*. (Interestingly enough, the abridgment cuts chapters dealing with the more humdrum aspects of Kurt's life but leaves the sexuality intact.)

The complete novel was reprinted in 1987 with an introduction by Hubert Kennedy. Its till then unknown author stepped forward to reclaim his work in his own name and to acknowledge that it was heavily autobiographical. As a result, it was reprinted in 1995 with photographs and the identities of the principal characters. Kurt was the author, Forman Brown (1901–1996). He was born in Otsego, Michigan. A graduate of the University of Michigan, he became a musical comedy composer and lyricist and a writer of plays for puppets. David was Richard Brandon (1905–1985); Derry was Brown's cousin Harry Burnett (1901–1993). The three of them founded the Yale Puppeteers and then the Los Angeles Turnabout Theatre, 1941–56. Their career was the subject of a 1993 documentary, *Turnabout*, by Burnett's nephew Dan Bassic. Tony was actor Alexander Kirkland (1901–1986). In 1991 Brown published a charming tale for young readers, *The Generous Jefferson Bartleby Jones*. He died of heart failure in Los Angeles.

[Brown, Forman.] *Better Angel*. By Richard Meeker. New York: Greenberg, 1933. *Boston: Alyson, 1995.

20 Rex Stout: *Forest Fire*, 1933.

Stout's novel has not been reprinted since its initial publication. It recounts the obsession of a forty-five-year-old Montana forest ranger, Stan Durham, for his nineteen-year-old summer helper, Harry Fallon: "There was something special about Harry, something that made Stan feel for the first time in his life that there might be something important about a man besides the work he was supposed to do" (32–33). He has never felt anything particular for women. He does not satisfy his wife, Elsie, sexually; she has turned to other men and labels her husband "a snub-nosed gelding" (21), *nose* descriptive of his face but metaphoric for another part of his body. She grows suspicious of the friendship between the two men. Other rangers observe it too, but as one tells Elsie, "Maybe I know when something's a little too peculiar, but it's just none of my damn business" (140). In trying to understand what is happening to him, Stan remembers "many of the forest and prairie epithets and phrases and jokes regarding intimate physical relations between men, or between men and boys, but knew nothing whatever of the actual facts on which they were based" (119). He fumbles his way through what is, at base, a courtship of the youth.

A summer visitor, Dot Fuller, also sets her sights on Harry, even though she is ten years older than he. She decides that she is not returning to the city a virgin. When Stan discovers the two together (innocently, but he does not know that), "he becomes aware of a startling and incredible fact" that he is crying (190). Dot grasps that he is her rival for Harry's affections. The emotional fires billow up into a very real fire. Dot, in her perpetual carelessness, does not verify that a cigarette she throws away is out. She even thinks, "when you're having an affair with a young man what's a forest fire more or less no matter who started it; quite possibly you did it on purpose so Stan Durham would have something to do" (249). Harry is killed when a burning tree falls on him. Discovering Dot's culpability, Stan, insane with grief, ties her up in Harry's cabin and tries to set fire to it to burn her alive. She manages to get to a revolver and tries to shoot him; Elsie shows up and succeeds. The two women ride off, leaving his body in the burning cabin. Despite the melodrama, the misogyny, and the heavy irony of the ending, the novel presents a fascinating portrait of a mid-life crisis brought on by sudden awareness of one's hitherto hidden sexuality.

The year after *Fire*, the first of the author's thirty-three Nero Wolfe novels appeared. Since the series features a household made up of four men and no women, some readers have wondered whether Wolfe and his amanuensis, Archie Goodwin, are lovers. Wolfe, despite his suggestive names and his pronounced misogyny, seems more asexual than anything. Still, he is a fervid lover of orchids, a flower which receives its name from the Greek for *testicles*. Archie well may be pansexual, were he out of the closet, but the evidence is skimpy. The factotum Theodore Horstmann is seen almost exclusively tending to the orchids, but the gourmet chef, Fritz Brunner, comes across as more than a little fey, whatever that might suggest about his sexuality. Rex Todhunter Stout (1886–1975) was born in Noblesville, Indiana, but grew up in Wakarusa, Kansas. He served in the Navy in the years before World War I, assigned to President Theodore Roosevelt's yacht. Fervently anti–Fascist and anti–Communist, he was one of the founders of the Vanguard Press and a mainstay of the Authors Guild. Married twice, he had two daughters. He died in Danburry, Connecticut, of natural causes.

McAleer, John. *Rex Stout*. Boston: Little, Brown, 1977. Chapter 25.
Stout, Rex. *Forest Fire*. *New York: Farrar & Rinehart, 1933. London: Faber, 1934.

21 Kennilworth Bruce: *Goldie*, 1933.

Badly written as it is, *Goldie* has historical significance. It provides an extensive tour of gay midtown Manhattan and Greenwich Village between the end of the war and the onset of the Depression. It offers the first lengthy fictional depiction of street hustling. Throughout (though this is not new in gay literature), there are long discussions of the origins and nature of homosexuality, with lists of homosexuals who are counted among "the world's greatest geniuses." Long before Kinsey, it brings attention to the sheer number of gays, claiming there are "more than four million others in the United States who dwelt in that twilight realm of sex" (95–96). And it sounds the call for a gay liberation movement: "Whereas sexual inversion is inherited and ineradicable in a majority of instances; and whereas so-called abnormal intercourse between male and female is tolerated just as much as normal intercourse; and whereas, France and Italy have ceased for a century to make inversion a crime and haven't suffered by it; Now, therefore, be it resolved that we do hereby organize under this Constitution in order to advocate a change in the laws of the State of New York, of the several States of the United States, to permit adults to dispose of their persons as they wish, providing that they do not disturb the public peace or give scandal to the young or the public at large while doing so" (248). The same group advocates a major shift in scientific research: "Science has always approached the problem of homo-sexuality from the wrong angle. It is not, it should not be a study of psychical pathology, but rather one in embryology" (244). A teacher even envisions a gay studies course in university settings and the assembly of "an anthology of poems on love among the inverts" (250).

The novel opens in contemporary New Orleans, where Paul Kameron has been brought before a judge for approaching a detective, presumably for sex since he is "indubitably" queer, only for it to come out that he wants to confess to murder. The rest of the novel is a flashback explaining what led up to this moment. Paul serves in the Army air force in Belgium during the war. There he falls in love with a nurse, Connie Wilson, but finds out that his remorseful best friend has had sex with her while she was drunk. In revenge he brutally rapes her. She vows that she is "going to have [his] baby" (69). As a result of meeting his first "pansy," he begins his education about homosexuality. While a POW in a German camp he pulls upon what he has learned and finds "gratification in bestial practices" (79). When he and his sexual partner are freed, they go to Paris. Paul is quickly taken up by an American furrier, Marcus Reubenhardt, and consents readily to becoming his kept boy: "Now he had entered the twilight realm as a professional and with his acceptance of a place in Limbo he brought his career as a soldier and a man to an ignominious close" (86). Back in New York, he learns how to dress the part, and with the help of "a very good [hair] wash then on the market," he metamorphoses into Goldie. His very body begins to change and becomes effeminate. He educates himself about gay history, and, "With the help of Havelock Ellis, he embarked upon a self-analysis" with the result that he determines, "He was not going to deny his body" (100). Caught in the act with Skinner, another of Reubenhardt's employees, both men are sent packing.

After a rapid tutorial on the streets by Skinner, Goldie sets out to support himself by hustling. His striking looks attract the attention of Emily, "an old queen" (129), who takes him under his wing and who introduces him to Mr. Gordon's establishment on Central Park West. He attends his first drag ball, becomes aware for the first time of the "particular branch of Limboism that embraced woman-woman love" (143), and afterwards participates freely in a private sex party with a condom-maker for a partner. As he extends his explorations, "Goldie came to know hundreds of people like himself" (169): "He made many friends [...]. Besides the group that frankly paraded their abnormality and lived for their own satisfaction alone, Goldie met that other group composed of staunch citizens of the larger world, who lapsed occasionally into Limbo and its pleasures" (171–72). They include a fellow hustler who has a wife and children to support, a dope addict, a gangster, soldiers and sailors who are "always ready prey" (174), "innumerable old men" (176), and Paddy, a gay man in love with a lesbian. He meets a returning war pilot who has become a heroin addict in the "unending search for thrills" that the war began (164). Goldie indifferently witnesses Emily blackmailing the son of a Boston blue blood, but when he accidentally learns how much money Emily has been taking from his johns for his services, he walks out of the establishment. On assessing his position, he takes refuge in the thought, "I at least have an established trade" (200), only to discover that Emily has started a rumor that he has syphilis, effectively ending that career.

It is now 1931. Even hustlers are suffering from the Depression. Paddy entices Goldie to join him in opening a restaurant in the Village: "Perhaps it was because Paddy and Goldie were themselves citizens of Limbo [...]. But it soon became evident that besides a restaurant they were also conducting a rendezvous for the most unusual lot of hybrids that could be found in any section of the world" (226). Among the various types who come there are the founders of the gay liberation movement, which calls itself the Twilight League. Like so many movements, they discover it "impossible to organize the adherents of Limbo" (253). One of the founders in essence destroys it when he outs its existence in a tabloid paper. The consequences are direr for Goldie: his picture adorns the front page. Once again he is vulnerable to Emily's machinations. Unexpectedly, the publicity also brings a letter from Connie in New Orleans. She faces death (probably from ovarian cancer), so if he wants his thirteen-year-old son, she says to "come and get him" (257). On the trip down Goldie reverts to being Paul. He envisions his son becoming a doctor who would use medicine "with its wonderous preventative and curative powers" to "develop means for preventing and correcting sexual abnormalities" (266). His fancy dissipates the instance his son makes a sexual pass at him and he realizes "this son of his was queer like he was" (270). In a melodramatic finale, Paul concludes, "He would rather see him dead!" (272). And so he kills him. The novel ends with Paul's hanging. All my attempts to discover who Kennilworth Bruce was have failed. It has crossed my mind, given the opposing views that the novel endorses, that perhaps more than one writer were involved.

Bruce, Kennilworth. *Goldie*. New York: William Godwin, 1933.

22 Charles (Henri) Ford and Parker Tyler: *The Young and Evil*, 1933. Djuna Barnes: *Nightwood*, 1936.

Ford and Tyler's collaboration is autobiographical in source, modernist in execution, and long a cult favorite. It is raw in language, more than suggestive in detail (there's quite a bit of obvious sex, often with three to a bed, including sometimes a woman), but hardly pornographic. In meandering fashion it recounts Julian's arrival by boat to New York, where Karel awaits him. Until this point the two rather flamboyant gays have known each other only via correspondence. Soon they meet the poets Gabriel and Louis in Greenwich Village, and the rest of the novel follows their various pairings, jealousies, disputes, and reconciliations. Karel breaks up their relationship by pairing with Louis, and Julian ends up for a moment "with Gabriel because he wasn't with Karel" (132). He picks up a guy he sees in a restaurant, "the kind that makes homosexuality worthwhile" (141). Louis and Gabriel get back together. Louis wants Karel's suit, leading to the bizarre ending: "He did not resist having his topcoat taken off, then his jacket, then his vest and, lastly, falling over on the bed, his trousers. Louis leaned over and Karel saw him kissing him before he felt the bite. Then Karel screamed" (215). Set pieces include a party, an appearance at a Communist meeting, an evening at a drag ball in Harlem (much anthologized), and a mugging, by sailors on Riverside Drive, and subsequent trial under a gay judge. Lots of names are dropped, including Barnes, Stein, Eliot, but the usual list of great gays of the past was not considered necessary.

At one point, Julian ponders love: "He was unbelieving when he saw lovers who were lovers in the complete sense and who slept night after night in the same bed. He was quite sure their love was a fabrication or a convenience or a recompense and he did not believe in their love as love" (72). Much later he pursues the thought that "my homosexuality is just a habit to which I'm somehow bound which is little more than a habit in that it's not love or romance but a dim hard fetish I worship in my waking dreams it's more a symbol of power than a symbol of pleasure not a symbol inducing pleasure but exemplifying it not a specific symbol" (170). The novel is not an easy read, being lightly punctuated, when at all, and eschewing all quotation marks. Yet, read aloud with voices, it is compelling. It was published in Paris, not appearing in the U.S. until its reproduction in the Arno Press series on homosexuality in 1975. When Sea Horse Books issued a facsimile edition in 1988, it included, for the first time, six paintings that the Russian painter Pavel Tchelitchew made in Ford's personal copy.

Charles Henri Ford (1908–2002) was born in Brookhaven, Mississippi, brother to the actress Ruth Ford. While still a teenager he launched an important little magazine, *Blues*. Traveling to Europe, he met Tchelitchew (1898–1957) in Paris. The two lived together until the painter's death. Primarily a poet, Ford also directed the film *Johnny Minotaur*, 1971. He died in New York. Harrison Parker Tyler (1904–1974) was born in New Orleans. He came to New York in the mid-1920s to become a reviewer and a poet. In 1945 he met Charles Boultenhouse (1926–1994). Like Ford, the two became involved in the underground film world during the 1950s and 1960s, including Andy Warhol's early work. Tyler wrote the biography *The Divine Comedy of Pavel Tchelitchew*, 1967, and an early book about homosexuality in film, *Screening the Sexes*, 1972. Another of his books about film was extensively quoted by Gore Vidal in *Myra Breckinridge*, 1968. Tyler also died in New York.

In 1932 Ford typed an early version of Barnes's *Nightwood*. It too is autobiographical, modernistic, and a cult favorite. It is more style than substance—at least from a gay perspective (a lesbian reader would have a different take). Championed by Eliot, it was first published in London, then in the U.S. a year later. (Cheryl J. Plumb edited *Nightwood: The Original Version and Related Drafts*, 1995.) A lesbian triangle centers the plot. The gay character is Dr. Matthew O'Connor, somewhere in his fifties, originally from San Francisco, now living in Paris. He served in the war. He likes to dress in women's clothing and uses perfume and makeup, even indicating that he wishes he had been a woman (98). He also calls himself a "member of a secret brotherhood" of the night (87) and says that, since "so God has made me, my house is the pissing port [...] I haunt the *pissoirs*" (97), a connoisseur of "the size and excellence" of penises (100). He says he is "simple" and does not "want a thing in the world but what could be had for five francs" (111), and he recounts his delight when an Arab "offered me five francs before I could reach for my own" (118). Djuna Barnes (1892–1982) was born in rural New York. By 1913 she was part of the Village avant-garde, a member of the Provincetown Players. She spent the 1920s as part of the expatriate circle in Paris and the 1930s in England. Dr. O'Connor is based on Dan Mahoney, who also served as a model for Robert McAlmon. In 1941 she returned to the Village, where she died. She had various affairs with both men and women.

Barnes, Natalie. *Nightwood*. London: Faber & Faber, 1936. New York: Harcourt, Brace, 1937. *New York: New Directions, 2006.
Ford, Charles, and Parker Tyler. *The Young and Evil*. Paris: Obelisk, 1933. *New York: Sea Horse, 1988.

23 Edgar Calmer: *Beyond the Street*, 1934.

The novel follows the lives of ten teachers and five students during a year at a large high school in New York. None of them is particularly happy. Some are downright miserable, in fact. One of the teachers has a mental breakdown and kills himself. The two gays that we meet seem relatively staple by comparison, though both crave unobtainable loves. Lloyd Quent, the English teacher, has a penchant for falling for male students, "the kind that were on teams and didn't ever study much" (171). His latest infatuation is with the handsome and utterly straight John West. West has a schoolboy crush on the history teacher, Stewart Cassall, very much a woman despite her name. (Cassall, clueless to reality, is hopelessly, comically in love with Quent.) The teacher is part cliché: his studio apartment is decorated in mauve. He has an active sex life. Some of the teachers and even students suspect he is gay. John gradually senses that the teacher's interest in him is more than tutorial. During the performance of a show that Quent has invited him to during the Christmas holiday, he has "suddenly the impression that Mr. Quent was too near him" (142); the same evening he is "disturbed somehow at the seriousness under the other's laughing tone" (145). Near the end of the spring semester John appears in Quent's classroom, saying he wants to ask the teacher a question about something he has been told: "This fellow told me you were—" Quent preserves his dignity: "He knew, without shock, without shame, yet as if for the first time really that this was to have been expected." He apologizes that the gossip "seems to have made you unhappy" (281–82). But to his credit he does not deny the unarticulated allegation. In a postscript the reader is informed, "Lloyd Quent is teaching at a high school in Queens, living much the same life" (303).

Alex Sadowsky is a student with musical talent. In love with Vicente Fabrigués, three years younger than he, he takes straight fellow student Donal Keefe into his confidence. Donal is quite at ease with sexuality in general. When another students says to Donal of Quent, "You know why he's nice to West," Donal replies, "Sure it's true. You can see it without proof. But what of it? There's a lot of people like that, only the other people are in the majority and they object to it—well, for no real reason at all." He goes on, "It's only he's living in the wrong age. With the old Greeks it was a regular thing." He also mentions Shakespeare's sonnets (242) and feels scorn about how dumb people can be about the real nature of the world. Alex meanwhile accepts that his courtship of Vicente, though it seemed to promise something at one time, is hopeless. In a final meeting, he tells the younger boy, "I can't make you understand it, what it is, our friendship, what I feel. I don't know myself, kid, what I ever wanted from you. I know—I only know…. I never got it." Moving more deeply into insight about himself, Alex does know, "He wanted to hold him close to his body, he wanted to kiss him" (289). Alex feels despair, but music will become his refuge. In the postscript we learn that he never graduates but he is "studying piano and theory" while he works as an usher in a concert hall (304). He continues to play the piano with his high school teacher at his apartment and frequently sees Donal. The latter has a job on a New York newspaper.

Edgar (Ned) Calmer (1907–1986) was born in Chicago. He attended the University of Virginia. He worked as a journalist for both the *Paris Tribune*, beginning in 1927, and the *Paris Herald*, becoming friends with Henry Miller and Hemingway. Later he was hired for CBS by Edward R. Murrow as a broadcast journalist and worked for the network as a newsman for twenty-seven years. This was his first book. Calmer was married three times and had two children. He died in New York.

Calmer, Edgar. *Beyond the Street*. New York: Harcourt, Brace, 1934.

24 Lew Levinson: *Butterfly Man*, 1934. Daphne Greenwood: *Apollo Sleeps*, 1937.

Ken Gracey, the protagonist of Levinson's novel, possesses bodily grace but little ken about himself sexually. In 1922 the Texas teenager is, more or less, bought from his father by a wealthy townsman who now lives in Pasadena, California, but who happens to hold the mortgage on Ken's family home. Discovering that Ken has the talent to be a dancer, he enrolls him in a Hollywood school that trains dancers for the movies and the theater. There, for the first time, he meets different people that he realizes are gay, leaving him wondering, "What fraternity of men was Ken entering? What were its ramifications? Its code? And in what manner had he been seduced into joining this monastic life?" (34). He turns his back on his benefactor and teams up with a fellow student, Anita Rogers, some ten years older than he. They leave for San Francisco together and start touring theaters as a dance act. Unfortunately for him, she is alcoholic and promiscuous. As they tumble down the economic scale, they end up dancing in a Tijuana dive. Fed up, Ken leaves her and heads for New York. Under the tutelage of producer Howard Vee he becomes the star of a musical comedy. They share an intense if platonic relationship until Howard must go to London. On tour, after the show ends its Broadway run, Ken begins to drink and more wantonly sample gay life: "He had quit the old scheme of things, entered a new and happier region where life raced by so speedily that one never learned how to care. And here he knew he would remain forever" (212). He likes to dance naked. A Chicago gangster gives him the name "*il huomo volante* … my butterfly man" (223).

And then the novel begins a series of psychological zigzags. After much madness and lost time, Ken concludes that he is "not really that way," that he "just never cared about girls" (257). That mindset lasts until he meets Tommy. He gives Ken syphilis. On a visit to a doctor, he admits that he is homosexual. The doctor reassures him, "You have nothing to fear from your inability to conform. You diverge from normal, of course. But that is not to say that you are abnormal. Perhaps you are a more complex organism than we others. Don't worry about that" (276). In a rage Ken throws Tommy out and returns to being promiscuous and to drinking. His dance director tells him, "You overdo everything" (281). Out of control, jobless, broke, he accepts becoming a nude model for a photographer. When he next comes to, it is already November 1930. His self-hatred intensifies: "I'm a dirty mouthed fag ... a disease! I'm a low stinking slut! I'm a rotten...!" (307). Trying to break free, still drunk, he decides to return to Texas. Since he is broke, he must walk, and the way leads across the Hudson River: "He was in a great hurry and he stepped right off the pier and into space." The final line of the novel reads: "Ken's hand stretched out, as if to grasp the city that had killed him" (318).

Greenwood's novel is also about an American dancer, Anatole Desmond. He is as feminine as Ken is masculine. (All the gays in Greenwood's book are effeminate.) At sixteen, the self-centered teenager is singled out by the dancer Gussie Graves, who says he is as beautiful as Apollo. Even though he is repelled by Gussie's appearance, Anatole resolves to learn everything he can from him. He accepts his tutelage for four years, "during which period Gussie initiated him into his own world of queer people, whose names were legion. Anatole found them interesting and exciting, thoroughly enjoying the new life into which he fitted so perfectly. It was not long before he had settled down comfortably in his new environment, casually adjusting himself; accepting their peculiar codes as his own, taking their standards for granted" (72). Ready to move on, Anatole announces his engagement to an elderly but wealthy widow. Overwrought, Gussie kills himself. The marriage lasts ten months, until she catches him giving a drag party for his old friends. A few years later, for undisclosed reasons, Anatole has to flee the city. He ends up in Tokyo, where he meets the married Diana Steele. She surrounds herself with gay men, but she quickly loses her head over the dancer.

Anatole is amoral, without scruples or regrets. Deciding to live with a Japanese student, he defends his decision to Diana: "After all, I'm only doing what you and all the other women are doing—living with a man for what you can get out of him." When she retorts, "But I'm married," he says simply, "Marriage is only another name for room and board, and you know it!" Finally she sees him as the talentless gigolo that he is and correctly predicts that he, like the fairies he has make fun of, will "himself be teetering and mincing seriously instead of in fun. He would not notice it, but the others would be quick to see the change in Anatole. It would be such a '*camp*,' dwindling gradually into '*Aunt Gloria*'—another 'Ella' or 'Hortense' or 'Pauline'!" (230–31). At this point the woman who, as a little girl living next door to Anatole, had a crush on him, shows up as a tourist. Mousy, unattractive, still single, still in love with him, and now a rich heiress, she seems the solution to his troubles. He drops his Japanese boyfriend to marry her. He cannot, however, shake off a fellow American, the aptly named Felix Gossamer, who has been hovering around him since his arrival in Japan. But as the three board a boat to take them away, Anatole is still alive, still scheming.

Lewis Levinson (1898–1985?) was born in Rochester, New York. He attended Columbia and served as an Army French interpreter during World War I. He was a press agent for Broadway musicals. In 1932 he moved to Laguna Beach while he worked as a Hollywood script writer. He also co-authored at least two plays with William Charles Lengle. He returned to New York and worked for the *Daily Worker*, then became a sportswriter. He was married and had children. Daphne McIntyre (1895–?) of Christchurch, New Zealand, married Michael Shathin, a Russian, in Yokohama in 1920. He was the Far Eastern representative for Warner Brothers. Imprisoned by the Japanese during the war, he died in an airplane crash in Singapore in 1954 at age sixty. Both writers seem to have disappeared from view before they died.

Greenwood, Daphne. *Apollo Sleeps*. New York: Messner, 1937.
Levenson, Lew. *Butterfly Man*. New York: Macaulay, 1934. *New York: Castle, 196-.

25 H. S. Kahm: *The Passion Expert*, 1935 (aka Jerry Cole: *Secrets of a Society Doctor*, 1950).

Kahm's novel was revised stylistically when it was republished under the Cole pseudonym, but the plot remains the same. Dick Weston, a recent college graduate with a degree in psychology, talks his best friend, Johnny Hadwell, into putting up a thousand dollars he has inherited to rent an office suite in New York; there Dick will pose as a psychiatrist. With publicity from another college friend, now a city reporter, he plans to rake in money from wealthy women with sexual problems. Soon *Dick* takes on new meaning in counseling. His life becomes more complicated when

Matt Johnson, a teenager working in the next office, tries to kill himself. When Dick sees the sobbing boy, he feels a "thrill of sympathy, deep and searching" (25), and invites him into his office. There Matt confesses that he is gay and has just been rejected by the boy he loves. Dick thinks, "This boy was suffering because he was convinced that there could be no love for him in this world, no outlet for his natural love impulses which were directed towards his own sex. If he could be shown concretely that the world hadn't died with Chris' rotten friendship, that it was still possible for him to love and be loved, that would restore his mental or emotional balance" (27). Telling himself that "he mustn't let his so-called normal instincts get the better of him," Dick invites Matt to share the apartment and the bed that he and Johnny have taken together, Johnny being relegated to the davenport. He assures Matt that "some of the best and finest people in the world have been—just like yourself. It's nothing to be ashamed of. You're not a fairy. Those fairies, or pansies, are only a small percentage of the people who are like you" (35–36). Given that this is a novel written for a straight audience in which all the other sexual escapades are heterosexual, the language becomes interesting.

While Dick is trying to keep up his strength to satisfy all his demanding women clients, he wrestles with the problem that Matt has, of course, fallen in love with him. He faces the idea that "Matt would sleep with him and probably try to make love to him. Homosexuals did that. [...] Could he stand it? Well, sometimes things just had to be done if you wanted to accomplish something" (40). When called upon to reassure Matt, Dick kisses him "slowly and thoroughly" (76). A second gay shows up seeking Dick's help. Arthur Merrick is searching for "a young man who could understand my nature, and who could respond to my love—it would make me unbelievably happy" (69). What is now the obvious solution to Dick's problem remains unobvious to our hero. It takes Matt's being wounded while trying to protect Dick from a jealous husband, a second attempt at suicide, and more heterosexual shenanigans before Dick thinks "that perhaps if he did a little really intelligent thinking about each of his patients instead of blindly worrying about what might happen something could be worked out of the chaos" (124). Finally it dawns upon him to pair Matt and Arthur up. Dick reflects, "I'll miss him. After all, he's been a pretty good friend on the whole; I'll sort of feel different when he's gone" (142). Matt writes from their honeymoon in Europe to assure Dick that he will always love him as a friend.

Kahm's obituary noted his lifelong support of sexual freedom. Unfortunately, he was not inventive enough to create the kind of soufflé he needed for the novel to work. It needs tightening (Matt seems to be forever sobbing). Johnny is never developed as a character, though there is obviously strong male bonding between him and Dick. The satire against the psychiatrist profession seems out of place. And chronological development is hopelessly messed up. Still, the novel is a reminder of the complex and varying attitudes towards homosexuality held by Americans between the world wars. Harold S. Kahm (1906–2000) was born in Chicago but moved to Minneapolis when he was six. He lived there the rest of his life. He never married, but his part in a *ménage à trois* with another man and a woman was important to his writing. His first novel was *Shared Woman*, 1934. Under the name Henry Sackerman, he published *The Crowded Bed*, 1967 (which may be a revision of *Shared Woman*), and *The Westbank Group*, 1970, which includes limited homosexual activity. He died of cancer.

Kahm, H. S. *The Passion Expert*. New York: Regent House, 1935. *Revised: *Secrets of a Society Doctor*. By Jerry Cole. Intimate Novel. New York: Designs, [1950].

26 Arion (Alan Campbell): *Starborn*, 1938.

Obviously autobiographical, the novel, never published in the U.S., describes James Macdonald's years between twelve and sixteen in San Francisco during the 1920s. There is something about his very appearance and mannerisms that label him immediately "sissy" (13), "hermaphrodite" (46), "fairy" (76). Hostile Father is "hounded by a revolting vision of his son's future" (33). He consults a doctor who advises him that without treatment "James might develop into a type of man who is regarded as undesirable by civilized society" (84). Doting Mother remains ignorant of her son's feelings. When James confesses that he has loved another boy, she says, "Rubbish! [...] Loving another boy! ... it is unheard of" (257). Only their servant, Martha, is sympathetic to the boy's loneliness.

When Father refuses to buy James *The Fairy Tales of Oscar Wilde*, she buys it out of her savings as a Christmas present to the boy. Father chastises her: "If you knew why Oscar Wilde spent a sentence in an English prison not so long ago, you would understand why I don't think any stories of his are suitable for James. He was a degenerate of the lowest...." Of course, this leaves his son "burning to know why Oscar Wilde was imprisoned" (28–29). Eliot Bender, the father of one of his classmates, recognizes an affinity with the boy when he comes upon him at his daughter's party: "I am your Brother ... don't you understand" (36). He is a composer, whose piece *Starborn* initially eludes James. Eliot kills himself. Slowly James begins "to understand why he had frequently been followed on the street by men with beckoning faces whose gestures repelled and attracted him at the same time." He recognizes, "There was an inner part of him, longing for the call of these outcast voices" (46).

He yearns to discover a kindred soul, someone who will accept him. His dream of such a boy produces his first nocturnal emission. He thinks of him as he discovers masturbation (even as he feels that he has "hopelessly defiled himself," having heard all the current theories about its harm): "He believed, even in the moments following his habitual surrender, in such a friend" (59–60). He thinks he has found his ideal in a boy four years older than he: Philip O'Day. Again Wilde is evoked: the two argue over *Dorian Gray*, with James contesting that the fairy tales and *De Profundis* are "of higher calibre" (114). (Later James reveals he also knows the story "The Priest and the Acolyte," wrongly attributed to Wilde.) Philip has a friend who met Wilde in San Francisco during his American tour. Philip himself is a curious creature. He declares, "Theocritus was a poet after your own heart, James" (133). He takes every opportunity to caress the boy, but he keeps making appointments and then finding excuses not to keep them. James is told that Philip is "diseased," in constant attendance by a physician, but the nature of his malady is not clarified. At one point, Philip announces, "You know, James, I understand you and all that sort of thing. Of course I am not bisexual or anything like that myself" (185); shortly afterwards, he says, "what a great pity I'm not queer ... what an amusing affair we two might manage together" (192). But Philip becomes smitten with an Italian poet whom James has met, "an extraordinary pervert" (187), and is vexed by the attention the poet pays James.

James impulsively writes the young Virgilio Cobelli just before he gives a poetry reading in the city. Father explodes about his son getting "mixed up with a degenerate dago who called himself a poet" and avows, "If there was a scandal, he would disown James" (153). Virgilio proves to be a better guide than Philip. He calls James "one of the elect" (155) and sets about "explaining and glorifying love between men" (160). He begs James, "do not suppress your feelings through false creeds ... do not let silly forms or conventions rule you" (167), for such is "endangering his health by emotional repression" (181). He argues, "What you call sin I should call destiny and spontaneous force of emotion" (169). Virgilio himself is a free spirit, dancing in the nude for his friends. He introduces James to others who "understand our nature" (163), most notably Peter Kerensky and Mark Wilkins. Peter remarks how much "we all enjoy the quest, though at times it is difficult for people like us ... so many doors are not open to us ... but that only makes the moments when we are together doubly sweet ... we know each other in any clime ... our language is of the eyes" (217). James offers himself to the poet: "He had given his lips and all the parts of his body to Virgilio, and he had touched with his own hands and lips, all the white nudity of his poet-friend. The experience had been most pleasurable" (203). Mark plays *Starborn* for him, and this time it speaks to him.

Virgilio returns to Italy; Peter and Mark take a cabaret job in Shanghai. Still a teenager, James briefly enters into a relationship with a ballet dancer only slightly older than he; it too becomes physical "as they read the desire in one another's eyes. They lay close beside one another so that all the parts of their bodies were in communion, so that the flow of love within them, which was the essence of their twin natures, mingled and made them as one" (242). James is last seen entering a sanatorium, having contacted tuberculosis. Yet the novel ends positively with a sense of rebirth in the offing. For a third time the music of *Starborn* is evoked and, along with it, memories of all the people who have helped him so far and "a promise that what had passed was but the beginning" (258). The novel is important as the first American work to have a gay teenager for its protagonist.

George W. Campbell (1910–1959) was born in San Francisco. He early adopted the name Alan Campbell. Noël Sullivan (1890–1956) was a patron responsible for a trip to India. The sexologist Havelock Ellis put him in touch with the married Harvard art historian Kingsley Porter (1883–1933); they became lovers shortly before Porter's disappearance from his Irish home. By this time Campbell had already written his one published novel. He returned to California, living for a time in Carmel, where he had a bookstore. On returning to San Francisco, he opened Studio Forty-Four, another bookstore and gallery. He died in his San Francisco home, the result of a fall down the staircase after having been somehow injured earlier in the evening while in a bar.

Arion. *Starborn*. Paris: Obelisk, 1938.
Costigan, Lucy. *Glenveagh Mystery: The Life, Work and Disappearance of Arthur Kingsley Porter*. Dublin: Merrion, 2013. 177–240.

27   Elliot Paul: *Concert Pitch*, 1938.

The straight narrator, Ernest Hallowell, an American music critic based in Paris, is intent on forming a relationship with the widowed American, Elizabeth Maura. He marries her and then loses her because she is intent only on her son, Robert. The gay French music critic and piano teacher, Lucien Piot, is intent on conquering Robert. He accompanies him on an American tour, makes a pass, and collapses when Robert brutally rejects him. Robert is intent only on Robert. His image must not be sullied; he uses poor Berthe, Hallowell's middle-aged concierge, to this end. Robert's former teacher, Eleanora Vallejo, who was in love with his father, now seems intent on his mother. The composer Gurevitsch is intent on making a splash with his avant-garde music. The post–Dadaist, Raoul Evrard, is intent on creating disruption. The last two habitually refer to Piot as a pansy, a nance, a fairy, while Berthe in speaking of him, says, "There are plenty of *tapettes* for him […]. There couldn't have been less than a thousand in the *Salle Gaveau* that evening" (255). But on the evidence of the novel, Piot is the sole homosexual in the city of Paris. The novel does not wear well. Elliot Harold Paul (1891–1958) was born in Malden, Massachusetts. He served in France during World War I. As a journalist based in Paris, he became friends with expatriates there and was one of the founders of *transition* magazine. He rode out the Spanish Civil War on Ibiza. Back in Paris and later in Hollywood he became a mystery writer. He was married five times and had a son. He died at the Providence, Rhode Island, Veterans Hospital.

Paul, Elliot. *Concert Pitch*. New York: Random House, 1938.

28   Carson McCullers: *Reflections in a Golden Eye*, 1940; *Ballad of the Sad Café*, 1943.

McCullers's first book, *The Heart Is a Lonely Hunter*, 1940, often appears on lists of gay novels. Certainly, there is a strong homosocial bond between the two deaf-mutes, John Singer and Spiros Antonapoulos, and gay readers can receive a great deal of pleasure from the work. But there is nothing explicitly gay about it. Likewise, in her final novel, *Clock without Hands*, 1961, though the seventeen-year-old Jester Clane begins to explore his attraction to men in his infatuation with the half-black, half-white Sherman Pew, a boy his age, it is not yet part of his sexual identity. Homosexual longing, however, is central to these two works.

Reflections was first published in *Harper's Bazaar* in October–November 1940. The short novel is gem-like in its brilliance. Serving on an unspecified Army base in the South, Captain Weldon Penderton becomes obsessed with Private L. G. Williams. He first becomes aware of the private when—in a scene that echoes Billy Budd's initial encounter with John Claggart—he spills coffee on the captain's trousers. They meet again when the private is assigned to yard work at his house. The fateful meeting, however, occurs, in a forest clearing, after the captain has sadistically mistreated the horse he is riding and turns to find his actions have been observed by the very naked soldier. Williams unties the suffering animal and leads it away. Penderton feels violated: "The Captain stumbled to his feet and started blindly through the darkening woods. […] In his heart the Captain knew that his hatred, passionate as love, would be with him all the remaining days of his life" (356). Williams is no innocent; we discover that he has killed a man and hidden his corpse. And now he becomes just as obsessed as the captain, but for the naked body of the captain's wife, Leonora. During the day Penderton stalks Williams, yearning for some way "to establish relations with the soldier whom he had come to hate" (370). In the evenings Williams enters the sleeping Leonora's bedroom and stands guard over her bed. The nervously overwrought wife of Leonora's lover witnesses the strange tableau and frightens Williams, but no one will believe her story. She is sent to a private sanatorium, accompanied by her effeminate Filipino houseboy; there she has a fatal heart attack, and Anacleto disappears. In the aftermath Williams returns to the house for a seventh time. He becomes disoriented and strikes a match to discover where he is. Looking out his window, the captain sees his face; he passively watches the private's approach and entry into the house. While Williams is kneeling beside Leonora's bed, Penderton shoots him twice through the heart. John Huston directed the 1967 film version. It was a box office failure but has since become a cult classic.

Ballad appeared in *Harper's Bazaar* in August 1943. An account of an unconventional lovers' triangle, it is no less powerful. The author defines love as "a joint experience between two persons," whom she labels "the lover and the beloved." Of these, she says, the lover is the more important because "the value and quality of any love is determined solely by the lover himself. It is for this reason that most of us would rather love than be loved" (417–18). But as the story demonstrates, the lover does not always gain his object. Miss Amelia Evans is the thirty-year-old proprietor of a café. Poe-like, the building reflects its owner in having "about it a curious, cracked look." Miss Amelia's face is "sexless and white, with two gray crossed eyes which are turned inward so sharply that they seem to be exchanging with each other one long and secret gaze of grief" (397). Masculine in her appearance and manner, a person who today would probably be seen as a transmale, she unexpectedly falls in love with a hunchback dwarf who claims to be her cousin Lymon Willis. Under his influence the café becomes a place for "fellowship, the satisfactions of the belly, and a certain gaiety and grace of behavior" (414). But the warm center does not hold. Long before Cousin Lymon's appearance, Amelia was married for ten days to Marvin Macy, who chose her "solely out of love" (419). Their wedding night was a disaster. When Marvin finally gave up, he turned to crime, and though the townsfolk continue to gossip about him, his name is never mentioned in Amelia's presence. Marvin returns while she is out on business. Lymon hears his approach: "He and the man stared at each other, and it was not the look of two strangers meeting for the first time and swiftly summing up each other. It was a peculiar stare they exchanged between them, like the look of two criminals who recognize each other" (436). Lymon falls in love with Marvin and invites him to move back in. The tensions among the three climax in a fight between Amelia and Marvin over the hunchback. Just as she is on the verge of winning, Lymon comes to Marvin's aid, and the two of them triumph over her. After destroying as much of the café as they can, they disappear. Despairing of their return, Amelia boards up the building and turns completely in upon herself. The novella ends with a mysterious but soothing coda: a description of the music that a prison chain gang makes as they work together on the road: "Just twelve mortal men who are together" (458). Edward Albee dramatized the story in 1963. The play became the basis for a 1991 Merchant–Ivory film directed by Simon Callow.

Lula Carson Smith (1917–1967) was born in Columbus, Georgia. Upon graduation from high school, she left for New York to study music, but ill health kept her alternating between the two places. In 1937 she married Reeves McCullers (1913–1953), and the two moved to North Carolina. Both bisexual, they divorced in 1941, and she became part of the February House commune in Brooklyn. They remarried in 1945; he committed suicide in Paris. She was friends with Paul and Jane Bowles, David Diamond, Tennessee Williams, Truman Capote. Jordan Massee was her cousin. Beginning in 1941 she suffered repeated cerebral strokes. She died in Nyack, New York, of a massive brain hemorrhage.

Carr, Virginia Spencer. *The Lonely Hunter: A Biography of Carson McCullers*. Garden City, N.Y.: Doubleday, 1975.

McCullers, Carson. *The Ballad of the Sad Café: The Novels and Stories*. Boston: Houghton Mifflin, 1951. *The Ballad of the Sad Café: The Shorter Novels and Stories*. London: Cresset, 1952. *Complete Novels. New York: Library of America, 2001. 395–458.

———. *Reflections in a Golden Eye*. New York: Houghton Mifflin, 1941. London: Cresset, 1942. *Complete Novels (see above). 307–393.

29 Harlan Cozad McIntosh: *This Finer Shadow*, 1941.

Shadow became a code word in titles and blurbs on book covers to indicate gay content. Sometimes the word promises more than is delivered, but homosexuality suffuses this posthumous novel. The text is elliptical, elusive, dreamlike—and fascinating. Set mostly in New York, it covers the period between the time Martin Devaud leaves the ship *Verda* till the time he returns to it months later. A widower, clearly bisexual emotionally, whatever he might be sexually, Martin sets out to find "where in the world a finer shadow was leading him—a search for mysteries without substance or reason" (27). It is a world in which religion is only fitfully useful and psychiatry not at all. After a drunken spree in which Martin ends up in a hospital to be examined by two psychiatrists, he roundly denounced the entire profession: "Theirs is a subtle lechery. They love this parade of erotics. Orgasms by proxy! Intelligent, perverted and ruthless!" (87). His world is now inhabited largely by gays, a "queer outfit" (261) with people falling obsessively in love almost instantly. Four men and one woman surrender to Martin's spell.

At an employment office, soon after arriving ashore, he meets an advisor, William Roberts, "a person hesitant in sex and yet requiring it" (30), who immediately assumes Martin is "one of us" (35) and whispers "one word" (32, 37), never heard by the reader. Roberts invites Martin to a party, at which he meets and falls in love with the widow Deane Idara—a woman fascinated by gay men, "conscious of the beauty of a sex that shocked her heart but held her mind" (220). Martin turns down a second invitation to go out with Roberts in order to be with Deane; in a snit, Roberts arranges to have Martin fired from the job he has obtained for him. Martin confronts him: "I respect the frank demands of the body. Petty intrigues disgust me. Your intricate desires have overruled your intelligence. As an invert I respected you. As a subverter I find you intolerable" (75). When nothing will convince Roberts that Martin does not love him in return, he deliberately, brutally, takes Roberts in his arms and "poured one bitter kiss after another—his teeth cutting the advisor's tender lips and cheeks, his sweat falling like molecules of light" until "Roberts screamed and turned his face away" (250).

Through Deane, Martin meets Drew Noland and Carol Stevens. From the beginning Drew holds an unexplained charm for Martin. At a drag ball that he hosts, "Drewena" begs for a kiss; "Miriam" responds and discovers that "a feeling had come over her during that kiss that she could not interpret. It was a half sick, half desirous mood of great intensity. And so, unaccustomed to tempering her emotions, she threw Drewena back upon the bed and held her tightly, her mouth pressing on her throat. Drewena did not resist until the desire had grown and Miriam groped blindly" (182). Martin tries to make sense of what has happened: "Desires that were new to her had come upon her without warning. Were her concepts changing? Or had they lain dormant, awaiting only the right moment to make her aware of another facet in her individuality?" (194). Drew flees Martin's intensity. Carol is not so lucky. In him Roberts sees an eminent threat, a dangerous rival. Suffering from a congenital defect of the brain, he fatally shoots Carol. While staring, Narcissus-like, in the mirror, he suffers a stroke. He dies in the arms of Martin, whom he has summoned to his bedside. Martin says: "Diseased, humiliated by our artificial sexual codes, he made his own world. Quite happily he lived and dreamed in this chimerical condition until unfortunately, I entered his last kingdom" (302). The shock brings Martin to renounce a life with Deane.

The one constant figure for Martin is his shipmate Rio. They arrive together on the *Verda*; they leave together on the *Verda*. The two men may or may not be lovers. Rio may or may not be gay. He demands to know whether Martin is: "Are you a god-damned fairy with your god-damned eyes and the way you look at people? You looked queer in that draggy dress at the party, and you acted queer. [...] If you're a queer, tell me! [...] And if you ain't—what are you?" Martin answers simply, "I am." Rio refuses to accept the statement and starts anew: "why d'you hang around them?" Martin accuses him of being afraid: "frightened of yourself, frightened of me, frightened of symbols" and suggests, "Before you ever ask another man that question, Rio, go to the mirror and ask it of yourself. Perhaps the answer will be—'thou, too'!" Martin sums up that homosexuality simply is: "It's part of life. It has its particular and its important position in the world. It has its stages and its stratas. Thus it is, Rio—this force was created [...] for balance." Rio blurts out, "'Balance,' hell!—those upside down bastards?" And Martin replies, "I didn't say they were balanced. I don't know that, because I don't know where the average begins or ends. I said they were created for balance. A necessary people forming a resilient salient between the rigidity of the sexes." His last words on the subject are, "I've looked at all of us and found us all so different—and yet so much the same" (263–65).

Harlan Cozad McIntosh (1908–1940) was born in John Day, Oregon. Dropping out of two colleges, he spent time at sea and vagabonding around the world. He came to New York in 1933, where he married and, where he, presumably, met John Cowper Powys, who was instrumental in getting the novel published posthumously. Disappointed by all the rejection slips he had received, McIntosh committed suicide by jumping from his apartment roof.

McIntosh, Harlan Cozad. *This Finer Shadow.* *New York: Lorac, 1941. New York: Dial, 1941.

30 Charles Jackson: *The Lost Weekend*, 1944; *The Fall of Valor*, 1946.

Weekend was Jackson's first novel. Its protagonist, Don Birnam, comes across as a repressed homosexual whose alcoholism grows out of his inability to accept his sexuality. As a boy he engaged in mutual masturbation with a classmate. One day he felt prompted to ask the other boy who he was thinking of "to aid the act." As a result, he became hyper-aware of the difference between the two of them. While his friend was thinking of a girl, Don was envisioning his own naked father (52). As a student at the University of Pennsylvania, he was "ushered out" of his fraternity for his "fatal infatuation" with an upperclassman (48–49), his having written him a "passionate" hero-worshiping letter, which was taken to the Senior Council (88). Early in the novel Don drops in on a mixed bar in Greenwich Village, whose singer takes delight in double entendres involving words like "*camping, queen, faggot, meat*" (28). While there, he becomes fascinated by a couple, attracted equally to the young man and his girlfriend: "It was all one to him, for the moment he was like a god who could serve either at will" (30). When he ends up in the alcoholic ward with a concussion from a fall, he spots the male nurse as being gay and reacts angrily: "They were always so damned anxious to suspect every guy they couldn't make of merely playing hard-to-get; so damned anxious to believe that their own taint was shared by everybody else." Showing more knowledge than one would expect from a straight or a closeted man about aspects of gay life, Don criticizes gays for putting down other "queens, but then goes on: "In the same breath that they ridicule their kind, they claim kinship with the great ones of the world," and he lists "Wilde, Proust, Tschaikovsky, Michelangelo, Caesar" (145–46). However, when he stumbles upon two men cruising each other in a men's room at the NYC subway, he is singularly clueless about what is going on (240–41). Charles Brackett erased most of the homosexual allusions from his 1945 award-winning screenplay, but the male nurse was played as gay as the Production Code would allow.

Fall, Jackson's next novel, set in June-July 1943, describes its forty-four-year-old protagonist's mid-life crisis. A New York university English teacher, he has been married for some ten years and is the father of two boys: "He had wanted to belong, fit in, find a place in social life which he could have found only in marriage" (259). But John and Ethel Grandin have started drifting apart, their problems beginning in the bedroom. John has lost sexual desire for her. They are to spend two weeks' vacation on Nantucket. On the boat over they meet Marine Captain Cliff Hauman, wounded in the Pacific, and his new bride. John falls in love with the young giant of a man. Cliff, on his part, sends out all sorts of mixed signals. He is constantly touching John, volunteering to put suntan lotion on him, offering him a photograph and then his military cap, joking to another man on the beach about an obviously gay man: "I want you to lay off that pretty boy over there, the fag. *You* can't have him—he's mine!" (202). A stray comment encourages John, but he is unprepared for his physical response: "to his horror, he felt a slow rude pressure growing in his loins." He understands "the danger he was in" (229). "He could not call it accident; events had shown it to be inevitable, perhaps, and even just" (237), "an extension or illumination of his nature. Very well; though he refused to give in to it, he would try to accept" it as experience (238). Ethel finds the cap and finally understands what she has sensed. She lashes out, calling it "perversion" (254), and leaves. Away from him, she realizes why she was drawn to John in the first place—that had he "been all male, they would not have met on common ground ever" (308)—and writes him a letter of reconciliation. Before the letter arrives, Cliff shows up at their New York apartment and again sends off mixed signals. John declares, "'I've grown very fond of you, I can't help it' [...] and he drew Cliff tight against him." With outraged masculinity, Cliff seizes the fire tongs (which are mentioned, in good Chekhovian fashion, in the opening pages of the novel) and swings them against his face. Like a stereotyped acquiescent queer, John "knew Cliff was not to blame, knew he had brought it on himself, asked for it" (307). He comes to, finds the letter pushed under the door, reads it, "and his sole emotion was a passionate regret that Cliff had not finished the job" (310). End of novel. The 1949 paperback edition was the first to unmistakably depict a gay encounter on its cover.

Charles Reginald Jackson (1903–1968) was born in Summit, New Jersey, but grew up in Newark. He attended Syracuse, where he joined a fraternity but left under the cloud of a sexual indiscretion with a brother (the episode appears in different ways in both novels). Throughout his life he had various male lovers. He worked as a journalist in Chicago and New York between bouts in sanatoriums for treatment of tuberculosis. He also suffered from alcoholism. He was married and had two daughters. He died in New York of an overdose of barbiturates. His last lover was a Czech emigrant, Stanley Zednik (1926–1998). His brother Frederick ("Boom") Jackson (1906–1971) was also homosexual, in a longtime relationship with physician Jim Gates.

Bailey, Blake. *Farther & Wilder: The Lost Weekends and Literary Dreams of Charles Jackson.* New York: Knopf, 2013.
Jackson, Charles. *The Fall of Valor.* *New York: Rinehart, 1946. *The Fall of Valour.* London: Hale, 1948.
———. *The Lost Weekend.* *New York: Farrar & Rinehart, 1944. London: Lane, 1945.

31 Kenneth Millar: *The Dark Tunnel*, 1944. John Ross Macdonald: *The Drowning Pool*, 1950. Margaret Millar: *Beast in View*, 1955.

The first novel by the writer who would come to be known as Ross Macdonald is a wartime thriller. Nazi spy Peter Schneider is blackmailing his father, who is on the war board of a Michigan university, into passing on sensitive material that may be of use to German planners. Peter's lover is Captain Carl von Esch, whom he has sprung from a Canadian prisoners of war camp. In the somewhat convoluted tale, they have tried to kill Carl's sister Ruth, newly hired to teach at the same university, so he can take on her identity (the two resemble each other like twins). When Peter realizes that the narrator, an English professor named Robert Branch, has known Ruth intimately, it becomes imperative that he kill him. He doesn't succeed, but he does murder one of Branch's colleagues who has found proof of Professor Schneider's perfidy. And he murders his father, who is mortified by his son's homosexuality: in Branch's words, "They could get around whatever political morality he had, but his sexual morality was too strong to curb, stronger even than his vanity" (236). Peter also has used Rudolf Fisher, whom he "met at a pansy drag" (221). An FBI agent who has interviewed him tosses off the comment, with "a contemptuous smile," that Rudy's "element is the boudoir. He wants to grow up and be beautiful like Hedy Lamarr. He intimated to me in his subtle feminine way that he could really go for me because I'm such a masculine type, if only I weren't so coldly professional in my attitude." Showing how he feels about such people, the agent "twisted his mouth sideways" and "spat in the road" (214). All these disclosures make Branch think "of Roehm, the homosexual chief of the SA whom Hitler murdered with his own talented hands in the bloodbath of 1934. I thought of the elegant Nazi boys I had seen in the Munich nightclubs, with their lipstick and their eye-shadow and their feminine swagger, and the black male guns in their holsters. I thought of the epicene white worms which change their sex and burrow in the bodies of dead men underground" (217). So much for an English teacher's sensitivity. When the novel was brought out in paperback in 1950, a subtitle was added: *The Story of a Homosexual Spy*. It was reprinted in 1955 as *I Die Slowly* by Ross Macdonald. It is a clumsy novel that foreshadows the Lew Archer series only intermittently.

A stereotypical gay man has a very small but catalytic role in *Drowning Pool*, the second in the Archer series. Sixteen years before the story begins, James Slocum knew that he "had a faggot tendency." He thought that marriage might "save him," and so he proposed to the college student who was typing for him as he worked on a graduate degree in drama. Maude was pregnant with her landlord's child and allowed herself to be persuaded (227–28). They go to live with his domineering mother, who controls the purse strings. According to Cathy, the daughter who has grown up thinking James is her father, "She twisted my father from the time he was a little boy, she made him what he is" (240). James is now in a relationship of some sort with an aspiring playwright, Francis Marvell. The wife, who is being blackmailed for her renewed relationship with Cathy's father, hires Archer to find out who is behind the threats. He quickly becomes aware of the tensions between husband and wife. She throws Francis up at him and goes on, "It chills a woman off, [...] being married to a fairy" (78). At a party, just after James finishes a song to entertain the guests, Cathy's real father sneers, "That was very nice, James. Now why don't you and Marvell sing a duet?" (52). Archer mentions James's "limp hand" (31); the police note Francis's "gestures" (68). The grandmother is the first victim. Her death sets off a series of others. James retreats from reality and enters "a circle of intimacy" with Francis (235). The man at the center of the maelstrom of passions remains blurred, undeveloped. Archer does manage to evoke pity for him. Just before leaving the two men alone over a chessboard, he tells Francis, "If you care about this man, you'd better get him a damn good doctor" (237). The novel was loosely adapted as a movie in 1975.

Kenneth Millar (1915–1983) was born in Los Gatos, California, but brought up in Kitchener, Ontario. According to his biographer, he had sexual encounters with other boys while still in school. Nolan suggests (125) that in reaction, "Some of his books showed homosexuals as evil grotesques" and goes on to say that "Millar was concerned that a homosexual tendency ran deeper in him than he'd imagined." He married Margaret Ellis Strum (1915–1994) in 1938. A native of Kitchener, she attended the University of Toronto, as did he, after graduating from the University of Western Ontario. He interrupted his studies at the University of Michigan to serve with the Navy during World War II, returning to take a Ph.D. in 1951. She established her name in the mystery field before he did. He said he changed his, going through an evolving series of pseudonyms, to avoid confusion with her. None of his novels won major awards, though he was given two lifetime achievement awards. *Beast in View* won an Edgar, and she too was given a lifetime achievement award. He died in Santa Barbara, California, of complications from Alzheimer's; she died there of a heart attack.

Her depiction of a gay man is pretty much of a piece with her husband's. Douglas Clarvoe is "a pansy," "a pervert," a mama's boy who was briefly married because "he wanted to prove he wasn't a fairy" (86, 88). The mother closes her mind to the facts, explaining away how "he hadn't finished college because of some highly exaggerated incident in the locker-room of the gym," refusing to understand what he means when he says, "Because I am, sweetheart, I am," in response to her question, "Why should you *want* to look different from other men?" (55–56). A perpetual student supported by the widowed mother, he has entered a sexual relationship with a photographer, Jack Terola, calling himself Jack's "wife." When the mother finally faces the truth about Douglas, as the result of a telephone hate message, he defends Jack, saying, "He's not an evil man [...]. He's like me," and denies that Jack "corrupted" him (94–95). The day of his twentieth-six birthday he tries to kill himself but actually dies accidentally. His ex-wife says of him: "Poor Douglas. In some ways he was the best of the bunch, of the Clarvoes, I mean. He at least had some warmth in him. Directed towards the wrong people, perhaps, but at least it was there" (134–35). The actual plot centers on the way a psychopathic split personality manipulates people, with a melodramatic twist at the end. Few, if indeed any, of the characters are appealing.

Macdonald, John Ross. *The Drowning Pool*. New York: Knopf, 1950. London: Cassell, 1952. *By Ross Macdonald. New York: Vintage, 1996.
Millar, Kenneth. *The Dark Tunnel*. New York: Dodd, Mead, 1944. *By Ross Macdonald. New York: Mysterious Press (Open Road), 2013.
Millar, Margaret. *Beast in View*. New York: Random House, 1955. *New York: Carroll & Graf, 2000.
Nolan, Tom. *Ross Macdonald: A Biography*. New York: Scribner, 1999.

32 William Maxwell: *The Folded Leaf*, 1945.

Though Maxwell denied that there was anything sexual about the two main male characters' relationship, so many gay readers have identified with the work that it has become, ipso facto, a gay novel. *Leaf* is set in 1920s Chicago. It describes the crush one schoolboy has on another. The uncoordinated and studious Lymie Peters meets the athletic Spud Latham in high school when the latter saves him from drowning. They become friends, and an emotional bond grows between them, especially on Lymie's part. Spud's mother feels uneasy about the two boys' relationship. They themselves feel at ease with their bodies (Lymie is enchanted by Spud's perfection), and when they end up sharing an unheated room at college, they sleep spoon-fashioned. Even after Spud joins a fraternity, he returns one evening to share Lymie's bed, and Lymie thinks, "All that he had ever wanted, he had now" (206). This occurs after Sally Forbes has come into their lives. She falls in love with Spud, but he thinks she is in love with Lymie, and jealousy ensues on his part. Spud seems to have no idea how Lymie feels about him, although Sally does: she says to Lymie, "Somehow I can talk to you about Spud because I know that you feel about him almost the way I do" (241). The two boys finally confront each other. Lymie tries to kill himself. On Spud's visit to the hospital: "They looked at each other with complete knowledge at last, with full awareness of what they meant to each other and of all that had ever passed between them. After a moment Spud leaned forward slowly and kissed Lymie on the mouth. He had never done this before and he was never moved to do it again" (284). Exactly what that knowledge, that awareness, is is never spelled out; nor do we really know the reason for the solitary kiss. The novel ends with Lymie receiving an invitation to a dance from a girl, rather heavily handed named Hope, which he will accept. There are many other characters and plots going on, but this is the thread on which a gay reading hangs or falls. William Keepers Maxwell, Jr. (1908–2000), was born in Lincoln, Illinois. He graduated from the University of Illinois and Harvard. He served as the fiction editor of *The New Yorker* for forty years, 1936–75. He was married for fifty-five years and had two daughters. Maxwell died in New York.

Burkhardt, Barbara A. *William Maxwell: A Literary Life.* Urbana: University of Illinois Press, 2005. Chapter 4.

Maxwell, William. *The Folded Leaf.* *New York: Harper, 1945. London: Faber & Faber, 1946.

33 Kenneth Fearing: *The Big Clock*, 1946. Carley Mills: *A Nearness of Evil*, 1961.

In *The Gay Metropolis*, Charles Kaiser devotes over six pages (19–26) and two photographs to the 1943 Lonergan murder case. He remarks that for the first time newspapers discussed homosexuality openly—this, several years before the Kinsey report. There have been two nonfiction books about the murder: Mel Heimer's *The Girl in Murder Flat*, 1955, and Hamilton Darby Perry's *A Chair for Wayne Lonergan*, 1971. Dominick Dunne recalled the story in a *Vanity Fair* article in July 2000. Almost at once the case influenced Fearing's conception of his first *roman noir*. James Baldwin abandoned a complicated 1948 fictionalized version, *Ignorant Armies*, but his efforts prepared the way for both *Giovanni's Room* and *Another Country*. Brion Gysin, a newly naturalized American citizen, tried his hand with his unpublished *I Am Out*, 1949. Certain aspects of Lonergan's relationship with his father-in-law probably colored Theodora Keogh's *Double Door*. With a major change (keeping the father-in-law alive), the case became the basis for Mills's only novel. Karl Flinders (Milton Saul) used the son as his jumping off point for *The Boy Avengers*, 1971. It was barely fictionalized by Gordon Merrick, in what was his last novel, *The Good Life*, 1997, completed by his partner, Charles G. Hulse.

Canadian, Wayne Lonergan (1918–1986) came to New York to work at the 1939 World's Fair. His good looks attracted the attention of the wealthy William O. Burton (né Bernheimer, 1897–1940), heir to the Bernheimer brewery fortune and aspiring portrait painter. He set Lonergan up as his lover, but unexpectedly died of a heart attack in 1940. Lonergan turned his attention to the daughter, Patsy Burton, who stood to inherit millions. They were married in the summer of 1941. Patsy loved New York's night life. They were frequently seen at such places as the Stork Club and El Morocco. Merrick and Gysin met him. The couple had a son, but the marriage was rocky from the start because of both parents' extramarital activities. Lonergan continued to cruise gay haunts; his wife took on lovers. The two separated, and Lonergan enlisted in the RCAF. On October 23, 1943, he flew back to New York on a weekend pass. In his confession he said he and his wife got together the next morning. According to gossip, she tried to bite off his penis (Dunne says there is no basis for the rumor). Whatever the cause, he bludgeoned her to death with a candlestick. He fled back to Canada, where he was arrested. As an alibi, he claimed to have spent the night having sex with an American soldier. Mills has one of his characters say, "He figured out it was better to be a queer than a murderer" (208). One of the detectives found the alibi so "degrading" that he could not believe it was other than true. The trial vied with war news in all the newspapers. Lonergan was found guilty of second degree murder and sent to Sing Sing. He was paroled in 1967 and deported to Canada, where he died. The news of his death made the *New York Times* obituary page. His son had meanwhile been assigned his mother's maiden name.

In Fearing's novel, Earl Janoth surprises his lover Pauline Delos just after she is dropped off by George Stroud, the main character. Earl sees George but does not recognize him. When he discovers that she has been with another man, he begins a verbal attack during which he also brings up her lesbian liaisons in the past. She retorts, "What about you and Steve Hagen?" When Earl acts surprised, she asks, "Did I ever see you two together when you weren't camping?" As their altercation escalates, she flings out, "Why, you poor, old carbon copy of that fairy gorilla" (430–31). At this point Earl picks up a heavy glass decanter and smashes it repeatedly against her head, killing her. Since at this point he is narrating the events, the reader is left to infer that she has struck such a nerve because she is telling the truth. Nowhere in the novel does Earl face the possibility that he is sexually attracted to his sub lieutenant. When he turns immediately to Steve for help, it is noteworthy that he does not tell him what caused his murderous outbreak. Steve speaks in his own voice in only one chapter. There he acknowledges, "I liked Earl more than I had ever liked any person on earth except my mother, I really liked him" (442). George's only comment about the relationship is his statement, "I knew he was almost as loyal to Janoth as to himself" (446). The circumstances of the murder are the author's only indebtedness to the Lonergan case. The rest of *Clock* details Earl's frantic attempt to discover the man he saw, who can place him on the scene, in order to eliminate him as a witness; he comes up with a cock and bull story about why he needs to locate the person and then ironically taps George to track himself down. Both the 1948 film version and its 1987 remake as *No Way Out* retain the homosexual angle in the minds of some viewers. (Gay actor Charles Laughton played Earl in the first version). Kenneth Flexner Fearing (1902–1961) was born in Oak Park, Illinois. After graduating from the University of Wisconsin, he settled in New York. He was an important poet as well as a pulp writer. He was married twice. He died of cancer in New York.

Mills's novel is more extensively based upon the Lonergan case. It begins with its straight narrator, the lawyer Alfie Fisher, calling upon Bobby Randall, né Rindshauer, at the request of his mother at his home in Villefranche on the Côte d'Azur. While there Alfie thinks back over his long association with Bobby since boyhood, including his early realization that sexually the two were different. He recalls the anti–Semitism that Bobby had fought as well as the homophobia. The purpose of his errand is to tell him that he is dangerously close to running out of money and to urge him and his ex-wife, Florence Becker, to remarry as a beard. He has been having too many scandals while abroad; his mother says to him, "Your being a fairy don't worry me so much as your being a damn fool" (94). Alfie's mission is a success. But the growing signs that Bobby and Florence's daughter, Diane, is also wayward are already worrisome. The second part of the drama begins at the World's Fair. Bobby takes Diane there; almost immediately he meets Neal Hartigan, one of the young men hired to push visitors in a wheeled contraption from attraction to attraction. They are quickly a pair, being seen frequently at a gay hangout called Chez Marcel. Diane is equally attracted to the handsome man, declaring pertly that "if he's good enough for Daddy he's good enough for me" (115). They start going out also, causing a catty society columnist to remark, "Hartigan is going steady with both Randalls" (117). As a result, father and daughter turn against each other. Bobby decides to evict Neal from the apartment he has set up for him. Letting himself in unannounced, he is shocked to find Neal in the company of Howland Jotham packing up his things: "*Neal* was walking out on *him*" (126). As a result of the escalating gossip, "Bobby's social prestige, which had never amounted to much, had fallen even lower" (128). Then comes the announcement that Neal and Diane are married.

Diane lets drop that marriage does not mean Neal has given up "Jothaming" (137). Soon, like him, she is taking up "the early draftees, the foreign service men, the reservists, the ROTC boys [...] with no connections, little money, and a natural hunger and thirst, and no objection to having someone else pick up the tab" (116). Diane's conquests, like her father's, include a high number of "pansies" (138). Shortly after their son is born, Neal departs for Canada to join the RCAF. Then on October 17, 1943, Diane is discovered murdered in her apartment. Neal returns for the funeral but is arrested when it is revealed that he had been back for that weekend. As an alibi he claims to have spent the evening visiting "gay bars," picking up an American soldier in one of them. Asked point-blank, "Then you admit you are an active, practicing homosexual," Neal replies, "Yes. I'm afraid I do." A female friend is asked to collaborate Neal's alibi: "When asked by a reporter of her opinion of Hartigan's story, she replied, giggling, 'I think it's a terrible fairy tale.'" In all this, Alfie's natural reaction is to protect Bobby, who is being presented by the press as "the evil genius who had touched off the whole chain of events leading up to the murder" (163–65). The transcript of Neal's trial takes up several chapters. Both Bobby and Howland are called, and the gay angle is pushed hard. Then the district attorney introduces the soldier with whom Neal supposedly spent the night; he emphatically denies that he ever met Neal, and Neal abruptly changes his plea to murder in the second degree. Bobby leaves town: "He had become inured to scandal—in fact, he liked it so long as he was the center of it; but ridicule was another matter, and he could not take it" (243). He settles first in Cuernavaca, but leaves it abruptly after one of his "guests" turns out to be "under eighteen" and a British general's son (245). By 1951 he is back on the Côte d'Azur. His old place now a shambles, he sells it. Finally he ends up in Tangier, where his houseboy cuts his throat. Florence summons Alfie to set up a trust that will protect Neal and Diane's son from being emotionally extorted by the father. She also insists the boy be told everything so that he will not one day be hit with the information from a stranger. The novel ends with Alfie's reflection that Florence has turned out to be the most solid member of the family.

Carley Mills (1897–1962) was born in Deal, New Jersey. He attended NYU. He was a song writer and musical comedy composer. Tennessee Williams lived with him briefly in 1942, but found the arrangement too restrictive. His songs "So Nobody Cares" and "If I Cared a Little Bit Less" were written for Williams. He is the basis for Rupert in Donald Windham's *The Hero Continues*. Mills enjoyed travel and lived in various places in Europe, Southeast Asia, and the Caribbean. He dedicated the novel to "Kenneth, my son." He died in New York.

Fearing, Kenneth. *The Big Clock*. New York: Harcourt, Brace, 1946. London: Bodley Head, 1947. *American *Novels: American Noir of the 1930s and 40s*. New York: Library of America, 1997. 379–515.
Mills, Carley. *A Nearness of Evil*. New York: Coward McCann, 1961.

34   Alfred Hayes: *All Thy Conquests*, 1946. Calder Willingham: *End as a Man*, 1947.

As homosexuality became more talked about, if not more visible, the figure of the treacherous, predatory homosexual became more common in U.S. fiction. Here are two examples vaguely associated with the war, the first taking place in occupied Italy, the second in an American military academy just before our involvement. Hayes harkens back to earlier American prejudices by creating a variation on the stereotype of the craven Italian villain. Willingham caters to the stereotype of the fairy. Neither novel offers any insight into gay identity.

Hayes's novel takes place in Rome just after the American troops arrive. In something of the style of Dos Passos's *U.S.A.*, it has alternate portraits of five people—two American soldiers and three Italians—set within a framing device that turns it into a three-part novel. One of the Italians is the Marchese Aldo Alzani, who is plotting the downfall of his hated father-in-law, a military bigwig during the war. The marchese has sat out the conflict in Switzerland, enjoying the favors of "the Greek refugee boy, Pepi" (55), whom he now misses. A gypsy woman prevents his picking up an Italian youth to replace him: "I know your kind. You'll dirty him" (172). We learn, "Once, without the Marchesa's knowledge, he was able to have two simultaneous affairs: one with a Jugoslavian boy who had robbed him, and one with a girl from the Trastavere who had infected him. He had managed to conceal, from the Marchesa, both the loss of his health and of his money. But he had not been able to conceal from her quite his sexual indifference to her long, rather flat and bony body" (65). So he is delighted when she begins an affair with the influential newspaper editor, Guido Cespa. After his father-in-law kills himself because of Aldo's treachery, he thinks again about inviting Pepi to join him: "It would be amusing: she and Guido, Pepi and himself" (269). Alfred Haas (1911–1985) was born in London but was brought to New York when he was three (at which time the new spelling of his name was adopted). Hayes attended what is now CUNY and worked as a journalist before serving in the Army during the war. He was a poet, novelist, and screenwriter (nominated for two Academy Awards). He was married twice and had three children. He died of meningitis in Sherman Oaks, California.

Willingham's novel is set in fall 1940 at The Academy in Port George (i.e., The Citadel in Charleston, S.C.). It has a large cast of characters who might be easier to distinguish if they were not so uniformly unlikeable. The central figure is freshman cadet Robert Marquales, whose personality seems largely fluid. A junior, Jocko de Paris, is the major disruptive force who propels what plot there is. Two of the cadets, Carroll Colton and Perrin McKee, are a couple—a heterosexual fantasy of just how awful homosexuals are. Perrin has a vision of a world in which gays will reproduce themselves, bringing "into the race a new blood, a virile, new man, and the present-day depravity, the limiting of growth, the oppression will all cease, to permit those who are born with the power, but die never knowing it, to live fully, to develop according to their tremendous capacities, and to people the earth like mountainous spore explosions with their own kind" (141). He hopes to initiate Jocko into this new order, promising that he is "gentle with virgins" (143). He also has designs on Robert, thinking he "might have the ability to learn" (129). Robert is strangely fascinated by the two men, so much so that he calls upon Perrin after the latter falls and breaks his leg. But then he feels compelled to avow his orthodox sexuality. He calls Perrin (truthfully) a "repulsive person" and goes on to assert, "your high opinion of yourself is mainly about a weakness. You are proud of being a pervert." He finishes up with a flourish, "healthy people would never have anything to do with you. [...] You're disgusting; you and all like you" (234). Perrin flings back at Robert that at least he is not a "repressed" homosexual—"like yourself" (236). The scene climaxes with Perrin begging Carroll not to leave him, and Carroll answering with a kiss, "I won't, darling" (245). Four-fifths of the way through the novel, Robert has one final encounter with Carroll. He brings him a note from Perrin, which maintains that everything he has said and written was only "literary exercises" and that he actually enjoys women (275). Carroll and Perrin leave the school to settle in New Orleans.

Willingham adapted the novel as a play for the Actors Studio in 1953 (with James Dean in a non-speaking role); he then adapted it in 1957 as a screenplay titled *The Strange One*. Thereafter, he continued to write scripts, being responsible entirely or in part for a series of ground-breaking films, including *The Graduate*. Calder Baynard Willingham, Jr. (1922–1995), was born in Atlanta. He enrolled in The Citadel but dropped out. After serving in the Office of War Information in Washington, he moved to New York, where he spent ten years writing before turning his attention to Hollywood. He was married and had six children. He died in Laconia, New Hampshire, of lung cancer.

Hayes, Alfred. *All Thy Conquests*. *[New York]: Howell, Soskin, 1946. London: Gollancz, 1950.
Willingham, Calder. *End as a Man*. *New York: Vanguard, 1947. London: Lehmann, 1952.

35 Willard Motley: *Knock on Any Door*, 1947; *Let Noon Be Fair*, 1966.

In these two novels, Motley's first and last, gays have secondary roles. The first traces the trajectory of Nick Romano from a Chicago altar boy to a convicted killer. Along the way, at age sixteen he hooks up with a "phoney" (the code word for homosexuals in the novel) named Owen. It is never clear whether anything physical happens between them, though one assumes it probably does. What is clear is that Owen is in love with him, and Nick uses him. But gradually something new arises between them: "Nick went over to Owen's house quite a bit; almost every time he needed money, and sometimes when he didn't. Sometimes Owen wanted him to stay, but not always. He seemed to like to have Nick near him. For Nick a certain liking and friendship had grown up. Owen was somebody who understood. Maybe because Owen, in his way, lived outside the law, too" (189). Owen accepts Nick's marriage, accepts him back after the wife kills herself, and visits Nick on death row. After Owen leaves, after they have come as close as possible to a hug in that setting, Nick ponders why he has remained faithful, in his own way, to the gay man for four years: "One answer presented itself: Because he was always decent to me no matter what I did. And liking, love, being pity, sympathy, half-understanding; liking being the recognition of faults along with the good; liking, love, being the circle that ties all things together" (481). Of course, Owen disappeared from the 1949 film, directed by the closeted Nicholas Ray, to the film's loss.

Motley's last novel is set in a coastal town in Mexico, Las Casas, as it is being discovered and subsequently ruined by American visitors and expatriates. The central character is the seemingly sexless writer Tom Van Pelt, who is pretty oblivious to any gays around him. There are three Mexican brothers. Andrés, twelve when the novel begins, is regularly sodomized by an American pederast, Chester "whom none suspected" (99). The middle brother, Rodolfo, fourteen, tries to join in for the money. Tomás, fifteen, as he becomes a young man, is willing to service women or men: "Only, the men would pay more" (329). As the town becomes a resort, a gay bar opens: Rondevous [sic]. Andrés frequents it. Another Mexican, Victor, presents a curious case. He worships his friend Jorge as a hero, to the point that he is jealous of Lupe when Jorge courts her. When Jorge lies dying of stab wounds, Victor promises to marry her and take care of their unborn child, but he resents her across the years until she confesses that it is Victor she has loved all the time. Thereupon, all is made right. There are glimpses of a few other homosexuals. But it is not a true gay novel any more than the author's first is.

Willard Frances Bryant (1909–1965) grew up in Chicago in the home of his Motley grandparents, whose name he adopted as his own. He worked as a free-lance writer for various projects before the success of his first novel. After the relative failure of his second, in 1951, he fled to Mexico. There he adopted Sergio Mendez, a street boy, to whom he dedicated his third, *Let No Man Write My Epitaph*, 1958, a sequel to his first. His last novel is dedicated to Matias Noriega, who was perhaps his lover. Other love interests included a Chicago bartender, Morris Glen, and an American relative of Noriega, Sammy Ramirez. Motley died in Mexico City of intestinal gangrene two weeks after completing *Noon*.

Motley, Willard. *Let Noon Be Fair*. *New York: Putnam's, 1966. London: Longmans, 1966.
———. *Knock on Any Door*. *New York: Appleton-Century, 1947. London: Collins, 1948.

36 Gordon Merrick: *The Strumpet Wind*, 1947; *The Demon of Noon*, 1954; *The Lord Won't Mind*, 1970.

Given his later status as a romance writer, Merrick's first novel comes as a surprise. The story of Roger Chandler is told by an anonymous Red Cross worker who encounters him on the way to the south of France in the summer of 1944. Chandler is a something of an idealist but also a homophobic U.S. intelligence officer assigned to work under Major George Meddling. The major, who has a "relish for all the romantic details of spy fiction," is "heavily male, overripe, decadent." Chandler "instinctively" distrusts him (39–41). His own work to disseminate false information to the German military is going well, though the method he is using creates moral issues for him. Hoping to find a way out of the ethical dilemma and simultaneously penetrate the enemy's local organization, he poses as a Nazi sympathizer. The local enemy agent suggests a meeting at the Café des Quatre Reines. It turns out to be a gay bar. As the agent explains, they are in the safest place to meet: "Nobody here dares inquire into his neighbor's business" (181). At just the wrong moment, Meddling shows up. Having failed to receive Chandler's communication earlier in the day, he assumes that Chandler is also gay and greets him effusively, in the process saying enough to arouse the contact's suspicions. The blown opportunity gives Chandler the opportunity to assert his independence of Meddling's control. Stating baldly, "I don't like to work with fairies," he threatens, "If I have any trouble with you, I'll make a complete report on your behavior tonight. You know what that would mean, Major." On the way back to headquarters Chandler ponders whether he should report him anyway: "Men like that oughtn't to be allowed in the Army. But no. He would wait. It would serve as a useful club to keep him in line" (188–90). In a last visit to the Red Cross worker Chandler claims, "The good Major Meddling is railroading me out of his territory." But Chandler is falling apart, having "been false to himself and to his victims on all counts." The last the narrator hears of the man he is "drinking heavily" (247–48). The novel was reissued in 1952 as a paperback under the title *The Night and the Naked*.

Merrick's next novel also has a homophobic protagonist: the American expatriate Stuart Cosling. But the authorial voice defends Stuart's gay teenage son, Robbie, in ways that are all the more remarkable given the blight of McCarthyism in full force at the time of the novel's publication. Set during the period between the world wars on the Côte d'Azur, the second half of the novel traces Robbie's sexual awakening, begun when he is not quite sixteen. With his family at a local nightclub he experiences an excitement when he sees two men in Mistinguett's entourage dancing together. On a yacht trip to the Greek islands, Robbie is stirred by a series of males whom he encounters—straight, gay, and bi; young and old—and in the presence of ancient Greek art finds the "meeting of the sensual and the spiritual" that he has been craving (154). Back in France he hangs out with a group his age, including "a pansy," and is "stunned that Richard bore no stigma upon him of his avowed inclinations" (170). He has his first sexual experience with an erotic dancer who is used to accepting favors from men and women alike. Toni teasingly calls Robbie a *pédé*: "Robbie didn't mind. The ugly word had been spoken and he didn't care, for Toni had said it as if he accepted him and for the first time he felt as if he were something. He had found his identity and discovered his world" (191). Toni is probably Stuart's illegitimate son. The father catches the two in a sexual act. He recoils, not because of incest but because of homosexuality. He argues with himself that, as a free spirit (he has never married Robbie's mother, Marthe), homosexuality should not bother him. But when Robbie stands up to Stuart, daring to cite Gide, the father threatens him with psychiatry and sends Toni away.

The results are the contrary to what Stuart had hoped to achieve: "Since he no longer had anything to hide, he could at least follow the dictates of desire"; Robbie "glimpsed salvation in physical satisfaction" (215). Stuart finds out later from Richard's sister, after he has been killed in the early days of World War II, that he and Robbie had an affair: "He said all Robbie cared about was sex and he tried to make him understand there was something more important. He said it was your fault that Robbie was so embittered." Stuart still refuses to admit the possibility of romantic love between men; the sister asks him why he cannot "just relax and accept life" and accuses him of being "cold and inhuman" (248). By then the parents have broken up and Robbie is in Paris in a relationship with a man attached to the Belgian Embassy. Then Carl von Eschenbach, a German friend from the Greek island days, reenters their life as a Nazi agent on a secret mission. Earlier he and Marthe had an affair. Now he initiates one with Robbie, who thereby enters into a collaboration with the enemy. Stuart faces the fact that Carl "had won his wife, he had won his son, he had won a war. But he wasn't finished. Stuart would not be defeated himself without a struggle" (255). He coolly kills Carl, in Robbie's presence, and disposes of the body. Some readers have interpreted the act as a further example of Stuart's homophobia, and certainly personal feelings enter the murder. But in the context it seems almost entirely politically motivated. When Robbie accuses him, "you always destroy everything," Stuart admits that on the day he sent Toni away, "Instead of trying to get you over it, perhaps I should've tried to help you face it and make it part of a decent life." He continues, "Whatever you are, you can make something good of it. It will never be easy for you. The world doesn't make any place for you. You must make your own place. You can do it only with self-discipline and a real belief in high principles, in decency, in love. You can't do it by defiling yourself. You can't allow yourself the laxness that's pardonable in others. You must accept the world's standards" (261–62). The novel ends with father and son planning their escape via Spain to volunteer in the war effort. It was reissued as a paperback under the title *Lovers in Torment*. In 1982 Merrick rewrote it as *Perfect Freedom*, making Robbie the central character.

There followed two more novels, then silence. Then, the year of the first Pride march the very title *The Lord Won't Mind* seemed to declare its own kind of pride. Set in the period just before and during World War II, the book did well in its hardback incarnation; as a paperback, it became a publishing phenomenon: the covers of it and its two sequels became part of gay iconography. The fact is hard to fathom given how unappealing its main character comes across. Charlie Mills is a bigot, making fun of blacks. He is a hypocrite, insisting that he is not "a fairy or a queer" because what he and his lover, nineteen-year-old Peter Martin, are doing is "perfectly natural" between friends (38), and he gets upset when he sees Peter in the company of a 'pervert'" (51). He thinks nothing of raping a woman because it is "what they really deserved" (50). He is spoiled by a doting grandmother and wants to match up with what she expects of him. The novel begins as high class pornography. In explicit detail, including repeated mentions of how huge their penises are, Charlie conquers Peter, and before the day is finished they are planning their life together. That does not stop Charlie from pursuing women. The two men quarrel. They make up. It is emphasized how huge their penises are. Peter decides, "If his idol was flawed, it was all the more important for him to be at his side, to defend him from danger; he sensed instinctively that Charlie's refusal to accept the nature of their relationship could lead to serious trouble" (65). Charlie paints Peter's nude portrait and, at Peter's request, does a nude self-portrait. It is mentioned how huge their penises are. They move into an apartment in New York together, but their different lives and hours causes them to share less of their life together.

Charlie meets Hattie Donaldson. He discovers the draft of a letter Peter has begun to the pervert—in which he mentions Charlie's huge penis—and become irate. Charlie is not a queer! They fight. They make up. Peter tells the grandmother that he loves Charlie carnally; she is horrified. Charlie assures her that he had no idea of Peter's feelings and that nothing physical has occurred. He throws Peter out. He has sex with Hattie. She admires his huge penis, and they get married. The grandmother tells Hattie they must never have children, but Hattie assures her she does not anticipate the marriage lasting long. Peter runs into Charlie. He is now stereotypically gay in his mannerisms and is hustling. Charlie is "shocked and repelled, drawn, held" (167). They attend a party in Harlem to honor the grandmother's former maid, who is now a musical star. Charlie is still a bigot. He leaves. Peter stays and has sex with the host. Peter, whom we now learn has been nicknamed the Growler because of the sounds he makes when he is sexually aroused, shows signs of becoming an interesting human. He begins an affair with lawyer Tim Thornton: "Peter adored him, but the feeling lacked the obsessive quality which he associated with being in love" (201). Meanwhile, Charlie and Hattie get parts in a new play, garnering the grandmother's disapproval. Charlie does not take direction well and is fired when he slugs the director after he calls Charlie a Park Avenue faggot. Harriet also calls him a faggot; he offers to prove his manhood by taking her anally. She counters with the offer of a blow-job. He taunts her, "Yes, we mustn't let Peter have all the fun," whereupon she "took the sex in one hand and opened her mouth and clamped her teeth into it" (214). The wounded Charlie runs to Peter. Peter instantly drops Tim and takes Charlie back, with the condition that he be honest with the grandmother. Charlie now learns that his great-grandfather was an African American. The novel ends with his accepting that he is "a queer" with a "bit of black blood" (253–54), whom it does not behoove to act so snottily. There is no indication of a sequel, but Charlie and Peter's story is continued in *One for the Gods*, 1971, and *Forth into Light*, 1974.

William Gordon Merrick (1916–1988) was born in a Philadelphia suburb. He left Princeton to become a Broadway actor. His big break came with *The Man Who Came to Dinner*, 1939. He was briefly the lover of co-author Moss Hart (1904–1961). Tiring of an actor's schedule, he turned to journalism. During the war he served as a counter-espionage agent in Algeria and France. After the war he lived for a time in Mexico. With the success of his first novel he returned to France, before settling on the Greek island of Hydra. In both early novels he thanked his lover Robert Paine Richardson. In 1956 he met his life partner, the former dancer Charles Gerald Hulse (1929–). He died in Colombo, Sri Lanka, of lung cancer.

Merrick, Gordon. *The Demon of Noon*. *New York: Messner, 1954. London: Hale, 1956.
_____. *The Lord Won't Mind*. New York: Geis, 1970. *Los Angeles: Alyson, 1995.
_____. *The Strumpet Wind*. *New York: Morrow, 1947. London: Davies, 1947.

37 John Horne Burns: *The Gallery*, 1947. Vance Bourjaily: *The End of My Life*, 1947. A. M. P. Stratton: *Lord Love Us*, 1948.

Allan Bérubé in his ground-breaking history of gay American men and women in World War II, *Coming Out under Fire*, discusses the huge impact that serving in the military had on their lives. He writes (6): "The massive mobilization for World War II relaxed the social constraints of peacetime that had kept gay men and women unaware of themselves and each other, 'bringing out' many in the process. Gathered together in military camps, they often came to terms with their sexual desires, fell in love, made friends with other gay people, and began to name and talk about who they were." Gore Vidal made many of these points in his *City and the Pillar*. His main character observes "a tight clique of fairies on the base who went everywhere together" (194); another character in the novel notes that "homosexuals, who might have remained hidden all their lives, who never practised but remained latent, have been caught in this hysterical desire for sex and have become known" (236). Bérubé points out (272–73) that, unlike after World War I, when "few gay characters had populated American war fiction," in the aftermath of World War II "the American soldier's private experience with homosexuality was confirmed, explored and exploited." As a result, "Some critics interpreted the trend toward discussing homosexuality more openly in literature as a sign that the war had had a corrosive influence on American culture and morality. Others believed that the war had helped emancipate American authors from sexual repression and hypocrisy." Bérubé demonstrates the links between gays' military experiences and the beginnings of a new political movement working for gay liberation from oppression.

One of the first, Burns's *Gallery* remains among the most important of more than ten wartime novels to feature gay military figures. It is a story cycle, influenced by Dos Passos's *U.S.A.*, composed of eight autobiographical sketches and nine portraits of people involved in the Allied occupation of Naples in 1944. The Galleria Umberto Primo, a covered shopping area, provides the focal point for the stories. The fifth portrait, "Momma," has deservedly received the most attention from gay readers. The title character, an Italian woman, runs a bar that caters to gay military personnel: "There was a heterogeneous quality about [her clientele]. They had an air of being tremendously wise, older than the human race. They understood one another, as though from France and New Zealand and American they all had membership cards in some occult freemasonry. And they had a refinement of manner, an intuitive appreciation of her as a woman. Their conversation was flashing, bitter, and lucid. More than other men they laughed much together, laughing at life itself perhaps" (130). She bristles when an M.P. threatens them: "Momma's boys had an awareness of having been born alone and sequestered by some deep difference from other men. For this she loved them. And Momma knew something of those four freedoms the Allies were forever preaching. She believed that a minority should be let alone" (133). Her habitués talk about what it means to be gay, a word they use; about the reasons for camping (but without ever examining their use of the feminine); about cruising and what is being sought. One of a pair of British sergeants wistfully hopes, "A new morality may come into existence in our time, Esther. That's one of the few facts that thrills me, old bitch that I am. Some distinction may be made between public and private sins, between economic and ethical issues. In 1944 you find the most incredible intermingling, a porridge of the old and the new, of superstition and enlightenment. How can we speak of sin when thousands are cremated in German furnaces, when it isn't wrong to make a million pounds, but a crime to steal a loaf of bread? Perhaps some new code may come out of all this.... I hope so" (149–50).

"Momma" has overshadowed other stories. The title character of the third portrait, "Hal," is sexless: "something had been omitted from his nature—some gland, some gonad" (54). But he cannot "be five minutes in a bar without being invited to join someone" (58). He is invited to share the New York apartment of a married couple. The husband accuses Hal: "He covers the waterfront and he's eating in chophouses and he's doing Pennsylvania Station at five in the morning." Husband and wife both hold that Hal should be on stage; he counters, "I look enough like a chorus boy as it is. I don't dare go to the beach at Fire Island" (60–61). Hal works at the Brooklyn Army Base. Evenings he spends "questing": "He was seeking something missing in himself, something like his own double, which would confront him with the image of something positive. He was always alone" (63). Overseas, he meets a paratrooper in a bar, a captain who has "an almost effete way of speaking, like poets in the Village," who seems as lost as he (76). He was a chorus boy on Broadway, but he asks, "Do you think I liked swishing my way through the American theater?" (88). Hal thinks of "the old tale of Narcissus" (81). He ends up in a mental ward convinced he is Jesus Christ.

The sixth portrait, "The Leaf," presents Captain Motes. He prides himself on being a very correct Virginia gentleman who has married a very proper, sexless Virginia belle. He immediately offers his service when war is declared. After serving incompetently as the company commander of "an all-Negro outfit," he is transferred to military intelligence and shipped to North Africa. There he becomes the overbearing head of the mail censorship division. Taking advantage of his inept command, Lieutenant Frank moves in to fill the vacuum. Then Lieutenant Stuki arrives. He sets out to seduce Motes, body and mind. Despite the difference in rank, they share the same room: "Stuki would lie nude under his mosquito netting and listen while Captain Motes read aloud from [his wife's] poetry. Stuki's body was black and sheathed in glossy fur. He'd squirm and groan with pleasure at [the] love poems" (179). The whole operation degenerates into farce, causing Captain Motes to fall into a nervous fit. Stuki is instantly beside him, massaging his writhing body: "Captain Motes fell asleep. The last thing he remembered was hands, kind hands that knew him as well as a mold informs a piece of clay to its own image" (183). Motes is promoted to Major. Then Lieutenant Mayberry moves in to make his own grab for power. After one particularly drunken celebration, Stuki "announced he was going out into the streets of Algiers to cruise up a little heavy lovin" (199). The "obscene comedy" continues even after they arrive in Naples. At end, Major Motes is sent home to be treated for nervous exhaustion, leaving Captain Stuki in charge: Motes "felt icy and empty and alone" (205).

Bourjaily's and Statton's novels have in common that the military person coming out is a secondary character, so that we do not see the actual process that he goes through. Their self-discovery, however, amplifies the straight protagonists' equally intense search for meaning to their existence. Bourjaily's novel focuses on Skinner Galt, who serves in an ambulance unit stationed in Syria. Two members of his group, Billy and Tommy, are "a pair of young homosexuals who spoke of themselves as actors, pleasant, conscientious boys who cheerfully allowed most of the daily routine work to be thrust upon them, and did it efficiently and uncomplainingly. They were thoroughly absorbed in one another, and were hardly noticeable unless they were having one of their periodic fallings out" (60). One of the straight soldiers, reflecting on Billy's resemblance to a woman, muses, "I can see how, if you were off someplace, away from women, you might really go for him" (82). To Skinner's surprise, his aptly named friend, Rod Manjac, does. Explaining why he intends to go AWOL, he tells Skinner, "I'm in love" with "a lovely, blue-eyed creature, with crispy golden curls, and a nice little pink set of male genitals" (198). Skinner asks why he doesn't try to get away from Billy by requesting a transfer. Rod responds, "This outfit's full of fairies. And this thing[']s been following me for a long time. I've been afraid of it, and I've fought it, and I've lost. I'd be a pushover for any fairy, anyplace." Rod queries Skinner about how it feels having "a nice fairy for a friend" and makes him admit that it creates a difference. Skinner later reflects that "you could hardly blame Billy for being true to his distorted nature. You could blame Rod, for being weak [...], if you wanted to, but it proved nothing. So what were you going to blame? Society for being anti-social? Humanity for being anti-human?" (201–04).

Stratton's novel follows the lives of Boston twins Ed and Persis Pearse from their college days in 1934 through their war experience 1939–41. Ed becomes the friend of Abe L'Hommedieu of South Carolina. He seems instinctively to sense that the friendship may go beyond the usual on Abe's part; he is hesitant, for example, to share the communal shower with him at school. Abe marries Persis. But during the war he discloses to Ed that he is gay: "I met a guy. An Italian. A prince" during the war; "I found the guy attractive." Ed does not handle the revelation well: "So, my friend, so my sister's husband—such as that marriage is—indulges himself in a—a minor deviation. After all, let's get this thing into the proper perspective. A great many worse things are going on" (285–87). When Abe dies alone in his room, "of a broken heart, though the medical name had something to do with occlusion" (306), Ed feels that he is partly responsible. He tells Persis that he should have gone to bed with him: "Maybe I could have kept him alive. [...] By showing him that I did not think of him as evil. By—loving him" (310). Persis has already said, "You can't hide, or dodge, or withhold, or disguise—you can't have any reservations in love" (290). There is also the strong possibility that their Great Uncle Percival Pearse was in a gay relationship with his butler Bunny. The novel's language is luxurious, sensual; that may contribute to its being so little known.

John Horne Burns (1916–1953) was born in Andover, Massachusetts. He attended Phillips Academy and Harvard. He taught for a number of years at a private school in Connecticut before being drafted into the Army, serving in North Africa and Italy. He published two more novels—*Lucifer with a Book*, 1949, and *A Cry of Children*, 1951—but neither had the success of his first. An alcoholic and depressed, he was then living in Italy with a veterinarian, Sandro Nencini (1922–2005). Burns died in Marina di Cecina after falling ill during a sailing excursion. Vance Nye Bourjaily (1922–2010) was born in Cleveland, Ohio, but grew up in Virginia and New York. He served in the ambulance corps and later the regular army during the war. He graduated from Bowdoin. He was a writer and a teacher. A gay reader should also check out *The Hound of Earth*, 1955, and *The Violated*, 1958. He was married twice and had four children. He died in Greenbrae, California, after slipping into a coma, the result of a fall. Arthur Mills Perce Stratton (1911–1975) was born in Brunswick, Maine. He was likewise educated at Bowdoin, and then Columbia. He had a varied career as a writer, a teacher, and a secret agent. He served in the war as an ambulance driver.

Bourjaily, Vance. *The End of My Life*. New York: Scribner's, 1947. *New York: Dial, 1961.
Burns, John Horne. *The Gallery*. *New York: Harper, 1947. London: Secker & Warburg, 1948.
Margolick, David. *Dreadful: The Short Life and Gay Times of John Horne Burns*. New York: Other, 2013.
Stratton, A. M. P. *Lord Love Us*. New York: Scribner's, 1948.

38 Gore Vidal: *In a Yellow Wood*, 1947; *The City and the Pillar*, 1948; *The Judgment of Paris*, 1952. Edgar Box (Gore Vidal): *Death in the Fifth Position*, 1952. Hugh Wheeler: *The Crippled Muse*, 1951.

Given the disdainful way homosexuals are generally treated in his early novels, it is difficult to understand the high esteem Vidal has held from early on in gay circles. The putdowns of gays begin in his second work. *Wood* is a dull book about a dull person, a "contented Babbitt" (146): the straight Robert Holton, Wall Street broker. We follow a little over a day in his life with small excursions into the lives of others he meets. In the evening he attends a cocktail party. There he meets George *Robert* Lewis, his middle name always italicized, presumably to remind us to pronounce it in the French fashion. The editor of an avant-garde journal with a French title, "Unfortunately for his family he had very early shown a passion for the artistic as well as a marked tendency toward Socratic love" (117). Lewis swoops down on Holton and the woman he is with, Carla Bruno Bankton. She is married to a gay artist who wants Carla "for camouflage" (150). Lewis invites them to join him at a gay club in the Village. Finding him "a funny little queer" (147), Holton accepts for the two of them. There, a comedian tells jokes about "fairies" for an audience "reveling in exposure," since "often their masks became too tight, too heavy. He removed them" (157). Of the evening, Holton remarks, "I never saw anything like this before. I used to hear a lot of stories but I didn't think there were really such places" (162). He and Carla leave to spend the rest of the night at her hotel. In the morning Holton returns home and naps. He dreams: "George *Robert* Lewis's voice sounded in his head and the clashing colors of the fairy night club glittered in his head" (200), but the voice has nothing to say: "It didn't matter because Lewis was just another little fairy. He was perverted in everything" (206). Finishing the novel, the reader understands why, as Vidal's biographer Fred Kaplan writes (210), his editor "assumed that his interest in the subject [of homosexuality] was impersonal, sociological, literary."

City, his next novel, created an explosion beyond its literary merit. Timing was in its favor. It appeared in company with Capote's first novel and the Kinsey Report. Suddenly homosexuality was news. In *Judgment* Vidal writes that the "last cherished area for intolerance was suddenly declared out of bounds by a celebrated statistical report which revealed that one third of the nation's men had, at one time or another, committed a homosexual act. This survey promptly lessened everyone's guilt and, if only by weight of the numbers given, it made the idea of pederasty much less remote, no longer exclusively associated with managers of flower shops or with a fearful fumbling in the back row of a darkened movie house. Those sturdy youths who had been ashamed of their secret practice now took much pleasure [...] in openly doing what they pleased and, with all the enthusiasm of zealots, they proselyted furiously" (272–73). One of the characters in *City* does argue that "the real dignity is the dignity of a man realizing himself and functioning honestly and according to his own nature" (140). Its protagonist, Jim Willard, comes to accept "the importance of being one's self, to make as few compromises with one's real nature as possible" (179); but he also knows "that it was a desperate thing to be an honest man in his world and he had not the courage to be that yet" (288). But the authorial voice seems conflicted. Throughout, homosexuality is referred to as *unnatural*, an *abnormal vice*, *twisted behavior*, a *natural narcissism*. Even after Jim finally identifies "himself as a member of the submerged world of the homosexual" (171), he still thinks "that should he ever have a woman he would be normal" (195). When he cannot obtain the man of his dreams, he murders him.

The novel is essentially a long flashback. It begins with Jim in a New York bar getting drunk, trying not to remember the murder. The great moment in his life occurred back in Virginia, before the war, when he was a teenager and had his first sexual experience with the victim, his friend Bob Ford. The weekend after graduation they spent together at a cabin on the river. The sex was apparently no more than frottage, and Bob dismissed it even then as "kid stuff," something "guys aren't supposed to do with each other. It's not natural." But for Jim it was (in an echo of Plato's *Symposium*) "his first completion, his first discovery of a twin: the half he had been searching for" (48–49). Emotionally, he never progresses further. His life is dominated by the "memory of a cabin and a brown river" (127). Looking back he turns into a pillar of salt. Sitting in the bar he recalls a series of events in his life. After high school the two boys go their separate ways. Jim ends up getting a job as messboy on a passenger liner. To prove himself to a fellow worker Jim tries to have sex with a woman, but fails, thinking that his weekend with Bob had not been "dirty like this; it was not unnatural like this" (91). In Hollywood he becomes movie actor Ronald Shaw's kept boy (giving the author the opportunity to make some piercing observations about the closet in Hollywood): "Jim felt like a whore but he was not unhappy" (104). Then he comes under the influence of the writer Paul Sullivan and lives with him in New Orleans, Merida, and Guatemala City. He is swept up into World War II. Upon discharge, he ends up in New York, where he reconnects with Shaw and Sullivan. Eventually, he meets the now married Bob Ford. He tries to recreate the magical weekend, to be rebuffed: "you're nothing but a damned queer!" In a fury, Jim chokes Bob to death: "Death was unimportant but the end of his love was important. He no longer cared what might happen to him. With Bob gone there was nothing left" (306–07). The novel ends with his staring at the Hudson River. At least he doesn't jump in. The ending was criticized by gay readers, as was the flat style that Vidal adapted. He decided to rectify both criticisms. His extensive revision was published in 1965. Now instead of murdering Bob, Jim rapes him.

Philip Warren, the main character in *Judgment* "had often thought that he might, at one time at least, have had a fling at pederasty if it had not been for his dislike of those aggressive masculine traits which inevitably kept him at a distance from his contemporaries" (130). Taking a year off after obtaining his Harvard law degree, he is entertained by three women that he meets in three countries: Italy, Egypt, and France. In both Italy and France he generally runs in homosexual circles, "proving, perhaps, that he has an inclination toward forbidden vice; a very slight one, however" (85). Clyde Norman takes him up in Rome and introduces him to Lord Glenellen, whose "hobbies" are bedding boys. He pushes Philip to go with an Italian youth at the Baths of Nero. Philip goes along with the charade, leaving the boy "a little bewildered that nothing had happened" (93). He meets a wider range of gays in Paris, where "business men from Kansas City, good Rotarians all, embraced bored young sailors on the streets at night or paid high prices for slim Algerian boys at those bordellos which catered to such pleasures. College boys, young veterans [...], athletes and aesthetes both, ran amok among the bars and urinals in search of one another" (272). Philip attends a party attended by "several middle-aged gentlemen in evening gowns and twenty or thirty young men in Brooks Brothers suits"—"their sibilants cracking like whips across the room no matter which language they spoke" (289–90). Philip is also introduced to a rite centered on the "only functioning hermaphrodite in Paris," the mysterious Augustus/Augusta (268). Norman and Glenellen both turn up. So does a male couple from Spartanburg, South Carolina, having a last fling before they return home to marry (after which their sex life will be reduced to hunting trips together). A handsome prostitute named Jim, a hopeless drug addict who dies before the end of the novel, could be Jim Willard. He says that he cannot return to the U.S. because he "got into trouble" (280) three years earlier. But "trouble" seems a weak euphemism for murder, and there are differences between the two characters. This Jim, in fact, is based on Denny Fouts (*q.v.*), whom Vidal met spring 1948.

Vidal wrote three murder mysteries under the pseudonym Edgar Box. The first is set in the world of ballet. The murderer is gay choreographer Jed Wilbur, "the hottest choreographer in town at the moment, the most fashionable ... not only in ballet but also in musical comedies" (8). He kills his scheming star after she threatens to expose his earlier membership in the Communist Party if she does not get her way. Rumors have flown about him, but so far he has managed to hide. Her threat, however, is more threatening since he is being summoned to Washington. McCarthyism is in full fury; the secretary of the United Veterans Committee proclaims that they "have spent close to a hundred thousand in the last year to root Reds and other perverts out of our way of life, in government, entertainment and the life of everyday … and we're doing it" (82). Wilbur is "a thin prematurely gray young man" with "a high nasal voice" (13). Jerome Robbins's biographer asserts that the character was based on Robbins in revenge for his putdown of Vidal's promiscuity. Vaill has no use for Vidal, but the novelist proved uncanny in his foresight of Robbins's damaging testimony before the House Committee on Un-American Activities the spring following the book's publication.

Wilbur's lover is the principal male dancer, Louis Giraud, French in origin. He is shrewd about his career and intent on making his own way rather than relying on Wilbur or anyone else. Peter Sargeant, the straight narrator, hired to handle public relations, is struck by how "masculine" Louis is: "He had a deep voice and he wasn't at all like the other boys in the company who were inclined to be rather tender" (17). He is always on the make: "He's had every boy in the company … even the ones who like girls" (24). Louis tries to get Peter into bed, but, when not putting Louis down, he is busily bedding the ballerina taking the dead star's place. Peter does admit that "there may be, who knows, not much difference between nailing a boy to the bed and treating a girl in like manner" (52). He admits too, "Thinking of Louis always puts me into a good mood … that is when he's not around to make me nervous" (68). After inexplicably spending an evening together cruising the bars from the Village to Harlem, ending up naked in a bathhouse, Peter even goes so far as to say, "I wasn't too sure of myself. Louis looked like one of those Greek gods with his clothes off, all muscle and perfect proportions" (132). Vidal's friendships with dancers Harold Lang, Johnny Kriza, and Leon Danielian undoubtedly contributed to his portrait of Louis. Vidal wrote the teleplay, *Portrait of a Ballerina*, for a 1956 CBS adaptation of the novel. Gays do not show up at all in the second Peter Sargeant mystery. There are only brief glimpses in the third: *Death Likes It Hot*, 1954, set in the near fashionable world of the Hamptons, where they are identified by the code word "sensitive," along with the observation that they are "tender with sibilants."

Eugene Louis Vidal (1925–2012) was born at West Point into a political family; his grandfather Thomas Gore was twice U.S. Senator from Oklahoma. In homage to him, upon his baptism Vidal added Gore to his names. Although he always insisted he was bisexual, the great myth that colored his life was a prep school friendship with James ("Jimmy") Trimble (1925–1945), to whose memory he dedicated *City* and who is important to *The Season of Comfort*, 1949. Vidal served in the Army. After the war, he became friends with Williams, Paul Bowles, John Latouche, and Isherwood—and Capote's perpetual detractor. He appears as the character Arial Lavalina in Kerouac's *The Subterraneans*, 1958. Vidal's *Narratives of Empire* novels receive praise, but his finest work is perhaps his trenchant essays. He also wrote plays and film scripts. Of his personal writings, *Palimpsest*, 1995, and *Snapshots in History's Glare*, 2009, are vital. For fifty-three years he lived with Howard Austen (1929–2003) in a variety of places, including a long sojourn on Italy's Amalfi coast. He died in Los Angeles of pneumonia.

Wheeler began his career as a mystery writer, working behind pseudonyms in collaboration with Richard Webb. The one novel he published under his own name is the gayest. Here the two victims are homosexual, killed for trying to blackmail the murderer. She rhetorically asks the straight protagonist, an American English professor named Horace Beddoes, "do you think I was going to let a couple of horrid little pansy boys strip me of everything I'd worked so hard to get?" (222). The setting is Capri, "the breeding-ground of perversity" (44). Horace has arrived hoping to gain permission to write the authorized biography of the now silent poet Merape Sloane, only to find that Michael McDermott has beaten him to it. He is a novelist "of the fashionable-dirty school" whose latest work "dealt with a delicate twelve-year-old boy's infatuation for a one-armed Mexican field-worker" (16). Horace is struck by his resemblance to portraits of Caligula when Mike regards him "with a bold, almost sensual appraisal" (26). Inadvertently, Horace destroys the murder weapon, casting suspicion on him. The second victim is a Latvian gigolo on the make for either sex if it will benefit him, equally willing to extort money from the murderer. To this end, Askold wants the notes that Mike made for his biography, which have passed to Horace. If he can get Horace at the same time, all the better. Recoiling, Horace strikes Askold and flees. He returns to find his dead body. He realizes that in order to save himself he must unmask the murderer. As in Vidal's mystery, homosexuality is incidental, not germane to the plot. It is puzzling why a gay writer should feel compelled to introduce gay characters in order to derogate them.

Hugh Callingham Wheeler (1912–1987) was born in London and attended London University. In 1934 he emigrated to the U.S. Renewing his friendship with Webb (1901–1966), the two began collaborating on a mystery series that Webb had begun earlier with other collaborators. The two traveled widely together and were probably lovers for a time. Wheeler dedicated *Muse* to him. Wheeler was naturalized in 1942 and served in the Army Medical Corps during the war. In 1961 he turned to writing plays and books for musicals, most notably with Stephen Sondheim. He also rewrote the book for Bernstein's *Candide*. His screenplays include *Something for Everyone* and *Cabaret* (uncredited). His partner was John R. Grubbs (1916–2006). He died in Pittsfield, Massachusetts, according to townsfolk of complications from AIDS.

Kaplan, Fred. *Gore Vidal: A Biography*. New York: Doubleday, 1999.
Vaill, Amanda. *Somewhere: The Life of Jerome Robbins*. New York: Broadway, 2006. 193–94.
Vidal, Gore. *The City and the Pillar*. *New York: Dutton, 1948. London: Lehmann, 1949. Rev. New York: Dutton, 1965. London: Heinemann, 1965.
[_____.] *Death in the Fifth Position*. By Edgar Box. New York: Dutton, 1952. London: Heinemann, 1954. *Boxed In*. Garden City, N.Y.: Mystery Guild, 2011. 1–143.
_____. *In a Yellow Wood*. New York: Dutton, 1947.
_____. *The Judgment of Paris*. *New York: Dutton, 1952. London: Heinemann, 1953. Rev. New York: Dutton, 1965. London: Heinemann, 1968.
Wheeler, Hugh. *The Crippled Muse*. *London: Hart-Davis, 1951. New York: Rinehart, 1952.

39 Norman Mailer: *The Naked and the Dead*, 1948; *The Deer Park*, 1955; *Why Are We in Vietnam?*, 1967.

In the twenty years between the closeted general in his first, World War II, novel and the closeted teenager in his Vietnam novel, Mailer made at least a 160 degree turn in his attitudes about homosexuality. The macho author, as he himself recognized, was fascinated by the subject. In a conversation with Mailer's biographer (596), Dotson Rader recalled that when he arrived in New York, "I was warned that he was homophobic. I knew Norman quite well [they were both activists in the peace movement] and I never had a sense of that, quite the opposite. I feel he was fascinated, intrigued, by homosexuals and homosexuality. He would go into the very specific, raunchy details, and to me very embarrassing details, about exactly what physically you did as a gay person. And he wanted the moist [sic] specifics about the encounter. Sometimes I provided them, sometimes I would get my back up and say this is too much."

In *Naked*, the deeply repressed Major General Edward Cummings is married, but in his lovemaking, "he fights out battles with himself upon her body" (416). Alone in Italy before the war, "he gets up on an impulse and walks the streets, ending up in an alley where he becomes drunk in a bar. There is a little man pawing him. Signor Maggiore you come home with me now? He staggers along dimly aware of what he wants, but he does not find it." He is mugged. "He feels as if he is breaking apart" (425). Unable to express his feelings, he plays a sadistic game with his aide, Lieutenant Robert Hearn. When Hearn retaliates, Cummings has him transferred to a post that he, almost consciously, knows will lead to Hearn's death. When the news comes, "it had hurt him, wrenched his heart with a cruel fist. He had almost grieved for Hearn, and then it had been covered over by something else, something more complex. For days whenever Cummings thought of the Lieutenant he would feel a mingled pain and satisfaction" (717). Hearn himself is sexually ambiguous. While at Harvard he had declared, "You know when nothing else is left I'm going to become a fairy, not a goddam little nance, you understand. [...] Bisexual" (340). But facing the dangers of an ambush, Hearn comes to realize that "deep within him he needed control and not mating" (580). The novel repeatedly shows up on lists of gay war novels, but if it belongs there, it should be mostly to demonstrate how the American military works to suppress male-male sexual feelings so thoroughly that they essentially cease to exist. Even this was subverted in the 1958 film in which Cummings acts as a father figure and Hearn returns to praise the altruistic fraternity of soldiers.

Barbary Shore, 1951, also has a homosexual villain, at least in Mailer's mind; he describes him as "a secret police agent named Leroy Hollingsworth whose sadism and slyness were essentially combined with his sexual deviation" ("Homosexual Villain," 44). *Deer Park* treats satirically the fallout from the Congressional investigations into alleged communism in Hollywood. Incidental to the story is an attempt by his studio to force gay actor Teddy Pope into a cover-up marriage: "A rumor about a fellow like you, it spreads like hot cakes" (268). The chosen starlet is saved from the "faggola" (275) when she reveals that she is already secretly wed. What makes Teddy so interesting, however, is the part he played in altering Mailer's personal prejudices against gays. In an essay he published in *ONE* magazine in January 1955, "The Homosexual Villain," he talks about the impact his reading of Donald Webster Cory's *The Homosexual in America* had on him. (Toby Schneebaum, who went on to write *Keep the River on Your Right* lent Mailer his copy.) Mailer says (46) that from it he gained "the realization I had been closing myself off from understanding a very large part of life." As a result, he continues (48), "I no longer believed in Teddy Pope as I had drawn him." He was not ready to jettison the novel, but he did try to flesh out the caricature that he had originally drawn for comic ridicule. Whether it was a result of Mailer's reading or something already in the manuscript, at one point Teddy says, "I would like [...] for something to happen where I could be true to myself. A moment of dignity." He adds, "I make a lot of people uncomfortable, but that's no reason for them to feel superior" (235). It is admirable the way Teddy stands up against his studio head when he proposes the marriage cover as well as his relationship with Marion Faye. A more important character in the novel, Marion is a bisexual pimp. He admits that in having sex with Teddy, he discovered "that deep down I'm half queer anyway, so it wasn't repugnant" (146). Near the end of the novel, we learn that, even with his career on the skids, Teddy was brave enough to assert his friendship with Marion and to visit him in jail (365).

Mailer was on the fringes of the Beats. He much admired Burroughs, both the man and the writer. His teenage protagonist in *Vietnam* pays explicit homage to him (and to media guru Marshall McLuhan). There is barely enough plot for a short story; the work is embellished by piling on detail after detail with many sentences going for almost two pages. Even more than *Naked Lunch* the novel would benefit from being released as an audiobook; in fact, the story is presented as a transcript of a tape recording. The speaker, eighteen-year-old Ranald (D.J.) Jethroe, is recalling the Alaska hunting trip that he and his best friend, Gottfried (Tex) Hyde, Jr., went on two years earlier as part of a group from Dallas. Repressed homosexuality and violence are the intertwined tropes that propel the narrative. D.J. describes himself as "a humdinger of a latent homosexual highly over-heterosexual with onanistic narcissistic and sodomistic overtones" and suggests that he and Tex have sublimated their sexual desires for each other by sharing the same girl. By turning the hunt into a Hemingway parody, Mailer demonstrates what a pathetic bunch the group of men are. The two boys themselves become aware of the fact. In disgust they discard all their hunting gear and set off alone into the Brooks Range. D.J. has the epiphany that the two of them are caught "on the knife of the divide in all conflict of lust to own the other yet in fear of being killed by the other." Therefore, they become "twins, never to be near as lovers again, but killer brothers" (203–04). The tape is being finished the evening before they are "off to see the wizard in Vietnam" (208). And so Mailer seems to hold, with the flower children generation, that we make war because we are incapable of making love. His one-act dramatization, "D.J." was performed but has not been published.

Norman Kingsley Mailer (1923–2007) was born in Long Branch, New Jersey. He graduated from Harvard and was drafted into the army. Always ready to promote himself, he was attended by controversy most of his career. He was married six times and had eight children, plus stepchildren. He died of stomach cancer in New York.

Lennon, J. Michael. *Norman Mailer: A Double Life*. New York: Simon & Schuster, 2013.

Mailer, Norman. *The Deer Park*. *New York: Putnam's, 1955. London: Wingate, 1957.

———. "The Homosexual Villain." 1955. *Come Out Fighting: A Century of Essential Writing on Gay and Lesbian Liberation*. Ed. Chris Bull. New York: Thunder's Mouth, 2001. 44–49.

———. *The Naked and the Dead*. *New York: Rinehart, 1948. London: Wingate, 1949.

_____. *Why Are We in Vietnam?* *New York: Putnam's, 1967. London: Weidenfeld & Nicholson, 1969.

40 Truman Capote: *Other Voices, Other Rooms*, 1948. Speed Lamkin: *Tiger in the Garden*, 1950.

Capote's novel is a coming of age story. It may also be a coming out story. Upon the death of his mother, thirteen-year-old Joel Harrison Knox is summoned to Scully's Landing, a gothic house falling into ruins in rural Mississippi, to join his father, Ed Sansom (the boy carries his mother's maiden name), and his stepmother, Amy Scully. He meets Amy's cousin, the strange Randolph (who calls Joel his Alcibiades), but, to his bewilderment, he is kept from seeing his father. After repeated requests, the two finally meet. The father is almost completely paralyzed, his ability to communicate limited: he lets fall a red ball when he needs attention. Randolph tells Joel the story of his own great love for Pepe Alvarez, the fighter for whom the father had been the manager, and his madness when Pepe decamped with a woman. It was then that he accidentally shot the father, apparently damaging the spinal cord. Randolph describes how he enchanted Pepe at a Mardi Gras ball disguised all in white as a countess in the court of Louis XVI. Still obsessed by Pepe, he periodically dons the costume and transforms himself into "the queer lady" whom Joel glimpses looking out the window, "smiling and nodding at him, as if in greeting or approval" (55). Randolph explains, "any love is natural and beautiful that lies within a person's nature; only hypocrites would hold a man responsible for what he loves, emotional illiterates and those of righteous envy, who, in their agitated concern, mistake so frequently the arrow pointing to heaven for the one that leads to hell." But, he continues, "so fierce is the world's ridicule we cannot speak or show our tenderness" (124).

Joel's own sexuality is still undefined; he remains puzzled by his memory of "two grown men standing in an ugly little room kissing each other" in New Orleans (54). He feels "as if his heart were beating all over his body" when he and Idabel, the friend he has made, come across a naked couple having sex (158). Idabel is probably equally uncertain of her sexuality, but quite clear about her gender: she is a boy. The two of them run away to see a traveling show. Joel falls ill as a result of the night excursion, a rite of passage though "nothing he saw concretely affirmed his suspicions of emerging manhood" (175). Randolph becomes for him an "X" (178) before he realizes "how helpless Randolph was: more paralyzed than Mr. Sansom, more childlike than [a midget they saw at the show], what else could he do, once outside and alone, but describe a circle, the zero of his nothingness" (191). But Joel? "'I am me,' Joel whooped. 'I am Joel, we are the same people'" (190). The ending is ambiguous. Randolph appears at his window in his white costume "as if snow were falling there." When he beckons to him, Joel "knew he must go: unafraid, not hesitating, he paused only at the garden's edge where, as though he'd forgotten something, he stopped and looked back at the bloomless, descending blue, at the boy he had left behind" (194). Most gay readers interpret the scene to mean that Joel has accepted his sexuality. But there are two details to note. The imagery recalls Hans Christian Andersen's "The Snow Queen," in which a little boy has his heart turned "into a lump of bitter ice" (10). And he must go where? The authorial voice does not specify. The novel became the basis for a film in 1995.

Truman Streckfus Persons (1924–1984) was born in New Orleans but grew up in Monroeville, Alabama, where he met Harper Lee, a model for Idabel (just as he was a model for Dill in *To Kill a Mockingbird*). He moved to New York, where he was adopted by his mother's second husband and took the name Capote. He quickly established a literary reputation with his stories in *Harper's Bazaar*. A photograph by Harold Halma on his novel's dust jacket created a sensation, leading to a famous invitation from Denny Fouts to join him in Paris. He was friend and sometimes enemy with Vidal and Williams. The English professor Newton Arvin (1900–1963), to whom he dedicated the novel (and who tragically killed himself as the result of a police raid for possession of "indecent" materials) was a lover. Capote's longtime partner was the Broadway dancer and novelist John Paul (Jack) Dunphy (1914–1992). But there were other lovers. Capote's slow downfall began paradoxically with his best book, *In Cold Blood*, 1966. He died in Los Angeles from liver cancer.

The composer Ned Rorem called Lamkin "the poor man's Truman Capote." The description misleads more than helps, but Lamkin's first novel, like Capote's, is the story of a Southern family, in the first third of the twentieth century, in which covert homosexuality plays an important role. The Richardsons are seen through the eyes of Henry Nelson, a cousin and their next door neighbor. The younger son, Percy, is gay—and thwarted. He tells Henry, "It's something inside me that keeps wanting to get out," and follows by saying, "I should have gone to New York or to New Orleans, where you can really live, maybe even to Paris with that friend of mine from college" (60–61, 65). He feels trapped in the small Louisiana town where he was born. Another cousin, a younger man, Stanley Wright, is also gay. Stanley's mother, who prides herself on being modern, periodically reports on Stanley's gay reading (Wilde, Proust) and his "effeminate friends" (133). She says with obvious relish, "Really, Henry, I sometimes fear that behind my back my Stanley will put Sodom to shame" (125). Later she implies that she fostered her son's sexuality by associating with "French Quarter pansies," "men-women" (150).

Apparently Percy, angry at the way Stanley's mother is flirting with his brother-in-law, gets "revenge" by seducing the son (150). He tries to justify his act by confessing to Henry that "it was wrong of me to do what I did with Stanley. But we couldn't help ourselves. How can you help yourself when both of you are thinking and wanting the same thing" (170). Soon afterwards Percy mysteriously drowns. Henry himself is an enigma. He professes to love a schoolmarm but denies the possibility of marriage with her because his mother is dependent on him. While in New Orleans, he does not hesitate to accept Stanley's offer to take him to a bar frequented by "men of both sexes" (208). He learns that it is the same bar Percy frequented when he was in town. While the two are there, Stanley tells him, "If one has the feeling, it is no more wrong to do the thing and enjoy it than to have the feeling pressing you to misery. [...] One must develop oneself, realize one's nature perfectly," a comment that he ascribes to Wilde. Stanley goes on to say, "Homosexuality was a cross that Percy bore," and attributes his suicide to his inability to accept his hometown's values. Henry holds, however, that "Stanley liked that bar more from a sense of rebellion than from a sense of pleasure" (210–11).

The novel subtly links the taboos of miscegenation, homosexuality, and perhaps incest in humans' blind search for love. It also explores the sanctity of family and records the rise of a nouveau riche and Huey Long's political hold on the state. An unattributed comment by Williams was often repeated, to the effect that Lamkin "doesn't write as well [as Capote] but is more agreeable." Hillyer Speed Lamkin (1928–2011) was born and died in Monroe, Louisiana. He attended Harvard. He lived in New York, London, and Los Angeles. He became friends with Isherwood, who appears as Sebastian Saunders in Lamkin's second novel, *The Easter Egg Hunt*, 1954. Lovers included Mike Steen (1928–1983), an actor and early Williams biographer, and actor Paul Millard. He was an avid art collector.

Capote, Truman. *Other Voices, Other Rooms*. New York: Random House, 1948. London: Heinemann, 1948. *New York: Modern Library, 2004.
Clarke, Gerald. *Capote: A Biography*. New York: Simon & Schuster, 1988.
Lamkin, Speed. *Tiger in the Garden*. *Boston: Houghton Mifflin, 1950. London: Macmillan, 1951.

41   Hubert Creekmore: *The Welcome*, 1948. Thomas Hal Phillips: *The Bitterweed Path*, 1950. Note on William Faulkner.

Set in a small town in Mississippi during the 1930s, Creekmore's novel depicts the effects same-sex desire has on the lives of two men born there: Don Mason and Jim Furlow. Coupled with pressure from society and family, his feelings so frighten Jim that he sets out to get married. An abandoned church that the two boys visit one evening takes on emblematic significance for Don. Though the moonlight casts strange "phallic patterns on the floor," it represents for him "our heritage—from the Puritans, the Victorians, the feminists—and their opposites"—that has forced women to forget they're human, "animals, too, like us." He predicts for Jim, "Some day you'll marry one of those women," and then, most tellingly, he adds, "Your wife, when she chooses you, will be like that church" (29). Indeed, Doris Furlow is emotionally and sexually frigid. She is also materialistic and pretentious, a prig, eliciting one of two homophobic slurs that Jim slings out during the course of the novel: "Too bad you didn't marry some aristocratic pansy" (108). She gives in to Jim's desire to have a child, which she doesn't want, if he will promise to buy her an expensive Lincoln automobile. Thereafter, she takes advantage of separate bedrooms: "She was the cold, empty church which Don pointed out to him years ago" (139).

Don left for New York before the marriage took place—"Big cities are excuses for people like me" (215)—but his mother needing him in her final illness, he returns. Old emotions stir just under the surface, but Jim is hopelessly trapped by social mores: "*I remember it all; I miss it; but I must pretend*" (178). Yet "he always knew how Don felt toward him" (248). On a hunting trip momentarily he gives in to his sense of despair at having lost this friendship and actually pleads with Don to kill him. Later, he begs Don to run away with him: "Let's be together, in some other town, in some city. We can both be happy then." But Don recognizes "both destruction and love" in Jim's desperation and rejects it as a cowardly proposal made "too late for both of us. What you should have offered of your own free will, years ago, you're now offering like some kind of desperate bribe" (255–56). Don renews his friendship with Isabel Lang, an intellectual who has given up hope of finding a suitable husband in the small town. Outcasts both, they regard themselves as potential spouses. Isabel tells him that she knows the truth about him and Jim, but declares that "my love hasn't been hurt by knowing you loved Jim" (288). Even as Don thinks about the "empty church" (285), even as he tells her that she cannot be sure of his fidelity, he comes to feel that the two of them can make a life together. Jim despairs at their wedding. And he reacts typically, calling Don a "damned little fairy" (306).

In many ways, the most intriguing character in the novel is the straight Gus Traywick, "still the Boy Scout [...] who wanted to show his affection and wanted a little in return; he went on loving people in a lumbering doglike way" (54). He assumes that Jim and Don will want to get back together the way they had been in school even though he has never understood the emotional basis for that friendship. Not at least until now: "In the first surprise of realization, Tray was a little dumbfounded, a little inclined to assume that such things didn't happen here in Ashton, to friends," but "after a moment's reflection, he saw that his only surprise was one of acknowledgment. He had really known all the time, but didn't want to admit it." But then in one of those generous moments than can occur in small towns, he decides, "There are worse things less frowned upon. People were too silly about their feelings" (199–200). He is taken aback by Don's anger when he suggests that Don and Jim may want to sleep on adjacent cots during the hunting trip. He begs Isabel to marry Don, arguing, "There's more than just the physical" (270). And he begs Jim, "At least let him try to be happy." In the final scene in the novel Gus holds Jim in his arms like a male pieta, calming him, "'If only people could forgive each other for loving.' And Tray, never having been taught how to be good, nor having felt any guilt for his lack of this knowledge, wondered for a moment what his own words meant" (306–07).

Creekmore's novel is far from straightforward in addressing sexuality, but Phillips's is even coyer. It is set near Vicksburg, Mississippi, at the turn of the twentieth century. Darrell Barclay is the son of a Faulknerian tenant farmer: a ne'er-do-well consumed with racial and economic prejudice, a member of the Ku Klux Klan. He becomes a tenant on Malcolm Pitt's place. Darrell first meets Roger during a schoolboys' race in which they are both entered. The Pitt boy is like some naked vision: "the light seemed to bounce away from the pale fullness of his loins" (4). Darrell is mesmerized by the Pitt family and home, and "Roger was the most beautiful thing he could imagine in a very real and beautiful world" (72). When his father is ambushed while on Klan activity, his demise provides relief and release for the boy. Malcolm begins to treat Darrell almost like a son and, by such, their relationship becomes strangely near incestuous. A decisive moment arrives when Malcolm and Darrell share a riverboat cabin on the way back from business in Memphis. In a symbolic gesture, though exactly what it symbolizes remains unclear, Malcolm renounces chewing tobacco and tries to clean his stained mouth with his handkerchief. Later, for warmth they share the same bed, "and Malcolm pulled him close so that Darrell could feel the great maleness of him, soft and warm and weighty. He shivered a little." Darrell now feels that he is "bound forever to the great strength against him" (83–84). Memory of the scene returns, but apparently nothing sexual ever occurs between the two.

Darryll and Roger's physical relationship intensifies, though to what exact degree we never know. They kiss. They sleep naked together, aware in the morning that they need to "put on some underwear" lest they be discovered thus by Malcolm when he comes to awaken them (104). They stay away from prostitutes while in New Orleans. But both accept marriage. Darrell is drawn to Roger's sister, Malcolm's daughter, but caste prejudice on the part of the girl's mother is sufficient to block such a union. Darrell finds another and sires twin sons, neither of whom "could be named Malcolm" for the same reason (253). Malcolm is accidently killed; Darrell's wife dies in childbirth; Roger and his wife separate. Darrell and Roger once again share a bed naked. This time they embrace: "Suddenly Roger whispered, 'Do you think it's right?' 'I don't know ... we're grown now'" But "the wild tenderness was now upon them." A chapter break immediately follows; the next chapter begins: "In the bright light of day their eyes burned with a tenderness against each other, as if to say: now it is done; we have reached the just-beyond; there is no going back to something less; there is no ending" (311–12).

Hiram Hubert Creekmore, Jr. (1907–1966), was born in Water Valley, Mississippi. He graduated from the University of Mississippi and Columbia. He served in the Navy during World War II. He lived in Jackson and New York, where he served as an editor for New Directions. He died of a heart attack in a taxicab on his way to the airport. Thomas Hal Phillips (1922–2007) was born on a rural farm near Kossuth. He received degrees from Mississippi State and the University of Alabama. During the war he served as a Naval lieutenant in north Africa and was part of the Italian campaign. He published five novels in the early 1950s, including the homoerotic *Kangaroo Hollow*, 1954, before engaging briefly in politics and then working in Hollywood. He played the judge in the 1980 television adaptation of Faulkner's "Barn Burning," to which the early chapters of *Bitterweed Path* bear comparison. He died in Kossuth.

Faulkner presents a special case of his own. Several of his works permit gay readings. Of the short stories, the often anthologized "A Rose for Emily," 1930, readily receives such a reading. But exactly what do the townsfolk mean when they report that Homer Barron (an interesting name in itself) "liked men" and that he himself had said "he was not a marrying man"? "Divorce in Naples," 1931, is an overt comic treatment of the relationship between two men working aboard a cargo ship plying between Galveston and Naples. Fellow sailors easily accept that young Carl, a mess boy, is "the wife" of the second cook, George. They are not surprised that George goes berserk when Carl loses his virginity to an Italian prostitute; nor are they surprised when the two men reconcile. Then there is Voyd Ewing in "Golden Land," 1935, a Hollywood story. The father, having caught him wearing women's underwear, calls him "a f...." Gay characters in the novels, if they exist, are less out. But Quentin Compson, the troubled Mississippi youth who focuses the Civil War romance *Absalom, Absalom!*, 1936, and who kills himself at Harvard in *The Sound and the Fury*, 1929, has marks of a closet case. Another character calls his roommate, Shreve McCannon, Quentin's "husband." There is also a tight male relationship between the half-brothers Henry Sutpen and Charles Bon in the Civil War part of *Absalom* to parallel Quentin and Shreve's. Then there are the McCaslin twins in *Go Down, Moses*, 1942, one of whom enters marriage only because he is trapped into it. Is there an incestuous relationship between them? And what role does the slave Percival Brownlee have in their life? Other works that have come under scrutiny include *Mosquitoes*, 1927 (Ernest and Gordon, the latter based on the gay artist William Spratling); *Sanctuary*, 1931 (Popeye Vitelli and Horace Benbow); and *Light in August* 1932 (Joe Christmas). Darl Bundren in *As I Lay Dying*, 1930, and Gaven Stevens, who appears in seven short stories, a novella, and five novels, should be considered. William Cuthbert Falkner (1897–1962; he added the *u*) was born in New Albany but grew up in Oxford, Mississippi. He received the 1949 Nobel Prize for Literature. He was married and had a daughter. Increasingly an alcoholic, he died in a sanitarium in Byhalia, Mississippi, after a severe fall from his horse.

Creekmore, Hubert. *The Welcome*. New York: Appleton-Century-Crofts, 1948.
Howard, John. *Men like That: A Southern Queer History*. Chicago: University of Chicago Press, 1999. Chapter 5.
Phillips, Thomas Hal. *The Bitterweed Path*. New York: Rinehart, 1950. London: Allen, 1951. *Chapel Hill: University of North Carolina Press, 1996.

42 Klaus Mann: *Pathetic Symphony*, 1948. Marguerite Yourcenar and Grace Flick: *Memoirs of Hadrian*, 1954.

From Alfred Cohen on, gay American letters have been enriched by the contribution of naturalized citizens. Escaping the menace the Nazis posed his family, Mann (with his sister Erika Auden) arrived in the U.S. in 1936 (their closeted father, Thomas Mann, came in 1939); Yourcenar (and Erika's husband) appeared in 1939. Yet, despite the one actually writing in English and the other having largely researched and entirely written her most important novel in the U.S., they have only rarely been recognized as American authors. Beyond having gay protagonists, these two works share in common that both are historical novels preoccupied with death (the sense of an expatriate's loss?). Ironically, the openly gay Mann created a protagonist ill at ease with his sexuality, while the closeted lesbian recorded one of the world's greatest same-sex love stories, albeit a tragic one.

Mann had published *Symphonie Pathétique* in 1935 (that is, two years after Hitler became chancellor), and it was translated into English in 1938. But after the war Mann himself recast it in English and published it as *Pathetic Symphony*. The story of the Russian composer Peter Ilych Tchaikovsky (1840–1893), it begins with his ill-fated lavender marriage and ends with his suicide. The novel makes clear that Tchaikovsky is gay, but the information is rendered obliquely. At the beginning we are told that the musician has married "for the definite purpose of silencing certain rumors—malicious, venomous talk about the emotional weakness Peter and Modest [Tchaikovsky's brother] had in common, and to which they were wont to refer mysteriously as "THIS" (4). Childhood crushes are recorded. There is a long scene in Paris in which Tchaikovsky becomes bewitched by a young man he encounters, but when it comes time to act, the composer deliberately gives a false name and the wrong hotel for their rendezvous (175–85). Leon Botstein, though not in a complimentary way, credits Mann (103) for being the first to emphasize the composer's "essential loneliness, despair, homosexuality, and failure to achieve lasting intimacy." Mann's biographer, Andrea Weiss, however, comments (120) that the novel "reveals more about the author than the composer." She goes on, "He dedicated it to his friend, Christopher Isherwood, who somehow missed the tragic autobiographical component." Mann was open about his sexuality, but he seems to have been driven by a death wish. Perhaps this explains why, of all his German novels, he chose this one to rework into English at the end of his life.

Klaus Heinrich Thomas Mann (1906–1949) was born in Munich, the second of six children. A drama critic and budding writer, he first visited the U.S. in 1927, in company with Erika. Back in Germany, Erika played the part of the drama teacher in the classical lesbian film *Mädchen in Uniform*. The two siblings' political action, along with their sexuality, brought them to the Nazis' attention. They left Germany in 1933; the following year he was stripped of German citizenship. With the help of Isherwood, whom Klaus had met in Berlin, Erika entered into a lavender marriage with W. H. Auden in order to gain British citizenship. Klaus was always searching for love; in the mid-1920s he had a brief affair with the French writer René Crevel. His longest relationship was with the American Thomas Quinn Curtiss (1915–2000), later a Paris film and drama critic. Once in the U.S. Klaus began turning himself into an American. To earn money he worked the lecture circuit. He began writing in English, including his autobiography. In 1941 he launched a literary journal, *Decision*. Once the U.S. entered the war, he applied for American citizenship (granted in 1943) and volunteered for the Army. Sent to Italy, he wrote war propaganda and was a staff member of the military newspaper *Stars and Stripes*. Again a civilian, he returned to his drug habit. He killed himself with an overdose of sleeping pills in Cannes, France, never knowing that much of his grief in the U.S. had been created by FBI surveillance of him and his family. Harold Fairbanks was one of his last lovers.

Although Yourcenar had envisioned the novel decades earlier, *Mémoires d'Hadrien* was reconceived in the U.S. Published in 1951, it was translated, with her "collaboration," by her lover, Grace Frick, and published in English in 1954. Taking the form of a long letter written as his death looms to the future emperor Marcus Aurelius, the emperor Hadrian (76–138) reflects on the form his life has taken and its meaning. Central to his musings is his love for the Greek youth Antinous, which means that he must also reflect on the meaning of his lover's death. Hadrian was captivated by the boy's beauty as soon as the two met at Nicomedia. Their intimacy swiftly grew. Hadrian records, "This adventure, begun casually enough, served to enrich but also to simplify my life." He also says, "Passion satisfied has its innocence, almost as fragile as any other" (156). But he also must acknowledge that he became restless under the burden of love: "Passing interests reappeared" (176). He tries to justify some of his more shameful actions. He remembers the hostility that developed between Antonius and Lucius when he reintroduced the latter back into his life, while he continues to laud Antinous's devotion to him. Finally, he is forced to admit that he ultimately has no real idea why the boy drowned himself. And he admits, "Even my remorse has gradually become a form of possession." He proceeds to deify the youth. One senses the twentieth century author speaking through her emperor when he says, "It goes without saying that I lay no blame upon the physical desire, ordinary enough, which determined my choice in love" (172–73). Throughout the novel we hear only the one voice: Hadrian's. There is no dialogue at all, no real action per se. The author's style is everything, though in a curious way the novel seems a reflection also of her life to that point and a foreshadowing of what is to come. Still, Royston Lambert wrote (12) that she had fashioned "the broadest, the most balanced and in many ways the most authentic interpretation" of the emperor so far.

Marguerite de Crayencour (1903–1987) was born in Brussels. In 1937 she met American English teacher Grace Frick (1903–1979). Frick invited Yourcenar (the pseudonym is an anagram of her birth name) to join her in the U.S.; when war came she was forced to remain. She supported herself by teaching at Sarah Lawrence, 1940–50. In 1947 she became a U.S. citizen. The two women lived in Hartford, Connecticut, for ten years (she made use of the Yale library for her research on the *Memoirs*), then moved to Mount Desert Island, Maine. Frick died of cancer just months before Yourcenar's 1980 election to the Académie Française, the first woman to receive the honor. At the same time she was granted dual citizenship by the French government. Jerry Wilson (1949–1986), a gay photographer, now became her partner, until his death from AIDS. In 1981 she published a study of the gay Japanese writer Mishima. She died at her home, which is now a museum.

Botstein, Leon. "Music as the Language of Psychological Realism: Tchaikovsky and Russian Art." *Tchaikovsky and His World*. Ed. Leslie Kearney. Princeton: Princeton University Press, 1998. 99–144.
Lambert, Royston. *Beloved and God: The Story of Hadrian and Antinous*. New York: Viking, 1984.
Mann, Klaus. *Pathetic Symphony: A Novel about Tchaikovsky*. New York: Allan, Towne & Heath, 1948. *New York: Wiener, 1985.
Weiss, Andrea. *In the Shadow of the Magic Mountain: The Erika and Klaus Mann Story*. Chicago: University of Chicago Press, 2008.
Yourcenar, Marguerite. *Memoirs of Hadrian*. Trans. Grace Flick with the author. New York: Farrar, Straus & Young, 1954. London: Secker & Warburg, 1955. *Memoirs of Hadrian and Reflections on the Composition of Memoirs of Hadrian*. New York: Farrar, Straus & Giroux, 2005.

43 Nial Kent: *The Divided Path*, 1949.

The novel is a bildungsroman, one that many a solitary gay boy growing up at the time could easily identify with. Early on Michael becomes aware, "He was so different from his parents that he was sure he was not their child. He was adopted" (17). As he becomes older, he remains "a person apart from his fellows, living behind the walls he had constructed around himself to keep out the things that might hurt. The walls were so high and so effective they also kept out many things that might have been beneficial" (23). Michael tries to conform by dating women, but he recognizes that his deepest bonds are with men. He early identifies with Alexander in his love for Hephaestion; he reads Petronius and Theocritus, "and Krafft-Ebing had brought them up to date, stripped of romance" (57). Yet he rejects all attempts on the part of both men and women to seduce him when he leaves the security of his home to study music at the state conservatory. He meets Paul Allen and "for the first time Michael knew the meaning of real desire [...] yet he feared the consequences." He realizes that "it was one thing to understand and accept the romantic fact that David and Jonathan could feel for each other a love 'passing that of women,' to know what Alcibiades had in mind when he lay on the couch of Socrates and crept beneath his cloak [...]. It was something else again to find within himself impulses about which he had only read, often as 'case examples'" (147–48). The two become intimate, often spending weekends in "Arcadian naturalness" at Paul's uncle's cabin (179), yet he cannot bring himself to respond sexually even when Paul seems to be offering himself. He loses his virginity with a woman and finds he desires a child. He realizes he is "standing on a divided path" (253). Instead of deciding which fork to take, he flees to New York. There—"pretending it was Paul" (276)—he has his first sexual experience with another man. Soon he is part of the city's gay scene. He is especially attracted to Nikki Bolton but their budding romance is put on hold by the war.

The psychiatrist who examines him is easily bamboozled, but a heart-murmur keeps him securely out of the draft. So he serves as a hospital orderly until the end of the war. Continuing to live in New York, he meets all types. Michael becomes something of a counselor to some of them. One chapter is given over to his naming all the great gays of history to a new friend who "had grown up with a feeling that sex was unclean," which, "added to his guilt complex about being 'gay,' threatened to wreck his happiness" with another man (360). But Michael has no success in his own love life. Nikki returns, and he thinks he has found happiness, only to be supplanted by another man. He decides it is time to return home. To this point, one suspects that the novel is autobiographical, even as it would appear that the author was influenced by earlier gay fiction. There are reminders of Meeker's *Better Angel* in the protagonists' interest in music; Paul even calls Michael his "good angel" (175). There are similarities with the New York medical scenes in *The Scarlet Pansy*. Two of Vidal's books lurk in the background. The title of Kent's novel reflects a line from Frost's poem "The Road Not Taken," the source of Vidal's title *In a Yellow Wood*. And the cabin in *City and the Pillar* re-emerges. Back home Michael discovers that Paul too has returned—not only that, but it sounds "as if Paul now stood at that division of the path where he himself once had paused" (440). They set up a rendezvous at the cabin where they had spent time together in childhood. And then, the author, for some reason, seemed compelled to play an unsatisfying game with the reader. We have already learned that Michael has made his will, that he is worried "about something that psychologists called the death wish, and how accidents sometimes went out of their way to happen to people who had it" (432). On his way to meet Paul, he has "the ghost of a smile on his lips" and feels "free at last." "Dead leaves" fall around the car as he drives "into the storm" (444). Eager to meet him after all this time, Paul walks the road that Michael will drive. He comes upon a car wreck and Michael's apparently lifeless body. He grabs the cold hand. The last line of the novel reads, "Limply it lay in his grasp, but slowly, imperceptibly at first, then unmistakably, it tightened on his fingers" (447). When the novel was published in paperback in 1951, the author heavily abridged the long work. He did very little rewriting; instead, he ruthlessly excised paragraphs and entire chapters, cutting the original ninety-three chapters to fifty-nine. It went through several reprintings during the 1950s. There seems to be no information available about him other than the assertion that his real name was William Leroy Thomas (1908–?).

Kent, Nial. *The Divided Path*. New York: Greenberg, 1949.

44 Ward Thomas (Edward T. McNamara): *Stranger in the Land*, 1949.

Though the author delves into the main character's psychology at length, the work falls into the class of the social problem novel: specifically, small town America's reaction to its homosexual citizens during the war. But the unusual denouncement that its protagonist engineers lifts the novel out of the ordinary. When the twenty-eight-year-old English teacher Raymond Manton coolly plots and kills his twenty-year-old would-be blackmailer, the corrupt Terry Devine, in a perfect crime, the act has to strike some cord in anyone who has felt impotent in the face of virulent prejudice. The novel covers four critical days, June 1–4, 1944. In this time the police arrest eight men accused of having relationships with teenage boys. One of Ray's students questions why he is handing out "all that pansy talk about poetry while real men are out giving their blood for their country" (223). The school principal plays the outraged protector of delicate morals; Ray's own mother lordly announces she would "rather see a son of mine dead than involved in such a scandal" (158). One of those arrested, a young bank clerk, hangs himself in his jail cell. Terry, who has used Raymond as a ready source of income in exchange for his sexual favors, ups the stakes and threatens blackmail. Raymond first contemplates suicide, then decides on murder. He lures Terry into a pond and drowns him. The author does not permit him to escape altogether: Ray feels "no redemption in his freedom and no possible peace for him ever, only the bare solace of survival for an uncertain while" (373). But it arguably the most audacious ending of all postwar gay novels.

Since he was going further than earlier writers in questioning attitudes about gays, much of the novel is given to polemics. His observations still hold validity, but the general acceptance of many of his arguments means that this important aspect of the novel now weakens it. He accepts that he is an outsider, always "potentially a victim" (145). Aligning himself with other minorities, he thinks, "The invert must copy from the Negro and the Jew all their tricks of survival in the stronghold of great white Nordic supremacy," but he acknowledges, "As society's chameleon, with his instinctive ambiguity itself a form of protective coloration, the invert was better equipped than either Negro or Jew to deceive his enemies and had made a peculiar art of survival," creating stereotypical images that "forced a puritan civilization to treat him as a joke on the burlesque stage, instead of lynching him" (189). He questions whether some of the most rabid haters are not actually deflecting attention from their own "favorite sins" (262). But it annoys him "that men who carried adultery and seduction in their minds should be relatively secure from prosecution and from social stigmas, while he was forced to plot a crime to cover up a relationship that was at least harmless in its consequences to others, however destructive it might be to himself" (293). He expresses defiance: "I want to be Raymond Manton, whatever that implies" (85). He observes that though gays "sometimes disparaged women as a sex" they never "reviled them, as Terry, who lusted them" does (87). And he is honest: Ray reflects how the very furtiveness of gay encounters keeps "the edge of anticipation always keen" (67).

Some of the cultural asides about Wilde, Whitman, Housman, and others demonstrate again how gays have sought solace in art. A few sentences about the last movement of Tchaikowsky's *Pathétique* are poignant: "This music was easy for the sexually twisted to understand, Raymond thought; it contained the code of their sorrow and the aesthetic catharsis of their tragedy. The composer had not dared to give it a program, but the program was in the music itself" (167). Edward Thomas McNamara (1915–1987) was born and lived most of his life in Danbury, Connecticut. He attended Yale for one year on a scholarship. In 1935 he was with the CCC. That was followed by two years working as a hatter, before he became employed by USPS in 1938. Under his birth name, he published one other novel, *A Waste of Shame*, 1967, about an immigrant family. He died in Norwalk, Connecticut.

Thomas, Ward. *Stranger in the Land*. *Boston: Houghton Mifflin, 1949. London: Secker & Warburg, 1950.

45 Michael De Forrest: *The Gay Year*, 1949. Harrison Dowd: *The Night Air*, 1950.

De Forrest's and especially Dowd's novels present Broadway life, backstage and offstage, from a gay perspective. In both, however, the protagonist's emotional, not his professional, life centers the work. Both men view gay life ambivalently: "not unhappy, though never really happy" (De Forrest, 57). Both end with the protagonist having reached some kind of resolution to their problems, although, given the circumstances, it is impossible to predict just how long that resolve may last. And both the soap operaish *Gay Year* and the fairly literary *Night Air* are entertaining reads. They differ in that De Forrest's novel follows the intertwined lives of a number of bohemian characters, not all connected to the theater, while Dowd's focuses on one character alone.

In *The Gay Year*, straight painter Lou Franklin insists that the twenty-three-year-old actor Joe Harris is not truly gay, but it is Joe's year that gives the novel its title—apparently the first time that *gay* appeared in a title with a homosexual meaning. He is friends with the Three Graces, "three of the most obvious gay boys Joe had ever met" (28): Wally Steinman, a budding musician from the South loaded with racial prejudices; Charles Evans, a Broadway gypsy who "bragged that he had slept his way into the chorus and was now sleeping his way through it" (30); and Harold Price, an aspiring painter with increasing psychological problems. After first insisting he is straight, then accepting that he's queer and "may as well get used to the idea" (27), Joe—until now a virgin—has his first sexual experience with Roger Stuart, actor Teddy Knight's boyfriend. Instead of being a one-night stand, a relationship develops, to the mutual pleasure and distress of both men, providing the novel's arc. Though Joe entrances Roger, Roger feels that Teddy needs him more. Therefore, when the actor receives a contract to star in a Hollywood film, Roger accompanies him to the West Coast. But "Roger had made Joe aware that he was a highly sexed young man" (126), and he resorts to a series of one-night stands. He also sets himself the goal to find a rich man to take care of him and to forward his career.

The producer Reginald Hartley may be physically repulsive, but he obviously fits the bill nicely. In return "Joe had only to respond to Reggie's rather maudlin lovemaking, and maintain a semblance of regard for his benefactor" (123). But when Reggie reneges on his promise to let Joe have a good part in a Cape Cod production of Emlyn Williams's *Night Must Fall*, giving it to Roger in order to get Teddy to agree to be its star, Joe severs their relationship. Now for the first time he considers the fact that he is selfish, "one of the world's 'takers,'" "not a very nice person" (159), and tries to drown himself. Alerted by her young daughter, Katherine Anderson saves him from the sea and decides to save him from himself, convinced that "this one was not meant for 'the gay life'" (174). Joe responds by imagining that she may be just what he needs, but it only takes his stumbling across Roger in the dunes—having sex with one of the locals (a mentally handicapped youth who, "breathless with delight," tells Roger that whatever they are doing "won't cost you anything")—to fall yet again under his spell (186). In the duel between Katherine and Roger for his affection, Joe concludes that "he didn't think half as much of Roger as he did of Katherine. But he was 'gay,' and it was silly to pretend he could ever have had the woman who'd saved his miserable little life" (197).

Meanwhile, things are happening to his old friends. Harold is rapidly losing his grip on reality as the result, first, of being the victim of a gay bashing and, then, of being seduced by a mentally disturbed woman he meets in the park. Wally becomes the pianist for a newly launched gay bar. Stopping in to see him one evening, Joe is persuaded to sing for the crowd. The effect is so electric that he is hired at once. For the first time Joe feels contentment. Teddy chafes under the fact that he can be himself while working in the theater but once Hollywood gets him, he can no longer "call my soul my own" (255). He arrives at Joe's club one evening. Seeing him following a plainclothes policeman to the toilet, Joe steps in. Thinking Joe is jealous, Teddy refuses to listen. He is saved only by the latter's cold-cocking him. Joe calls Roger to come get his lover. In seeing him again, Joe realizes that "Roger had been the beginning of a new way of life for him. Roger brought him closer to the feeling people called love. Roger introduced him to a new self, Joe Harris, homosexual." But he realizes also, "A part of his life had ended tonight" (242). He auditions for a role in a new musical that he is almost guaranteed to get. Then in a bizarre twist that seemed required for books to be published at the time, he deludes himself that "maybe there'll be a girl, a girl I'll love who'll love me." At least the novel ends, "Whatever happens from here on in, he said to himself, I'm going to be all right. I know" (267).

It takes far longer to realize that Andy Moore, the central character in Dowd's *Air*, is gay. When we first see him, he is married, chaffing under his financial dependence on his wife's small wealth, a forty-three-year-old failed composer, has-been actor, and recovering alcoholic. Quite early he encounters a lesbian friend; she brings up the name Sam North and says, "He certainly had a crush on you" (44). But it takes many pages before it is made clear that Sam was his lover and fellow addict. Andy gets a part in a new play, a chance to renew his life. He separates from his wife. He falls in love with a bisexual fellow actor, Quentin Burke. The picture Andy paints of the homosexual's lot is a pretty dismal one. Even as he brings Burke out, he tells him, "Nobody ever really accepts it, Quent." When Burke responds that some do, "Flaunt it, even," Andy replies, "Most of them are putting on an act." He continues, "No matter how well you may have it figured out, unless you're one of those who haven't anything to lose, there's always fear. So you pretend, and if you're like me hate yourself for pretending. Finally, because hatred is somehow easier to put up with than fear, you come to value it; it's the only way you can assure yourself that you're superior" (170). In one of Andy's strangest musings, he thinks: "Maybe Housman's responsible for all this. Ought to be a law. No Shropshire Lad served to soft boys under eighteen. No, too easy, why blame Housman? You did it yourself, Narcissus, looking at your body as a man looks at a woman's and wanting it" (255).

Not realizing the consequences of his action, Burke starts Andy drinking again. In a replay of Don Birnam's role in *Lost Weekend*, he becomes a falling down, blacking out drunk. As with Don, it is not clear what role, if any, hatred of his homosexuality plays. Andy starts showing up at performances drunk. After he misses an entire performance, having spent the night with men he has met in a gay bar, he is fired. Encountering Sam, he gets into a physical fight with him: "but it wasn't Sam's face under his fists now, it was the nobody he'd wanted to kill for so long, the thing, the shadow that talked like Andrew Moore" (301). Having hit bottom, he accepts, "I'm all those things still, in the order named: dirty, little, a monster. The only difference is that I recognize it. Even if I were sure I were a good artist I'd still have to forgive myself. On the other hand, self-hatred's no good either, that's equally stupid. The accusation still holds. And the guilt. All I have to do is learn to live with it." He realizes that "forgiving myself" is the "one thing I've never done" (324–25). Throughout the novel Andy's thoughts keep reverting to the Acadian New England farmland where he grew up. Broken, he returns there even though he thinks the trip is futile. It turns out to be liberating. He encounters the boy on whom he had a crush, to find that he has gone to seed, far from the image he has carried in his mind. Even before their meeting, he has had an epiphany: "He didn't have to be a serious musician" (329). He realizes that his forte is light lyrics, the stuff of musical comedy and radio. And though he accepts, "He hadn't come home," the land leaves him a sense "of green, inextinguishable life" (337–38).

This seems to be the only novel Michael Jean De Forrest (1924–) wrote. It was minimally updated and reprinted in the early 1960s, both in hardback and paperback, with the author listed as "M. de F." According to the World Catalog, he also wrote a number of nonfiction works and provided the screenplays for two of Radley Metzger's films. He was for a time an editor at Award Books, in which capacity he met Joseph Hansen. Frank Harrison Dowd (1897–1964) was born in Madison, Connecticut. He joined the Navy in 1918 but was still in training when the war finished. He was a musician and an actor. He was with the Provincetown Players, then moved on to Broadway and Hollywood. He spent much of the 1920s in Europe. Though he published poetry and short stories, this was his only novel. He married (the novel is dedicated to his wife) and moved to Woodstock. He died in New York.

De Forrest, Michael. *The Gay Year*. New York: Woodford, 1949.
Dowd, Harrison. *The Night Air*. New York: Dial, 1950.

46 Isabel Bolton: *The Christmas Tree*, 1949. Grace Zaring Stone: *The Grotto*, 1951.

When provoked by a crisis, two mothers with gay sons react quite differently as a result of very dissimilar dynamics in their relationships. All the characters in Bolton's novel suffer under the burden of contemporary psychological theories about homosexuality. Mrs. Danforth reflects that "if she had had to endure having everything explained to her in these bald Freudian terms, being called to look at herself as the primal cause of all the misery, still she had, with reservations naturally, for she was sick to death of all the clichés, accepted the verdict that Larry was the victim of a mother-complex or fixation (one could take one's choice)" (29). She remembers her son's first love affair as a teenager while they were living in France and wonders: "If she'd acted differently, if she had made an issue of it, might she perhaps have altered the sequence of events in Larry's life?" (37). Larry himself excuses his actions because "it was this obsession with his mother that was doing him in" (95). His ex-wife, Anne, underwent psychoanalysis while they were together. As a result she accepts her husband's sexuality "with such disarming frankness, coming out so boldly with all the facts; for, it seemed, there were today no secrets one must bury in the heart." She admits that he is "the type she always fell for—the invert, the schizophrene, the artist" (30). For Larry and his mother there is also a religious aspect at work: Larry thinks in terms of demons and angels fighting over his heart as lines from Eliot's *Waste Land* run through his mind. He feels anger against "this lunatic world in which we lived" and longs for "some great triumphant declaration of faith" (163).

The crisis occurs at Christmas 1945. Anne has just gotten a divorce in Reno and married a war hero. The two are returning to New York to pick up her son, left in Mrs. Danforth's keeping. Larry for reasons unclear even to himself is on his way up from Washington, where he is working still as part of the military. He is using the occasion to break up with his current lover, Gerald Styles, another of the "young men he was always getting entangled with and who seemed so capable of adoring him, no matter how badly he might treat them directly his infatuation was over" (110). He recognizes his cruelty, acknowledges that it is a pattern, even as he excuses his inconsiderate actions. On the train he irrationally promises to be a guide to a farmboy soldier who asks him where one can find women for the night in New York and gets drunk with him. Meanwhile, Gerald has impulsively followed Larry to the city. They all converge at Mrs. Danforth's apartment. There Anne's husband proves what a consummate homophobe he is in his macho posturing before Gerald and Larry.

He goes out on the terrace, sixteen floors above the street. Larry follows and pushes the offensive man over the railing to his death. Anne, who has witnessed the murder, Gerald, and his mother are all ready to lie in order to save Larry. But Larry will have none of that. He calls the police and confesses his guilt; presumably he will be executed for his crime. The novel ends with Mrs. Danforth declaration that "the facts, the headlines, the shocking public story" are not the reality: "It was elsewhere one searched for meaning and message—for reality" (209).

There is no mention of current psychological theories in Stone's novel, but her main character could serve as a case history of the domineering mother who comes close to destroying her son. One of the other characters tells her: "It's natural to have a certain amount of fear for those we love but yours has a special quality. At times it seems almost pathological" (137). Shortly after the war, Mrs. Thorne brings her nineteen-year-old son, Evan, on a European cruise in order to get him away from another boy she considers an unhealthy influence. They are momentarily stranded in Naples by a boat strike. There she bumps into Freddy Foliot, a writer she has known in New York. He has sublet a villa farther down the coast and invites the two to stay with him while they wait for the strike to be settled. Freddy is discreetly gay; his male servant was the teenage boyfriend of the former tenant. In the five days Evans is in their company he comes to the decision that he must free himself from his overbearing mother, who more than lives up to her last name. Mrs. Thorne initially fights his decision, declaring that "it would be better for him to be dead" (140) than for him to accept his sexuality. But in the womb-like grotto under the cliffside house she has an epiphany that she must let him go: "The making of life is a separation, and the mystery of birth and identity is that whatever lives must go on creating new life out of itself" (188). But when she discovers that Evan intends to share an apartment in Venice with Freddy, she loses control and tries to murder the writer—and is dismayed when she discovers she has failed. The shock is too much for her weak heart, and she dies. She leaves behind the woman servant in the house, whom Freddy has already identified as her "deputy," her "doppelgänger," an extension of herself (217), and who now seems ready to prey on Evan's grief to her own advantage,

so there is no assurance that Mrs. Thorne's death brings a happy ending.

In a long interview between the mother and Freddy, one that takes place earlier before she is aware that he is gay, Freddy makes a series of statements that are even more interesting when one thinks about the novel's date of publication. Of moral law, of which Mrs. Thorne is fearful, he takes a relativist position, saying that it is "simply one we've agreed to accept in our time and place." When she avows that she wants her son "to be a complete, a whole human being," he retorts, "You want him to be *a certain kind* of human being. One *you* as a woman like other women can understand. One whose experience would complement your own and not set him apart from you." She reasserts, "I don't want him to be maimed and crippled," whereupon Freddy commonsensibly says, "No man is maimed or crippled who lives according to the truth of himself" (142–43). Throughout the novel homosexuality is always referred to as "it." But it would take a dense reader not to understand what "it" refers to.

Both authors were in their sixties when they published their novels. Mary Britton Miller (1883–1975) was born in New London, Connecticut, but grew up, an orphan, in Massachusetts. She spent some time in Europe, particularly Italy, but lived the greater part of her life in New York. She never married. Grace Zaring (1891–1991) was born in New York. She married Ellis S. Stone, a Commodore in the Navy; they had a daughter. She spent much of her life in Stonington, Connecticut, and died in a nursing home in nearby Mystic. She also wrote under the name Ethel Vance.

Bolton, Isabel. *The Christmas Tree.* *New York: Scribner's, 1949. London: Chapman & Hall, 1949.
Stone, Grace Zaring. *The Grotto.* New York: Harper, 1951.

47 Eugene MacCown: *The Siege of Innocence,* 1950.

Set in Paris and Venice in the 1920s, the novel is a *roman à clef* that compresses time and otherwise arranges historical fact. It is the story of the coming of age of Bruce Andrews, twenty-one years old but acting at times like "an awkward adolescent from the prairies" (237). In Paris, studying to be a painter, he is besieged by two women who hope to bed him but whose advances he finds repugnant. At the end of the novel the reader is given the understanding, however, that he will set his cap for a third, the painter Lily Dunham, who has a studio in the same building as his. When one remembers that he had earlier thought he was in love with the inaptly named Felicity—until her hand suddenly descended "in wanton abandon to his darkest and most secret places, where it clung in hidden anthropometry" (222), whereupon he fled—one must wonder what happens in the next, unwritten chapter. All the signs point to his being closeted. When he needs the help of the gay Dr. Leclerc, Lily insinuates that part of the payment might be sex and asks, "Would you deliver the goods?" When Bruce stutters that he is uncertain, she scorns his reticence: "What's a toss and a tussle more or less?" (92). At a party an ambiguous "spectacle of sly connivance" promised by a "willing young butler" plunges him into a "state of sickened weakness" (200), though nothing comes of it. A worldly archbishop compares Bruce to Ganymede. Other gays play more important roles in his life.

They include the American poet Whit Niblett, clearly modeled on Hart Crane. An alcoholic, Whit mourns, "I've discovered I can't write when I'm not drinking" (139). He makes no attempt to hide his sexuality. A long set piece is based on an incident that happened to Crane in MacCown's presence in July 1929. Bruce comes upon Whit, already drunk, at the Café Select. When he describes how he has stumbled upon a gay working men's bar whose patrons refer to each other with the feminine *elle*, Whit wants to go there at once, especially when he finds out there may be sailors there. Preparing to pay his large bill, he discovers his wallet missing. Bruce has already confessed that he has no money on him. In the ensuing fracas, the gendarmes are called, and Whit is taken away and forced to stand trial. Felicity thinks it would help to obtain "testimonials to Whit as a poet." She suggests Abel Guise, Copeau, and Martin Swann— i.e., Gide, Cocteau, and Proust (in 1929, the last was dead, of course, but the first two actually did write character references for Crane). This permits the author to pen three send-ups of the three writers, including a witty parody of Proust's style. The list of people, by first name only, who attend the trial (not altogether the author's invention) outs a number of couples, once one supplies the last name, including "Eugene and René" (137). Whit ends up rooming with Bruce in Venice. The city is buffeted by waves of sexuality from gondoliers, the adolescent hustlers on the Piazza, and the German tourists who descend "from the cities of the plain" (173–74). Whit becomes entangled with sailors, receiving two black eyes from one he picks up. He spends an evening with one of the dancers with the Ballet Russe. He courts a gondolier, one Romeo, but loses him to Monty Jerome (Cole Porter?). In one of the more comical scenes in the novel, Whit's attempt to kill himself fails miserably when the hook to which he has tied his rope pulls lose from the ceiling just as Bruce enters the room. He calls Dr. Leclerc, who is also vacationing there. At several points the author parodies Crane's style. One wonders what he was implying in having "the last words of America's most promising poet" be a limerick (215).

Other gays and a transwoman appear in lesser roles. When Bruce's *femme de ménage*, Mme Jaloustre, becomes ill, he secures the services of Dr. Leclerc. But it is too late, and she dies. Afterwards Leclerc confides to Bruce, "Mme. Jaloustre wasn't a woman at all. She was a man." He continues, "A fine-looking fellow she was, too, not in the least epicene; muscular and well developed and all that." To preserve her secret and her husband's honor, he has "tampered with an item or two in the records" (103–04). Whit's gangster friend from New York, Gigi Ruby, shows up. He unburdens himself to Bruce, recalling his days as a teenage boxer and his happiness with his partner, Gene, doing exhibition matches: "all night long we'd lie together. I'm not ashamed of it, and I can tell you that I've never been as happy in my life as I was in those days." Gene has died of double pneumonia; Gigi's only regret is that the only gift he gave "to the only person in my life I've ever loved" was a "lousy jock strap" (242–43). He now vows to Bruce that he is going to embrace his sexuality and live honestly. As for Romeo, discharged from his employment after Signora Jerome becomes jealous, and still as greedy as ever, he delivers the final catastrophe that ends the two women's siege on Bruce's innocence.

William Eugene McCown (1898–1966) was born in Eldorado Springs, Missouri. He attended the University of Missouri. By 1921 he was in Paris, where he remained until 1933. There he painted and, for a while, was a jazz pianist at Le Boeuf sur le Toit. He was briefly bedmates with the musician Virgil Thomson (1896–1989), then the lover of the surrealist writer René Crevel (1900–1935) from 1924 until 1927. A painting by McCown was used for the cover of Crevel's novel *Détours*, 1924, and the artist was the model for the character Arthur Bruggle in *La Mort difficile*, 1926. McCown's friends included Stein (who wrote a portrait of him and Thomson), McAlmon, Kay Boyle, Harry and Caresse Crosby, Crane, Nancy Cunard, Klaus Mann, and those in Cocteau's circle. Of special interest is Paul Mooney (1904–1939), later Richard Halliburton's lover. Mooney's biographer asserts (50) that "MacCown based his novel [...] on Paul's life [...] despite its dedication to one Frank Richard Urbansky." Back in the U.S. MacCown (as he was now spelling his name) continued painting. During World War II he served with Army Intelligence in London as a French translator. He died in New York of testicular cancer.

MacCown, Eugene. *The Siege of Innocence*. New York: Doubleday, 1950. London: Allen, 1950.
Max, Gerry. *Horizon Chasers: The Lives and Adventures of Richard Halliburton and Paul Mooney*. Jefferson, N.C.: McFarland, 2007. Chapter 4.
Roditi, Edouard. "Introduction." *Putting My Foot in It*. By René Crevel. Chicago: Dalkey Archive, 1992. xv–xxvi. Online.
Unterecker, John. *Voyager: A Life of Hart Crane*. New York: Farrar, Straus & Giroux, 1969.

48 James Barr (James Barr Fugaté): *Quatrefoil*, 1950; *The Occasional Man*, 1966.

The Quatrefoil Library in Minneapolis–St. Paul chose its name to honor "the first modern book to portray homosexuals positively." Never mind that it was not the first; for many it remains one of the most esteemed of all those 1950s gay novels that have not yet quite achieved canonical approval. Set in Seattle and a fictional town in Oklahoma immediately after the close of World War II, it details the charged relationship between Ensign Phillip Froelich and Lieutenant Tim Danelaw. Tim is unhappily married and seeking a divorce. Phillip is unhappily engaged but determined to go through with the marriage: "He had read enough of the machinations of the diseased mind to know that he was suffering from something that might easily destroy him. No normal mind was beset with melancholia, emotional frigidity, or the homosexual symbolism that he found in himself" (40–41). Later, the reader is told, in connection with an emotional attachment Phillip had with a friend, "He had read enough on the subject, from Freud through Proust, Gide, and Mann to Sinclair Lewis, to understand what it was" (70). But he has what seems an almost morbid fear of psychiatrists. Allan Berube's account of gays in World War II (*Coming Out*, 25) helps explain why Phillip would "rather enter a dark room with a blind copperhead than submit himself to a psychiatrist." During the war, Berube writes (33), for the first time in U.S. military history, psychiatrists "introduced to the military the idea that homosexuals were unfit to serve in the armed forces because they were mentally ill"; their sexuality "defined the person, even when there was no sexual act, as disruptive of morale." On his own, Phillip maneuvers out of the engagement and accepts Tim's love. He argues, "The best psychiatry is that which we work out ourselves" (313).

Accepting himself in both his simplicity and his complexity, Phillip finds that after all "it was easy to laugh, to live, to love" (355). Then, as if to test him to the core, Tim dies in a plane crash. Phillip contemplates suicide, but he realizes that "he was strong enough to face the ordeal of living." Instead of taking the great swim out to sea that he initially envisions, "Phillip put his clothes on again and slowly climbed the hill" (373). With that symbolic ending, the author, as he revealed in an afterword to a 1991 edition of the novel, tried to bestow a happy ending to the life of the person on whom Phillip was based. The real Phillip, he tells us, was killed on his wedding day in a collision with a train, presumably a suicide. Curiously, unlike many an inferior gay novel from the period, it was not reprinted in paperback until 1965, with an introduction by Barr. It came out in 1970 in England under the hideous title *Other Than a Man*. It was reprinted in the U.S. again in 1982, with an introduction by Samuel M. Steward, and then in 1991 with a reprint of Barr's introduction and the new afterword.

There followed a collection of seven gay stories, *Derricks*, 1951, set mostly in the Midwest—one ("First You Take a Live Goat") a humorous sendup of psychiatry. Next came a drama of ideas, *Game of Fools*, 1955, in which four gay youths are arrested for political reasons on trumped up charges of sodomy (an offense, of course, in all forty-eight states at the time). Published under his full name, the play and its preface are more militant than the rest of the author's fiction in attacking America's legal, religious, and medical views on homosexuality. Meanwhile, he was contributing essays to

ONE, *Mattachine Review*, and *Der Kreis*. Not until 1966 did he bring out a second novel.

Occasional Man was very different in kind. More complex and, arguably, better written, with less intellectualizing, it is also less interesting. The protagonist, David—age forty-two, a failed suicide and a recovering alcoholic living on the largesse of his family after being dumped by Claude, his lover of fifteen years—engages in a sexual dance in New York with four strikingly different men: Gus Akropolis, a young moving man who otherwise acts like a straight; Hermie, an African American owner of a gay bar for which David plays; Pretty John, a young ne'er-do-well who holds that "the best cure for a broken heart" is a "stiff joint" (114); and Count Giulio de Groa, a wealthy ex-Nazi and sexual connoisseur who understands the difference between "love-making that depletes and exhausts the reserves of strength" and "the rarer kind of experience that invigorates and renews" (124). He meets the last two at a drag ball that Hermie has taken him to. Claude also returns and tries to reconnect, but too much has changed. All in all, David is relatively well adjusted. His attempted suicide and his drunkenness stemmed from Claude's unfaithfulness, not from any turmoil about his sexuality. De Groa says of him that he knows "*more* than just the rules of the game," that he knows "*why* the game was being played in the first place" (194). Because David is seeking "a natural aristocracy of man, based on virtue and talent" (162), in a melodramatic finale the more interesting, rough-hewn, but unacceptable Gus is decisively passed over for the sophisticated de Groa. With a new freedom missing from the earlier works, some of Barr's sexual descriptions were so explicit for the time that paragraphs and even whole pages were dropped from the British reprint.

James Barr Fugaté (1922–1995), according to Herbert Kennedy, was born "in an oilfield boomtown in either Texas or Oklahoma." He probably attended the University of Oklahoma. He served in the Navy during the war. He moved to New York, then worked for a time in the movie industry in Los Angeles. During the Korean conflict he returned to active duty but was given an honorable discharge when it came out that he was the author of *Quatrefoil*. He was briefly lovers with Jim Kepner (1923–1997). He became involved with con artist Albert Ross Puryear (1926–?), who was the cause of a riff in the Mattachine Society on the west coast. During the 1970s Fugaté worked in hospitals in New York and Oklahoma. His writing reveals that he held no racial prejudices, only sexual ones, and that he had an intense sense of class. He died in Claremore, Oklahoma, of liver cancer.

Barr, James. *The Occasional Man*. New York: Paperback Library, 1966. Abridged. London: Rodney Books, 1968.
―――. *Quatrefoil: A Modern Novel*. *New York: Greenberg, 1950. Boston: Alyson, 1991.
Kennedy, Hubert. *A Touch of Royalty: Gay Author James Barr*. San Francisco: Peremptory, 2002. Online.
Sears, James T. *Behind the Mask of the Mattachine: The Hal Call Chronicles and the Early Movement for Homosexual Emancipation*. New York: Harrington Park, 2006. 358–63.

49 Loren Wahl (Lorenzo Madalena): *The Invisible Glass*, 1950. Martin Dibner: *The Deep Six*, 1953. Dennis Murphy: *The Sergeant*, 1958.

The trope of the officer obsessively fixated on an enlisted man under his command fascinates writers. The English writer D. H. Lawrence formalized the dynamics in his short story "The Prussian Officer," 1914; ten years later it was revealed that Melville had anticipated him in his posthumous novella *Billy Budd*, 1924. McCullers picked up the trope in *Reflections in a Golden Eye*; it applies to Mailer's *Naked and the Dead*, and it shows up in Purdy's *Eustace Chisholm and the Works*. It dominates Wahl's and Murphy's novel and forms an important subplot in Dibner's. The trope provides a study in the power differential and its misuse and indirectly critiques the military closet.

Invisible Glass is a radical reworking of Shakespeare's *Othello*. Set in a segregated African American Army unit under the command of white Southerners in northern Italy in April–May 1945, the Othello figure is the very heterosexual Chick Johnson. He is perpetually in trouble with his captain, who perceives the Los Angeles born private as "uppity." The captain would be irate if he knew about Chick's liaison with a local woman, Anna Castiglione. The twenty-six-year-old Italian American Lieutenant Steve La Cava plays the Iago role. Though refusing to acknowledge that he is gay, Steve becomes morbidly obsessed with Chick. He spends a drunken evening with Anna's brother, Angelo, just returned from the front. The Italian is more than willing to pursue a deeper relationship, but Steve is too fixated on Chick. When his attempt to seduce the private fails, he plunges into an Italian gay bar. There, too late, he faces the truth about the nature of his desires: "He hadn't really 'come out' yet, although he'd had various affairs. He was still fighting it off. That was why he kept running. Each time he came face to face with the fact that he was gay, he took off in terror, refusing to realize that he was a homo. It was incredible" (213). Seeking to justify his sexuality, he blames his religious upbringing. His first instinct is to start living honestly: "If the Almighty had seen fit for him to be homosexual, then he'd accept it. He wouldn't have to let himself go completely and be 'Nellie,' like the corporal and the sergeant in the bar. But at least he'd be man enough (or should he now say 'woman'?) to admit what he was. And make the best of it" (217). But as soon as he realizes that he cannot have Chick, he melodramatically kills himself. Unfortunately, the circumstances of his death lead the captain to assume Chick has murdered him. The novel was reprinted in hardback by the gay Guild Press in 1965. The 1950 paperback edition was titled *Take Me as I Am*, while the 1952 paperback edition was titled *If This Be Sin*.

Dibner's *Deep Six* is set on a Navy ship stationed off the Aleutians. Ensign Mike Edge is an example of the villainous homosexual. On another ship he raped and perhaps murdered one sailor. He now has his sights set on a mentally disturbed radioman, Harry Hudson Gray. He fantasizes that the teenager's "insane blue eyes looked tenderly on Edge, filled with the love that Edge craved and never in his vulgar lifetime had known" (209). A Japanese attack on the ship, which almost takes both their lives, in "splendid irony" creates the impression that Edge saves the boy from death. Thereafter, Gray worships the psychopath. Another member of the crew wryly notes, "Mike Edge, the most contemptible scum on board, will get a Purple Heart and a Bronze star. [...] he'll also get Gray. If he hasn't already had him" (297–98). Gray disappeared from the 1958 film version of the novel; Edge remained, villainous in a different way.

In Murphy's *Sergeant* a forty-three-year-old master sergeant, Albert Callan, becomes obsessed with Private Tom Swanson, to the point of stalking the twenty-year-old across the French countryside where they are stationed after World War II. Though Swanson has a French girlfriend, he becomes like one bewitched by "the red magic of the man's strange force" (192), and the two men go out and get drunk together night after night, letting Callan use the pretext of being drunk in order to cling to the youth. When Swanson finally tries to escape the sergeant's spell, Callan attacks him: "The hand clawed at him, at his belly, and as it went down into his crotch the boy roared with lightning strength that came clean as a vision" (238). The resulting fight puts Swanson into the hospital. Upon his release, the sergeant is there waiting, this time to be sure that Swanson is watching as he moves into a grove of trees to kill himself. Instead of the remorse Callan had hoped to evoke, Swanson "breathed deeply and his breathing was steady and clear" (254). The very simplicity of the story permits contradictory readings. Is the sergeant a homosexual monster preying on an innocent? Or is the novel a tragedy resulting from a man's inability, because of background and setting, to admit to and act on his deepest desires? And how should one read Swanson's capitulation to Callan's entreaties to join him in evenings of drunken carousing? One could suspect the private of being a closet case. The reader must decide.

Lorenzo J. Madalena (1919–1983) was born in San Diego, California. He graduated from San Diego State and Claremont Graduate School. Between schools he served as an officer in an African American unit of the Army during World War II. He also served during the Korean conflict. He was a teacher in different high schools in southern California. He published one other novel, under his birth name, about the Little Italy district of San Diego. He died in Rialto, California. Martin Dibner (1911–1992) was born in New York. He served in the Navy during World War II. He attended the University of Pennsylvania and Rollins College. He wrote eight other novels and the texts for two books of photographs. He was director of the Westbrook College art gallery and then became the first head of the California Arts Commission. He was married and had two children. He died of heart failure in Casco, Maine. Dennis Murphy (1932–2005) was born in Salinas, California. His father was friends with Steinbeck (rumor had it that Dennis and his brother were the models for the brothers in *East of Eden*). He attended Stanford but left to join the Army, serving in France. The novel was a bestseller; he also wrote the screenplay for the 1971 film. He was married three times and had two children. He died in San Francisco of cancer.

Dibner, Martin. *The Deep Six.* *Garden City, N.Y.: Doubleday, 1953. London: Cassell, 1954.
Murphy, Dennis. *The Sergeant.* *New York: Viking, 1958. London: Muller, 1958.
Scambray, Kenneth. *Queen Calafia's Paradise: California and the Italian American Novel.* Madison, N.J.: Fairleigh Dickinson University Press, 2006. 51–61. On Madalena.
Wahl, Loren. *The Invisible Glass.* New York: Greenberg, 1950.

50 Edward Ronns (Edward S. Aarons): *State Department Murders,* 1950. David Karp: *The Brotherhood of Velvet,* 1952. Gerald Sykes: *Children of Light,* 1955. Allen Drury: *Advise and Consent,* 1959.

By 1950 the so-called Red Scare and Lavender Scare were underway. Senator Joseph McCarthy made himself notorious by his pursuit of Communists in the State Department, but (perhaps because he was a closeted homosexual himself, like his aide Roy Cohn) he left it to others to ferret out gays. David Johnson in his account, *The Lavender Scare,* asserts (2) that "many politicians, journalists, and citizens thought that homosexuals posed more of a threat to national security than Communists." He goes on (7), "When not referred to directly as homosexuals or sex perverts, such persons were often called 'moral weaklings,' 'sexual misfits,' 'moral risks,' 'misfits,' 'undesirables,' or persons with 'unusual morals.' But the most slippery and euphemistic term of all was 'security risk.'" Though exact figures are impossible to come by, Johnson estimates (166) that "as many as five thousand suspected gay or lesbian employees may have lost their jobs with the federal government during the early days of the Cold War."

An otherwise unremarkable book, Ronns's *State Department* is noteworthy for incorporating the atmosphere of the time so quickly into a murder mystery. The protagonist is a member of the department, straight Barney Cornell. He is in love with industrialist Jason Stone's wife, Kari. In retaliation, the all-powerful and menacing Stone has set out to destroy him by creating the suspicion of his having passed classified information to the Soviets. Not being able to take further grilling in a Congressional hearing seeking to purge government of Communist sympathizers, Cornell determines to confront Stone face to face. He has a rendezvous with Kari in a restaurant filled with men and women, not a one of whom "would be found at a ball park or football stadium" (16). The waiter puts the make on Cornell. He becomes aware that Kari is flirting with a woman at the bar. Then his supervisor, Paul Evarts, shows up, and the waiter speaks to him "as if they were old friends." The truth about the situation strikes him "with a sudden explosive sense of revulsion—Kari and the girl at the bar, Paul's knee against his, the soft unnaturalness of the other people around them" (20). Though Evarts has been married (and divorced) three times in an attempt to establish a cover, Stone has discovered that he accidentally killed another man in a fight over a third man. Stone, threatening to expose him, has forced him, for reasons never made clear, to become a traitor to his country (thus uniting the red and the lavender scares). Now Evarts moves to kill Stone before Stone can eliminate him. The FBI cannot prove that Stone was "a master spy," and since Evarts is killed in the final showdown, the case is closed, with Cornell's good name restored. Interestingly, the FBI agent, though he speaks of Evarts's "moral failings," seems sympathetic to his need "to present a normal front to the world he had to live in" (152–53).

Three other novels show how men leading straight lives could be targeted in the oppressive climate right-wing politicians had created in Washington if even a hint of homosexuality could be dredged up about them and exploited. In Karp's *Brotherhood,* a mysterious group called the Brotherhood of the Bell wants to replace government worker Clark Sherrell with one of its own; it hands James Watterson, the "youngest undersecretary in the United States government," the incriminating evidence to use. Watterson instantly realizes, "With the temper of official Washington as it was, nothing could save Clark's job once I started making the phone calls." The accusation? That at age fifteen Clark and three other boys had engaged in adolescent experimentation while on a camping trip: "Clark would be torn apart by the senatorial wolves. They had gone berserk through the State Department. I had seen the faces of men let out of State as 'poor security risks'" (42–43). Watterson decides to save Sherrell from the humiliation and bungles everything. The Brotherhood strikes back: Sherrell is publicly outed; Watterson is fired and reduced to a miserable existence in New York. His sexually insatiable wife divorces him. In his last moments of freedom he is propositioned by Seymour, a gay dancer hired by the Brotherhood to prey "on my loneliness, my kindness, my sense of sin" (146). At the end the reader discovers that all the while Watterson has been in Bellevue's psychiatric ward and that his analyst suspects his entire story is "a homosexual fantasy" created by a man "split between wanting homosexual relations and despising them" (157). At that point the reader is forced to reconsider the entire novel. When Karp fashioned the script for a 1970 TV movie *The Brotherhood of the Bell*, he eliminated the gay angle altogether and turned the story into a simple thriller.

In Sykes's *Children* "guilt by association" (139) is used. The novel is set in 1950 in the imaginary town of Trimble, Ohio, showing how the red and lavender menaces had power in the hinterlands. State legislator Hank Trimble's political image "had been increased, and favorably, when he had widened his drive against Reds in the schools and colleges to include homosexuals" (70). Now in his campaign for Congress he is in a struggle with his own father, who distrusts him. The visit of gay playwright Cairo Thornton to his father's home gives him the opportunity to start a smear campaign. The hotel detective searches the playwright's room while he is out and finds a journal that frankly records his sexual adventures. It is photostatted and returned; Thornton is hastened out of town, and the rumors are launched. Thornton makes one further appearance in New York. He reflects, "Humanitarians spoke up boldly for the black man, the red man, the yellow man, and even for the killer man; they said never a word for his kind of man." He lays it to the idea that "puritanism was their safeguard against destruction. Also against life" (253–54). The plot is muddled, but Sykes exposes how in postwar America the meanings of political terms were distorted as the right consolidated power. The playwright is based on Tennessee Williams: physical description, adaption of a pen name from a geographical entry (the city in Illinois for Thornton), citation of his favorite expression *En avant!*, mention of a play that sounds much like *The Glass Menagerie*, paraphrase of actual lines from *Summer and Smoke*, an anachronistic allusion to his work on a film (*Senso*), reference to a book review (for Paul Bowles), and so on. The link between the two men was Sykes's first wife, the painter Buffie Johnson (who painted Williams's portrait).

In Drury's *Advise* Utah Senator Brig Anderson kills himself when his political opponents are set to disclose a brief liaison he had with another military man in World War II. It occurred "when the whole surging loneliness of the war, his own tiredness and questioning of himself, the burden of so much agony everywhere in the world, the need for a little rest and little peace without fighting any more with himself or anybody, had seemed unbearable" (288). He does not regret the interlude, indeed feels that it made him stronger, but "nothing ever again induced in him quite that combination of restlessness, uncertainty, impulse, and desire" (294). Anderson opposes the President's nomination of liberal Robert Leffingwell to become Secretary of State when he discovers that Leffingwell has earlier been a Communist sympathizer and lied about it. Just at this point an inscribed photograph turns up that leads Anderson's enemies to his wartime lover, who provides the damaging testimony for money. Anderson's dying thoughts flash back to that "beach in Honolulu on a long, hot, lazy afternoon" when the two met (447). The novel was a Pulitzer Prize bestseller; it became the basis for an equally successful play in 1960 and a 1962 motion picture that, unlike the novel, sensationalized the men's relationship. In *The Lavender Scare* Johnson sums up the importance of *Advise and Consent* to the burgeoning dialog about gay rights (141–42): "Drury's explicit contrast of the two men's pasts offered a critique of a security system that weighed political disloyalty and deviant sexual behavior equally." He goes on, "In Drury's novel the gay-baiters are the unprincipled menace to the country, using every available tool for partisan advantage. By portraying their victim as a courageous man whose homosexual experience was limited to one wartime encounter, Drury effectively spotlighted the excesses of Washington's obsession with homosexuality for millions of readers."

Edward Sidney Aarons (1916–1975) was born in Philadelphia. He attended Columbia. He served in the Coast Guard during World War II. He was a prolific writer of murder mysteries and spy thrillers, under his own name and the pen names Paul Ayers and Edward Ronns. Married twice, he had no children. He died in New Milford, Connecticut, of a heart ailment. Allen Stuart Drury (1918–1998) was born in Houston, Texas. He grew up in California and attended Stanford. After a brief stint in the Army during World War II, he became a deeply closeted Washington-based journalist. He died in Marin, California. David Karp (1922–1999) was born in New York. He served in the Signal Corps during the war. He graduated from CCNY and began working in television, winning an Emmy. He was married twice and had two sons. He died in Pittsfield, Massachusetts, of emphysema. Gerald Sykes (1903–1984) was born in Peterborough, Ontario, but grew up in Covington, Kentucky. He attended the University of Cincinnati, Columbia, and the Sorbonne. He was a playwright during the 1930s. He served in the Office of War Information. He was married twice and had a daughter. He died in New York of kidney failure.

Drury, Allen. *Advise and Consent.* *Garden City, N.Y.: Doubleday, 1959. London: Collins, 1960.
Johnson, David K. *The Lavender Scare: The Cold War Persecution of Gays and Lesbians in the Federal Government.* Chicago: University of Chicago Press, 2004.
Karp, David. *The Brotherhood of Velvet.* New York: Lion, 1952. *New York: Banner, 1967.
Ronns, Edward. *State Department Murders.* New York: Fawcett (Gold Medal), 1950.
Sykes, Gerald. *The Children of Light.* *New York: Farrar, Straus & Young, 1955. London: Heinemann, 1955.

51 Theodora Keogh: *The Double Door*, 1950. Vin Packer (Marijane Meaker): *Whisper His Sin*, 1954. Note on Patricia Highsmith.

Both these novels are *romans à clef*. In Keogh's novel Duke Charles de Tudelos owns adjoining houses on 65th Street in Manhattan. A double door, which only he is permitted to use, links them. No. 7 is for his private homosexual life. There he entertains special guests, and there stays whatever boy is in favor at the moment. The current occupant is eighteen-year-old Giovanni Puchini, a former laborer "who wanted a life of ease, or rather who had stumbled blindly into that want, simply out of accident, because Charles had noticed him on the street" (118). No. 5 is for display to society. There live his wife, his fifteen-year-old daughter, Candy, and his lecherous private priest, Père Laborde. They will be joined by Nigel, aka Neju the Sorcerer, homosexually predatory. Charles sees himself as a patron of the arts. He relishes his social power and cultural prestige. He adores his daughter (conceived in a moment of transferred ardor visited upon his wife by the image of a luscious Indian boy he saw earlier in the day). All goes well till Candy spies Giovanni, the two fall in love, and she manipulates him into taking her virginity. Giovanni feels no betrayal of Charles: "Of what had happened once he got upstairs to the room at the top of No. 7, Giovanni thought quite casually. Everyone knew about such people, and if that was what the old fool wanted and was willing to pay for, well that was all right, O.K." (38). But when Charles learns about it, Giovanni's days are numbered. It does not help that, in a fit of revenge against Neju's culpability in the death of his mother, he destroys all the puppets that Nigel has been fashioning for a marionette theater Charles wishes to produce. Charles, Nigel, and Laborde conspire to set Giovanni up for charges of corrupting a minor. His replacement has already been installed in No. 7.

The story was inspired by tales told about the Chilean born George de Cuevas (Jorge Cuevas Bartholín, 1885–1961), who formed the Grand Ballet de Marquis de Cuevas. Though homosexual, he married the heiress Margaret Rockefeller Strong, with whom he had two children. He owned adjacent town houses on East 68th Street in New York with a door between them. Dominick Dunne published a profile of him in *Vanity Fair* in 1987. Onto that story Keogh grafted elements of the Wayne Lonegan–William Burton–Patsy Burton triangle, though no murder (save perhaps Mrs. Puchini's) occurs here. Theodora Roosevelt (1919–2008) was born in New York, the granddaughter of the twenty-sixth president. She became a dancer. Her first husband was the ballet costumer Tom Keogh. They lived in Paris, where she met the writers associated with the *Paris Review* among others. She later lived in Rome, before returning to New York. She married twice more. She died at her home in North Carolina.

Packer's novel is the study of a parricide. Ferris Sullivan's mother is about as loathsome a parent as one could imagine. Appalled that her own brother has turned out to be "queer" (33), she is vigilant to the extreme in trying to make sure his nephew does not follow in his steps: "We merely want a nice, *healthy* son!" (30). Ferris's father respects his brother-in-law's intellect but offers only minimal resistance to his wife's hysteria. The older

Paul Lasher, a military veteran, meets Ferris upon the latter's matriculation at "Jackson University" in Virginia and is instantly smitten by him. The deeply repressed Carter Fryman IV recognizes his own hidden yearnings in Ferris and Paul and sets out gratuitously to destroy them. Ironically, save for an innocent summer camp incident (which had set his mother aflame), Ferris is still inexperienced. Back home in New York for the Christmas holidays, he ends up, almost by accident, at a gay party. As a result, he begins to transform: "Should I live my whole life out in a state of abject misery and loneliness, just so strangers who don't give a hoot about me won't talk about me? Is that a *life*?" (99). He accepts Paul's invitation to spend the night with him, with the result that "Ferris Sullivan became a man. The kind of man his mother always thought he would be" (100). In a whirlwind of events, the gay uncle commits suicide, Fryman sends an anonymous letter to the Sullivans, which sets the mother off on another series of recriminations, and Paul convinces Ferris to kill his parents. Paul considers the murders a matter of self-defense: "A threat to expose a man's abnormality before a society that mocked, persecuted, and prosecuted abnormality was, to Lasher's mind, a threat as real as the black butt of a loaded revolver." Supposedly celebrating Ferris's engagement to be married, he offers his parents champagne laced with potassium cyanide. They die as "Silent Night" plays an ironic counterpoint on the radio. Ferris convinces the police they killed themselves, despondent over her brother's death. Paul becomes keenly aware that the two of them are now "bound together from then on, whether it was desirable to them or not" (120). The money Ferris inherits, and shares with Paul, goes to their heads. They buy too lavishly. Ferris throws drunken gay parties which annoy neighbors. Then Fryman, who has been expelled for his harassment of the two men, shows up and admits that he understands he behaved the way he did with Ferris because "I was afraid I was like him" (131). Guilt sets in, and both men confess. Ferris is sent to a mental hospital and Paul is sentenced to the electric chair.

As the author acknowledged in her introduction to the 2006 reprint, the novel was based on the 1953 "champagne cocktail murder case," in which Harlow Fraden (1932?–1960), a recent NYU graduate with a degree in chemistry, poisoned his parents with the aid of his roommate, would-be novelist Dennis Wepman (1930?–). Marijane Agnes Meaker (1927–) was born in Auburn, New York. She attended the University of Missouri. An editor for Fawcett's Gold Medal series, she began turning out novels under the name "Vin Packer." *Spring Fire*, 1952, has been credited with launching lesbian pulp fiction. She has written under a number of other pseudonyms as well as her birth name. *I'll Love You When You're More like Me*, 1978, by "M. E. Kerr," is an early example of a gay novel for young adults. For two years, 1959–61, she and novelist Patricia Highsmith were lovers.

Both novels share more than a little similarity with Highsmith's distinctive style and general outlook. *Strangers on a Train*, 1950, and the Ripley pentalogy, beginning with *The Talented Mr. Ripley*, 1957, show up often on lists of gay novels, sometimes with the qualification that they have a "gay subtext." Certainly all six works have a gay feel to them, as do Hitchcock's iconic 1951 film *Strangers on a Train* with a screenplay by Raymond Chandler and both the 1960 René Clément film *Plein soleil* and the 1999 Anthony Minghella film *The Talented Mr. Riley*. Charles Bruno's psychopathic infatuation with Guy Haines and Tom Ripley's with Dickie Greenleaf, leading Tom to murdering the object of his obsession, never move into any acknowledgment of a gay identity, but Sally R. Munt makes the interesting observation that "gay readers, themselves positioned in an uneasy relation to the law and its regulation of permissible behavior, find in Ripley the antithesis to state-sanctioned Christian virtue. He pushes transgression to the limit" (Summers, *Literary Heritage*, 364). Perhaps the gayest of the Ripley novels is the fourth, *The Boy Who Followed Ripley*, 1980, with scenes in Berlin's gay bars and Ripley appearing in drag. Born Mary Patricia Plangman (1921–1995) in Fort Worth, Texas, Highsmith was adopted by her mother's second husband. She graduated from Barnard. The title for *Strangers*, by the way, came from an English friend, Marcus Beresford (1919–1994); as Marc Brandel, he wrote *The Barriers Between*, 1949, about an American journalist in Mexico who thinks he has killed a gay friend after the latter makes a pass at him. Highsmith had a number of lovers. She died in Locarno, Switzerland, from cancer.

Keogh, Theodora. *The Double Door*. *New York: Creative Age, 1950. London: Davies, 1952.
Packer, Vin. *Whisper His Sin*. New York: Fawcett (Gold

Medal), 1954. London: Miller, 1959. *Whisper His Sin / The Evil Friendship: Two Novels.* Eureka, Calif.: Stark House, 2006. 7–141.

Schenkar, Joan. *The Talented Miss Highsmith: The Secret Life and Serious Art of Patricia Highsmith.* New York: St. Martin's, 2009.

52 George Sklar: *The Promising Young Men*, 1951.

Though a gay has a major role in the novel, it is a straight male's reaction to him that provides the main interest. The novel follows the twists and turns of the career of tennis star Steve Kropa, aka Steve Krowe, from 1927, when he was fourteen, until 1948, age thirty-five. During his last tournament he mentally sums up his life: "He'd been a bad son and a bad brother, a faithless husband, an irresponsible father and a manless being. At each turn he'd taken the easy, opportune way and in the slick, money-greased maze, he'd lost his way." Now, in this final match, before his ex-wife and his son, "he was struggling for re-identification with the kid he'd been, for a token grasp on the potential he'd promised as a boy" (296). In those days his mentor was "Ken (The King) Calder, next to Tilden the winner of more Nationals than anyone in tennis" (85). Calder is homosexual, and Steve's reaction when he understands that fact becomes another of his failures: "He felt a deep guilt toward Calder. He'd acted pretty shabbily at a moment when he needed him most" (302).

The recent downfall of tennis star Bill Tilden must have prompted the author's use of a gay coach, but Frank Deford's biography of Tilden provides little—other than the fact that he like Calder had "protégés" but was generally very discreet around them—to lead me to think that the fictional player was modeled on the real. Steve observes "Calder's mannerisms and effeminate affectations" (146) but initially refuses to believe the rumors could be true. Once the seed has been planted by his jealous girlfriend, his suspicions that they are grow and seem confirmed when he sees Calder with a dancer with the Ballet Russe who has reprised Nijinsky's role in *L'après-midi d'un faune.* Upon being confronted, Calder concedes that he is "not a normal person." He explains, "I've never been able to have a relationship with a woman" (107), and goes on to say that he gets the same enjoyment from being with the dancer that Steve does from being with a woman. While Calder is away, word comes that his mother is dying.

Steve seeks him out and discovers him at a drag party with the dancer. Their split is now inevitable, but in a curious turn Steve blames the girlfriend for taking Calder away from him.

The two players next meet in a match which Calder desperately wants to win. Steve is tempted to give him the victory: "He felt that he owed it to him." Then competitiveness takes over. Calder generously praises Steve. Afterwards, "Steve turned away and walked quickly into the showers. The hot water washed away the betraying tears. He felt like a heel who'd knifed his best friend" (178). Calder sends a catty note to Steve upon his marriage. But the two do not meet again until Calder is invited to deliver an exhibition match at the resort where Steve is now working as a teaching pro. When the two face off on the court, Steve realizes that Calder wants revenge for his earlier loss to his protégé: "Suddenly Steve didn't care about winning. [...] It had no meaning for him; it seemed to have every meaning for Calder. Why deny him?" (304). It is noteworthy that there is no mention of sexuality in their reacquaintance. This fact in itself must have carried a subliminal message to readers during this time of intense American homophobia.

George Sklar (1908–1988) was born in Meriden, Connecticut. He attended Yale's drama school; during the Depression he wrote a number of protest plays with the Federal Theater Project. He then wrote for Hollywood, until he was blacklisted for his socialist sentiments. He was married and had three children. He died in Los Angeles of a heart attack.

Sklar, George. *The Promising Young Men.* New York: Crown, 1951.

53 Paul Goodman: *Parents' Day*, 1951; *Making Do*, 1963.

According to Taylor Stoehr, Goodman finished *Parents' Day* in 1949 but could not find a publisher. A small private edition was printed by a friend. It is not hard to discern why no mainstream publisher was interested. The setting is a private school where the unnamed thirty-something-year-old narrator secures a teaching post early during the war. He and his wife have split, and the narrator is taking care of their young son. The reader has barely started the novel when he announces that he is "homosexual" (10). By the second chapter he is telling the reader, "*I* was happy in my love for

Davy Drood" (37). We are left clueless, however, why he has fallen for the seventeen-year-old, save for the fact that the boy is "beautiful" (29). He is willing to abet Davy when he wants to lose his virginity with one of the girl students and argues with the school's head that they should "encourage them by furnishing contraceptives and also by giving them a convenient occasion together" (115). When he meets Davy's mother on Parents' Day, he ponders, "Should I tell her right off that I was sexually attracted to her son?" (150). He manages to have sexual relations with one of the women by thinking about Davy. Later we learn that he has "masturbated him thru the blankets and then, sick with longing, fell on him and came in my pants" (232). Another student, Jeff Deegan, has a crush on the narrator. He fights Davy on Parents' Day and, sometime later, begs to sleep on the floor beside his bed. Out of jealousy, he betrays the narrator, who is fired. Poems he has written are interspersed throughout the text. Basically we seem to have Goodman's personal apologia masquerading as fiction. The parts do not quite hang together to produce a satisfying whole.

Making Do continues the same vein of authorial introspection and self-doubt, now keyed higher because of Goodman's growing reputation as a social thinker. Much franker about the main character's sexual relationships with men, it is a mark of the changing times that it was published by a major house. Here the unnamed narrator falls in love with a slightly older student, Terry, when they meet during a panel discussion at Ohio State. Though we know almost from the beginning that they have a sexual relationship—"'Of course I have sex with him,' said Terry [much later, to his girlfriend], 'I love him'" (175)—again we see little of them in each other's company and are given Terry's descent into drugs-induced schizophrenia almost elliptically. Far more interesting is a character named Harold, who suffers from impotence. He yearns after at least one woman, but his heart goes out to teenage Puerto Rican hustlers who work at New York's Union Square, and he always has a number of them sponging off him till his fifteen-year-old favorite is tricked into betraying him. Most of the action occurs in Vanderzee (Hoboken), New Jersey, where many of characters have sought artistic and cultural refuge after being forced out of New York by rising prices and rigged evictions. There is more talk of community in this novel. In a bit of metafictional play, we are told that Terry has encountered the idea in "Goodman, the anarchist writer, whom he had newly added to the pantheon alongside Nathanael West and Mailer." In a bit of self-criticism, the author notes that another character "respected Goodman but thought that his books had no juice of life" (113–14). Structurally the novel alternates between first and third person narrators, adding to the problem of keeping straight a relatively large cast. The novel retains interest mostly because of its author's prescience about the directions the 1960s would take.

Paul Goodman (1911–1972) was born in New York and graduated from CCNY. He received his Ph.D. from Chicago. He taught for a year at a private school, being let go because of his bisexuality; he had the same experience at Black Mountain College after the war. He was rejected by the draft board during the war. One of the founders of gestalt therapy, his book *Growing Up Absurd*, 1960, brought him widespread fame and new teaching posts. He entered into two common law marriages and had three children. The accidental death of his only son in 1967 plunged him into depression. He died of a heart attack on his farm outside North Stratford, New Hampshire. Others novels and much of his poetry have gay subject matter. He was the subject of a 2011 documentary film, *Paul Goodman Changed My Life*.

Goodman, Paul. *Making Do*. New York: Macmillan, 1963.
_____. *Parents' Day*. Saugatuck, Conn.: 5x8, 1951. *Ed. Taylor Stoehr. Santa Barbara: Black Sparrow, 1985.

54 Fritz Peters: *Finistère*, 1951. Gerald Tesch: *Never the Same Again*, 1956.

Novels about romances between adults and adolescents disconcert American readers. When they find they like the book regardless of its content, they sometimes go out of their way to discover that the work is anything but a romance. Peters's novel has been subjected to that treatment; Tesch's has been generally ignored and never reprinted after its 1958 paperback revision. But both have much to say about the havoc an unsympathetic world can wreak upon those who transgress its cultural standards. Neither, however, bothers to examine what effect, if any, their acts have on the adults on either side. The authors' objective seems to be arousing sympathy for the teen-aged boys rather than kindling serious discussion.

Finistère is the region of Brittany that stretches farthest west into the Atlantic; it comes from the Latin "end of the earth." In 1927 Matthew Cameron, almost thirteen, is brought to France by his mother so she can obtain a divorce from his father and marry a Frenchman, Paul Dumesnil. Also in France is his father's best friend, Scott Fletcher, on whom Matthew has a schoolboy crush. The boy is enrolled in a school near Rouen. He engages in the usual sexual play in private schools, discovers masturbation. One day while swimming in the Seine he is caught by a rip current and almost drowns. The new athletic director, Michel Garnier, rescues him. Michel is gay, has been out since 1922: "He did not attempt to deny his own perversion, he could do nothing about it; it existed, definitely and irresistibly" (154). Matthew falls in love with him, and Michel responds in kind, though aware, in a way the now fifteen-year-old Matthew is not, of the dangers. A blissful year passes. Then Françoise Lauret, Scott's lover, catches on and makes the mistake of telling him. Scott writes Matthew a letter to "satisfy [his] conscience [...] with no thought of the consequences for him" (264). It arrives at a fraught time: Matthew is becoming aware that happiness is not easy in the world he inhabits. Paul, who, it turns out, is quite happy to play both sides of the bed, has recognized that Michel is "a pansy" (203). He realizes that Matthew is "standing perilously close to the edge of the precipice" and decides that it would be amusing "to give Matthew the slight shove necessary to push him over" (298). He throws himself literally on the boy. Even Michel turns against him, accusing him of having "asked for it, or Paul would never have done it" and berates himself for having fallen in love with a "little mama's boy" (313). Mother, of course, will hear nothing against her husband and announces to her son, "you and Michel ... it's unthinkable, it's horrible!" She finishes with the grand gesture, "I'd rather you were dead!" (320). Matthew obliges her by drowning himself. The book has been reprinted several times. A 1964 paperback edition was retitled *The World at Twilight*, echoing Peters's 1949 novel set in a mental institution, *The World Next Door*, which has some gay elements.

With Tesch's novel the reader moves from the privileged world of rich Americans in France before the Depression to the lives of people just squeaking by in the American Midwest in 1946. Despite the class differences they share common moral outlooks. Johnny Parish is thirteen, living in a household of women, floundering. He gets a summer's job working at thirty- year-old Roy Davies's gas station. He develops a crush on the man, though that does not stop him from engaging in petty theft. Roy's own emotional makeup is muddled. They engage in mutual masturbation in a parked car, progressing to sharing a motel bed in weekends at a lake. Neither identifies as gay. Roy loses the station for lack of sufficient sales. A closeted leader of a boys club picks up on the relationship and manipulates Johnny, projecting his own undeniably perverted desires on the two. In a surprising move, Roy instructs Johnny, "Tell him the *truth*. Everything" (287). Under the strain of questioning from the judge whom the club leader involves, Johnny breaks and labels Roy a "homosexual fairy *queer*" (304). Afterwards he has a violent reaction: "Jesus Roy I'm sorry for selling you out. I really am but they put words in my mouth that tasted so bad I had to spit them out and they came out wrong" (310–11). His mother is unsympathetic: "the filthy nasty *evil*ness he's done to you eliminates what very little good he *did* do" (308–09). Roy leaves town. Johnny is lost, feeling unloved, beat down. The novel ends enigmatically: "That was the first time Johnny Parish died" (318). It is not nearly so polished a work as Peters's, but it raises even more questions. The 1958 paperback edition is an "uncensored abridgment." The chapters involving Johnny and Roy are untouched; extraneous passages about the family were cut, to the novel's benefit.

Arthur Anderson Peters (1913–1979) was born in Madison, Wisconsin. When he was eleven, he was taken in by his aunt, the editor Margaret Anderson, and her lover, Jane Heap. They enrolled him in the Fontainebleau school run by the mystic G. I. Gurdjieff. Peters served in the Army during World War II. He was briefly friends with Samuel Steward and Edward Field, who devoted a chapter to him in his book *The Man Who Would Marry Susan Sontag*, 2005. He was married twice and had two children; his lover for four years in the mid–1960s was Lloyd Lozes Goff (1908–1982), a painter and a former model for Paul Cadmus. (Cadmus's 1952 painting *Finistère*, by the way, seems to have no relationship to the novel though the themes are similar.) An alcoholic, Peters died in Las Cruces, New Mexico, of heart disease. Jerry

Tschappat was a member of the Handy Writers' Colony in Marshall, Illinois, working with James Jones. While there he wrote apparently his only novel. Norman Mailer fired off at least one letter (March 22, 1956) to Jones about him. Is he the Jerry Mccullen Tschappat (1933–1986) who was born in Richland, Ohio, and died in Santa Monica, California? If so, he was married and divorced and had at least one son.

Hendrick, George, et al. *James Jones and the Handy Writers' Colony*. Carbondale: Southern Illinois University Press, 2001. 103–06. On Tesch.
Peters, Fritz. *Finistère*. New York: Farrar, Straus, 1951. London: Gollancz, 1951. *Ed. Mark Macdonald. Vancouver: Arsenal Pulp, 2006.
Tesch, Gerald. *Never the Same Again*. New York: Putnam's, 1956.

55 Russell Thacher: *The Captain*, 1951. Ralph Leveridge: *Walk on Water*, 1951. Jim Barbee: *Young John*, 1954. Marc Rivette: *The Incident*, 1957.

These four novels, in essence, critique the military policy of excluding gays from service, thus forcing men and women who wish to serve into the closet. They show the pernicious effect hiding one's sexuality can have on morale and on performance. The problem, they suggest, is not homosexuality but the policy. Incidently, the association of music with homosexuality in three of the four novels is intriguing. Being musical served as a code term for a long time.

Thacher's *Captain* deserves to be better known. The novel is about many things, especially about the way men operate under stress, but it is especially about the perils and the rewards of male-male affection. The title character, whose name is never revealed, commands an LBT during the seizure of the Japanese-held island of Kia Orta (a thinly disguised Iwo Jima). A Naval Reserve lieutenant in rank, the young but complex figure suffers from both a mysterious physical malady and a spiritual malaise. Too sensitive to his men's varying and conflicting drives, too much a humanitarian to be a good officer, he ultimately creates a situation where his commander has little choice but to relieve him of his command despite his considerable abilities. He is nominally straight, but there are indications more is going on psychologically than the captain wishes to reveal. He is aware that his bosun, Esposito, "has one great god, S-E-X" and that "he isn't too fussy about how it comes, as long as he gets it" (50)—or, as the quartermaster puts it, "a dog, Pearly, Mr. Swett, battered up old whore, Lana Turner, adds up the same to him" (150). During a night swim with the captain, Esposito gets a cramp. In helping him to shore the captain becomes unduly "hot and bothered" when apparently Esposito has an erection (32–33). He seems captivated by fellow lieutenant Dudley Gilmore, whom he compares to Andrea del Sarto's painting of a sculptor. The captain is involved in divorce proceedings; he is quite indifferent to a camp follower who throws herself at him. And he is disproportionately jealous of the fact that Gil turns to Esposito for comfort when he receives a Dear John letter. Gil's own homosexual leanings are conventionally telegraphed by his love of Shakespeare's sonnets, Whitman, and music. Crew members suspect that something physical is going on between the two: "it isn't right, him and Esposito always hanging around together [...], prowling around together in the dark" (105). The captain confronts Gil: "You and Esposito are too chummy. Maybe you like each other too much; and the boys say that isn't good. How would I say it? It isn't natural." At that moment "an identification of himself with Gil took possession of him with such force that he felt tears in his eyes" (185–86). His jealousy moves him to interfere more, sullying whatever has developed, unseen, between Gil and Esposito. During an assault on the LBT as it unloads at the island, Gil is killed. The now ex-captain and Esposito confront each other one last time as the former leaves. Esposito curtly dismisses him: "Keep yur feet dry, Capt'n. Ain't no one gonna be around to take care of ya" (280). Lothrop Russell Thacher, Jr. (1919–1990), was born in Hackensack, New Jersey. He graduated from Bucknell. During World War II he served as an ensign in the Navy. He published two other novels. Though he became a movie producer, this novel was never filmed. He married and had two sons. He died in Los Angeles of complications following surgery.

Leveridge's *Walk* is another compelling read. Set in the last days of the Philippine Campaign in 1945, it details the life of one squadron, under the leadership of Sergeant Bill Hervey. Central to several intertwined stories is the fate of Lorry Adams. All the men suspect that he is gay: "He reminded them of things they had run away from, of dirty stories and marked-up psychology books, paragraphs slyly pointed out" (31). The straight Hervey is the only one to talk frankly with him, to point out that he's "not unique" (34), to learn that Adams hopes to be killed—so "nobody can hurt me any more" (39), and to encourage him, while they are on base, to entertain the men with his ability at the piano. During combat, expediency requires Hervey to put Adams in the same foxhole as the sadistic, power-hungry, yet strangely magnetic Tuthill. Hervey warns the latter not to take advantage of Adams, but Tuthill discerns that not only can he inveigle Adams into giving him a blowjob but that on some level Adams wants to lose his sad virginity. What Tuthill is not prepared for is that Adams will then leave the safety of the foxhole under cover of darkness to court death with the Japanese. He is captured and tortured, his fingers cut off one by one down to the third finger, so he will never play an instrument again. Hervey recognizes Tuthill's culpability and confronts him: "I don't condemn you for what you did. You had to do that, same as you'll do it again and again. Know why? Because you're really that way yourself." Then, unexpectedly, he asks, "Why couldn't you have been decent? A little tenderness would have made you his idol forever." He sums up, "You're without the courage to be decent or tender" (287). Interestingly, another officer blames not war for what has occurred, because "nobody gave a good goddam, unless it was some of the stupid people who had stayed home." He blames the "small Michigan town" where Adams had grown up as the true "degenerate and the killer" (270). Hervey's friendship with Bob Cailini is equally intriguing. There is nothing sexual about their relationship, but such an intense bond grows between the two men that when Cailini is killed, Hervey sacrifices himself in order to take out the encampment that launched the fatal mortar. The novel is shot through with religious imagery, much of it originating from Cailini's musings. Common to almost all the squadron's stories is a search for the meaning of various kinds of love. Their final sacrifices are seen in terms of Calvary. Presumably Tuthill will survive the campaign, to suffer for his inability to love anyone, not even himself. The 1958 paperback edition was retitled *The Last Combat*. It seems to be the author's only novel. I can find no information about Ralph Leveridge (1922–).

Though not strictly a military novel, Rivette's *Incident* fits with the others. It is built on a strange conceit. A peacetime merchant marine ship is torpedoed by a mysterious submarine in the Pacific soon after the cessation of war. As if the author wanted to square Stephen Crane's crew in "The Open Boat," here there are sixteen survivors. By novel's end, they have dwindled to three: Beaumont, the radio officer; Durant, a crew member; and Looseley, the purser. Only now is it revealed that Looseley is a repressed homosexual. Thinking they are doomed, Durant uses him for one last moment of sexual gratification; overcome with guilt or some undefined emotion, Looseley mutilates his genitals and bleeds to death. When Durant confesses his guilt to Beaumont, the latter argues that it was Looseley's self-repression that was the actual cause of his death: "He could not let himself believe that about himself, so when it finally got too strong and he couldn't fight it any more, he had to kill himself." Then Beaumont makes an unexpected connection: "The only thing Christianity tried to do with the sense of guilt was to imbue it with love. But love and guilt don't mix. There can be no love where there is guilt. Sex becomes something nasty and foul then, just as the prudes want it to be." He goes on to theorize that "homosexuality is the logical and overwhelming sense of guilt that is the ultimate end of all morality" (290–91). He holds that there is hope for mixed up humans: "It takes only two things: the ability to talk, and the desire to see yourself as you are, rather than how you'd like to be. It all boils down to one thing really. Know yourself" (293). Marc Rivette (1916–1982) was born in Chester, Massachusetts. He attended Sacramento College. An insurance broker, he was married. He died in Monterey, California. This was apparently his only novel.

Eaton Smith in Barbee's *Young John* is another sailor relatively open about his sexuality. He shares the fo'c'sle with the protagonist, John Griffits, and the sexually ambiguous George Lucio. He feels he has discerned a kindred soul in the former and falls in love with him: "Someday, Giffits, I'll tell you all about yourself." He tangles with the latter in a brutal fight that leaves him badly damaged. Young John is indignant: "Just because you're ... 'different,' that's no reason to abuse you." Smith is philosophical: "our kind are outside the confines of the law. We have no redress for crimes committed against us. To be vilified and abused is our expectancy. It's been that way for centuries. To turn the other cheek is our only protection" (107–09).

Before he can come through with his promise to Griffits, the ship is torpedoed; he and Griffits are the only survivors. Upon recovering, they are flown back to the States. Smith gives Griffits a telephone number where he can be reached: "Perhaps I can help you find yourself ... if you know what I mean..." (139). We already know that he plays the concertina and reads Verlaine. Now the reader finds out something of his background in Chicago and the fact that he "consumed books, all kinds, obscene, religious, psychological and philosophical in his efforts to find everything was known about his 'kind'; delving into the Greek, the works of Ulrich, Freud and Stekel and the writings of Krafft-Ebing and Ellis and Hartmann of Berlin" (137). Griffits is intent on reconnecting with his fiancée. Her sister, however, is obsessed with Griffits; she reveals to him that his fiancée has been her boss's mistress all the time he thought they were in a relationship. He wants nothing to do with either of them. He pulls out the telephone number that Smith has left him and goes to make "the most important call he would ever make" (154). The last paragraph of the novel comes out of nowhere. One wonders if it was imposed by the publisher. The call is to a steamship line, where he asks for a name never mentioned before and asks to be signed up for a berth on a ship. According to the dust jacket, Jim Barbee (dates unknown) was born in North Carolina and grew up in Kinston. He entered the Maritime Service in 1942. He was married and had three children. At that time he was living in Greenville, South Carolina. I can find nothing more about him.

Barbee, Jim. *Young John.* New York: Exposition, 1954. *New York: Pan, 1957.
Leveridge, Ralph. *Walk on Water.* New York: Farrar, Straus, & Young, 1951.
Rivette, Marc. *The Incident.* *Cleveland: World, 1957. London: Cassell, 1958.
Thacher, Russell. *The Captain.* *New York: Macmillian, 1951. London: Wingate, 1952.

56 Jay Little: *Maybe—Tomorrow,* 1952; *Somewhere between the Two,* 1956.

Had Little's first novel appeared twenty years later, it might have been marketed as a young adult novel, for it is a classic coming of age / coming out story. While hardly the most polished novel from the period, it remains the most affirming. The author understands the struggle that a boy who realizes he is different from most of society goes through, including boys from "Cotton" (El Campo), Texas. Seventeen-year-old Gaylord Le Claire knows he is perceived as a sissy (although it turns out that ironically he has one of the largest penises in his high school). He is also aware that he far prefers the school jock Robert Blake to Joy Clay after he has some form of sex with both. He asks himself one of the more unusual worded questions to be found in gay fiction: "Why was the creation of life so repulsive to him" (152). Some of his questions are resolved on a trip with his parents to New Orleans. He is picked up by Paul Boudreaux, ten years older. He becomes his guide into gay life as it is seen in a New Orleans bar and at a party and initiates him that evening fully into sex. Before they part, Paul advises Gay, "Do what seems natural for you" (229). Thinking back on the evening, "Gaylord knew that he had no wish to conform to a standard alien to his nature." He finds comfort in Paul's "idea that the shadow world might be one of Nature's experiments. He saw Nature as the great designer, the great creator, fashioning the earth and all that is therein, experimenting, revising, working with vast numbers. He remembered that Paul had said there were thousands of such men and women in the United States alone" (320–21). He later expresses his faith that "nothing could keep the good from God, because they, too, were his children." Bob has never been introspective. But jealousy of Paul unlocks his natural reticence to display his emotions. He tells Gay that he loves him: "There was going to be a tomorrow now.... The sun would come up, life would go on ... his life" (345).

Little's second novel is darker, more somber, and less interesting. Picaresque in structure, there is no emotional arc to pull the reader into the story. Set in the world of female impersonators, it follows the life of Terry Wallace across two decades. An illegitimate child, he discovers his "aunt" is his actual mother only on her deathbed. Stifled by the unnamed Southern town he grows up in, he departs for Los Angeles. There he is picked up by Kent Stewart. Phil Carlton arrives at a party in Kent's house with his troop of female impersonators, and Terry finds his calling. Phil's advice for success on stage is to give the audience what they expect: "Be a whore but be a high-class one" (89). Kent and he have problems, and Terry moves on to Phil and to San Francisco and New Orleans. But then they drift apart, and Nick Lazzo enters his life. Off to Baltimore. Nick becomes unhappy, and Terry drives him away. Chicago. New York. Kent calls out of the blue and invites Terry to accompany him to Europe. Return to Los Angeles, where Kent dies of cancer. Terry decides to return to the drag circuit and heads to New Orleans. The moment when someone gasps, "Do you mean to tell me that's a boy [...], to the impersonator, was more than adequate compensation for all the uncertainties and disappointments, rude remarks, corruptions, the anxieties and the heartaches and heartbreaks, with which their lives are beset" (148). The novel ends with Terry meeting Gaylord Le Claire.

Both books were reprinted by the Paperback Library in the 1960s. Clarence Lewis ("Tex") Miller (1911–2001) was born in El Campo, Texas. After graduation from high school, he worked for a Houston radio station, toured the South with a band of female impersonators (sometimes performing under the name Jay Little), then moved to California to perform at the Pasadena Playhouse. A bisexual, he was married at the time. He met Charles Lester Yoder (1923–1973) in California, and they lived together until Yoder's death from a heart attack. He returned to Texas in the early 1950s and opened a restaurant in El Campo. He had also worked as a florist in Beverly Hills and later ran a fabric business in Houston, where he died.

Little, Jay. *Maybe—Tomorrow*. New York: Pageant, 1952.
———. *Somewhere between the Two*. New York: Pageant, 1956.
Peters, Brooks. "A 'Little' Romance." *An Open Book*, 2010. Online (no longer available).

57 Chester Himes: *Cast the First Stone*, 1952. Christopher Teale: *Behind These Walls*, 1957.

Don Carpenter in his 1966 prison novel *Hard Rain Falling* (q.v.) writes (177), "Sex in prison is a matter of three choices: abstinence, masturbation, and homosexuality." The last is sometimes innate, more often situational. In either case, because of the dynamics of incarceration the relationship is close to being a parody of that between different-sex partners. In mentioning how "Goldielocks had found his Corydon—a dark lad called Blackie," George Sylvester Viereck in his 1949 novel *All Things Human* describes them thus: "Goldielocks was the more feminine of the two. Though hovering on the borderline between the two sexes, he was not [...] a congenital 'queer.' Blackie represented the male element in this romance. He was normally sexed, but his experience, like Goldielocks,' was confined to punks and wolves. Since their teens they had never been on the street long enough to form deep-rooted attachments to women." Speaking through his protagonist, Viereck concludes that "these crushes are safety values" (132–33). Himes defines the prison terminology for these cases: "Everyone was either a wolf or a fag. The wolf is the so-called male of the species, a rare and almost obsolete animal. The fag is the female. And there were those who did not want to be associated with the fags, but were not actually wolves, who were loosely classified as wolverines." (*Punk* and *gunsel* were also used.) Himes quotes the prisoners' rewrite of Cole Porter's lyrics: "Slugs do it, bugs do it, even funny looking mugs in jugs do it." He goes on to say that they "treated degeneracy as one does normal sex, with no more shame attached to it than one attaches to promiscuousness" (72–73).

Viereck's novel is mainly about political and legal corruption in the U.S. Though his protagonist does bond with another inmate as closely as males depicted in nineteenth century novels about romantic friendship, I hesitate to call it a gay novel. I feel no such qualms in thus labeling Himes's work. In 1928 Hines was sentenced to 20–25 years of hard labor in Ohio State Penitentiary for armed robbery; he was paroled in 1936 and began working on the autobiographical manuscript that became *Cast the First Stone*. Its narrator, Jimmy Monroe, mirrors prison life realistically, but he is quite unreliable when it comes to describing his own emotional relationships with the other prisoners. As soon as he arrives, some of them start jockeying to size up his sexual availability. Quite early Jimmy holds a conversation with another inmate, Mal, in which the two sneer at the sexual degenerates they are among. But it is not long before the narrator confesses, "I was startled at the femininity a man's face could assume when you're looking at it warmly and passionately, and off to yourselves in prison where there are all men and there is no comparison." When Mal muses, "I wonder how it would feel to do something like that," Jimmy quickly turns the conversation, without cluing the reader fully to his internal reaction (41). Later when Mal accuses him of having changed, Jimmy reacts heatedly. But a later exchange, though cloaked in sarcasm, may reveal a truth. Jimmy says, "Screw Burns" (another inmate, whom he is tired of hearing about), and Mal retorts, "You and Chump." Jimmy answers smartly, "He's been after me to, but I haven't got to the place where I can do that yet. But give me time. It's so common around this joint it sounds almost natural" (97). When he and Mal escape a massive fire that kills nearly three hundred inmates, Jimmy is so happy to find Mal safe that he kisses him and shortly thereafter says, "I want you for my woman," only to feel suddenly "repulsed" (136, 140).

The bulk of the novel is taken up with quotidian affairs interspersed with extraordinary events—attempted escapes, a riot, an execution, a flu epidemic, the fire (based on a real event) and resultant prison reform. But situational and bona fide homosexuality abounds. We learn about prisoners in drag and glimpse some of the liaisons. Another friend, Metz, contends that "any form of perverted sex was both physically and spiritually degrading, and I'd say, just to make an argument, 'They tell me that married people do everything; they say that's part of the sex act itself.' And he'd grin and say, 'But these convicts aren't married.' And I'd grin and say, 'Don't be too sure about that'" (127). He finds himself momentarily attracted to a "cute little nurse" in the hospital (72), and something stronger for the effeminate Chump leaves him "with an excruciating ache" when he refuses the invitation offered (179). Then in the last third of the novel Jimmy meets young Duke Dido. The attraction between them is almost instantaneous. Dido argues that there is nothing wrong with sex between men "unless you feel that it's wrong," that is what "makes it queer" (255). Jimmy wavers, but he cannot bring himself to commit. Foreseeing that he will play the unfaithful Aeneas, he converts any possible relationship into an emotional S/M game. The night before he is to be paroled he tells Dido, "I've loved you from the first," and kisses him. "It was the first and only time I had ever kissed him. There was no passion in the kiss but it had a great tenderness" (300–01). But he does nothing to stop Dido from falling into despair and hanging himself, even taking pride "that he had done it for me." When one of the cons asks whether he plans to hang himself too, another retorts, "Not him […]. He likes himself too much to do anything like that." And indeed, as soon as he arrives at the prison gate, "I quit thinking about Dido" (302–03). In 1998 *Yesterday Will Make You Cry*, an earlier and more autobiographical version of the novel, without the melodramatic suicide, was published.

Teale's novel, also based on real experience, resembles Himes's in its choice of incidents and likewise is narrated by the main character. But Teale's has a much stronger and more focused plot. The two main characters are straight, not engaging even in so much as a kiss. Tex, a repeat offender, on his return to prison meets sixteen-year-old Red. The kid is beautiful, the perfect mark for a wolf. Tex almost against his will feels compelled to protect and to educate him. He secures him a place in the print shop, where he works, so he can look after him. He does blurt out, "If I ever decided to become a jocker, I'd want someone just like you, Red." Afterwards, he admits, "I wondered at my own motives" (50). Though he tells himself that his motivation is at base paternal, his honesty forces him to accept "that there were times when I looked into his eyes or felt his hand on my shoulder as we headed for the mess hall when my feelings were not paternal" (136). When he discovers that it makes it easier to let everyone think Red is "his punk," he accepts the masquerade. Homosexuality permeates the storyline from the beginning. We meet various couples, including one whose bond is so tight that when the wolf has a chance to escape, he cannot leave his boy. We overhear their quarrels and jealousies, leading even to murder and suicide. We attend a "Jocker's Ball" for which the queens are permitted to dress in full feminine attire. We come upon two in bed (Tex complains of the smell of cold cream mixed with "that other"). Two of the secondary characters are gay. One of them is Clyde, the head of the print shop, who takes pride in the fact that he has "never brought a kid out" (31). The other is Ramona, by trade a prostitute, who keeps getting busted. Tex says of him that "he was an honest, likeable kid" whom he finds it impossible to censure "for the way he got pleasure out of life" (204). Even though Red has a life sentence, Tex and Clyde prepare him to become a topnotch printer and then start plotting to gain him early parole. Once out, Red keeps in touch via letters. He writes about falling in love and marrying a woman, promising Tex that their first child will be named Francis or Frances, after him. At that point Tex makes a decision based totally on his own brand of altruism. Calling a favor from the mail clerk, he asks him to return the letter marked "Deceased." He consoles himself with his memories.

Chester Bomar Himes (1909–1984) was born in Jefferson City, Missouri, but largely grew up in Cleveland. He attended Ohio State for two years before his arrest. While in prison he became lovers with another inmate, Prince Rico; they continued to correspond for some years after his release. He lived in Los Angeles, San Francisco, and New York, before moving to France in 1953, then to Spain in 1968. He is best known for his series of detective novels set in Harlem. He was married twice. He died in Moraira, Spain, from Parkinson's Disease. Frank Earl Fleck (1904–1970) was born in Pittsburgh, but grew up in Texas and Kansas. He attended St. Benedict's in Atchison for two years, but mostly he was in and out of various state prisons for a series of petty crimes and counterfeiting. He was released from Alcatraz in January 1956. The next year he published his only book under the name Christopher Teale; it was dedicated to the two models for Clyde and Red and to "Alvin," whom Brooks Peters identifies as possibly Alvin Karpis, part of the Barker gang. In 1963 Fleck was arrested again, this time for armed robbery. He died in the Huntsville Texas State Prison of liver cancer.

Himes, Chester. *Cast the First Stone*. New York: Coward-McCann, 1952. *London: Allison & Busby, 1990.
Margolies, Edward, and Michael Fabre. *The Several Lives of Chester Himes*. Jackson: University of Mississippi Press, 1997. Chapter 5.
Peters, Brooks. "The Word Man of Alcatraz." *An Open Book*. Online.
Teale, Christopher. *Behind These Walls*. New York: Fell, 1957.
Viereck, George Sylvester. *All Things Human*. Lanham, Md.: Evans, 2014.

58 Mary MacLaren: *The Twisted Heart*, 1952. Alexander Randolph: *The Mail Boat*, 1954. Deborah Deutsch: *The Flaming Heart*, 1958.

A surprisingly large number of novels followed the line begun by Alan Dale in having a gay man enter into a relationship with a woman but continue to have sex with men. Most were simple propaganda. One of the most vitriolic was penned by Wilma M. Prezzi (1915–2002). Her basic premise, which she states at the beginning of *Dark Desires*, 1953, was simple: "The rapid-fire intransigents are always arguing that there is no such thing as normalcy! […] if this were so, the bleak despair of the enveloping immensities that *such inverted beings* suffer would not compel them time and again to create independent systems of personal hypocrisy. […] Nor would they suffer the torment of psychological frustration for living as organisms and failing to fulfill the biological function of reproduction as society requires it. For, no matter how they revert to the jungle of animal desire for itself alone, there is, there always will be, *there must be*, a sense of extravagant incompleteness, a hopeless feeling of disability, a dread concern for those diseased parts rendered useless" (7–8). In comparison these three novels seem benign.

McLaren's novel is so bad that one can read it as unintentional camp. It chronicles the recently widowed Barbara Moray's obsession with Dee Richards during the early years of World War II. The owner of a rooming house, she recognizes that her roomer Carlos McCann is gay. But she misses the fact that Dee is likewise, even as she wonders how he can make "such ardent love" to her without getting an erection (28). (He explains that he has been in an accident.) She notices that he eyes every male, attractive or not, and often disappears with another man without explanation. When he returns, he is sometimes unaccountably trembling, but she has to witness marks on his body before she snaps to the fact that Dee likes to be dominated in S/M sex. She finally confronts him: "You're queer, aren't you?" (86). Undergoing analysis, she receives the current interpretations of homosexuality. When told to give him up if she wants to have a healthy life, she acknowledges the validity of the counsel. But she cannot act. It takes finding him and Carlos having sex in her home for her to break with Dee. Even then she hopes that he will change. Barbara verbally attacks Carlos for his part in the affair, citing scripture and concluding, "Jesus himself would have condemned such goings on." Carlos responds, "That's where you're wrong! Jesus leeved 'ees life according to a higher morality, just as I am leeveeng mine," for, he explains, "Jesus nevaire married because 'ee 'ad no use for women. 'Ee 'ated them, just as I do. […] He was queer, as you call eet, queer. Just like me!" (205). Dee moves into a motel room, which he shares with another man. There his naked corpse is discovered, his genitals mutilated. The author provides enough clues for the reader to realize that the brother of a sailor whom Dee seduced during his brief stint in the military has tracked him down and enacted revenge. The novel was written by a silent film actor. Mary MacDonald (1896–1985) was born in Pittsburgh, Pennsylvania. She began her stage career at the Winter Garden in New York in 1914. Two years later she was in Hollywood as Mary MacLaren. Married three times, she died in poverty in Hollywood. Her novel was dedicated to James M. Cain, appropriately enough given his scurrilous depiction of gays in *Serenade*, 1937.

Randolph's *Mail Boat* is an epistolary novel. It presents fifteen letters written by Martha Baker to various people back in the U.S. and nine by her lover, Oscar Tower, all to Andrew MaCloy in Venice. The couple have taken a house on an island in the Tyrrhenian Sea, where Oscar intends to finish his novel. Martha becomes aware that something is amiss in their relationship and catches on that Oscar is smitten with thirteen-year-old Mario. In a surprising moment, she writes to the man she really loves, "I think that if he would just *do* something with the boy, go ahead, and stop procrastinating, and stop analyzing the little midget, it would all be over in no time at all." Making a common mistake, she cannot believe, however, that Oscar is "one of those people" because "he is not effeminate" (87–88). Mario dies; it comes out that he has been hustling tourists all summer. Martha departs. Oscar picks up another boy, the fifteen-year-old Angelino. Martha herself dies in Rome, leaving Oscar floundering. His last letter, claiming that he did love Martha, begs Andrew to join him in Rome. He writes: "And always there will be that question: how much did she really know? how much did she guess? (My dear André, I hope you understand what I am talking about, and that you will not be tempted, ever, to ask for degrading details.)" (177–78). Alexander Randolph (1922–2004) was born in Czechoslovakia, where his American parents were traveling. He attended school in Switzerland and lived in a variety of places, including Boston and Venice, Italy, where he died. He became renown for the board games that he invented. The novel appeared two years after his Italian marriage.

Deutsch's novel is part fiction, part primer on homosexuality. It is such a bizarre production that it leaves one wondering whether it is just a dreadfully written book or a wayward parody of the trashy stuff found in magazines like *Confidential*. One can even wonder if the author is actually a woman or a gay man playing with gender expectations—or perhaps a collaboration. Moments of unexpected playfulness occur as the protagonist moves into a "world peopled by legions of svengalis and phallicists." When he is first taken anally, his seducer "pushed him down on the sod" to *sod*omize him (42). Describing oral sex, he turns slang terms for the penis into simile: "He played me like a piccolo and when he hit my high note!" (87). He continues, "As time goes by (like the song) we crave more stimulus and excitation and other pendants besides our own. That beautiful male instrument, that organ of exquisite physical melody, stimulates the—orchestration" (90). At times homosexuality is justified: "How could such sensational thrills that caused such an inexhaustible flow of energy from the glands and lured one so irresistibly, be so entirely contrary to nature? What was nature, anyway? It was all nature, for that matter" (181). But such a passage as the following is just as common: "A world of sordid intrigue and subterfuge. A gigantic *manmade* exchange mart of lust and flesh, unrequited love, unfulfillment. A phrenetic compulsion to withdraw from life, not to return to the mother's womb for safety, but to retreat to the veritable microorganism of creation, the spermatozoon in the father's loins" (105). There are moments of horror in the novel, such as occurs when the boy sees "a Mexican wistfully project a portion of his anatomy through a man-made knot hole in the next stall" (it being parenthetically explained that these are "called glory holes") whereupon "a straight man, seeing the projectile, suddenly pulled out his jack knife and whacked off the offending intrusion" (45).

Starting with their childhood, *Heart* follows the blind obsession that Linda King has for Hilary Jay Wertzman. Leaving their Colorado homes, they both end up in San Francisco, where they marry—a case of bigamy, since she has run away from her first husband without securing a divorce. Hilary does not slow down in his pursuit of men. He takes trips back to Denver and to New York, where he has multiple encounters. He cruises the baths, the YMCA, the toilets, the parks, the streets, and he disappears from their home for long stretches to be with someone he has met, finally leaving her altogether. All the time an unmarried friend, Tess McTeague, a nurse "born on the Isle of Man" (more playfulness on the author's part?), puts down Linda and abets him in his pursuits. The novel ends melodramatically: Linda, she of the flaming heart, hires a detective to find him. She purchases a gun. Arriving at Hilary's apartment on New Year's Day, she shoots him several times, then turns the gun on herself. Hillary survives, gaining his minute of fame when his face is splashed across "all the San Francisco newspapers" (271), joining the likes of the actor John Gielgud, the tennis star Bill Tilden, and the parricide Harlow Fraden. Lying in the hospital, he hears a song "from a distant radio, 'Where is Your Heart?'" (271). The book had unexpected publishing popularity. It first appeared in hardback, was republished in 1964, still in hardback, by Guild Press in its failed attempt to create a gay library, and again in 1966 by the gay-friendly Paperback Library.

Deutsch, Deborah. *The Flaming Heart*. Boston: Humphries, 1958.
MacLaren, Mary. *The Twisted Heart*. New York: Exposition, 1952.
Prezzi, Wilma M. *Dark Desires*. New York: Padell, 1953.
Randolph, Alexander. *The Mail Boat*. *New York: Holt, 1954. London: Heinemann, 1954.

59 John Goodwin: *The Idols and the Prey*, 1953; *A View of Fuji*, 1963. John Cromwell: *A Grain of Sand*, 1953.

Goodwin's novels, published ten years apart, both describe an American's international, interracial affair that ends in failure with the American having gained no real insight into himself or the other as a result. The first takes place in Haiti; the second, in Japan. In the first, the richer of the two, the American is the one who loses at love; in the second both do, but the Japanese, reenacting the role of Butterfly with Pinkerton, is totally victimized. John Blair Linn Goodwin (1912–1994) was born and died in New York. He was a poet, a novelist, a painter, and an art collector. A world traveler, he was friends with Bowles, Isherwood, Denny Fouts, Williams, and Cocteau, among others. His last lover was Anthony P. Russo, to whom he dedicated his second novel and left his estate.

There are three protagonists in *Idols*: Hugh Cannery, an American writer in his sixties, and his third wife, Faith, whose boat has broken down, stranding them there; and a twenty-nine-year-old painter, Boyd Knowles, in search of local color and spiritual enlightenment. Hugh is an alcoholic who, in the end, deserts Faith for a local masseuse. Boyd tries to go native. He wants to be initiated into the mysteries of vodun. He lusts after the beautiful Yatice, nine years his junior, but he hesitates to make overtures to the youth because he belongs to a powerful religious figure, "father, priest and lover all in one" (180): "If it had not been for Héraclite Boyd would have pursued [Yatice], forcing him off the path and pushing him down among the bushes" (143). The effeminate Musset has no such compunctions and not only goes after Yatice but uses Boyd's home for their trysts. Yatice, however, wants Boyd now that he realizes "that the White wanted him" (181), and he makes the first move. The two have sex. Musset is not happy. "In the early days of meeting, Boyd had sought to make plain to Musset that, outside their sharing certain predilections, they had nothing in common," but he "allowed the relationship to grow into a mutual but disparate dependence." Betrayed, "Musset was in open rebellion" (278–79). To complicate matters further, a young girl falls in love with Boyd. Faith tries to warn her; Musset tells her bluntly that "he doesn't want what you can give him" (60) and later announces, in "wishful thinking," that the two of them, he and Boyd, are lovers (128). Unfortunately, Boyd kisses her, convincing her that Faith and Musset are wrong. Finally, he cruelly tells her that he is "in love with" Yatice (294). The two men openly begin living together, but the affair is short-lived, and Yatice is soon back with Héraclite.

It is never clear what has produced the spiritual void Boyd feels or why he would turn to voodooism for fulfillment. The reader does learn that he feels "maneuvered" by a world "of escape and search and discovery and disappointment, of France on someone else's money, and of the war years spent in captivity." He wants to belong to another race: "in a very complicated way he both expiated the guilt he felt almost atavistically and built up his ego simultaneously. He was eating his cake and having it too. A cake, to be sure, as hypothetical as the motives for his guilt or his tolerance, and as illusory as his search for atonement and martyrdom" (200–01). Faith analyzes him thus: "His potentialities are constantly abnegated by his inability to let himself go. He is always trying to find himself and always comes face to face, in a sort of puritanical dismay, with himself" (213). Boyd "considered himself worthless and yet he had an inordinate respect for himself for having discovered how worthless he was" (35). But as he comes more and more under the spell of Yatice, this self-knowledge is replaced by self-delusion, rationalization for all his actions based on desire, "an occupation at which he was becoming adept" (316) to the point that he ceases to live objectively in reality. It is not clear whether even Yatice's final "giggle" (341) will snap him out of his lavender illusions.

The forty-eight-year-old narrator of the short novel *A View of Fuji*—"Farry" is the Japanese "approximation" of his name (18)—is on the Grand Tour of Eastern Asia. He describes his mission: "I was looking, I thought, for personal liberty and honest beauty and perhaps a love affair that would take the taste out of my mouth of all those vulgar disasters" (11). He meets a twenty-six year-old barman who holds "an obsequious awe for the Occidental" (42): Seami Shigeji. Since the narrator is a tourist, the affair is to be a short one. But he has no sooner got to Hong Kong than he feels drawn back to Kyoto. His re-entrance into Seami's life completely disrupts it, and Farry dismally fails him: "I had to face the fact that I was not prepared for love. I had not grown up to it for I could only perform the acts of love under the threat of its impermanence; I could bear with love only so long as I was trying to save it from disaster. When it had become a fact, a fact as pure and simple as the mountain we saw every day, then I didn't know how to accept it, longed to rid myself of it. Acts of love I knew; the art of love, I realized, I had been ignorant of all this time" (88–89). So he abandons Seami, paying him off with "an envelope fat with dollars" (127).

Another international relationship seems to be on the verge of occurring in Cromwell's novel. In alternating chapters, the reader follows an American student, John Frost, and a Greek English translator, Constantino Thanatopsis, who come together in Athens. With the model of a childhood friend, Spyro, to help, Constantino begins to explore his sexuality, living in "a Kavafis dream." After his first sexual encounter with an American sailor, "At last he had something of his own, an experience to remember and boast of in the right circles. For the first time he felt fully grown up, fully a man" (159–60). John seems to be clueless about his own sexuality: "He felt strange to have traveled all this distance and to still be himself" (181). The two men meet up socially several times, and John wishes that he "could be worthy of this man" (209). They go to the beach, where briefly they meet Spyro with an Englishman. Whereas Spyro's earlier encounter with an uptight American, Eugene Potter, comes to naught because of the American's fear of a sexual encounter with a man at the same time that he ardently desires it, leaving his conflicted "middle-aged body shaken by sobs" (88), this Englishman is obviously at ease with himself: "Best thing they do in this country, I always say—beer and boys" (213). What John thinks is never told. Instead, for no good reason, he decides to dive from a cliff into the sea and is drowned. The novel puzzles. The names seem symbolic, but the novel does not. John Cromwell (1914–1979) was born in New York. He quit Harvard to pursue a career in acting, making his Broadway debut in 1935. He was also a playwright. He died in London.

Cromwell, John. *A Grain of Sand*. London: Peter Owen, 1953.
Goodwin, John. *The Idols and the Prey*. *New York: Harper, 1953. London: Weidenfeld & Nicholson, 1954.
_____. *A View of Fuji*. London: Spearman, 1963.

60 John Lee Weldon: *The Naked Heart*, 1953. Flannery O'Connor: *The Violent Bear It Away*, 1960.

Southern settings, religious fundamentalism, death of a guardian, confused but straight adolescent protagonists, resistance to the idea of God, the brief appearance of a homosexual predator—these elements both novels hold in common, but for different thematic reasons; thus they arrive to different conclusions. Curiously, O'Connor's homophobic caricature leaves a more powerful imprint on the mind than does the gay Weldon's grotesque stereotype, perhaps because the violation of the teenager in O'Connor's novel leads to his spiritual renewal, whereas same-sex and masturbation lead to death in Weldon's.

Weldon's novel is set in and near Birmingham, Alabama. Christy Livingston, its main character, loses his faith after the girl he unknowingly impregnates dies trying to destroy the fetus within her. Then he loses the father he hates in an accident at the steel mill. During Christmas he visits his aunt and twenty-two-year-old cousin, Kenneth, who suffers from epilepsy. Nicknamed Kissie, he likes to cook and to crochet and embroider. He disdains women, holding that "like the ancient Greeks" they should be used "for reproductive purposes only." He argues, "All love is love of oneself or the reflection of oneself; and the mirrored self is, in a way, the self. What woman can be a man's other self? They are too different!" (113). He holds the Bible and Freud have equal validity when read symbolically, and he praises Proust. One evening Kissie steals into Christy's bed and kisses him all over; Christy remembers, "I feel a sensation that is in itself far from unpleasant" (117). The experience seems meaningless; he later records simply, "*Kissie clouded me*" (210). He does not remember an earlier, more crucial incident till after a series of events hammer him: his mother's death, three years later when he is twenty; his own nervous breakdown; his family's continued efforts to get him to rededicate his life to his namesake; his aunt's incestuous overtures; and his self-aborted baptism, which sets free a chain of mental associations. Then he remembers that, when his mother caught him masturbating at age six, she threatened, "I oughtta cut that thing off and throw it away!" (209). Christy literally crucifies himself (though, of course, he can drive in only one nail) in the woods and dies. What happens to Kissie we never learn. John Lee Weldon (1924–1997) was born in Birmingham. He attended CCNY and began a career as a writer and painter. He also wrote *Fabulous: A Parakeet*, 1971, and *Memory Touches Memory*, 1989. He is buried in a veterans' cemetery, having served in the Navy.

O'Connor's novel is set in rural Georgia and the city of Atlanta The unnamed and otherwise unknown homosexual predator appears almost at the end; his violation is the culmination of a series of acts of violence that drive the story. Francis Marion Tarwater, the fourteen-year-old protagonist, having drowned his mentally retarded cousin in the act of trying to baptize him, is returning to the homeplace where he grew up (which he destroyed by fire after his great-uncle died). On his way he is picked up by a driver of "a lavender and cream-colored car," a man wearing "a lavender shirt." He is "a pale, lean, old-looking young man with deep hollows under his cheekbones," lavender eyes, and remarkably white lips. When Tarwater sees him, "an unpleasant sensation that he could not place came over him." As they travel down the road, the man gets the boy high on marijuana and whiskey. Tarwater passes out, whereupon the man turns off the road and parks in "a secluded declivity near the edge of the woods." He carries the boy into these woods; when he emerges, alone, vampire-like, "His delicate skin had acquired a faint pink tint as if he had refreshed himself on blood." The boy awakens, naked, his hands "loosely tied with a lavender handkerchief." He sets fire to the leaves on "the evil ground" where he was raped. He interprets the experience as the final sign that he should accept his calling as a prophet: "He knew that his destiny forced him on to a final revelation" (227–33). As her biographer Brad Gooch wrote (309), "In her extreme theology, this pederast Satan triggers grace." Mary Flannery O'Connor (1925–1964) was born in Savannah, Georgia. She graduated from the Georgia State College for Women and the University of Iowa. She was a strong hater, expressing her distaste for Capote, Williams, Baldwin, and the like in her personal letters. Curiously, she had a long running correspondence with a lesbian friend, as well as the poet Alfred Corn, while Gooch felt compelled to write a biography. She died in Milledgeville, Georgia, of lupus.

Gooch, Brad. *Flannery: A Life of Flannery O'Connor*. Boston: Little, Brown, 2009.
O'Connor, Flannery. *The Violent Bear It Away*. 1960. *New York: Farrar, Straus & Cudahy, 1960. London: Longmans, 1960.
Weldon, John Lee. *The Naked Heart*. New York: Farrar, Straus & Young, 1953.

61 John Selby: *The Man Who Never Changed*, 1954; *Madame*, 1961.

The title *The Man Who Never Changed* is misleading. While it is true that Denis Sandzen unswervingly follows his goal to become head of the New York City Symphony before he is thirty-five, he does become humanized through his association with two people, both of whom are in love with him even though he will never satisfy the needs of either. Though he admits to having had sex once with a man and once with a woman, charming and desirable as he seems, Denis is asexual. He frustrates both a woman he has known since the two of them were young and Terry Metoyer, a New Orleans journalist whom he meets when he takes over as conductor of the city orchestra. Of the latter Denis says, "I honestly feel a little ashamed that I can't be physically closer to him." He muses, "the idea of being that way isn't distasteful. It's just that I can't, quite. And the whole thing does not change the way I feel toward him" (174). Their easygoingness with each other is remarkable; for example, the two men have no problem being naked together. The portrait of Terry that emerges, even buried as it is to some extent in this long novel, seems far ahead of the usual depiction of gays at the time of the novel's publication, and it is certainly radical (though perfectly believable in the way it is presented) for the time period in which the novel is set: the Depression years and the beginning of World War II—a time, the novel reminds us, of not only economic upheaval but also political and racial turmoil.

The two men remain close even after Denis leaves New Orleans, first for "Lakeland" (Cleveland), and finally New York, their often getting back together, spending extended periods touring Europe. Terry is troubled: "sometimes I'm afraid our ... friendship ... might be dangerous to you. People might talk" (303). In a moment of depression, he takes an overdose of sleeping pills but survives. Denis charters a plane to speed to his side. Terry's mother, whom Denis barely knows, confronts him: "I hope you haven't destroyed him, Denis." She continues, "He told me everything from the first [...]. I've always known—about him. And when the two of you met, I knew how he felt. [...] Denis, couldn't you have given him more?" She sums up: "I think my son's life with sex is, quite simply, his own affair. And I think he is a worthwhile person, and should be accepted for what he is, and not condemned for what he can't be" (318–20). Terry quits his newspaper job, which he feels has become a dead end, and accepts the post of Denis's personal assistant. They begin a collaboration on a musical drama, *Louisiana*, which they conceive as something new, different, with an all African American cast, but far different from *Porgy and Bess* as a way of combining book, music, and dance (think of a black *Oklahoma!*). Straying from the straight to the gay side of Fire Island while on holiday, they meet their future producer, and soon Denis is juggling his roles as symphony conductor and musical theater composer.

Out of town tryouts are so shaky, however, that they consider canceling the show. Then, at the eleventh hour a *deus ex machina* appears in the figure of Glen Rhodes, "a pharmacist's mate first class in the tightest uniform possible; without a zipper the blouse could never have been entered, or once on, could never have been shed" (427), "so tight that one could almost see the nipples on his chest" (433). (The reader is left to imagine what fills the trousers.) He points out the problem: the orchestration is too sophisticated. Denis enthusiastically tackles re-orchestrating the entire score. Glen begs to help copy; he can get an extended pass from his commanding officer because "I know him very well, accent on the very" (430). The result is a roaring success on Broadway. For the romantically inclined, the author offers the possibility that something may develop between Terry and Glen. Terry makes the point of inviting him to stay over after the first night party for the reading of the reviews. Glen reiterates, "It's nice to know your boss real well in the Navy." The last we hear from Terry is his "laugh, cut off as a door closed" on the two men, presumably entering the bedroom they will share.

By comparison *Madame* seems almost by a different author, save again for the novel's easy acceptance of homosexuality. The title character is Gertrude Olivier Donner—G.O.D. as her monogram lordly declares. Widowed, she has three children. Her oldest is a married alcoholic son; her middle is a bitter, six times married daughter; and the youngest is her beloved Larry, gay. She records details about each of them, in these, the last days of her life in 1957, as she dictates her life story about her climb to fame and wealth as a syndicated columnist. She thinks back to her first inkling that Larry was different when he and his best friend, Johnny Wile, at age fourteen, showed up dressed as girls. She acknowledges that she refused to think anything could be going on between her son and the man she hired to redecorate her newly bought New York townhouse; she admits, however, "I cared less about what they might have done than about what the world might think if it knew" (261). Because of her fear of the neighbors she threatens the female impersonator, Alberta Dole, if he ever hooks up again with the sixteen-year-old Larry, whereupon Larry summarily moves out of the house. She packs him off to a series of boarding schools, the first of which he is expelled from after having been caught three times in "a 'compromising position' with another student," each time standing up "for his right [...] 'to live as God made me'" (273). At age twenty-three he brings home the blind Martin Lamb. Madame sets them up in an apartment in Paris, where they live happily for eight years before Martin dies at the beginning of the German occupation. Then in 1950 Larry is accosted by Don Noble, his hitherto unknown nephew. Larry offers on the spot to share his apartment with the youth: "the rest of the day was devoted to moving Don, and to celebrating, and to a good many other things" (280). Despite their fondness for each other, Don leaps at the chance to handle one of Madame's New York publishing ventures. Larry remained in Paris, "happy, he and that one, whatever his name was" (86), an unknown never mentioned again. Madame, facing that her death is more imminent than she expected, summons them and their spouses for what is in essence her reading of her final testament. Her summation of her youngest, the only one of the six present who understands that she is dying, comes almost at the end. She admits that he has always been her favorite child: "I used to think it was because certain things about you set you apart, that you were the one to be protected. I was wrong. You are stronger than the lot of us and always will be" (305).

John Allen Selby (1897–1980) was born in Gallatin, Missouri. Upon graduation from the University of Missouri, he served as music critic for the *Kansas City Star*. After three years in Paris, in 1932 he became the New York based music and arts editor for the Associated Press. In 1944 he began a fourteen year association with Rinehart publisher. His wife died in 1945; they had no children. In 1965 he moved to Taormino, Sicily, where he died.

Selby, John. *Madame.* *New York: Dodd, Mead, 1961. London: Allen, 1962.

———. *The Man Who Never Changed.* New York: Rinehart, 1954.

62 Christopher Isherwood: *The World in the Evening,* 1954; *Down There on a Visit,* 1962; *A Single Man,* 1964; *A Meeting by the River,* 1967.

The first part of Isherwood's career belongs to England—or, perhaps more accurately, to Berlin, the setting of much of *The Memorial*, 1932, and almost all of *Mr. Norris Changes Trains*, 1935, and *Goodbye to Berlin*, 1939 (the last two collected as *The Berlin Stories*, 1946). Isherwood emigrated to the United States in 1939 and became an American citizen in 1946. One of the stories in *Goodbye to Berlin*, "Sally Bowles," took on new life in the U.S., first as a dramatization, *I Am a Camera*, 1951, by the naturalized American John Van Druten; then as a film with the same name, 1955; next as the musical *Cabaret*, 1966, by Joe Masteroff, Fred Ebb, and John Kander; then the triumphant film version of the musical with a script by Jay Allen, 1972; and finally the revision of the stage musical, 1998. *Prater Violet* was Isherwood's first novel written in the U.S., but it was set in Vienna before the war. *The World in the Evening* was his first novel set in his new country.

It has a bisexual narrator, Stephen Monk, an expatriate Englishman living in Hollywood. After catching his second wife in adultery, he flees to an aunt living in a small Quaker town in Pennsylvania. As part of his recuperation process Stephen puts his memories into order. These include his own adulterous relationship with a young German, Michael Drummond, during his first marriage. Michael has a crush on Stephen from their first meeting in England. They encounter each other again on La Palma. The two men take a trek to an isolated part of the island and have sex. Stephen describes the moment as akin to "the adolescent, half-angry pleasure of wrestling with boys at school" (194). Afterwards, he is cruel to Michael, and they come to blows. That does not prevent their going to bed one more time. Afterwards, Stephen remembers, "I felt horribly trapped; and for the first time I fully realized just what it was I'd done to Michael" (205). Michael forces the relationship to a conclusion by telling Stephen's wife what has happened. She understands Stephen too well and tries to let the boy down gently. The two meet a final time in 1937 in St. Luc. Michael has been wounded in the Spanish Civil War; his French lover, Henri, killed. Stephen behaves aggressively once again. He cannot credit Michael's argument, "When two men stick together, they can do anything" (202).

We learn of this affair late in the novel. It makes Stephen's relationship with a gay couple in Pennsylvania seem more textured. As a result of being struck by a truck soon after his arrival, he meets Dr. Charles Kennedy and his lover, Bob Wood. Bob is the first militant to appear in American fiction since the group in Bruce's *Goldie* in 1933. Recognizing that same-sex relationships are against the law in all forty-eight states, Bob self-identifies as "a professional criminal." When Stephen chides him for being "so aggressive," Bob argues that gays are actually "too damned tactful. People just ignore us, most of the time, and we let them. We encourage them to. So this whole business never gets discussed, and the laws never get changed." People don't want to think about the fact that some of their neighbors are gay because "then they'd have to *do* something" (104–05). Charles says of Bob, "He'd like for us to march down the street with a banner, singing 'We're queer because we're queer because we're queer because we're queer'" (112). Though a Quaker, Bob reenlists in the Navy when the war breaks out. He realizes that "if they declared war on the queers [...] I'd fight. [...] So how can I say I'm a pacifist?" He gets secret pleasure out of undermining straights' claim "that us queers are unfit for their beautiful pure Army and Navy—when they ought to be glad to have us." He also holds, "Compared with this business of being queer, and the laws against us, and the way we are pushed around even in peacetime—this war hardly seems to concern me at all" (281).

The novel holds other historical importance. Although the terms *camp* and *camping* had long been associated with queerness, through Charles's voice, Isherwood offered the first discussion of the meaning, in the process distinguishing between Low and High Camp. Charles says that Low Camp is "a swishy little boy with peroxided hair, dressed in a picture hat and a feather boa, pretending to be Marlene Dietrich. [...] It's all very well in its place, but it's an utterly debased form." In contrast, "High Camp always has an underlying seriousness. You can't camp about something you don't take seriously. You're not making fun of it; you're making fun out of it. You're expressing what's basically serious to you in terms of fun and artifice and elegance" (110).

It was eight years before his next novel appeared. Another story cycle like *Goodbye to Berlin*, it is composed of four novellas, the first three set in pre-war Europe. The last, "Paul," takes place in California. "Christopher Isherwood" reappears as the main character. He meets Paul—"the notorious, the 'fabulous' Paul" (192)—in 1940 in Beverly Hills. He has already heard talk of the man, "'the last of the professional tapettes' and 'the most expensive male prostitute in the world'" (194). By the time they meet, Paul says he has come to hate sex. He admits, "I used to be good for something—for sex. I was really good for that. All kinds of people used to get hot pants for me, and that excited me—even when I found them totally unattractive, which I usually did. I got a terrific kick out of giving them pleasure, and I was proud that I nearly always could" (218). But he is now more interested in the spirit than the body. He and Christopher meditate together. Though they sleep in adjacent twin beds and regale each other with stories from their pasts, there is no indication that they have sex. Paul is arrested after he is involved, drunk, in a car wreck. He is falsely accused of molesting a young girl. As a conscientious objector, he is sent to a forestry camp but mustered out because of a heart murmur. The two men drift apart; the last Christopher sees of him before Paul's death, he has become a drug addict.

Paul is based on Denny Fouts. For someone not a writer himself, Louis Denham Fouts (1914–1948) had an astounding impact on the literary world. Born in Jacksonville, Florida, he early cultivated the attention of Glenway Westcott, George Platt Lynes, and their circle. He met Brion Gysin, Jane and Paul Bowles, Cyril Connolly, Stephen Spender, Jean Marais. In his career as a male courtesan he was supported by Evan Morgan (the future Viscount Tredegar), Prince Paul of Greece, English patron of the arts Peter Watson, Nazi Luftwaffe officer Wolfram von Richtofen, RAF officer Anthony Watson-Gandy, painter Michael Wishart, and writer John Goodwin. His story forms a major thread in Capote's novella "Unspoiled Monsters," 1976, a part of his unfinished *Answered Prayers*. Fouts influenced Vidal's portrait of Jim in *The Judgement of Paris*, and he is the central character, Elliott Magren, in Vidal's 1956 short story "Pages from an Abandoned Journal." Gavin Lambert claimed his 1966 novel, *Norman's Letter*, was based on Fouts though no one character seems to correspond closely. It has also been claimed that he was the basis for Sophie, the French prostitute in Somerset Maugham's 1944 novel *The Razor's Edge*. He died in Rome of congenital heart problems.

In 1964 Isherwood's finest novel appeared. *A Single Man* recounts the final day in the life of a fifty-eight-year-old, British born English teacher living in Los Angeles. George goes about his usual activities, carrying with him memories of his happiness with his dead lover, killed in a car accident. He shares many characteristics with Bob Wood. He too feels that homophobic lawmakers and guardians "understand only one language: brute force. Therefore we must launch a campaign of systematic terror" (38). He uses the opportunity of teaching Aldous Huxley's *After Many a Summer Dies the Swan* to launch a dissertation on the complexities raised by the perception of people as minorities. He feels a gap between him and his generally indifferent students. Yet one, Kenny Potter, challenges him. This evening he meets him, not by accident, at his favorite bar. Kenny has come deliberately hoping to run into him. They go to George's home. George passes out; Kenny puts him to bed and leaves. When he comes to, George masturbates and discovers he is happy. Why then Isherwood felt compelled to kill George off at the end is mysterious, especially given his criticism of Vidal's melodramatic ending to *The City and the Pillar* (he dedicated this novel to him). Perhaps he wanted to sound a *carpe diem* alert to readers. The fact remains, the book would have been just as satisfactory (more so for many readers) without the final section. In 2009 Tom Ford's film adaptation brought new attention to the novel.

Isherwood's final novel only marginally belongs to American letters. The story is told through a series of letters written by Patrick, an English publisher living in London with a wife and children, and a diary kept by his brother Oliver, a convert to Hinduism. The setting is India. Patrick is visiting Oliver in an attempt to dissuade him from entering a monastery on the banks of the Ganges. One of the recipients of Patrick's letters is his lover, Tom, who lives in Los Angeles. Tom has given Patrick an early gay pulp novel to read. Isherwood thus became the first writer of status to acknowledge the impact pulp writing was having on gay readers. He had, in fact, already anticipated the pulp explosion with his own very effective sexually explicit story, "Afterwards," written in 1959 and unfortunately still unpublished. Isherwood and his partner, Don Bachardy, dramatized the novel. At its performance in 1972 (under the direction of James Bridges), one of the actors was Gordon Hoban (1941-1993). He went on to become a successful pulp writer himself, generally working under the pseudonym Tom Hardy.

Christopher William Bradshaw Isherwood (1904-1986) was born in his family home in Cheshire. He attended Cambridge without taking a degree. He was friends with the poets Auden and Spender; before the war he sought lovers in Berlin. American lovers included William Caskey (1921-1981), Fouts, and finally Bachardy (1934-), but all relationships were nonmonogamous. He was briefly Dr. Evelyn Hooker's tenant. Isherwood's diaries are a fascinating record of the time. He died in Santa Monica, California, of prostate cancer. Jaime Harker has written a study of him as an American author, *Middlebrow Queer*, 2013.

Isherwood, Christopher. *Down There on a Visit*. New York: Simon & Schuster, 1962. London: Methuen, 1962. *Minneapolis: University of Minnesota Press, 1999.
_____. *A Single Man*. *New York: Simon & Schuster, 1964. London: Methuen, 1964.
_____. *The World in the Evening*. New York: Random House, 1954. London: Methuen, 1954. *Minneapolis: University of Minnesota Press, 1999.
Parker, Peter. *Isherwood: A Life Revealed*. New York: Random House, 2004.
Vanderbilt, Arthur. *Best-Kept Boy in the World*. New York: Magnus, 2014. On Denham Fouts.

63 Edmund Schiddel: *The Other Side of the Night*, 1954; *Break-Up*, 1954; *The Girl with the Golden Yo-Yo*, 1955; *The Devil in Bucks County*, 1959; *The Good and Bad Weather*, 1965; *Good Times Coming*, 1969.

Though himself gay, the author never created a gay protagonist, only admitting gay secondary characters into his fiction. In *Good Times* he posits that readers "are curious about homosexuality, even though they may regard it as a disease or a sin. It fascinates them. America's hung up on diseases and sin. It's a puritan country still" (130). Schiddel's problem is that he tried too hard to be trendy, though, paradoxically, across fifteen years of fiction his characters could be flipped from one novel to another and no one would notice. None of his books remain in print.

The Other Side chronicles the events that trouble an assortment of New Yorkers connected by blood, sex, and friendship on one New Year's Eve. One of them is Adrian Murray. He actually lives on Gay Street in the Village. His mother very early decided that "if Adrian was to be a fairy, at least he would be hers and no other woman would possess him." As a result he develops "the incestuous love-hatred of a boy for his mother" (61-62). We first meet Adrian in the act of picking up the Baron Hansi d'Alpenbourg outside a Harlem fortune teller and installing him in the place of the decamping Stepan Konolai "(*né* Joe Skewes), a ballet boy who had fallen on evil days" (56), just in time to recoup most of the things he is stealing from

Adrian. Adrian is a talented performer: "He was entertaining in an epicene and transvestitic way; he could get himself up to be Mistinguette or Bernhardt at a moment's notice and his imitation of Cocteau receiving was a marvel" (63). He and the baron go to Adrian's half-sister's party; there he performs as Queen Victoria and then as a stripper. The baron steals some money, ends up playing a single turn of baccarat and winning, whereupon he replaces the original money and exits. All the big dramas, one ending in the sister's murder, are heterosexual.

More interesting is the story of an Ohio English professor in *Golden Yo-Yo*. One of several characters whose lives intertwine, he arrives in New York for a long weekend in pursuit of a dancer. Dr. Norris Bates has met Mikhail Taracz when he was on tour, his company playing at his university, and proposed they go out for dinner the next time Bates is in New York. The lonely dreamer knows about "the queer bars for men—he had once spent a hopeful and rather dreary evening doing the 'Bird Circuit,'" a cluster of gay bars in the East 50s near Third Avenue, but had ended up with people he knew from Ohio, "who were slumming, and to whom he had, in self defense, attached himself, lest they suspect that he was not slumming too." He has heard rumors about the baths and he is aware of streets "where charming and chance encounters could, and did happen—to others, but never to him. He was aware, and often rued the fact that his temperamental fears and rigidities quite precluded such adventures. What Bates longed for and needed was not sex, not depravity, not 'interesting sensations,' but love." And yet, "No one knew better than Bates the sadness, the ridiculousness, the improbabilities involved; but his cells drove him on, a slightly stertorous, middle-aged party, to an endless pursuit—of what?" (49). When he arrives, Bates discovers Mikhail is sharing an impoverished apartment with a woman and another man, Ernie Slocum. His first act is to buy them all a meal. They go bar-hopping, get drunk, become involved in a brawl, with the result that they are thrown out and Bates takes a cab, alone, back to his hotel room. The next evening Mikhail shows up at his hotel; they go out again for a meal and a performance of *Cat on a Hot Tin Roof*. Bates finds the portrait of life Williams draws "depressing, and its language frightening and pornographic" (141). After the play, Mikhail excuses himself to go into a drugstore to make a telephone call. The building has two street doors. After a long wait, Bates realizes he has been ditched: "On this night, at four minutes before midnight, Norris Bates, Ph.D., an assistant professor of English, accepted the fact of his middle-age with private resignation and humility." He utters a sigh "that had in it a deep relief, almost a contentment" (143). He returns to his dreary life.

Gays appear in small roles as comic relief in the first and the last of his satiric Bucks County (Pennsylvania) trilogy. They are all superficially drawn but mildly amusing. The county, we are told in *Devil*, "always had been tolerant of homosexuals but now accepted them" (230). It boasts two gay-friendly bars. The Wharf sponsors Fancy Dress Nights featuring female impersonators, one of whom specializes in impersonating T. C. Jones impersonating various stars. Fletcher's caters more to rough trade, but "sexual predilections were less easily recognized" in the gays now frequenting the area "than in their counterparts of a quarter century earlier" (231). In one of the three intertwined plots that make up the novel, three campy drinking buddies volunteer to be in a locally written and produced spoof of *Hiawatha*, titled *No, No, Nokomis*. Edgar Akers is "a canceled priest" who is also a trained dancer (38)—and whom the director begs "to wear a jock strap" on opening night (191). Lloyd Widney, who plays a firefly, specializes in turning found objects into sculpture. His current boyfriend is an unnamed student at the Juilliard Music School. The third cast member is Willie McGeehee, who will play the lead. Opening night does not bode well for a variety of reasons, including the presence of "the Widney boy friend and his supporters, who had been so merry at dress rehearsal; the group had expanded since then to include a number of Fletcher strays, all of whom, [the director] observed in a quick, backward take, seemed to have been on a bat ever since" (292). As if in response to her thought, a very real and very live bat hidden in the theater rafters decides to become part of the play. The results are an earlier curtain than planned. "The only ones who wanted to indulge in post-mortems" at the after-play party held at the Wharf "were Akers and McGeehee and the Juilliard boy, who regaled their table with how it had looked out front" (314).

In *Weather* aging lovers Teddy Hubbard and Bo deWillig are caricatures. The couple is tolerated mostly because of Teddy's wealth, but one of their neighbors attacks him for "taking away some girl's chances of getting a good husband! *You're* the reason there's so many old maids, you and your morphadite molly friends!" (325). The Swedish born Bo is "always chasing either jailbait or trade." The older Teddy is willing to look the other way: "the lonely path of queer old age stretched ahead, and, aging though Bo also was, at least he was company" (49). While cruising at the Wharf, Bo's eye is blackened by a very heterosexual specimen of male virility who descends on the bucolic village and leaves happiness and havoc behind. Later, he hooks up with a Gypsy who, "once he had obliged, not only took the money, but, being both older and stronger than he first appeared, relieved Bo of his gold Cartier watch and both his brown diamond and seal rings" (302). Teddy's mother lives with them: "She disliked her son's parties, and though (as the exclusively male guests always said) she was 'wise' to what went on, she had never really accepted *les boys* or anything she supposed they did after she was carted back upstairs" (172). Her birthday celebration becomes an occasion for a party. In one of the funnier moments in the novel, having been promised "a surprise," she thinks one of the uninvited guests who have shown up dressed in drag is her son's long hoped for fiancée, while he, in total confusion, assumes that she is another male in drag: "How was *I* to know she was for real?" (403). Feeling the episode is the final straw—earlier she has "wished Oscar Wilde could see what he had started" (348)—Mrs. Hubbard's nurse gives notice on the spot.

Writer/editor relationships intrigued Schiddel. A writer who is a minor character in *Break-Up* does not manage to seduce his editor before the latter kills himself. Upon hearing the news of Kevin Benbow's death, Grevin Townsend, an author of children's books, remembers him as "*one sweet man*" (191). But a writer who is an important character in *Good Times* not only succeeds but, in a strange way, saves the editor's marriage. The thirty-five-year-old Galey Birnham is presented as "a man without emotional allegiances" who gets his kicks by seducing straight men, particularly relishing it when he can get his quarry "to assume a passive role" (237–38). Succeed he does with Anson Parris, two year younger than he. But Anson gets his own back and discovers that, for him, sex with another man is "a double-gaited way of making love to oneself" (365)—"The ultimate, physical journey into the self" (367). He returns to his wife, and the knowledge "he had brought back from his experience was his enduring passion for Faye and his love for that mysterious, extended part of himself," his son (466). The epiphany arising from this unusual example of anal intercourse as marriage therapy becomes caught up for him in some reassuring way with Rimbaud's orphic statement *Je est un autre*. He tells his wife: "I may have betrayed myself many times; I may betray myself many times more, but that part which is you. It's love" (506).

Edmund Schiddel (1909–1982) was born in Chicago. He graduated from William and Mary and worked first in the Department of Labor, then in radio, before becoming a full time writer. His longtime partner was painter Beveridge Moore (1915–2004), to whom he dedicated *Other Side* and *Devil*. He died in Princeton, New Jersey.

Schiddel, Edmund. *Break-Up*. New York: Avon, 1954.
_____. *The Devil in Bucks County*. *New York: Simon & Schuster, 1959. London: Cape, 1960.
_____. *The Girl with the Golden Yo-Yo*. New York: Berkley, 1955. *New York: Avon, 1967.
_____. *The Good and Bad Weather*. New York: Simon & Schuster, 1965.
_____. *Good Times Coming*. *New York: Simon & Schuster, 1969. London: W. H. Allen, 1970.
_____. *The Other Side of the Night*. New York: Avon, 1954. *New York: Manor, 1965.

64   Richard McKaye (Richard K. Brunner): *Portrait of the Damned*, 1954. Marietta Wolff: *The Big Nickelodeon*, 1956. Pamela Moore: *Chocolates for Breakfast*, 1956. Walter Ross: *The Immortal*, 1958. Ronn Marvin: *Mr. Ballerina*, 1961. Richard Sale: *The Oscar*, 1963. Gavin Lambert: *Inside Daisy Clover*, 1963.

Throughout the 1950s Hollywood remained closeted. It was the era of the Hollywood blacklist, and the red scare became intertwined with the lavender scare in Los Angeles as in Washington. In McKaye's *Portrait*, scriptwriter Dan Seers meets British actor Cyril Hathaway. He is returning to England to make a movie, but "it was almost a certainty that he would not be allowed to return to the country because of the unfavorable publicity incurred as a result of certain actions with a young chorus boy which certain members of the congress viewed dimly." Not for the first time in his distinguished acting career his "fetish for young male ballet dancers" has brought him "social ostracism" (46–47). Seers is engaged in a series of heterosexual liaisons of varying kinds as he works on a religious epic. Revising the script unleashes his troubled past: "From his earliest recollections the writer had been unable to discern between his father and Jesus. Seers, the boy, had never been able to accept Jesus without first accepting his father, whom he despised" (18). Near the end of a series of crises, including being fired from the production, Seers runs into Ronald Morrison, the actor portraying Jesus, in a bar. Earlier, he has witnessed Morrison sharing "a love seat with a tow-headed sailor" (61). Now Seers wonders "what had become of the sailor [...]. Somehow he hated that sailor and he didn't know why" (135). As the two men drink, "Seers remembered his horror, when as a child a man had accosted him in a public lavatory using vulgar gestures to communicate his crude idea. Then, as in defiance, Seers brought his eyes up to the level of Morrison's, his traumatic badge of courage suspended there somewhere in the twenty-four inches of charged air which separated his face from the actor's. And then a smile, born of his inability to stare the actor down and of the pungent stink of remembered women he had known, spread across his face. And in this smile of acquiescence the apex had been reached." The flesh does not resolve his anguish, however: "Much later, when the twisting, turning of his body was quiet and he lay nestled in the sheets of the actor's bed, Seers realized that the orgies of the body could never exorcise the thoughts that continually ate at his brain" (137). The novel ends in a holocaust of Seers's creation.

Whispers and innuendos about closeted actors are always part of the Hollywood scene. James Dean's early cult status allowed speculation about his sexuality to become especially potent grist for the rumor mill. Ross's *roman à clef* was out within three years of his death. The novel consists of eleven documents about Johnny Preston, an idol for disaffected teenagers. While it becomes clear that Preston was willing to sleep with men and women, with "money and ambition" as his driving forces (186), we never know whether he was gay, straight, bi, or, as one woman accuses him, just a "male whore" (165). Two of the informants are former sexual partners. The seventh document is a transcript of an interview between Harry Costello, a Hollywood agent, and the ghost writer for his autobiography. Costello skirts the subject of Preston's sexuality and conceals their relationship. He does say, "I don't know that Johnny was a switch-hitter or anything like that, but I do know that he played the role of that queer schoolboy in *The Inward Gate* [i.e., *The Immoralist*] with great conviction." In answer to the ghost writer's direct question whether "Preston had any homosexual experience," Costello says that "he might have dabbled. To round out his experience" (113–14). The ninth document is more forthright. It is a psychiatrist's case history of New York actor Hairston Sklar, who feels guilty, as if somehow he was responsible for the airplane crash that killed Preston by having seduced him in the first place. He describes how he began his intrigue: "I said, 'There is a group of likeminded men who share a common attitude toward life quite far above the usual bourgeois conception of existence. [...] We're a group that is, well, more sensitive than the herd, and so we stick together. We help one another. If you are one of us, we will help you." In answer to Preston's question about sex, "'Likeminded people never have any difficulty about sex,' I said. 'It's just a natural thing'" (181). Sklar and Preston began living together. Sklar tells the psychiatrist, "He had an instinct for love-making. It never seemed to disgust him at all. The only thing he ever said was, 'It's all a part of living'" (191). When it seemed advantageous to his career to move on, Preston left with producer Charles Lucas and his wife, then changed to rich Alec St. Prieux, and eventually, after "a window-display boy, a real screaming swish," "a couple of actors," and "a girl" (202), to Costello. The novel now seems a curiosity; it is a lot less fun read than any one of several biographies.

Some gay actors, whether operating from studio pressure or out of their own confusion, seek to prove they are straight. Moore's Barry Cabot uses teenager Courtney Farrell, the daughter of a fading movie star, to try to break out of his fag image. She is warned not to become entangled with him, but she succumbs to his charm. Barry takes her virginity and feels like "a man" (102). They continue to see each other until Barry's lover, George, demands he end the affair. He says: "She doesn't mean anything to me. She's just—a convenience." He thinks, "Christ, where had it gone, his courage, his manliness, his loyalty?" (108). Cabot begs Courtney for her help, but she spurns him and disappears with her mother to New York, where the rest of the novel occurs. Lambert's Wade Lewis is too cryptic when he warns teenaged Daisy Clover about his predilections. She is too innocent or too dumb to understand what he means when he tells her, "I'm a cripple" (157). It is not clear she realizes the truth even when he desserts her on their honeymoon without going to bed with her. Her divorce lawyer says, "I don't understand how you could know Mr. Lewis so long and actually marry him without having any suspicion that he was sexually abnormal" (174–75). Wade flees to Acapulco with his lover, Malcolm; the two of them later open a hotel in Tangier. Briefly back in the States, they catch Daisy's comeback performance, and all ends happily. As Daisy tells us: "He looked better than I'd ever seen him, not quite sober, but a kind of new brightness in those dark warm fatal eyes" (243). When the novel was filmed, with a screenplay by Lambert, Wade became bisexual at Robert Redford's request, but even that concession was played down to the point of practically disappearing. As the author pointed out, at least Wade did escape the requisite death scene for gays onscreen.

Other actors, much like Vidal's Ronald Shaw and Mailer's Teddy Pope, struggle little if at all with their sexuality. The results are not always happy ones. Young actor Dick Whitfield falls under the influences of an amoral drifter known only as Stush in Wolff's sprawling *Nickelodeon*. Though chiefly a womanizer, Stush is willing to sponge off him. Pathetically in love, Dick becomes a homebody taking care of Stush, while Stush comes and goes as he pleases. After a physical fight between the two, triggered by Stush's womanizing, Dick says, "I've been gay all my life, but I always felt clean and decent. You make me feel like a faggot" (206). But he cannot throw him out, even though his fidelity jeopardizes his career. His straight friends, fearing for his emotional and professional well-being, work to free him of Stush's pernicious influence. Stush, trying for an acting career of his own, leaves. Even then, Dick says that if he ever needs "a place to go or someone to take care of him," he will be there (354). By this time, however, both men have become peripheral to the main story line: a straight screenwriter's inability to function. Sale's *Oscar* delves into the political jockeying that goes into winning the Academy Award for best male actor. Of the five nominees, one—the thirty-year-old, Polish born, English reared Brett Chichester—is in a relationship with eighteen-year-old Arlington Powell though he knows, "The love life of a homosexual in Hollywood was perilous, at best" (69). Two of the other nominees search to see how they can use Brett's sexuality to ensure he will lose. An attempt is made to trap him in a scandal by introducing Arly to a minor named Sidney Flower. It fails: the minor turns out to be "Sidney Coxey, who was mustered out of the Navy on a Section Eight, for homosexuality, at the age of twenty-one years which makes him twenty-three. So since the Powell boy is eighteen, that makes the corrupter the corrupted" (190). Arly's tenure having ended, we catch Brett with his "arm around a handsome young man with a black widow's peak, tremendous shoulders and an overripe mouth" (330). Brett does not win the Oscar, of course.

Marvin's is the gayest of these Hollywood novel. It actually begins in the San Francisco dance world, but then moves to that of the Hollywood musical. When dancer Dana Bates reports to the studio, "Lee Apollo, dance director supreme at Hemisphere, left no room for doubt in Dana's mind that he was mad, hysterical and queer" (65). The novel is also as depressing as the rest. The police raid an all-male party that Lee throws. Dana manages to escape, but two of the ones caught are spiteful enough to turn him in to the police. Lee loses his job for violating his contract's morals clause (104). Dana faces that he may likewise be fired. Dana's lover is a musician, Ralph Matthews. He is convinced that his mother and then Dana turned him into a homosexual, but really he is straight. It's just that he has these intense sexual needs, and Dana plays on them. He turns to a woman who is trying to save her mother from a lesbian relationship. Contemplating starting up a Homosexuals Anonymous program (126), Ralph breaks up with Dana, breaks Dana's nose when he protests, has sex with the woman, and proposes to her. We only need a fiery holocaust to feel we have come full circle.

Richard K. Brunner (1920?–) grew up in Reading, Pennsylvania. He was a prolific journalist and, for a while, a public relations officer for Muhlenberg College. He is married. One would have hoped for more from Gavin Lambert (1924–2005) since he was a Hollywood insider. He was born in East Grinstead, England. A schoolmate was future filmmaker Lindsay Anderson. From 1950 to 1956 he was editor of the influential *Sight & Sound*. In 1956 he relocated to Los Angeles with his lover, director Nicholas Ray (1911–1979), and became a U.S. citizen in 1964. His first publication was a Hollywood story cycle, *The Slide Area*, 1959. He was nominated for two Oscars for screenplays. His friends included Williams and Isherwood. He died in Los Angeles of pulmonary fibrosis, naming his former lover, playwright Mart Crowley (1935–), as his executor. Ronn Marvin (1919–1998) began as a dancer in San Francisco. He was in four movies. His dancing career ending with a foot injury, he turned to writing television scripts and novels. He died in Los Angeles. Pamela Moore (1937–1964) was born in New York. She attended Barnard. She was married and had a son. She published four more novels before she killed herself. According to the dust jacket, Walter Ross (dates unknown) graduated from Rutgers in 1936 and attended the University of North Carolina. He worked in public relations and wrote a number of other novels. Married, he had two children. (The dust jacket itself received attention because it reproduces a drawing by Andy Warhol.) Richard Bernard Sale (1911–1993) was born in New York. He attended Washington and Lee. He began as a writer for pulp magazines, then became a writer-director in Hollywood, the force behind several important movies. He was married three times and had three children. He died in Los Angeles of complications following strokes. Maritta Martin Wolff (1918–2002) was born in Grass Lake, Michigan. She attended the University of Michigan. She was married twice and had a son. She died in Los Angeles.

Lambert, Gavin. *Inside Daisy Clover*. New York: Viking, 1963. London: Hamish Hamilton, 1963. *London: Serpent's Tail, 1996.
Marvin, Ronn. *Mr. Ballerina*. Evanston, Ill.: Regency House, 1961. *New York: Macfadden-Bartell, 1968.
McKaye, Richard. *Portrait of the Damned*. New York: Twayne, 1954. *New York: New American Library (Signet), 1954.
Moore, Pamela. *Chocolates for Breakfast*. New York: Rinehart, 1956. London: Longsman, Green, 1957. *New York: Harper Perennial, 2013.
Ross, Walter. *The Immortal*. New York: Simon & Schuster, 1958. *London: Shakespeare Head, 1958.
Sale, Richard. *The Oscar*. *New York: Simon & Schuster, 1963. London: Cassell, 1964.
Wolff, Maritta. *The Big Nickelodeon*. New York: Random House, 1956.

65 Lonnie Coleman: *Ship's Company*, 1955; *Sam*, 1959.

The title character in *Sam* is a publisher. One evening he is asked why he has never published a gay book. He answers, "The only ones I see are trashy or sentimental. A dream world of television drama with the sexes changed a little. They all end with a suicide or a murder," despite the fact that, as he says, "How many of us do you know who've killed themselves, or each other?" (55). *Sam* is the kind of book he would want to publish. The oblivion into which the author has disappeared is inexplicable. One searches in vain for his name in the standard reference guides. The very funny story "The Theban Warriors" used to be anthologized (as in *Calamus*, 1982), but even it seems to have vanished.

The story is the fifth episode in a story cycle, *Ship's Company*. Based on the author's own experience, the novel describes life aboard the U.S.S. *Nellie Crocker* during her service in World War II in both the Mediterranean and the Pacific and at port. "The Theban Warriors" begins in Norfolk, Virginia. William Montgomery is open about his interest in men from the moment he comes on board and meets the narrator, Barney Casper: "Contrary to what all of us expected, Montgomery got along fine. Everybody in the division heard about him right off, and within a day everybody on the ship must have known about him. He seemed to enjoy causing a stir, and didn't change his way of talking much, no matter where he was" (115). Barney does not catch on that he is Montgomery's target until the bosun tells him bluntly, "I've got my eye on you, and I'll get you sooner or later" (119). They get all the way to Algiers before he succeeds. After the two visit local prostitutes, Montgomery says to Barney, "Don't you know that most women hate men and use their sex to insult them and dominate them? I'm offering you something better than that, you damned fool. I'm offering you myself, and I'm promising you that I'll take you and hold you and keep you as long as—such promises last. I love you, Barney." Barney admits, "It was that that made me cry" (134). The two men are not recurring characters, but later, when a pair of sailors are discussing a shipmate who escapes to the forecastle to sleep, one muses, "You suppose he meets anybody up there?" When the other asks, "Who like?" he responds, "Oh—Montgomery. You know." With that, "They laughed" (199).

Sam is a very different order of art. The thirty-seven-year-old New York publisher Samuel Kendrick has had for years an ill defined relationship with his former editor, Addie. She is sexually attracted to him, even knowing that the case is hopeless. Probably as a consequence, she has entered a marriage with a man, Toby (they are the only two characters with no last name), who can satisfy her sexual, but not her emotional needs. Toby is threatened by Sam and hates him, hates all gay men by extension. Sam is not sexually attracted to Addie, but he is emotionally bound to her: "they were family to each other" (207). For whatever reason, Sam chooses men who are not good relationship material. Addie thinks it is a question of age; his current lover, a narcissistic actor, Walter Roland, is nine years younger. After he meets Richard Redman, who is his age, that seems plausible. But in watching Richard, the reader becomes aware that it is more. Both men are successful in their professions; that is important. But Richard arrives at the heart of the matter: "There's something we have to know and believe: that *we* are more important than you or I—[...] unless it involves our work." He continues, "You can have any friend you want, as long as it's understood I take precedence over everybody else" (216–17). In the opening scene Sam more or less ignores Walter; in the final scenes Richard makes it clear that will not happen with the two of them.

The novel presents a fascinating view of New York gay life among professionals at the time. Richard and Sam meet at the baths. When Sam later asks him why he was there, Richard replies, "I found you there, didn't I? There were nights I went and found nothing, or found things I didn't want. Sometimes I just found good, mindless, bang-bang sex. I don't apologize. To say I'm sorry would be to deny a lot of nice men I met there to whom I am grateful and of whom I have pleasant memories. But I was looking for Sam" (215). Sam has understood that he can bed a woman—"if I shut my eyes and thought of a man." But he says, "*That*, I realized, was wrong, *that* was evil. I swore then I'd be true to myself and not try to be true to the cant of society." He concludes, "Why should I go to bed with a woman and make both of us unhappy when I can go to bed with a man and make both of us happy?" And so, "I began to go to bed with men without shame or fear. I made them happy, and I made myself happy. I felt whole and healthy for the first time. For the first time I was a man." A friend wants to argue that one can't "buck society." Sam answers, "I'm not trying to. But I insist on having my place in it. Not theirs. *Mine*" (35). In refusing to succumb to straights' expectations, he also rejects gay stereotypes. As part of his growth process, he breaks decisively with a friend who is a gay caricature and, in so many words, lays to rest a "ghost" (226). Sam even owns a male cat, reminding the reader how seldom gay men in fiction seem to have pets.

William Lawrence Coleman (1920–1982) was born in Bartow, Georgia. He graduated from the University of Alabama and served in the Navy during World War II. After the war he worked as a magazine editor for more than ten years. His *Beulah Land* trilogy, 1973–80, was his most successful novels; the first two were filmed as a television miniseries. *Mark*, 1981, his autobiographical final novel, traces the sexual development of the title character. A pre-war romance with Edgar Jean Brasco was dashed when Brasco married. In the 1950s he met Gordon Reekie (1920–1987), with whom he lived the rest of his life. He died of cancer in Savannah, Georgia.

Coleman, Lonnie. *Sam*. *New York: David McKay, 1959. London: W. H. Allen, 1960.
———. *Ship's Company*. Boston: Little, Brown, 1955.

66 Virginia Rowans: *The Loving Couple*, 1956. Patrick Dennis: *Tony*, 1966.

In his review of Myers's biography of Edward Tanner, Robert Plunket (*Advocate*, Nov. 21, 2000, 112) wrote: "If you grew up gay in the '50s and '60s, chances are that you loved Patrick Dennis. You felt he was talking to you, clueing you in on a secret world where fabulous people said witty things and had adventures both ridiculous and hilarious. I remember *Auntie Mame* as having the first jockstrap joke I ever encountered. This is perhaps Tanner's most lasting accomplishment: He introduced gay sensibility to popular American taste." A gay reader at the time simply knew *Mame* was a gay novel without its introducing any obviously gay characters. We loved it as a 1955 novel, as a 1956 stage play, as a 1958 movie, and as a 1966 musical (with music and lyrics by Jerry Herman), and tried to love it as a 1974 movie musical.

When it came to portraying actual gays in his novels, however, the results were darker, more disturbing. *The Loving Couple* appeared under a different pseudonym the year after *Auntie Mame* made its dazzling debut. An unusual novel, it recounts the day when a married couple decide to divorce by letting you read first either "His Story" or "Her Story" and then, after flipping the book over, the other's side. In the course of the evening both John and Mary encounter Randolph Carter Lee. Born Randolph Leroy Skaggs in Virginia, he is the son of the woman who did the washing for the rich Lee family. When at age sixteen he impregnated a girl, he felt it imperative to leave. In the process he took on the persona of the heir. Getting a job at a twenty-four hour bathhouse, he was plucked up by Norbert Bessamer, an elderly gay male who "offered him steady employment of a more specialized nature." They stayed together for five years. Unfortunately, "Randy had one failing, hazardous to his position; Randy preferred women" ("Her Story," 78–79). The older man caught Randy in bed with his niece and promptly suffered a fatal heart attack. His will left only "a paltry five thousand dollars for 'my faithful companion'" (His Story," 99). Randy became a gigolo, with time out "with a successful English dramatist." There were further vicissitudes: "Then came a time of cruising the Bird Circuit" ("Her Story," 81–82). Encountering Mary in a club, he sets his sights on her. While in the men's room, he encounters John. The husband identifies Randy as his unknown rival and tries to get his address. Randy, of course, thinks he is being propositioned: "Not that he had ever minded that. [...] Randy was the veteran of numberless encounters in toilets ranging from the subway to the most expensive restaurants in town and 'No' was a word which Randy found almost impossible to pronounce" ("Her Story," 105). But he and Mary leave together, returning to the apartment rented by the woman presently keeping him. She is supposed to be out of town but returns just as Mary realizes she has to get out of the situation. Randy's character is so well drawn that when Mary puts him down with a cheap shot ("How shabby you are [...]. How *pathetically* shabby"), the reader feels for him ("Her Story, 124). Mary also runs into Gerald Updike and his lover, Ronny, who replaced her at the interior decorating firm where she previously worked. Tanner's biographer offers no clue to what joke lies behind the author's throwaway line about a ballerina who is "working on a very symbolical ballet based on the writings of Donald Webster Cory. Completely revolutionary" ("Her Story," 56).

Myers observes (218) that "Pat usually had a gay character or two in his books; they were there for comic effect and were all fairly stereotypical in their nelliness. In *Tony*, Pat finally created a gay character who engenders sympathy." This is Tatham Purdom, another Southerner, who falls for the title character. Unfortunately for him, Tony is a con artist, interested only in being a "kept gentleman" (117). To fulfill that role he is willing to be gay or straight. And when Tatum's mother offers him enough money, he is willing to skip off to Palm Beach, leaving behind a note for Tatum. Poor Tatum takes the obligatory gay exit and kills himself. The mother stops the check, but to her chagrin, Tatham's will leaves everything to Tony, permitting him to carry on in style, mourning the loss of the "great friend of his" (211). The best thing about the chapter "Tony in Sodom" actually is the pretext it gives the unnamed narrator, now a book editor, to satirize the would-be chic gays in New York: their posturing, their "pansy" tastes, their conversations, the gay names they drop, and the autobiographical novels they dump upon him. I suspect many of the habitués who hang out at Tatum and Tony's parties are thinly disguised portraits of people the author knew. Myers confirms that the title character was based on Guy Kent, the man that Tanner had fallen in love with and to whom he dedicated the episodic novel.

Edward Everett (Pat) Tanner III (1921–1976) was born in Chicago but grew up in Evanston, Illinois. During World War II he served as an ambulance driver in North Africa and the Mideast. At the end of 1948 he married; the couple had two children. Between 1953 and 1972 Tanner published sixteen novels. In 1962 he met costume designer Guy M. Kent (1922–1990s) at the Luxor Baths and fell in love. He and his wife separated in 1963 but never divorced. Other lovers came and went. In 1972 he opened an art gallery in Houston with a gay couple he had met in Mexico. His novels out of favor and his earnings pretty well depleted, from 1973 to 1976 he served as a butler for three different households, including that of the founder of McDonald's. Suffering from pancreatic cancer, he returned to his wife and died in New York.

Dennis, Patrick. *Tony.* *New York: Dutton, 1966. London: Barker, 1966.
Myers, Eric. *Uncle Mame: The Life of Patrick Dennis.* New York: St. Martin's, 2000.

Rowans, Virginia. *The Loving Couple.* *New York: Crowell, 1956. London: Muller, 1957.

67 James Baldwin: *Giovanni's Room*, 1956; *Another Country*, 1962; *Tell Me How Long the Train's Been Gone*, 1968.

Giovanni's Room, Baldwin's second novel, is the tragedy of a man who cannot love: a fairy tale about an unworthy suitor who cannot release his prince from the room in which he is trapped because he cannot give fully of himself. While his girlfriend Hella is in Spain, in the company of Jacques, his sometimes fairy godfather, David meets Giovanni, a barman working in a gay bar in Paris. The attraction between the two men is immediate. An old fairy queen comments on it, but David insults him and is ceremoniously cursed: "I fear that you shall burn in a very hot fire. [...] You will be very unhappy. Remember that I told you so" (252–53). Jacques councils David to "love [Giovanni] and let him love you. Do you think anything else under heaven really matters?" Otherwise, he warns him, "you'll end up trapped in your own dirty body" (267). David fails: "Even at my most candid, even when I tried hardest to give myself to him as he gave himself to me, I was holding something back" (283). He moves in with Giovanni in his tiny room. But fearful of social disapprobation—"What kind of life can two men have together" (337)—heedless of the pain he is inflicting on others, David continues to try to convince himself that he is straight, or at least bisexual. Apparently jealous of David, Giovanni's boss fires him, throwing the two men even more on each other. David bolts and joins Hella upon her return. Hearing the two men are no longer together, Giovanni's boss seems willing to take him back as barman, but something goes wrong and Giovanni strangles him. David convinces himself that it would serve no purpose to visit him in prison while he awaits his execution. He spends several nights with a sailor he has picked up. Hella catches them together. Honesty peeps out for brief moments. He tells her, "I wasn't lying to *you*. [...] I was lying to myself" (355). He even admits, "I loved him. I do not think that I will ever love anyone like that again" (311). But he records Giovanni's statement: "You do not [...] love anyone! You never have loved anyone, I am sure you never will! You love your purity, you love your mirror" (336). Ultimately the novel is one of the most withering indictments of American hypocrisy in the gay canon. As a mark of the impact the book had, in 1973 a gay and lesbian bookstore in Philadelphia was named after it.

Baldwin depicts David and Giovanni's polar opposites in his next novel, *Another Country*. Though he is mentioned earlier, Eric Jones is actually introduced about a third of the way through this long novel. He is an American actor in France. He has met and fallen in love with Yves, a streetboy surviving by his wits, straight only for pay. They are well adjusted, unashamed, and as honest with each other as possible. The chapter that introduces them describes their Edenic last days together in a house on the Mediterranean. It is a celebration before they must momentarily part as Eric is returning to New York to take a role in a play. During its course the reader learns about Eric's upbringing in Alabama and his instinctive turn to African American males for something missing in his emotionally cold family as well as about Yves's survival during the Nazi occupation with a mother who used the invaders to keep alive. The author's discussions of the meaning of love and the standards that each gay must "make for himself" if he is "to find out who he was" (555) are as lyrical as Carson McCullers's. One can regret that Baldwin did not feel compelled to expand Eric and Yves's story into a complete novel of its own. Instead, they become two of some eight characters, none of whom is as well adjusted—one might even say, as normal.

The bisexual black actor Leo Proudhammer suffers a heart attack on stage at the beginning of *Tell Me*. He reconsiders his life, all that has brought him to this point: "I gathered that I had an interesting reputation in the streets. Some people considered me a fagot, for some I was a hero, for some I was a whore, for some I was a devious cocks-man, for some I was an Uncle Tom" (339). (The sense that the author is describing himself here is inescapable.) More is seen here of white hatred and pettiness—the dark side of American life exposed at greater length in Baldwin's powerful essays. Some of it is almost funny, as when Leo has to entertain his white acting partner and best friend's Kentucky family, but the greater part is gut-wrenching ugly, a reminder of how little matters have changed in almost half a century since the novel's appearance. Leo's other meaningful relationship has been with Christopher Hall: "When

Christopher first met me, he decided that he needed me: that was that" (331). Christopher is an activist; he engages Leo's skills as an actor for an important rally in the fight for civil rights. Leo reflects, "It certainly had not occurred to me that love would have had the effrontery to arrive in such a black, unwieldy, and dangerous package" (338). With all his anger, Christopher is another singularly well adjusted gay man. The novel received mixed criticism at the time; in the second decade of the millennium it seems perhaps the most relevant.

Almost all of Baldwin's gay characters retreat at some moment or the other to the apparent comfort of bisexuality without ever evolving a sexual philosophy or even illustrating an emotional base that would convince the reader of the reality of the moment. David and Leo affect the pose from the beginning. Eric, while waiting for Yves's arrival, beds an old friend, a married woman having her requisite marital crisis. Christopher feels compelled to bed Leo's white friend. The first third of *Another Country* concerns the bisexual black jazz musician Rufus Scott (who kills himself not because of his sexuality but because of the way he has abused a white woman). These momentary lapses seem more gratuitous pandering to readers than realistic or insightful.

James Arthur Jones (1924–1987) was born in New York. He took his stepfather's name in 1927. Still a youth, he became a Pentecostal minister. Countee Cullen was a school teacher; future photographer Richard Avedon was a classmate. He formed a lifelong friendship with the artist Beauford Delaney. During the war Baldwin lived in Greenwich Village, where he met Richard Wright. He began honing his writing. In 1948 he moved to Paris. There he met Lucien Happersberger (1932?–2010), against whom all other lovers were measured, even though the Swiss native was bisexual and thrice married (including the actress Diana Sands). *Giovanni's Room* was dedicated to him. For the rest of his life Baldwin alternated between the U.S. and Europe, buying a home in the south of France. During the 1950s he became involved in the struggle for civil rights. His last gay novel was *Just above My Head*, 1979. He died in St.-Paul-de-Vence of throat cancer. In his novel *The Tenants of Moonbloom*, 1963, Edward Lewis Wallant included a character, Joe Paxton, that resembles Baldwin.

Baldwin, James. *Another Country*. New York: Dial, 1962. London: Joseph, 1963. *Early Novels and Stories*. New York: Library of America, 1998.
———. *Giovanni's Room*. New York: Dial, 1956. London: Joseph, 1957. *Early Novels and Stories* (see above). 217–360.
———. *Tell Me How Long the Train's Been Gone*. New York: Dial, 1968. London: Joseph, 1968. *Latter Novels*. New York: Library of America, 2015. 1–362.
Leeming, David. *Baldwin: A Biography*. New York: Knopf, 1994.

68 Mary Orr: *Diamond in the Sky*, 1956. Roy Doliner: *Young Man Willing*, 1960. Basil Burwell: *A Fool in the Forest*, 1963. Russell O'Neil: *The Devil's Profession*, 1964.

These four theater novels have in common their use of gay stereotypes relegated to largely secondary roles. Burwell clearly drew upon his own experience for his novel set in 1930. The straight narrator recalls his teenage apprenticeship in Cape Cod summer stock. The self-acknowledged fool of the title, he is warned to watch out for his director, Cyrus Lowell, by his fellow actors, including Cyrus's current lover, the bisexual Don Francis. When he encounters the two for the first time, he realizes, "I had never before, knowingly at least, been in the presence of two men who were lovers. Even though I admired them for associating with a Barrymore, the thought of their having sex together made me as queasy as if I had been handed a human foetus with two heads" (34). The two men bicker throughout; the narrator offers, "With Cyrus the obnoxious quality may partly have been the bitchiness that is so often the occupational disease of the homosexual" (305). Don drops Cyrus for an actress, leading to the director's collapse and dismissal from the company. After his fall, the narrator finds, "I no longer felt disgust because that kind of love was unnatural; it just made me feel sad and sorry" (389). A campy female impersonator, Larry LaTouche, also briefly shows up. He gooses the narrator; it is a measure of his growth that, instead of repulsing him, he dilutes the situation by quipping, "Don't do that too often, I might get to like it" (393).

The other three novels allow the gay cast members to speak for themselves. Orr's records the preparations to mount a new costume drama about Nell Gwyn. The first twelve chapters are devoted to a different member of the production team. Rodian Liss is the gay set designer who uses his position to have Lyle Andrews hired as costume designer in order to seduce him away from his other admirers: "He trusted that he would show his gratitude in the proper manner" (153). The last five chapters follow the short life of the play on stage. Even though it is a flop, Lyle succeeds so well with costumes that he is offered a job in Hollywood. The pathetic Rodian tries to hold onto him. He is devastated when Lyle informs him, "You're more attractive than Harold [Lyle's former patron], but you're far too possessive and jealous. I want my freedom" (290). Both men are such cardboard figures that it is impossible to care about either. Almost as bad is Doliner's similar work. It recounts the rehearsals and out-of-town tryout of a Broadway-bound play "written by a fairy" that, one of the backers argues, needs a fairy director to make it work (57). So a Southern-born director with the improbable name of Bubber Frick is hired: he "thinks everybody that's not gay is crazy" (22). He is having an affair with the leading man, the bisexual Hollywood idol Tony Amali. They spend much of their time bickering. The best scene occurs when a depressed Bubber, in the company of a man Tony has cuckolded, taunts a pair of homophobic policemen at a cafeteria. He begins his jeers in his best Rita Hayworth manner before "becoming Shirley Temple" (103). The last we see of Bubber and Tony, the director is reviving the fully clothed, drunken actor under the bathroom shower at the after-show party.

The best of the four novels (though that's not saying much) is O'Neil's. It follows the careers of a number of actors after their last performance together in summer stock. One of them is straight, twenty-year-old Buck Tone. Strikingly good-looking, with a narcissistic awareness of his physical assets, he is willing to do anything to get a Hollywood contract. If this means becoming agent Archer Gordon's kept boy, so be it. Archer tells him, "'An actor who knows he hasn't a great talent, yet is determined to get to the top, has to be prepared to pay some high prices.' 'So far,' Buck answered, 'I haven't found a single price too high, and I don't think I will'" (95). It takes some disciplining, however. After he is rude to Archer's guests, he lays down a number of rules that Buck has to accept. Archer maintains that "generally, people in the theater don't give a damn about your sex life as long as you don't throw it in their faces and as long as it doesn't interfere with your work"

(203). Once Buck gets his Hollywood contract, he delivers his parting shot to Archer: "You're not a man; you're a queer. What do you think this has been, 'Younger Than Springtime'? Take a look at yourself, Archer. You're an aging, influential fairy who was able to do me a lot of good. And was able to keep me, give me expensive gifts, in return for which you were able to get your rocks off a couple times a week, doing something I couldn't bring myself to do if I was dying of the hots. Disgusting? You don't know what disgust is unless you know how much you disgust me [...] you and all your limp-wristed faggot friends" (400).

Basil Burwell (1911–1997) was born in Chelsea, Massachusetts, and died in Belfast, Maine. He was married and had three sons. Roy Doliner (1932–2015) was born in New York. He served in the Army during the war and then attended NYU. Married, he had two sons. Russell O'Neil (1927–1991) was born in Conshohocken, Pennsylvania, but grew up in New Jersey. He was a paratrooper in the war. He attended the Faigan School of Drama in New York. His one Broadway show, 1975, was a failure. In the late 1970s he lived with musician Eric Brown, who has left a brief sketch of him in connection with Brown's cousin Stella Adler. He died in New York of respiratory failure. One would have expected better from Mary Caswell Orr (1910–2006), a New York born actress. She attended Syracuse and the American Academy of Dramatic Arts. She was married to British director Reginald Denham, to whom she dedicates the novel. He brought Patrick Hamilton's homoerotic play *Rope* to the New York stage in 1929. Orr also wrote the story that was the basis for the film *All about Eve*, 1950.

Burwell, Basil. *A Fool in the Forest*. New York: Macmillan, 1963.
Doliner, Roy. *Young Man Willing*. *New York: Scribner's, 1960. London: Weidenfeld & Nicolson, 1961.
O'Neil, Russell. *The Devil's Profession: A Novel of the Theater*. New York: Simon & Schuster, 1964. London: Muller, 1964. *New York: Pocket Books, 1965.
Orr, Mary. *Diamond in the Sky*. *New York: Crown, 1956. London: Cassell, 1959.

69   Milton Rebow: *Oh Dear!*, 1957.

Campy fiction is not an American forte. Many authors have tried it and failed. Readers, too, often miss the point: Rebow's soufflé has been badly misunderstood. The author has taken one fairy cliché after another and run with it to create a novel that is far funnier than Patrick Dennis's. Take the perception that all gays in fiction must come to a sad end. The novel's opening sentence is, "He was committing suicide" (9). And the hero? He is one Andrew Thess, twenty-five. We are told (pulling upon another cliché, this one from gay pornography): "Everything about his figure was petit, except for his jack-o-lantern which was not"—to his expressed dismay (18). As to his profession, he is, of course, a department store window dresser, an interior decorator manqué with an exalted estimation of his own worth. Think of someone akin to Mr. Humphries in the British TV comedy *Are You Being Served?* but more childlike, "an extreme introvert" (28).

The entire novel takes place in or near his apartment in New York on Monday, October 28 (1946?), the day he has chosen to kill himself. He is not quite sure which hour he will choose, nor which method he will use. While trying to make up his mind, he begins recalling, in chronological order, events from his past. He is convinced "that was the price one had to pay when committing suicide—one's whole life passed before him"—though it bothers him that maybe that happens "when one was drowning. He couldn't quite remember" (29). He recalls his high school graduation, his unhappy attempt at college, the embarrassment of his army physical (he is dismissed for having "a weak heart"), his first sexual experience and moving in with Louis Parsons, a fellow worker in a department store, and his clumsy experience with a woman, followed immediately by his acceptance of the truth about himself when he realizes the all too obvious effect a young man in a subway car is having on his overlarge endowment (50–51). As he thinks much later in the novel, "His way of life was molded for him. He certainly didn't choose it before he was born. He is this way" (152). All the while, he drifts in and out of jobs, quitting whenever he thinks his true worth is not being appreciated.

Upon leaving one job, Andy impulsively buys a ticket to Montreal. There he runs into Lou again. He in turn introduces Andy to Johnny Turner, who immediately hires him to be his "personal secretary" with special duties. After two happy years together, the idyll ends with the noisy arrival of the police. In trying to escape out the back way, Johnny is shot, but Andy makes it back to New York, to learn from the newspapers that he has been living with a "very highly paid spy for an international ring" (95). He suffers a further series of ups and downs. He finds he is his former landlady's sole heir. After failures as a window dresser and a bank teller, he lands a job in a small department store and becomes the protégé of Julius Whee, who takes more than a fatherly interest in the "very good looking young chap whose presence he liked" (135) but then flees back to the safety of his wife. Then a certain Norman Lang chooses Andy as ready prey for a con job. Homophobic to the max, Norman dissembles enough to talk Andy out of his entire inheritance. When Andy realizes how he has been tricked, he decides the only thing left is to kill himself. The hour of midnight passes. Andy is still waffling about how to off himself, when he realizes he has not checked the mailbox. There he finds an invitation from Lou to attend a fashion show. That causes him to remember that he has an invitation for later on to a cocktail party at the Waldorf Astoria. He reconsiders his pending suicide: "Well it would just have to be postponed until his schedule wasn't so hectic." With that, our hero "mince-stepped to bed exhausted" (181). Milton Rebow remains unidentified. The 1940 census records a person with that name as having been born in New York in 1924. But the name could be a pseudonym.

Rebow, Milton. *Oh Dear!* New York: Key, 1957.

70 David Stacton: *Remember Me*, 1957. Robert B. Asprey: *The Panther's Feast*, 1959.

Both these novels are set in Middle Europe in the nineteenth century. In Stacton's portrait of Ludwig II of Bavaria (1845–1886), his protagonist's attraction to other men provides the story's central thread. The novel becomes a meditation on the nature of love, including the role of desire. For Ludwig, "The lower desires were abominable. At the time they meant everything. Afterwards they meant the loss of everything. They worked against the Self. And sex is not love. One will never find love down there" (48). Yet he recognizes, "Release he must have of some kind, or else explode" (47). Whenever the tension builds to such a point that "he had to satisfy the desires of his body, he would satisfy them in some anonymous place where nothing could touch him" (65–66). Of those people with whom a king may openly consort, none satisfy. Though the mythological figures who propel Wagner's music remain Ludwig's constant symbols in his search for love and purity, the heterosexual composer himself fails to answer his needs: "To Ludwig love was a necessity. To Wagner it was only a convenience" (49). His boyhood friend Paul von Thurn und Taxis seems eager to please, but Ludwig's horror of himself when he makes a physical overture to Paul spells the end of their relationship: "We can never forgive others for their participation in our own sins" (73). Actors—first Emil Rohde, later Josef Kainz—likewise fail since Ludwig is attracted to the character each is playing rather than the man behind that character and an actor can maintain a role only so long. Then there are servants, who "have more uses than one" (48). His longest relationship with one of them is with a groom, Richard Hornig: "Of all those to whom Ludwig appealed only Richard answered him" (120). Yet even he must eventually fail simply because he is human and cannot measure up to Ludwig's ideal. So Ludwig blunders on: "After each sexual act, each cloudy white outlet of the self, he was down another step" (165). Ludwig's great building mania becomes an attempt to arrest that decline. But for the king, love finally equates to death as he deliberately drowns the physician who, for political reasons, has declared him insane and then drowns himself.

One wonders to what extent the portrait of the king was a portrait of the author. Arthur Lionel Kingsley Evans (1923–1968) was born in San Francisco. He attended Stanford but graduated from the University of California after the war. During the war he was a conscientious objector. He legally changed his name to David Derek Stacton in 1946. His partner for many years was John Mann Rucker. He spent much time in Europe; most of his books were published in London. He died of a heart attack in Fredensborg, Denmark. Under the pseudonym Bud Clifton, Stacton wrote a contemporary potboiler, *Muscle Boy*, 1958, that allegedly grew out of a blackmail ring that worked in San Francisco. Set in the milieu of the physique photography culture and its association with all-male pornographic films and other illegal activities, the novel follows the ensnarement of a naive straight teenager, Jerry Carpenter, into their ugly schemes. One of the artists, Reveille, is gay (he bears a superficial resemblance to Quantance, though Reveille comes to a very different end). The novel promises more than it delivers.

Asprey's work is a hybrid. It was marketed and cataloged as a biography, and it comes complete with photographs, lengthy bibliography, and index. But it is written like a novel, with invented dialogue and even whole scenes, and it shows a fictional flair for pacing the story. Allen Dulles included a chapter from it in his anthology *Great Spy Stories from Fiction*, 1969, writing in his introduction how it "departs from being a biography and becomes imaginative literature when Asprey ventures to create episodes for which there is no documentary evidence." The very title is telling: it comes not from the life of its subject, the Austro-Hungarian Colonel Alfred Redl (1864–1913), but from Wilde's *De Profundis*. The author follows Redl's rise—from cadet school to head of the counter-intelligence sector of the empire's Intelligence Bureau—and fall—when he is blackmailed into becoming a Russian double agent. The Tsar's Intelligence discovers that Redl is gay and prone to outspending his income to please his youthful lovers. As a novel, and even as a biography, the book is not very satisfactory since it provides no insight into Redl's own understanding of his desires and drives. It seems baffling that a man who is so good at following trails through the murky worlds of international espionage fails so markedly to fathom his own murky psychology. The best the author comes up with is: "To hide the horrible fact of his calculating being, to impress none of the truth and all of the fiction of his distorted existence on society, required a force of will so great as to almost defy human imagination" (173).

The greater portion of the book is taken up with the political and social maneuvers of the period. But the author follows the homosexual thread throughout, beginning with Redl's adolescent fixation on a fellow cadet and ending with his fatal infatuation with a straight youth half his age. The language of his first encounter demonstrates how the biography constantly shifts into fictional mode: "Alfred laughed even while he felt the warm hands of Hans lift his nightgown and slide up his body to stroke his buttocks and roll him over and tickle the light growth of hair. When Hans' soft hand took it and pressed it Alfred could stand no more and he threw his arms around Hans and pressed wet kisses on him and pulled the body tight to him and worked his hands over that body and they did this until they panted and stiffened and clutched and slowly fell away" (30–31). Once he graduates and becomes an officer, his sexual encounters become more varied even as he fights for control: "loneliness was joined by aloneness. And with the feeling came the admission of physical man into his mind by every means the senses could provide: by the eyes as they searched high-cheeked Slavic faces to run furtively down the broad shoulders and straight backs to the classic mold of muscular buttocks and the tight mound of genital in the close-fitting trousers [...]; by the nose as it caught the heady dark smell of the male in a crowded salon; by the ear as each note of the sonorous voices sang to this troubled man; [...] by the feel of hips and legs brushing in the crowd of a roulette table" (91–92). For a moment he loves a woman, a circus performer, but when she infects him with both gonorrhea and syphilis, he becomes a confirmed misogynist—though the Russians discover he likes to "dress Joseph [his servant] like a woman and make love to him" (135). Ironically, the sheaf to a penknife that his last, straight lover, Stefan Hromodka, has given him provides the means to unmask his treason. Real life proved to be as inventive in its reliance on phallic symbolism as literature.

Asprey's book became the primary basis for English playwright John Osborne's drama *A Patriot for Me*, 1965. The play in turn influenced the German language screenplay by Hungarian director István Szabó for *Oberst Redl*, 1985. As with Stacton, one wonders about the attraction of the handsome Galician for his biographer. Robert Brown Asprey (1923–2009) was born in Sioux City, Iowa. He served as a Marine during the war. After the University of Iowa, he briefly joined Army Intelligence working in Austria before returning to the Marines to serve in the Korean conflict. He became a military historian. He died in Sarasota, Florida.

Asprey, Robert B. *The Panther's Feast.* *New York: Putnam's, 1959. London: Cape, 1959.
Stacton, David. *Remember Me.* London: Faber & Faber, 1957. *London: Faber & Faber, 2012.

71 William Talsman: *The Gaudy Image*, 1958.

This campy novel inevitably invites comparison with *The Young and Evil*, not so much for its, likewise, Paris publication, as for its free-wheeling embrace of the pleasures (and some of the torments) of sexuality in all their vulgarity. Set in New Orleans, the main character is a transplanted Californian, Thomas Schwartz, aka Titania Queen of the Fairies, Tit for short. He has a number of lovers, sex buddies, and one-night tricks: "Titania seeks the conditions of love in man, in men, because they hold the possible, all the gaudy delights of the opposite" (143). Sir Denis, a short order cook, accuses his friend Rose, who works in an antique shop, "Why, the way you carry on with your own sex is positively incestuous" (58). This is a world in which women are a parody, not much of a reality. We follow some of Tit's sexual partners even after they move out of his life. (One of the funniest of these extraneous episodes occurs early in the novel when Nickie and Gunnar, two petty criminals, hide out in a rooming house. A boxer and a wrestler have rooms on the same floor. The four men soon prove that all kinds of sexual variations are a lot of fun. Even the sudden appearance of the landlady while two of them are *flagante delicto* does not throw them out of sync.) Plot is minimal. Through a series of flashbacks we learn about Thomas's first sexual experimentations with another boy and how he fled his smothering mother after his father's suicide. Upon his arrival in the French Quarter he finds his milieu and takes on his persona. His friends have various kinds of hangups, but guilt is not one. Nor is image all that important, though creating an aura is. Superficiality is a norm. We see the men's interactions not only in the bed but at a pool hall, a gay club, a private party, the racetrack, Sparafucile's Bar and Grill. There are reminders of the darker aspects of being gay even in New Orleans. Rose is brutally beaten during Mardi Gras and dies. Denis is "grateful to Rose for dying, for the death gave him an opportunity to circulate, a chance to dispatch the details of a sudden tragedy" (225). Finally it is too much for Tit. Exhausted, he feels it is time to depart New Orleans. So he leaves on the train, taking the "gaudy image" of the ideal male with him (270), "curried, combed, clipped, and cured—ready to take his place among the monuments of Twentieth-century America" (275). The novel was published in the U.S. in 1967 in a pirated edition. The author also published a chapbook, *Notes from the Underworld*, 1961. The publisher identified him as James M. Smith (dates unknown), who was born in the Midwest. According to the chapbook, he graduated from Iowa State in 1950. He lived in New Orleans, Paris, and Cleveland. Further information about him has escaped me.

Talsman, William. *The Gaudy Image*. Paris: Olympia, 1958. *New York: Hard Candy, 1995.

72   Herbert D. Kastle: *Koptic Court*, 1958.

The novel describes the residents of seven apartments in a Brooklyn complex, devoting three chapters to each group, these chapters alternating in a regular pattern. The closeted homosexual, Elliot Wycoff, appears in chapters 3, 10, and 17. Though they share the same building and occasionally cross paths and comment on each other, basically the various inhabitants go their individual ways. The only moment they share in common comes at the end when a repressed teenager's joke accidentally blows up the building. Elliot is the thirty-three-year-old reader for a publishing company. He knows he is homosexual, but he wants to conceal that fact from everyone—and wishes he could conceal it from himself. He perceives his sexuality "as great a misfortune, a sickness, as a malformed spine" but resents that "they'd given up ridiculing hunchbacks and cripples, but homosexuals were still fair game" (26). Hearing gossip about his distaste for women, he deliberately beds one of his colleagues to squelch any idea that "he was—queer" (35). Still, Alex Fernol, a twenty-three-year-old proofreader, troubles his thoughts. The youth is obviously gay. He comes on to Elliot, who finds himself responding. But even though he "wanted to give in and end the fight, the long fight that meant only pain and loneliness and absence of love," he refuses the boy's overtures: "Elliot shook his head, as he had all his life, and walked out" (134–35). Part of him wants to say, "*To hell with what people think!*" (250), but his fear of public opinion leads him more actively to seek an explanation that he can present to the world that will justify his "staying clear of women" (240). Thus he welcomes losing an arm in the explosion: he will no longer "have to fake interest in women; he finally had his excuse for not wanting to be with them" (333). Alex gives up on him. The portrait seems designed to elicit pity from the reader, but Elliot is so self-centered that it is difficult to care for him. The novel was published in the U.K. as *Keys to Seven Rooms* and in the U.S. in paperback as *7 Keys to Koptic Court*. Herbert David Kastle (1924–1987) was born in New York. He attended the Washington Square College of Arts and Sciences. He worked in publishing and as a scriptwriter. During World War II he served in the air force. He was married and had a daughter. He died of a heart ailment in Los Angeles.

Kastle, Herbert D. *Koptic Court*. *New York: Simon & Schuster, 1958. *Keys to Seven Rooms*. London: Allen, 1958.

73   Reginald Harvey: *Park Beat*, 1959.

The novel covers eight summer hours, from 3:45 until 11:45 p.m. in New York's Central Park. The peregrinations of various people cross or parallel the path of a cop on the beat, a straight policeman named Hal Barton. They belong mostly to two groups, one defined sexually: gays; the other ethnically: Puerto Ricans. Hal is unusual in that he questions his own purpose: "What is the answer for the desperate men and women yearning for a moment of passion, for the outlawed homosexual hunting illicit affection in the dark pathways, for the bewildered Puerto Rican nursing humiliation and insult and plotting revenge? What laws can fill the void of a loveless city? Is compassion to be forgot and replaced by the night stick and service revolver?" (8). He despairs of his fellow cops who have become "just a law enforcement machine" (15). Jerry Masters, one of his best friends on the force, assigned to the vice squad, also becomes sensitive to the fact that "the type of homosexual we are supposed to watch are nothing like those we used to tell dirty stories about as kids," the stereotypes are inadequate (50). When a gay propositions Jerry, though he calls his a "goddam pervert," he lets him go, simply threatening him with a "sodomy rap" if he runs into him again (114). Later, in describing the scene to Hal, he comments on the ridiculousness of it all: "A police badge never scared a sex maniac or a homosexual out of his basic purpose. It may have delayed him a little, that's all" (123). And he tells his homophobic partner on the beat, "I understand why these poor fools have to go out even in the Park at night and pick up whatever or whoever they can to get that little bit of love or understanding. It makes 'em feel needed and necessary" (160).

Bert Shire (né Schiretzky), an advertising copywriter seeking a new position, and Joe Hilliard, a hustler originally from Evanston, Illinois, are two of the men cruising the park. Joe is basically a healthy young organism who does, as he says, "what I can do best." Sometimes he does it for the money; sometimes "because I like the guy" (181). Bert and Joe hook up, and it appears that something more than a single fling may come out of their encounter. Joe is willing to let whatever happens happen. For Bert the eight hours becomes a coming out process. The first step occurs in a job interview when he realizes that the agency head is gay and has recognized that Bert is, almost certainly guaranteeing that he will get the job. The next steps come as the results of accidently running into an old girlfriend from college. Seeing Kathy underscores for him his lack of sexual interest in women. That understanding gives him the courage to cruise the park. Though nervous that Joe may mug him, he invites the young man to join him for a meal at his nearby apartment. They are just moving into something sexual when Kathy unexpectedly rings up. When she arrives, he tells her bluntly that the young man she met while climbing the stairs had been with him, that in fact, "We were making love on this couch just a few moments ago" (77). In a strange convolution, he admits to her that his Jewishness bothers him more than his sexuality does. Still searching for understanding about herself, Kathy suggests they attend a band concert going on in the park. As they continue to talk, Bert's acceptance of himself grows: "I need friendship, companionship, maybe even love. I realize that. And the more I realize my needs and the more I look at them objectively, the more I find I don't have them." With a smile, he concludes, "I want other things to harden right now, not my arteries" (129). Never knowing that the whole time they have been stalked by a murderous Puerto Rican mugger, even after they stumble upon his latest victim, they separate, and he goes searching for Joe. When he finds him, he is finally able to act "without his having to think twice" (182).

The name Reginald Harvey must be a pseudonym. The novel was reissued in 1960 as an abridged paperback, *The Park Jungle*, with the author given as Robert Chessman. The copyright lists Hyman Lindsey. The cuts were all made in the homosexual sections of the novel. The Puerto Ricans and the upper middle-class Americans alike verge on being stereotypes, but the middle and lower-class gays and the cops provide a fun read.

Harvey, Reginald. *Park Beat*. New York: Castle, 1959.

74   Ben Travis: *The Strange Ones*, 1959.

The exposé-like title of Travis's novel was likely the publisher's invention, designed to sell books. The novel traces Ray Dobson's progression as he comes to accept that he wants money and he wants sex with men, and if the two combine, "he didn't care, and he knew now that he never would" (157). It opens in a small town in Ohio just after his discharge from the Navy. Frustrated by his failure to sell the rundown home he has inherited from his parents, he sets it ablaze, only to discover his father had cancelled the insurance. With only a few hundred dollars left from his severance pay and his temporary job as a lifesaver, he leaves for New York. Almost at once he is picked up by Bruce Carton. Bruce gains his livelihood serving as a gigolo for Amelia Hoppert, a "vicious and scheming" monster (142). He is just the latest in a string of male escorts she has kept; as with the ones before, she encourages his homosexual liaisons but will not permit him even to glance at another woman. She has become bored with Bruce. When he appears with Ray, without hesitation she shows Bruce the door and takes Ray to fill his place. This exchange only temporarily ruptures the two men's relationship. Although Ray has denied that he is gay, explaining away memories of his adolescent fascination with male bodies as "only natural" (86), with Bruce, "The awakening had come over him fully, and he felt awed. He was no longer afraid; instead, he was relieved and filled with desire. This was a beginning" (72). Unfortunately, Bruce puts money ahead of everything; he hopes to find another patron, "a rich man this time" (58). When such a catch shows up, Bruce drops Ray. Meanwhile, Amelia starts imagining things. Convinced that Ray is bedding the young actress starring in a play she is producing, she dismisses him, to find that he will not easily go. She goes to the actress to inform her that "Ray is abnormal." To her surprise, the actress takes the news lightly: "Don't you know that many of Hollywood's and Broadway's most handsome stars are homosexual?" she asks (140–41). Totally rattled, she returns home and gets drunk. In trying to stoke the fire in the fireplace, she sets herself ablaze and dies. Her lawyer is instantly upon the scene; he forces Ray out with only what he is wearing and what little money he has in his pocket: "it occurred to him how cleverly and distinctly fire had cheated him twice in his life so far" (154). But Ray is resilient: "he was no longer concerned with the past. He was thinking entirely of his future" (155). He heads for a gay bar and hooks up with model

Jimmy Wilcox. When Jimmy sees Ray naked, he proposes that he consider entering the market (clearly pornographic) for nude photographs and films. Ray does not hesitate to accept the idea. This is the only novel published under Ben Travis's name, almost certainly a pseudonym.

Travis, Ben. *The Strange Ones*. New York: Beacon, 1959.

75 Martin Mayer: *A Voice That Fills the House*, 1959.

The author, for no particular reason, introduces a gay police inspector into his story of the rise to stardom of its narrator, an unnamed American baritone at the Teatro San Carlo di Napoli and the Metropolitan Opera. His best friend's father, to the son's chagrin, is Inspector Charles Sellars. He is completely open about his relationship with a young Detroit born African American, Sergeant August Andrews. The two policemen show up first in Naples, where Sellars is working a narcotics smuggling case. Sellars is cultivated—his daughter-in-law is also an opera singer, and he loves the opera world. The two men, along with some of their friends, re-enter the narrator's life when he has his Metropolitan debut. Invited by them to attend a séance at which Oscar Wilde's spirit is to be summoned, he stalks out when something apparently sexual occurs. That same evening Sellars dies of a stroke. He leaves his Murray Hill house and his entire collection of rare pornography to Andy. The last we see of the young sergeant, he is arriving at a party, uninvited, with drunk friends to prove to them that he knows Sellars's daughter-in-law, now also a star at the Met. The narrator's lawyer maintains that Andy was "normal till he came to New York. Charlie picked up that boy and *changed* him, just as though he'd taken a knife to him." When the narrator questions how this could be possible, the lawyer replies, "Never is but one way—pornography." He continues, "Theory is: what God has wrought, let no man put to rights. But this is nasty. This is just wanton malfeasance for the sake of kicks" (128). Unfortunately, the novel does not hold up well. Martin Prager Mayer (1928–) was born in New York. He graduated from Harvard. He is a novelist, a writer about finance, banking, and the justice system, and was a music reviewer for *Esquire*, 1951–75, and *Opera Magazine*, 1985–2004. Married twice, he has four children.

Mayer, Martin. *A Voice That Fills the House*. New York: Simon & Schuster, 1959.

76 William S. Burroughs: *The Naked Lunch*, 1959. Alexander Trocchi: *Cain's Book*, 1960. Irving Rosenthal: *Sheeper*, 1967.

The intertwined lives of Burroughs, Kerouac, and Ginsberg have created such a mythos—perpetuated by memoirs, biographies, films, and blogs—that it is nearly impossible to read their works, based as they are on those lives, as simply fiction. Kerouac's *On the Road*, written in 1951 but not published until 1957, has been appropriated by readers as a gay novel because of what we know (or think we know) about the relationship between Kerouac and Neal Cassady—between Sal Paradise and Dean Moriarty in the novel. With more reason, we want to read Burroughs's *Junkie* (published in 1953, revised and retitled *Junky* in 1977) as a gay novel since its protagonist, William Lee, is obviously Burroughs, and Lee fleetingly acknowledges his homosexuality. The reading is reinforced by our knowledge of its sequel, with the telling title *Queer* (not published until 1985 but parts of which had ended up in *Junkie*). But *Junkie* really is about *junk* (its original unused title), that is, drugs, not about desire or sexual identity. *Naked Lunch*, his second published novel, is a different matter. Although likewise about drugs, it is filled with gay, or at least queer, scenes; in the words of scholar Jamie Russell (46), Burroughs "conflates two underworlds of 1950s America: the drug world and the gay world." A narc in the novel says, "I spent the night in the Ever Hard Baths—(homosexuality is the best all-around cover story an agent can use)" (180). For Russell (43), the entire work is "a *queer* satire/social protest novel in which the overriding emphasis is on the role of sociopolitical power in the regulation of identity and marginal sexualities." Seeing Burroughs as one of the leaders in the fight for gay liberation, he praises him (2) for "having produced a queer fiction that is unabashed in its sexuality, unafraid of its explicit lusts, and uncompromising in its condemnation of the oppression and restriction of sexual freedom undertaken by the heterosexual dominant."

Although Burroughs referred to it as a novel, it is far from conventional. It now consists of twenty-five sections that the author called "routines." In "Atrophied Preface" (placed at the end) Burroughs describes the work thus: "The Word is divided into units which be all in one piece and should be so taken, but the pieces can be had in any order being tied up back and forth in and out fore and aft like an innaresting sex arrangement" (191). The sections were assembled by his friends, particularly Kerouac and Ginsberg, so any sense of plot is arbitrary. All is in flux. The whole seems like a series of hallucinations—much of the novel was written on drugs—in which characters morph into one another. So do settings: mainly Mexico, Tangier, and a menacing Interzone. Likewise religions. Because of those qualities that Russell singles out, the work has sometimes been classified as dystopian science fiction. As satire, it makes ample use of irony, parody, and pure comedy. Sections from the novel appeared in the U.S. in little magazines, 1957–59; the first edition came out in Paris in 1959 under the title *The Naked Lunch* (the name it retains in England). It did not appear in the U.S. until 1962, with *The* dropped. Thereupon, it provoked one of the important law cases that expanded freedom of literary expression. The 2001 editors inform us that the two "first" editions are different in multiple ways, the American version was based on an earlier assemblage of the manuscript in Ginsberg's hands, while the French edition came from Burroughs's latest revisions. When David Cronenberg turned *Naked Lunch* into a movie in 1992, he created yet another work, part biography, only some part novel.

In one bow to conventionality, it opens and closes with William Lee on the run from narcs. There is, in a sense, a brief resume of *Junkie* as we follow Lee across the U.S. and into Mexico. There he is assigned to Doctor Benway, who runs a Reconditioning Center that seems vaguely to espouse many of the current theories about homosexuality and its cure. Scenes presenting him at work are momentarily interrupted by vignettes introducing other characters, some of whom will show up again. Hassan is the first major figure to appear (we are now in Morocco). His bar is essentially a brothel in which anything goes. One of the clients is A.J. After an abrupt interlude in a classroom at the Interzone University, we attend A.J.'s annual party. He projects a blue movie that involves an elaborate and complicated series of sexual acts among three performers: Johnny, Mark, and Mary, the latter armed with a strap-on dildo. We next turn to Doctor Schafer, a counterpart to Doctor Benway. He advocates lobotomies (a treatment actually performed on gay men at mid-century). There follow various scenes, still in the Interzone, including a meeting between Benway and Schafer in which Benway recounts one of Burroughs's more famous routines, the story of the talking asshole (110–12).

We return to A.J. He is now identified as an "international playboy and harmless practical joker. It was A.J. who put the piranha fish in Lady Sutton-Smith's swimming pool, and dosed the punch with a mixture of *yagé*, hashish and yohimbine during a Fourth of July reception at the U.S. Embassy, precipitating an orgy. Ten prominent citizens—American, of course—subsequently died of shame. Dying of shame is an accomplishment peculiar to Kwakiutl Indians and Americans—others simply say '*Zut alors*' or '*Son cosas de la vida*'" or blame Allah (123). A.J.'s exploits are intercut with others' and a long digression about Interzone political parties. A sidetrip taken by Lee lands us in rube country, U.S.A., with its strange heterosexual doings, followed by another overview of Interzone politics. Next, we go with Carl Peterson, supposedly heterosexual, for questioning by Benway about his homosexual proclivities, during which the unfortunate cases of gays who are pressured by society to marry women is mentioned. We meander back to William Lee's flight. Throughout the novel, sex is pervasive, almost always homosexual, and violence lurks everywhere. Political correctness is a nonexistent concept. The novel is impossible to sum up, but Burroughs seems to be saying to gays that, though you may not be able to beat heterosexuals' power, nor be able to understand their atrophied logic, you can make fun of them and, in the process, let your own erotic imaginings go wild.

William Seward Burroughs II (1914–1997) was born in St. Louis. He graduated from Harvard. He was briefly in the military during World War II before being given a discharge on psychological grounds. In New York, through his St. Louis friend David Kammerer's lover, Lucien Carr, he met Kerouac (1922–1969) and Ginsberg (1926–1997), both students at Columbia. He married twice, the first time to rescue a woman from the Nazis, the second time apparently out of love. He had a stepdaughter and a son, but proved to be a lousy father. He fatally shot his wife in Mexico City, an act that became central to the Beat myth alongside Carr's murder of Kammerer. He left Mexico for Tangier and the expatriate group surrounding Paul Bowles. After *Naked Lunch* he became internationally famous, showing up in surprising venues, and had a major impact on writers, painters, filmmakers, and musicians, especially punk rockers. Part of this influence derived from his use of the cut-up technique that he perfected with the English painter Brion Gysin (1916–1986). He had a tendency to fall in love easily; Ginsberg rejected him, but he had a number of intense affairs with other men. He died in Lawrence, Kansas, where he had moved with James Grauerholz (1953–); his death came just four months after Ginsberg's, his having lived the longest of any of the Beats' inner circle despite his lifelong drug habits.

Cain's Book, a novel much admired by Burroughs, comparable to *Junkie* in its reflections about drugs, invites passing mention. It too is autobiographical. It describes a period in the life of the Scot junkie Joe Necchi while living on a scow in the Hudson River. Basically heterosexual, though not new to having sex with men, Necchi describes an encounter with a Puerto Rican named Manuelo. Each barely able to speak the other's language, Necchi thinks, "it was better that way. There were no common memories between us; we shared our male sex only, our humanity, and our lust." Afterwards he reflects on the encounter, feeling "profoundly satisfied, physically with the mute certainty of my body, intellectually because I had broken through another limit and found that I could love a man with the same sure passion that moved me to women generally" (65–66). There are also several homosocial bondings throughout the work. Alexander Whitelaw Robertson Trocchi (1925–1984) was born in Glasgow and attended the university there. He lived in Paris after the war; there he translated Apollinaire's homosexual novel, *Les onze mille verges*, under the pseudonym Oscar Mole, 1953. From 1956 to 1961 he lived in New York and Venice, California. He was married twice and had four children. He died in London of pneumonia.

For better or worse, Burroughs's style had an enormous influence on other writers. Harold Norse wrote in his *Memoirs of a Bastard Angel* (414) that Charles Henri Ford thought Rosenthal's *Sheeper* went "a step further than Burroughs. Better than Genet. It's like nobody else. He's like Lautréamont." Norse himself seemed less enthusiastic, and indeed Rosenthal's novel can strike one as self-indulgent. The narrator himself accepts that the "book is about style and that's all it's about," though he insists that "the style of this memoir is the style of my life as I lived it" (69). At another point he writes, "The bulge in the book and the pants is the same," and goes on to say, "This prose is a new space I built special for an eager hand to plunge through" in search of the author's genitals (180). Homosexuality and drug use are conflated, without quite the hallucinogenic quality of Burroughs's writing: "One week he thinks he's a homosexual, and the next week he's a teahead" (29). True and fictional incidents intertwine, with some weird shifts in nomenclature. At one point, Sheeper (Rosenthal) depicts himself and Allen (obviously, Ginsberg) "crocheting a passage in Marrows' great novel from twelve different manuscript versions" (73). In the next chapter *Marrows* is dropped to record straightforwardly "Allen's epiphany on collating the Olympia *Naked Lunch* with our manuscript: With the end of the novel Burroughs passes from the world of nothing (no glot) into the empty door frame of the honey-Buddha, whose agent Lee has always been" (76). Besides Ginsberg, Sheeper is enthralled by Hubert Huncke, the man who gave Kerouac the term "Beat" and of whom he famously says, "Never was a criminal more petty and unsuccessful" (112). He recalls Marrows/Burroughs's depiction of Hunke in his first book, *Adder* (i.e., *Junkie*). Much of one chapter of *Sheeper* is given over to shooting up in Trocchi's apartment in Venice (219–37). Paul Bowles is outed in a parenthesis within a parenthesis (212), much to the expatriate's displeasure.

The novel contains many observations about sex and ego, and it offers criticism of political and religious oppression. One passage argues, "St. Paul of Tarsus would have been a different man had he known Jesus, and the world would have been spared another angry ruthless politician." It continues, "There is more sublimity in the life of Nero than in all the Pauline epistles"—which "Groucho Marx could not have outdone" (270). Repeatedly the novel sounds the call for gay pride, sometimes in unexpected ways as when the narrator muses, "According to Darwinian theories homosexuality should have wiped itself out the instant it showed its ... gentle interesting face" but it remains a fact; therefore no "auntie" should "cry about having no children" since he has "a karmic fertility that would put a shad to shame. A dozen queer babies will be born with the flames of your funeral pyre flashing" (115). There is even a glimmering of a conventional plot: we know that Sheeper feels oppressed by his Jewish mother, that he is having relationship problems with David, among others, and that Professor X poses a series of threats to his security. The book itself was beautifully designed by Dave Haselwood, with drawings of insects and arachnids scattered across its pages. But it seems a pale reflection of Burroughs's achievement, and despite periodic praise and translations into German and French, little has been written about it, and it has never been reprinted.

Irving Rosenthal (1930–) was born in San Francisco. He attended Pomona College and the University of Chicago. He became editor of *The Chicago Review*, which printed sections from *Naked Lunch*. When the university censored the journal, he resigned and created *Big Table*, which printed drafts of both Burroughs's novel and Rechy's *City of Night*. In New York he hobnobbed with Ronald Tavel and Jack Smith, becoming involved with Smith's films *Flaming Creatures*, 1963, and *No President*, 1967. He lived in Tangier and Athens 1962–64, writing his one novel while abroad. In 1967 he moved back to San Francisco with George Harris (aka Hibiscus, 1949–1982), the founder of the Cockettes. There he became the leader of the Kaliflower Commune.

Burroughs, William S. *The Naked Lunch*. Paris: Olympia, 1959. *Naked Lunch*. New York: Grove, 1962. *The Naked Lunch*. London: Calder, 1964. *Naked Lunch: The Restored Text. Ed. James Grauerholz and Barry Miles. New York: Grove, 2001.
Miles, Barry. *Call Me Burroughs: A Life*. New York: Twelve, 2014.
Rosenthal, Irving. *Sheeper*. New York: Grove, 1967.
Russell, Jamie. *Queer Burroughs*. New York: Palgrave, 2001.
Scott, Andrew Murray. *Alexander Trocchi: The Making of a Monster*. 2nd ed. Kilkerran, Scotland: Kennedy & Boyd, 2012.
Trocchi, Alexander. *Cain's Book*. New York: Grove, 1960. London: Calder, 1963. *New York: Grove, 1992.

77 Alexander Fedoroff: *The Side of Angels*, 1960.

Set during the years 1945–51, Fedoroff's novel is a sprawling work that tracks the intertwined lives of a large cast of characters. Five, however, focus the work: "Tiger, the radical; Steve, the easy-going liberal; Warren, who wanted to turn history back to what he thought of as a nobler time; Marvin and his dedication to advancing himself for his progeny"; and Helen "and her long battle to build something substantial and good" out of herself (518). Warren Taggert is the gay one of the five. We first meet him as he is getting out of the Army, "oppressed with loneliness, an uncertain troubling sense of incompleteness, of undefined, unworded dissatisfaction" (75). He realizes that the engagement with a woman that he has tumbled into in his hometown Cleveland is not really for him. But he sees nothing to take its place: "He was as he was, for some reason he never hoped to understand he had been cast to play out his life in hunger and alone. Oh, there was the perverts' underworld, he knew; one poor queen had given him a blowjob in the last row of a movie house one night in his sophomore year in prep school; boys he had known in adolescence had gone on to the orgiastic world of the unnatural. But that was furtive and filthy—he shrank from it at the same time that it slyly drew him. If he should give in, if he should ever join those hidden ranks—not hidden really, there were always plenty of people who could point them out—the penalties were too great" (109).

He flees Ohio and eventually ends up in New Orleans. There he lives a celibate life, seemingly ignorant of gay bars and incapable of feeling any kinship with "silly queens"; masturbation is "his only physical outlet" (232). One theme recurs in the chronicle of Warren's life: his distaste of "flissy types." He holds, "If you want to attract a guy who's gay, the first principle to keep in mind is that he likes men, not women. Why go around aping the very thing that's distasteful to him?" (256). Then during Mardi Gras he meets Mike Cowan, "a cleancut, well-spoken guy, patently of a background as privileged as his own, whose demeanor bore no trace of the soft or the effeminate—not even such hidden inclinations as Warren's did" (239). The two fall into lust and then into love. After only a day together, Warren accepts Mike's invitation to join him in Washington: "Why shouldn't it be possible? For God's sake, he pointed out to himself, you're a privileged character, a healthy sane American with every possible advantage of education and breeding. Why shouldn't you build a life for yourself that you can stomach?" (244).

But Mike's father is a judge, and most of his friends work for the State Department, having "to be really horrifying cautious about what they do and whom they see" (224). Mike accepts that, in order to be who he is, he must live in a "prison of discretion" (312). Warren pushes back, ignoring the realities of political changes and chaffing that "he was no more a free agent than he had been before. He was as shackled by Mike's fear of public disapproval as he had been by his parents' aspirations for him or his own surreptitious throttling of desire" (339). Following the curious zigzags that his psyche dictates, he decides that "the whole gay-marriage idea is shit" (341) and that he is tired of "imitating respectability, aping monogamy." On a trip together to New York, he splits with Mike after a quarrel whether to tour the Bird Circuit or not. Warren reasons, "If the very essence of you put aside any chance you had at a lasting happiness, you could have to the full whatever satisfaction your body with its incompleteness offered you" (343). So he embarks on a life of promiscuity. He feels some "self-disgust" when he is mugged yet again (416). But the pointlessness of his life is what truly troubles him: "He had to have point to his New York life or wither irretrievably into a mincing auntie of the antique shops and the ballet openings. He couldn't let that happen" (419).

Warren's solution takes him almost full circle: "Once, when he had broken away from Mike Cowan, he had vowed he would not let decorum shackle him. He had paid heavily for that vow, and assuming conformity like a uniform, he turned his back forever on the lawlessness of a homosexual's desperate existence" (430). Warren falls under the sway of a powerful right-wing editor of a national magazine and decides to work for him: "In the hunger that set his life off-balance there was as much need for identification as for sexual release, he knew. If he could not make a love relationship endure—such a relationship as he had had with Mike Cowan—perhaps he could find in [this editor] the lover who was not a lover, the *maître* who answered his need for identification with a man, even if there was involved no sexual link between them" (426). This means accepting most of the right-wing agenda, including its infatuation with Senator Joseph McCarthy, who briefly appears as a character. "He felt himself a part, at last, of the moving world" (431). His very success evokes a haunting sadness unlike that of other novels from this era. The author presents multiple attitudes about homosexuality during the period, including current psychological theory. And Warren and Mike are not the only gays the reader encounters, just the most prominent. Alexander Fedoroff (1927–1979) was born and died in New Orleans. He attended Loyola and Tulane. He served in the Army during World War II. He was also a playwright and worked in various capacities for Broadway. In his *Notebooks* (April 7, 1954) Tennessee Williams mentions a sexual encounter with him. Married, he had two sons.

Fedoroff, Alexander. *The Side of the Angels.* *New York: Obolensky, 1960. London: Barker, 1961.

78 Donald Windham: *The Hero Continues,* 1960; *Two People,* 1965.

An aging character is the focus of both novels. Denis Freeman, the hero who continues, is gay. Quite early, he says, "I knew I was being a whore when I moved into Rupert's" (11). He goes to the baths for "climax and exhaustion" (48). Throughout, he is always eying attractive males. We briefly meet a boy that he has spent the night with (161–62). While on a visit to a doctor, he thinks how "the puritan strain in his character, and more especially his belief that his life was limited and that in the limited time left it was necessary for him to control and conserve the greater part of his energy for work" has given way to the conviction that if "he could give in completely to lust he would know the pleasure of finding oblivion in others and his whole existence would become like those days after nights of debauchery when all his senses were tingling for contact and all the people he encountered were ready for love." Instead, he discovers, "His dependence upon his body for pleasure became repugnant," to the point that "he hated those to whom he made love" (158–60). But *Hero* is an example of a gay novel in which gayness is almost unimportant. A *roman à clef* based on Tennessee Williams's career, it is a study in the ways celebrity destroys, or at least perverts, creativity and interpersonal relationships. This spiritual loss is symbolically marked by Denis's physical losses: an eye (68), an arm (142), even sexual potency (184). Despite having all the resources of fiction to pull upon, Windham fails, however, to deliver a portrait of great interest. He dedicated the novel to Williams. The character Morgan is a self-portrait; Rupert is based on Carley Mills. The title comes from Rilke's first *Duino Elegy*; Hart Crane and García Lorca are also important.

Considered by many to be his best, Windham's next novel, *Two People*, tells the story of a spring and summer romance between a married American in Rome after his wife has returned to the U.S. and an Italian teenager half his age. The affair begins for Marcello as he is questioning whether he is capable of loving and then becomes a means to outwit his miserly father and gain money. For Forrest it expresses a part of his life he has closed off and at the same time allows him "to forget about himself and become a part of the convivial people around him" (16). The problem of communication worries him: "The trouble in understanding a language not your own is that you can never be sure that the syllables mean to you what they mean to the native who uses them" (89). Both men, but particularly Forrest, waver in sorting out what the relationship means personally. At one point, Forrest picks up a quite different sort of male, convincing himself "that to take him home was the natural way out of the predicament that he was in. If he could not rid himself in one way of the illusion that he was involved in something unique and unfathomable, then he would rid himself of it in another" (144). But the attempted cure does not work. Even as he comes to realize that he loves the boy, Forrest understands that he will return to his wife and Marcello will have an existence without him. Marcello makes some degree of peace with his domineering father. The two men part in the way of "friends and relatives," not lovers, their last words to each other the multi-meaning *arrivederci* (181). And yet the reader gains the impression that both men have surpassed their earlier personal limitations as a result of the experience.

Donald Windham (1920–2010) was born in Atlanta, Georgia. He moved with his lover Fred Melton (1918–1992) to New York in 1939. He met Williams, and the two collaborated on a play, *You Touched Me!* In 1943 Sandy Campbell (1922–1988) became his life partner. For two years he was editor of *Dance Index*, becoming friends with Lincoln Kirstein and his circle. His novel *Tanaquil*, 1972, is another *roman à clef*, this one based on George Platt Lyons. He also published a number of gay short stories. A 1987 memoir, *Lost Friendships*, recounts his friendships and quarrels with Williams and Capote. He died in New York.

Windham, Donald. *The Hero Continues*. *New York: Crowell, 1960. London: Hart-Davis, 1960.

———. *Two People*. New York: Coward-McCann, 1965. London: Joseph, 1966. *New York: Mondial, 2008.

79 Julian Green and Anne Green: *Each in His Darkness*, 1961.

Julian Green (generally given the French spelling Julien) has been virtually ignored as an American author. The reason is understandable: he was born and died in Paris and wrote in French. He was elected to the Académie Française in 1971, the first foreigner to be inducted. But he remained an American citizen his entire life; when President Pompidou offered him French citizenship, he declined. Julian Hartridge Green (1900–1998) was the son of Protestant American parents. While a teenager, he converted to Catholicism. Too young to serve in the military at the beginning of World War I, he volunteered for the American Red Cross, then enlisted in the French army in 1918. He enrolled in the University of Virginia, his first direct encounter with the South, from which both his parents came. There he fell in love with a fellow student. Upon his return to France, he began his writing career. He and the journalist Robert de Saint-Jean (1901–1987) became a couple. After the fall of France to Hitler, Green returned to the U.S.; in 1942, serving with the U.S. Office of War Information, he began broadcasting messages to France. He returned to France after the Armistice. In his old age he adopted the gay writer Éric Jourdan (Jean-Éric Green, 1938–), the author of *Les mauvais anges*. Other Green works were set in the American South, including his play *Sud*, 1953, which premiered in London in his own translation, *South*, in 1955. His sister Anne Green (1890–1978), a novelist in her own right, translated much of his work into English.

Chaque homme dans sa nuit was published in 1960 and then translated by his sister. Its settings seem made of cardboard and its characters are wooden. Yet it is a haunting novel, perhaps because of its oddity. It takes place in unnamed New York and a rural home seemingly in the South. The time is the 1950s but, though there are now blood tests and an easy cure for venereal diseases, television is nonexistent and a horse and cart is still used alongside cars. Its protagonist is the twenty-four-year-old woman-and-religion obsessed Wilfred Ingram. Its great conflicts are between the spirit and the flesh, faith and its loss—whether belief can "hold its ground before desire" (226). After the death of his uncle Horace, Wilfred is the sole Catholic in his family. He falls in love with his married cousin Phoebe Knight. But Wilfred's good looks entice men. His slightly older cousin Angus Howard feels a strong attraction to him, as does a mysterious Slav who calls himself simply Max. Wilfred's boss, Mr. Schoenhals, takes more than a fatherly interest in him. Even some of the customers in the men's clothing store where he works come on to him (154–56). All the men in the novel struggle with various kinds of darkness, but in a twist on the usual formula, here it is heterosexuals, not homosexuals, who end up dead. In fact, Tommy, a young man whom Wilfred has influenced to question his faith, ends up happily working in an art gallery for a "charming" dealer twice his age whom he has met—"By chance. In the street."—and with whom he makes "love every night" (296–97). Green shows that only the object of desire differs; the carnal drive is the same. Indeed, Wilfred wonders at one point about Angus: "What makes you so sure that he isn't better than you?" (140).

The womanizing uncle warns Wilfred away from Angus: "He's not the right kind for you to know" (36). Wilfred finds himself both drawn to and repelled by him, a gift of gloves taking on a disproportionate importance to both men. Whether to protect himself or to protect Wilfred, Angus decrees that they should not meet again. And then he reenters his life after the reading of their uncle's will. On this meeting the Protestant Angus asks him, "Does any possible salvation exist for people like me in your system?" When Wilfred answers, "God forgives everything," Angus retorts, "But how was it God's will that I should be made the way I am? What does it mean? I didn't ask for anything, I wasn't given a choice" (258–59). Later he writes a letter in which he says, "Wilfred, what my body wants is not what I want, for I too have known a life that was chaste and untroubled by desire, and in early youth had an inkling of what faith could be" (267). Angus enters into a sexual relationship with his mother's chauffeur, Ghéza, who worked for the dead uncle. Probably instrumental in directing Angus to a male whorehouse, the perfidious Ghéza sets him up for blackmail. In classical fashion, Angus worries, "If my mother hears of all this, it will kill her" (302). The reader is left unsure what Angus's future will bring.

Though not by his own will—"My profession has been imposed on me by circumstances"—Max apparently works as a prostitute (272). Wilfred meets him first when the Slav returns his missal, which he left behind in church. The two forge a strange bond forged of equal parts antipathy and need, with Max becoming Wilfred's dark angel. Their third meeting is at the docks, the notorious gay cruising area where Wilfred has wandered in seeming innocence and where Max is obviously on the prowl, as evidenced by his comment about a sailor "in a uniform designed, cut out and sewn by the devil." We are told, "Almost everything that Max said that night had a meaning that Wilfred preferred not to go into" (182). But he seeks him out as his confessor each time that he sins, for he recognizes on some level that the devilish Max is in love with Christ: "Wilfred thought of him with a compassion he had never felt for anyone, not even Angus" (325). He confesses to Max, "I've been wanting in love." The authorial voice comments, "He meant to say: in charity, but the word seemed weak. Charity was not what people wished for" (318–19). Max has said on that night at the docks, "You don't know yourself. That's where your real tragedy lies" (186). At a later meeting, he tells him, "Platonic love is what you want." When Wilfred scoffs, "Don't be absurd. What use would the body be?" Max answers, "For suffering" (268–69). It is inescapable that the dance to the death between Max and Wilfred, between homosexual desire and the Catholic faith, reflects the author's own personal demons.

Green, Julian. *Each in His Darkness*. Trans. Anne Green. New York: Pantheon, 1961. London: Heinemann, 1961. *Each Man in His Darkness*. London: Quartet, 1990.

80 Thomas Doremus: *Latitudes of Love*, 1961.

Hector, from the vantage point of adulthood, recalls a decisive period in his life, 1939–40, when he accompanied a dying man to Paris. In recreating the affected voice of his fifteen- or sixteen-year-old self (a kind of anti–Holden Caulfield rhetoric that Holden would have labeled immediately as phoney), style often obscures sense. Not for nothing does the narrator tell us, "it had been the year for *Sebastian Knight*, *Oblomov*, Denton Welch" (60). Basically, the novel's intertwined themes are the time-honored one of the son in search of the lost father (in this case, lost to death) and the relatively new one of a boy becoming aware of his homosexuality. The half-orphaned Hector, with his mother's reluctant permission, is informally adopted by a couple, Bill and Mary. They pull him out of his private school, which is not meeting his needs, and allow him to take a factory job for the experience of manual labor. The job does not last long: dying of cancer, Bill wants to make a last pilgrimage to his natal country, France. Hector is to accompany him. Mary begs the teenager to "have pity. Don't be afraid to show your heart! Give Bill your heart! Make him happy while there's time. He loves you" (49–50). As she says farewell onboard ship, she observes, "I have seen so many friendships like this work out. There is great, oh, tenderness, in a relationship between an older man and a young boy" (56). It is left to the reader to puzzle out her meaning: is she talking about emotional support, pushing him to share her husband's bed, or just what?

For Bill comes across ambiguously, our understanding of him not helped by being filtered through the memories of the adult and the hormones of the teenage boy. Is he saying what he seems to be saying when he tells Hector, "I love you powerfully and would go broke for you in a trice. You can have a piece of my meat anytime" (68)? Is Hector correct when he interprets their fights as a way "to make love, really, in the only way he knew how" (129)? Basically, Bill seems heterosexual. In fact, he has come to France in order to continue his affair with Hector's godmother more than to revisit childhood memories. Meanwhile, Hector is charting his own sexuality. Early on, he overhears Bill say, "I think he likes men" (34). Certainly it is mostly men that Hector notices. He is "enchanted" by a housebreaker who awakes him (15). At the factory he meets Pappas, a Greek who overwhelms his senses with "the perfection of his body, the mindlessness of his beauty" (26) and who, he consoles himself while in France, "is waiting for me back home" (115). He records in his shipboard diary, "A friendly steward named René made passes at me" (80). He notes Bill's nakedness on various occasions, but feels compelled to announce to the ship doctor, "I am not his boyfriend" (64). Later, however, he says of Bill, "Poor thing, I was making him become more of a pederast than he realized" (89). He begins to confound his father and Bill, remarking particularly on which side each wore his penis (111). In a pique Hector loses his heterosexual virginity to his godmother—and then proceeds accidentally to kill her in a car wreck. But he has already concluded: "I had turned queer, that's the truth" (113).

It is a fairly enjoyable read, one probably different for each reader, depending upon what is brought to it. The same year the author published another novel, *To Beaucock, With Love*, about a handyman, his eponymous psychiatrist, and a gay couple he works for. The sexuality all bubbles just at the surface without going anywhere. An earlier novel was *Flaw Dexter*, 1947. Thomas Edmund Doremus (1922–1962) was born in Columbus, Ohio. He worked for various New York magazines and newspapers, as well as for a U.S. Department of Immigration radio series and briefly for a Pittsfield (Mass.) newspaper. He died in Praia de Rocha, Portugal, of a cerebral hemorrhage.

Doremus, Thomas. *Latitudes of Love*. New York: Potter, 1961. *London: Deutsch, 1961.

81 Lou Rand (Lou Rand Hogan): *The Gay Detective*, 1961. William Gingerich: *The Gay American*, 1965.

Both these novels are genre firsts: the first gay private investigator, the first admirable secret agent (albeit one only temporarily tapped for that position). One could also argue that "Bay City," California, private investigator Frank Morley—"the gay detective"—is the first gay protagonist of heroic stature to appear. Who before him possesses such elan, such *savoir faire*, such honesty? He inherits the Morley detective agency and decides to try out the business. Frank is a protean figure. A former actor, he is also adept in sports, especially boxing. When he is called upon to engage in physical battle, he proves that he can more than hold his own. But when he applies for a gun permit, on being asked "what he needed a gun for, he just rolled his eyes, put his hand on his hip, tossed back his wavy hair and shrieked [...] that he'd have a helluva time beating off some attacker with a mascara brush" (10). He can camp with the best. He can also mimic the straight world: "his words were now clipped and sincere, and his tone distinguished by a dangerous steely quality." He is keenly aware that his inherent ability to change as the occasion demands provides him not just a general asset as an investigator in a town as gay as Bay City, but a resounding advantage over the local police and government agencies. As he says to a federal narcotics agent, "I understand [...] that you tried to work your way into a few places, but just didn't seem to fit. The point here seems to be that I look to be more the type, and can probably crash this outfit somewhere" (62). His ability to make "a flashing display of limp-wristed gesture" (57) and to fight with the most dangerous criminals is an irresistible combination that his straight sidekick, Tiger Olsen, attempts to emulate—until Frank puts him firmly in his place: "Just for the record, Mr. Olsen, let me do the camping in this act. I'll make with the gay talk. You just be big and beasty. Okay?" (131). Frank's unabashed affirmation of gay pride must have been a revelation at the time for readers starved for positive role models. Though he accepts from the start that homosexuals can also be villains, he gives readers glimpses of a gay-based political awareness just learning how to articulate its goals and purposes. His setting is largely the demimonde of a barely disguised San Francisco immediately after the McCarthy era. As he notes, "I seem to recall that several hundred federal government employees have been loudly bounced in Washington lately, and for just such little preccadillos" (60). His investigation takes him into after-hours nightclubs and gay baths. In two days' and a night's hard work, he cracks an intertwined case of murder, blackmail, and narcotic dealing that effectively dramatizes the way criminalizing human sexual drives invites organized crime to move in with increasingly disturbing consequences, including corruption of high government officials in addition to the horrible destruction of lives. Curiously, Tiger as well as other gays engage in sex, but Frank remains teasingly chaste throughout the case. It has been reprinted under its original title and as *Rough Trade*.

The Gay American, set in the same post–McCarthy Cold War period, has a necessarily more guarded hero coping with domestic suspicion within the diplomatic corps and counter-espionage in Eastern Europe. A minor official in the American consulate in Hamburg, Germany, Walter Gordon is under surveillance by a higher-up who has noted his penchant for visiting gay bars (though he apparently misses that Walter is sometimes accompanied by two friends also from the consulate, probably because both of them have wives). Walter, as narrator, is generally discreet, leaving the reader to divine his secrets largely from obviously inside knowledge of gay life in the city, his arch comments about men he encounters, and his taste in reading (largely Roger Peyrefitte, who was in the French diplomatic corps). On a personal (but not sexual) level, Walter came to know Franz Medam, gay, a former thriving dealer in fake antiques who sought sanctuary in the Eastern Bloc to avoid arrests for his activities and ended up working for the East Germany Ministry of Information. Franz finds life difficult: "The East Germans aren't at all sympathetic to his little weaknesses." He is willing to smuggle information to the Americans if he can receive "assurance that he can come back to Hamburg to live" (66–67). It turns out that Franz can potentially access quite important information: "The only possibility for our obtaining the entire documentation would be for him to somehow come into possession and then flee" (108). A rendezvous between him and Walter (now carrying a passport in the name William Galway) is set up for Belgrade. The documents are passed over (in a bottle of shaving lotion). Now the trick is to get Franz out, a dangerous task since the local authorities have become suspicious of their activities. Walter "borrows" a car, and they set off for the Austrian border. Even with their safety threatened, the irrepressible Franz picks up two young Yugoslavs: "The strain of life in East Germany and the sterilities of travel up to now had told on his temperament" (160). Ever circumspect Walter tells us only that one evening "we came within inches of arranging a first class all in orgy" (165). They make it across the border, only to wreck their car under a fuselage of bullets from the Yugoslav guards. But the information Franz got turns out to be useful indeed. Walter says, "I seemed to emerge from the fracasso as a sort of black sheep qualified hero who could neither be commended or cashiered" (184). He heads for safety in Spain.

Both novels are apparently the authors' only venture into fiction; both are fun reads. Lou Rand Hogan (1910–1976) was a San Francisco chef; under his birth name he published *The Gay Cookbook*, 1965, and wrote food columns for magazines. He served in the RCAF. Under the pseudonym "Toto le Grand," he published his memoirs, "The Golden Age of Queens," 1974, in the *Bay Area Reporter*. He died in Long Beach, California. William F. Gingerich (1919?–) was born in Okmulgee, Oklahoma. According to the dust jacket, he served in World War II, graduated from Georgetown University, and held a wide array of jobs.

Gingerich, William. *The Gay American: The Memoirs of a Reluctant Diplomat.* New York: Vantage, 1965.
Rand, Lou. *The Gay Detective.* Fresno, Calif.: Saber, 1961. *Ed. Susan Stryker and Martin Meeker. San Francisco: Cleis, 2003.

82   David Loovis: *The Last of The Southern Winds*, 1961. Susan Sontag: *The Benefactor*, 1963.

These two novels, neither of much consequence, share in common having a straight narrator who is profoundly influenced by a gay novelist he meets. In Loovis's novel, Carl Solon is an emissary sent by his uncle to Key West, Florida, to report back whether The Southern Winds, a hotel run by an old college buddy, is worth investing in. Carl has such an equipoised mentality as to render him ineffectual. Typical is his encounter with a sailor who propositions him and whom he turns down: "He also felt ... somewhat ... as if he had refused a request that he might very easily have granted" (226). His encounter with novelist Alan Houlton—whom he does not even realize is gay until their final evening in a bar together, when Alan comments on the available trade and picks up a sailor—provides him an epiphany: "Truly this business of self-discovery was a staggering thing, but Houlton had made it obvious that it was not so difficult an undertaking as to cause human strength to quake and fail. [...] It was one thing, Carl realized, to blithely and intellectually talk about attending to one's needs; it was quite another to risk the recognition, to seek the fulfillment, to live with oneself afterward" (286–87). Carl survives a tragicomic holocaust that brings the novel to its conclusion by finally taking control of his life. Tennessee Williams, incidentally, makes a cameo appearance under the name Emmette Colliers.

In this, her first novel, Sontag chose as protagonist a sixty-one-year-old Frenchman named Hippolyte, who recalls events of thirty years earlier. One of his friends was a writer, Jean-Jacques, who supplemented his income by petty thievery and hustling. Fascinated by his exploits, Hippolyte often shadowed him while he was cruising the streets and took to hanging around cafés which gays frequented and visiting *pissoirs* where they met up. Describing "the waiting, gossiping sisterhood of men" Hippolyte says, "They knew only two emotions, jealousy and love, and their talk, which was often spiteful, was only of beauty." At the other extreme, he avows that he "cannot think of a more perfect example of understanding without words" than that evinced by swiftly consummated sexual encounters at urinals and in "the back rows of cinemas." He professes to see "this world of illicit lust as a dream," while Jean-Jacques regards it "simply as theatre [...], a kind of playfulness with masks" which "induces a welcome detachment" from self (55–57). He also argues "that homosexuality was both guilt and humor, revolt and convention." The two men have "an impromptu sexual encounter" one evening that changes nothing (60). Actually, for all the talk and glimpses of action, sexuality remains almost an abstraction in the novel. The bulk of the work is taken up with Hippolyte's dreams and his interpretations of them. As when one is forced to listen to a friend's dream, one's eyes may glaze over.

Since Vidal, to whom he dedicated his first novel, and Williams served as literary mentors to David Loovis (1926–2008), the fact that he chose a straight protagonist for this, his second novel, may be more evidence of the pressures writers perceived publishers putting on them at the time. Loovis was born in New York and was a graduate of Colgate. He served in the Navy, then became a journalist, a textbook sales representative, and an advertising copywriter. In 1953 he worked as a waiter at Key West's Trade Winds Restaurant. He wrote two nonfiction works: *Gay Spirit*, 1975, and *Straight Answers about Homosexuality for Straight Readers*, 1977. He died in Hialeah, Florida. Susan Rosenblatt (1933–2004) was born and died in New York. After her widowed mother's remarriage while she was a child, Sontag took his surname. She graduated from the University of Chicago and Harvard. She was friends with Alfred Chester, who may have played some part, along with Genet and Artaud, in the creation of Jean-Jacques. Sontag was married and had a son; after their divorce she became a partner first with the playwright Maria Irene Fornés and later with the photographer Annie Leibovitz. An essayist, her "Notes on 'Camp,'" 1964, has garnered too much attention.

Loovis, David. *The Last of The Southern Winds.* New York: Scribner's, 1961.
Sontag, Susan. *The Benefactor.* *New York: Farrar, Straus & Giroux, 1963. London: Eyre & Spottiswoode, 1964.

83 Roger Davis: *Always Love a Stranger,* 1961. Charles Wright: *The Messenger,* 1963. Joe Leon Houston: *The Gay Flesh,* 1965. Alexander Goodman (George Haimsohn): *Handsome Is...,* 1966. Seth Young: *A Choice of Passions,* 1968.

In the 1960s bisexuality becomes trendy in American fiction. These five novels run the gamut in content and in worth. None of the characters in Davis's New York novel is appealing: neither Mark Reevey, the bisexual protagonist; Paul Delaney, the one gay; nor any of the several straights. Mark tries to maintain relations with both the older Paul and his latest pickup, Janet Morris, who is tired of a jealous husband and ready for a bout of adultery. Paul is growing equally tired of Mark, but blackmails him into continuing their relationship by promising him a parting gift of five thousand dollars when Paul is ready to give him up. Janet sums up Mark's failure: "You want me to wait until you get that money, and then and only then can we settle down together" (159). With this quarrel, the two part, but there has never been any indication that Mark has outgrown the crush he had on a fellow serviceman in the Navy and is ready to move into the straight world. Some interesting contrasts are made between straight and gay relationships; the constant quarrels between Janet and her husband, fueled by his possessiveness, have frayed their marriage bonds, but Paul argues that such quarrels can sustain a long-lasting gay relationship: "How do you think two men can go on living together? By perpetually fighting and arguing with each other, by stirring each other up constantly. God, how I love it when we fight and I get you up there in my bed at last." Paul has also said that what he loves about homosexuality is, "The camp of it, the perversity of it" (100–01). But most moments of introspection in the novel focus on the narrowly personal. The author's name is a pseudonym.

Houston's *Gay Flesh* (almost certainly the publisher's title) is set in and near Houston, Texas. It is a strange story. The twenty-three-year-old Carl Wolfe has accepted that he is gay since he was raped by a burly truck driver when he was a teenager. While in his favorite bar in the city, he meets Charles, "new to the gay life" (47), and the two fall in love. There is a narcissistic aspect to their mutual attraction: the two could easily pass for brothers. Their life is idyllic. Then they are busted in a bar raid conducted by sadistic policemen. Because of something the local preacher says, Carl's father forbids Charles to come to the house. As a result of Carl and the Reverend Hayes's confrontation, the mealy-mouthed minister broadcasts Carl's sexuality to his neighbors. (Carl tells him, "All the homosexuals I've ever known have more integrity than you do" [86].) Charles splits, and Carl faces the most intense loneliness he has ever experienced. He gets blindly drunk, and comes to in Janis Black's home. Carl is bewildered to realize that the two feel an attraction toward each other. Jan assures him that it does not matter to her he is gay: "To me what two people want in the realm of sex is normal for them. There's no right and wrong" (113). She also asserts that she has never had any lesbian instincts (which for some reason is important to Carl). The two get married. It quickly becomes apparent that Janis is cold and possessive. She aborts their child without consulting him. In a classic cliché, Carl makes it with a door-to-door insurance salesman: "It had been too long. Did I really think I could live without it forever?" (149). The affair improves the relationship between the husband and wife. Then, out of the blue, Charles calls up a mutual friend. Carl checks out all the possible haunts where he might find him. Discouraged, he returns home to find Charles having sex with Janis. He overhears enough to realize they were former lovers, that indeed Janis picked up Carl because she mistook him for Charles. Carl says: "I felt like a man watching a bad play" (157). To his credit, he heads for the gay bar to start anew. When the novel was released as a paperback in 1966, it was given an even worse title: *Desire in the Shadows.* The author's name is likewise a pseudonym.

In Goodman's short novel young Lilian Matthews meets the actor Tony Mason when he is in summer stock on Cape Cod, and they fall in love. They part, with Tony returning to Hollywood, but then she receives a telegram begging her to meet him at a New York apartment. Arriving, she discovers the body of an unknown man. For reasons she cannot explain, instead of reporting the murder to the police, she plays detective. She discovers that her boyfriend is really Tony Parmanelli, and she begins to suspect that he is gay. Asking one of her leads point blank, "Is Tony a homosexual?" he counters, "He's trade. A boy who might not really like men sexually, who could possibly enjoy the love of women, but who allows himself to be enjoyed by men" (35–36). In fact, Tony is virtually the captive of the sadistic Hollywood star Paul Mason. Then he meets Robbie Parks, who is serving as a temp bartender at one of Paul's parties. For Robbie, "in almost every way I'm normal and quite respectable—I just happen to like boys. And I'm not ashamed of it. I don't think homosexuality is a sickness, or even that it's an aberration," since for him, "Men have sex for pleasure. Some having it with women, some with men" (75). Having summoned up the courage to leave Paul, Tony searches Robbie out, and they flee to New York. For the first time with a man Tony has reciprocal sex. It is a test for him, and he concludes: "It's just not enough, not enough for me anyway." He decides he wants Lilian and "the chance of leading a regular, everyday life, of being a husband, having children" (89). Paul seeks revenge. He sends out his chauffeur, Helmut, a former Nazi whom he saved after Germany fell, but Helmut kills Robbie by mistake. His is the body Lilian discovers. The couple reunite on Fire Island and discuss marriage. Tony takes the position, "I could never let you marry me, Lilian, until I was worth marrying, until you could have some kind of respect for me. But first I have to learn to respect myself. Only then could I consider loving you, Lilian" (115). George Haimsohn (1926–2003) was born in St. Louis. He served in the Navy during World War II. After graduating from the University of California at Berkeley, in 1952 he moved to New York, where he lived the rest of his life. His play *Dames at Sea*, 1966, launched the career of Bernadette Peters. Working under the name Plato, he was a photographer of male nudes, much of his camera work appearing in the physique magazines controlled by Guild Press. Via this relationship he launched his career as a gay writer using the pen name Alexander Goodman. He died of a massive aneurysm.

In describing himself to an older lover, Holden Malloy, Mickey Bannon, the main character in Young's *Choice*, says near the end of the novel, "I look at myself as being sort of bisexual. I mean, maybe I'm, say, seventy-five per cent hetero and twenty-five per cent homo, or something like that. I like it with you. And I like it with girls too." When Holden, who runs a modeling agency, replies that he has known many young men who feel like Mickey, the teenager asks, "Did they stay AC-DC? I mean, for life?" Holden responds that he thinks not, "that, as they grow older most men find themselves compelled to—well, to decide, to cast their lot with one side or the other, to make ... a choice of passions" (144). Having made his choice by novel's end, Mickey thinks of the problems that aging gays suffer in a youth-adulated society and concludes: "I'd change if I could. I tried already. But this is the way I am. I'm as hooked as any mainlining addict is hooked. I tried the straight route but I fell off" (191). His journey to this point has been a winding one. It begins in Miami Beach, where he recognizes he is reacting differently from the other teenagers when they entice a homosexual to give them all a blowjob. He teams up with Don Stratton, an employee at a fitness center, who introduces Mickey to the money to be made from hustling. They tell each other they are straight: "What you and I do in bed is one thing. That fruity business is something else" (112). But sharing a bed in New York, Don comes increasingly closer to being honest. They break up when Mickey is invited for a screen test in Hollywood, only to spoil his chances by slugging the gay director. Meanwhile, Mickey has genuinely fallen in love with Holden's secretary. He marries her, but discovers that she is unaccountably terrified of sex. They struggle to preserve their marriage but finally give up. Mickey returns to Miami Beach and opens a gym. Don is already back, married, still cruising but "buying more often than he's selling" (190). It sounds like a sad novel, but it really is not. There are moments of low comedy, such as the time a client wants a group of hustlers to enact a naked corrida with his playing the part of the bull. And there are moments of high comedy, such as the director's explanation about why he was beat up badly enough to land in the hospital. The name is yet another pseudonym.

Charles Stevenson, the protagonist of Wright's autobiographical New York novel, stands apart from these four. Near the end he admits that, "to tell the truth, I'm bored with sex scenes" (207). Shortly afterwards, he records, "at twenty-nine, I am not expecting much from this world. Fitzgerald and his green light! I remember his rich, mad dream: 'Tomorrow we will run faster, stretch out our arms farther.' But where will this black boy run? To whom shall he stretch out his arms?" (209). His friend Nick introduces him to "the rich world of queerdom," but for him, "It was an experience, nothing more. And if I felt like it, I'd do it again" (23, 25). At another point he says, "I'm rather free sexually, but I'm a little sick of the queer scene. The queers are not really honest and their fear has nothing to do with it." In Charles's eyes, "The greatest problem of the American male is proving his masculinity" (128–29). He works as a messenger. On the side he hustles. He makes it with a woman while her husband watches. He is the play thing for rich women. He meets married men in the subway. "I've scored fairly easily with men and women, though the competition is great. You'd be surprised how my color helps business. Though I've missed out several times because, of course, I just wasn't dark enough" (102). But in the end it all seems meaningless: "There was horror in the knowledge that nothing was going to happen to me" (215–16). The messenger has no message for himself, and not much of one for readers. Charles Wright (1932–2008) was born in New Franklin, Missouri. He served in the Army during the Korean conflict and then moved to New York. He published two more books before succumbing to alcoholism, which ultimately killed him.

Davis, Roger. *Always Love a Stranger*. New York: Hillman, 1961.
Goodman, Alexander. *Handsome Is....* Washington, D.C.: Guild, 1966.
Houston, Joe Leon. *The Gay Flesh*. Los Angeles: Argyle, 1965.
Massengill, Reed. "Carnal Matters: The Alexander Goodman Story." *1960s Gay Pulp Fiction*. Ed. Drewey Wayne Gunn and Jaime Harper. Amherst: University of Massachusetts Press, 2013. 167–89.
Wright, Charles. *The Messenger*. *New York: Farrar, Straus, 1963. London: Souvenir, 1964.
Young, Seth. *A Choice of Passions*. New York: Paperback Library, 1968.

84 Vladimir Nabokov: *Pale Fire*, 1962.

The novel presents itself as a critical edition of *Pale Fire*, a poem in four cantos by John Francis Shade, with a foreword, commentary, and annotated index by Charles Kinbote. As one reads the notes, which reveal little about the poem and much about the commentator, one becomes aware that Charles is homosexual, ludicrous, probably insane, and unreliable. His gay side shows up at once. Throughout the foreword he alludes to a "rather wonderful boy," "radiant lads," and "charming identical twins," the latter of whom were involved in some undefined play on Ping-Pong tables in his basement, and "bad Bob," his "roomer," who betrayed his "trust" by entertaining a woman in Charles's absence and was consequently thrown out. Among glimpses that Charles shows of himself, he mentions his depiction in a students' skit "as a pompous woman hater with a German accent, constantly quoting Housman and nibbling raw carrots"; he describes a photograph of him wearing "a pair of lilac slacks" (449–53). The poem is filled with sly allusions to Nabokov's own career. The commentary is best described as hypertext, a maze of reflecting mirrors. One quickly discovers that Charles reads the poem as a sort of allegory, a reflection of his life as King Charles Xavier of Zembla, pursued by a hired assassin, Jakob Gradus, who accidentally kills Slade instead. This melodramatic plot becomes the basis of often absurd comedy.

Charles peppers the commentary with allusions to his affairs with boys from the time he was a boy himself to the present day in exile. Early on he was urged to "renounce sodomy" (514). But Charles remembers with pleasure his sexual experiments with his playmate Oleg, Duke of Rahl, whose "bold virilia contrasted harshly with his girlish grace" (525). He writes that after one period of play, when they were sent to wash up, their high spirits were soon replaced "by another sort of excitement. [...] Both were in a manly state and moaning like doves" (528). He remembers his problems with his newly wed queen, whose "anterior characters of her unfortunate sex kept fatally putting him off." He swore he would renounce "the practices of his youth; but everywhere along the road powerful temptations stood at attention. He succumbed to them from time to time, then every other day, then several times daily—especially during the robust regime of Harfar Baron of Shalksbore, a phenomenally endowed young brute." The queen catches him in a particularly wild scene and departs, "leaving him to amuse himself with a band of Eton-collared, sweet-voiced minions imported from England" (589). In the U.S. there are the series of students and, after he sends Bob packing, a gardener. The last, however, turns out of be "completely impotent which I found discouraging" (650).

How much of this approaches truth? Take one example where a series of shifts within a homoerotic description occur within a short space. In describing Gradus's pursuit of him Charles records how the assassin looked up Joseph Lavender, who collected *ombrioles* that "combined exquisite beauty with highly indecent subject matters" (580). There Gradus met Lavender's nephew Gordon, "a slender but strong-looking lad of fourteen or fifteen" who "had nothing on save a leopard-spotted loincloth." Gordon shows Gradus the garden. They visit the Grotto, where Gordon's night with a friend has left "a dark stain" on the collapsible mattress. After taking a sip from the spring he wipes his hands on "his black bathing trunks." They pass by an outdoor privy, and Gordon strikes "his flanks clothed in white tennis shorts." At the swimming pool he takes off "his Tarzan brief" and sprawls on the pool's edge naked. After Gradus leaves, he spies on the estate from a height, glimpsing "a pair of sandals on [the pool's] marble rim— all that remained of Narcissus" (582–84). Charles complains often of dark migraines. He notes that one of his colleagues has written that he "is known to have a deranged mind" (578).

Vladimir Vladimirovich Nabokov (1899–1977) was born in St. Petersburg, Russia. The family became European exiles in 1919. His gay brother, Sergei (1900–1945), settled in Paris, living for a time with the painter Pavel Tchelitchev and his lover, Allen Tanner, before falling in love with the Austrian Hermann Thieme; he died in a Nazi concentration camp. In 1940 Vladimir began his association with the U.S., becoming an American citizen in 1945. He taught at Cornell for many years. After the *succès de scandale* of *Lolita* and financial independence, he resigned in 1959 and moved to Switzerland. He was married and had a son. He died in Lausanne after suffering a fall and a series of illnesses. Grossman says Vladimir was homophobic but quotes his son's defense of his father: "He had a sense of justice, a homosexual brother, and not one but two homosexual uncles. [...] He had a number of homosexual friends. I also know he would have been less than happy had his son inherited those genes."

Grossman, Lev. "The Gay Nabokov." *Salon*, May 17, 2000. Online.
Nabokov, Vladimir. *Pale Fire*. New York: Putnam's, 1962. London: Weidenfeld & Nicolson, 1962. *Novels 1955–1962*. New York: Library of America, 1996. 427–667.

85 Paul Mandel: *Mainside*, 1962. Roderick Thorp: *The Detective*, 1966.

Mainside covers eight days on a Navy base outside Jacksonville, Florida, in 1956. Lt. Fletcher ("Fish") Howland is found dead of a gunshot wound, apparently a suicide. Lieutenant Sam Marks is assigned to investigate. Howland, it turns out, is a Jacksonville native. His father was a U.S. Senator who killed himself during the Depression. His mother still holds a high position in the community, enough so that she and her lawyer were earlier able not only to induce the Navy to hush up a homosexual scandal involving Howland and a civilian but to keep him in the service by evoking possible repercussions during the period when "the Navy had been having all kinds of loyalty board troubles" as a result of McCarthism (340). They now want the death to be ruled as a suicide "for unknown reasons." His commander urges Marks to arrive at such a conclusion but will not order him to do so. This comes after Marks discovers that a naval steward, Coley, not only witnessed Howland kill himself but knows, along with others, that Howland was "a queen" (207) and that his death was the direct result of a quarrel and subsequent breakup with Ensign Robert Wood. An interview with Wood confirms Coley's story.

Still trying to squelch a looming scandal, while maintaining the letter of Naval rules, authorities permit Woods—who identifies himself as AC-DC and holds that he "could have been straight for a while" if Howland had left him alone (230)—to resign with an honorable discharge without benefits. In a last-ditch effort to convince Marks not to tarnish Howland's reputation, his mother summons him for an interview. In a virtual monolog, two hours in length (taking up nearly a fifth of the 370 page novel), she details her son's sexual life from his first experiences with boys at a military school through the 1955 cover-up. She blames herself for causing or at least permitting him to become a homosexual; not once does she disclose that she accepted him—though she does admit that a French woman was right when she charged "that I was a no good mother and a no good person and that if I had any decency left I'd leave my poor son alone and let him lead his own life" (331). At the end of her summary, she asks Marks, "Is it really going to help the Navy or Fish or the world or you or anybody, or is it just going to be a chance to get even with a stupid bunch of scared men who didn't have the sense enough to leave you alone?" (349). But it is clear that it is her own reputation in the community that disturbs her the most.

There is still Coley. The question comes down

to whether he wants to testify about what he saw or not, realizing that the consequences may be unfavorable for him in the long run. Coley is African American. He lost his wife and unborn child when the white Officer of the Deck refused to grant him special liberty to take his hemorrhaging wife to the hospital. He is tired of being treated as if his existence does not matter. Marks is the first, he says, to show respect for him as a person. Marks is Jewish. Just before his interview with Mrs. Howland, a Marine chaplain, ironically named Goodman, pays him a visit. He admits that he would not have interfered had Marks been a gentile but he feels it his duty to admonish him that "a Jew must be careful about stirring up a scandal in his community" (283). Throughout, the novel makes clear that racial prejudice and anti-Semitism are akin. Nowhere does it equate homophobia explicitly to the same mentality. Indeed, at one point Marks hazards a guess to one reason Coley may want to testify: "Who knows, maybe he doesn't like the idea of fairy officers. I don't either" (255). The purpose of the novel is puzzling.

There are a number of similarities between Mandel's and Thorp's novels. *The Detective* is also a quite long (598 pages), quite busy novel. The present time is fall 1954, but much of the story takes place earlier. The suicide of a homosexual likewise sets its plot into motion. Colin MacIver has jumped to his death from the roof of a racetrack. His wife wants to know whether it was suicide or something else. She hires Joe Leland since her husband knew him; the two men briefly served in the same unit during World War II. Not until the very end of the novel do we learn, via a tape recording that MacIver has left in the care of his psychoanalyst, that there may have been another reason MacIver was very aware of Leland. While working for the police in March 1948 he had extracted a confession from Felix Tesla to the grisly murder of his roommate, Theodore Leikman. That confession landed the hapless drifter in the electric chair. But the actual murderer was the closeted MacIver. (The rambling confession also reveals another overly possessive mother.) As with *Mainside* the narrative interest centers on the straight protagonist's compassion warring with his strong moral sense. In this case, he must stand up to the analyst, who argues that no good can come of revealing the truth at this date. Political pressures also play their part in the narrative. Apparently the author is also trying to make some sort of parallel between Leikman's murder in the past and the kidnapping and rape of a seven-year-old girl in the present; otherwise, why so many mentions of the new case? But the novel's purpose is equally puzzling. Homosexuality actually plays such a small role in the development of the story that it is debatable whether one can even label it a gay novel. One is better off seeing the 1968 movie with Frank Sinatra. The scriptwriter Abby Mann, by the way, concocts a telling note for MacIver: "I was more ashamed of being a homosexual than a murderer."

Paul Mandel (1929–1965) was born in Long Branch, New Jersey, but grew up in New York. He graduated from Harvard, studied at the Law School there, and then joined the Navy. He joined the staff of *Life* magazine and accidently became something of a key figure in conspiracy theories about the Kennedy assassination. He was in on launching the London *Observer*. Married, he had three children. He died of cancer and is buried in Clinton, Connecticut. Roderick Mayne Thorp, Jr. (1936–1999), was born in New York. He attended CCNY and worked for his father's private detective agency, among other jobs. He was married and had two sons. He died in Oxnard, California, of a heart attack.

Mandel, Paul. *Mainside*. *New York: Random House, 1962. London: Joseph, 1963.
Thorp, Roderick. *The Detective*. *New York: Dial, 1966. London: Barker, 1967.

86   Thomas Baird: *The Old Masters*, 1963.

When aging New York art dealer Edward Maule offers a newly discovered Watteau for sale, he unwittingly creates a tangled set of often comical complications that nearly undermine his career and have all sorts of unexpected consequences, including one potential buyer toying with the idea of murder. What is most remarkable about the novel, from our viewpoint, is how little is made of the fact that Maule is gay. The others seem quite aware of his sexuality; one potential client in a pique calls him (inaccurately) a "pederast" (149). The Broadway actor Peter Dane is Maule's former lover and still "the emotional axis of Maule's life" (165–66). Maule paid for his drama school training. When the daughter of one of Maule's clients sees the two of them dining together, she describes Dane as "flaming" (47) but is clueless why Maule would be with him. But most of what slurs there are come from gays themselves as a form of self-deprecating humor. Maule's African American assistant, Thackeray, is Dane's current infatuation and Maule's professional protégé. At a party with gay theatrical folks, at which he is called "a real Peeping Uncle Tom" by one of the two hosts, "All three laughed, for here Thackeray was truly accepted as an equal, there being a community that quite transcended color" (72). Thackeray is on the make and willing to use Dane to help realize his dreams. But he saves Maule's reputation several times during the course of events: "Thackeray had a good instinct for what was important and what was not" (211), and Maule is more important than Dane. Thackeray's need to call his mother at least once each day serves more as a comical moment than Freudian insight. At the end Thackeray is posed to open his own gallery, his first show to be the work of an artist who dresses as Mimi when inspired to paint, as Thackeray has discovered through his "peeping" activities. Thomas P. Baird (1923–1990) wrote out of his knowledge of the art world. Born in Omaha, Nebraska, a graduate of Princeton, he taught art history there and at Trinity College in Hartford, Connecticut. He worked for the Frick Collection (which he speaks of admiringly in the novel), the National Gallery of Art, and Dumbarton Oaks. This was his second novel. Baird served in the Naval Reserve during World War II. He died of a heart attack.

Baird, Thomas. *The Old Masters.* *New York: Harcourt, Brace & World, 1963. London: Faber & Faber, 1964.

87 John Rechy: *City of Night*, 1963; *Numbers*, 1967.

Grove Press stirred up the publishing world by its series of successful lawsuits against censorship that permitted the first American publications of *Lady Chatterley's Lover* and *Tropic of Cancer*. But these were heterosexual novels. When Grove also released *Naked Lunch* and *City of Night*, it created a furor. Rechy's first novel is so tame by today's standards that it is difficult to remember the fervor with which it was denounced at the time. It was not so much that sex is the driving force for the plot as it was that its main character is a hustler who is unapologetic and unrepentant about his profession. Though readers had been taught not to confuse authors with first-person narrators, it seemed inescapable that the unnamed narrator was in some sense Rechy. *City* is an autobiographical novel. It is also a picaresque novel—a quest for meaning and for identity and to some extent for America. The outlaw hero explores the dark side of New York, Los Angeles, San Francisco, very briefly Chicago, and New Orleans with retreats to his hometown, El Paso. One wonders if critical discomfort also stemmed from the fact that, despite unorthodox orthography (no apostrophes), the novel was clearly literary in every sense of the word from its title's allusion to a largely ignored Victorian poet to the sense that here was a writer who probably knew Proust and Dostoevsky better than he knew Whitman and on whom Milton and Tennessee Williams had obviously had a major impact.

Sections of the novel started appearing in various little magazines as early as 1958. The finished novel is organized into four parts; each part consists of four short sections entitled "City of Night" and three much longer chapters named after a character the narrator encounters, for a total of twelve portraits and sixteen connecting vignettes. This structure gives the misleading appearance that the novel is a story cycle, but the "I" continues just as strong through each portrait, and the importance of the twelve is their impact upon this "I." Eleven of the portraits are of men: drag queens, other hustlers, and johns. Miss Destiny, with her unending search for a husband, seems to have had the greatest impact on the unnamed narrator; he keeps remembering her quest as he continues his own. But others are as memorable: Chuck, born in Georgia but in love with horses and the life of the cowboy; the beautiful Skipper, who was discovered by a photographer (i.e., Bob Mizer) and became for a while the favorite boy of a famous movie director (i.e., George Cukor); Lance, another would-be actor who tried sleeping his way to fame and failed. The painful portrait of Sylvia, the one woman of the twelve, stays in the mind. The owner of a New Orleans gay bar, she is trying to atone for the sin of having cast out her own son when he came out of the closet to her: "It's just—just not possible—to love too much. Too little—okay: The whole screwing world loves too little. But too much?" But she concludes that perhaps she had loved her son too much—"except when he needed me" (312–13). And now she wants to apologize.

The novel begins in childhood. A crucial moment arises when the otherwise loving mother informs her son that his beloved dog will not go to heaven because dogs "havent got souls" (11); the last words of the novel are, "It isnt fair! *Why cant dogs go to Heaven?*" (380). Throughout there seems to be some connection between *eros* and *thantos*. Early in his pilgrimage he senses "that this journey away from a remote childhood window was a kind of rebellion against an innocence which nothing in the world justified" (55). He is aware of his "narcissistic obsession with myself" (120) and the premium that he places on "Youth" (128). Like Chance Wayne in *Sweet Bird of Youth* he feels that the loss of youth is a kind of death. He wants to find "some undiscovered country within the heart itself" and accepts that to do so he must "drop my mask, to try, at least, to face myself at last" (340). In the last portrait, Jeremy tells him, "You want, very much, to be loved—but you dont want to love back, even if you have to force yourself not to" (346). Jeremy is the only man that the narrator kisses in the entire novel, even as he rejects the promise of love being offered (368). It is a sad novel. There are many insights, but the major epiphany the narrator longs for never occurs.

Though there is never any doubt about what sexual acts are being performed in *City of Night*, the descriptions are far from graphic. Illustrating how much American publishing changed in just four years, those in *Numbers*, though never pornographic, are explicit, enough so that the novel was not published in Britain. Here the main character has a name: Johnny Rio. Its similarity to the author's own, plus a photograph of Rechy in hustler stance on the dust jacket, reinforced the feeling that the narrative must be factual. In a bit of metafictional play that reinforces the confusion of author and protagonist, Johnny meets an old client who tells him, "You probably remember him— this young number that used to hang around the *bars* and *Pershing Square? Well!* He wrote a *book* about *Main* Street and *hustling* and Pershing *Square* and *queens*." The novel is shorter and more sharply focused than *City of Night*. The narrator leaves Laredo (i.e., El Paso) to return to Los Angeles. Johnny isn't sure why he has returned. "To prove to myself that I can still hustle? Once, it had been the most liberating of experiences" (25). He acknowledges his narcissism, his love of mirrors, his fear of losing his youth and thus his appeal. Cruising Griffith Park, he allots himself ten days to make thirty contacts according to certain arbitrary rules that he strictly adheres to. The final results are thirty-seven contacts, with twenty-one ejaculations. Two of the chapters describe barely disguised meetings with Christopher Isherwood, Don Bachardy, and Gavin Lambert. Isherwood was not amused by his appearance as Sebastian Michaels, a rather surprising stance given his own predilection for following the same method in his fiction. And his character is the one to issue the challenge that most troubles Johnny: that he goes for numbers because he is afraid of accepting one person only and "sharing mutually" with that one (236).

Juan Francisco Rechy (1931–) was born in El Paso with Spanish as his first language. He graduated from Texas Western and served in the Army in Germany. In New York he became a hustler, an occupation he pursued (sometimes with amusing results) even after he established himself as a successful author and university teacher. In 1999 he received the William Whitehead Lifetime Achievement Award. *This Day's Death*, 1969, is based in part on his arrest in Griffith Park in 1966. Another gay novel—perhaps his best—is *Rushes*, 1979. Important nonfiction includes his treatise *The Sexual Outlaw*, 1977; his collected essays, *Beneath the Skin*, 2004; and his autobiography, *About My Life and the Kept Woman*, 2008. His husband is the movie producer Michael Earl Snyder (1956?–).

Casillo, Charles. *Outlaw: John Rechy: The Lives and Careers of John Rechy*. Los Angeles: Advocate, 2002.
Rechy, John. *City of Night*. *New York: Grove, 1963. London: MacGibbon & Kee, 1964.
_____. *Numbers*. New York: Grove, 1967.

88 Burt Blechman: *Stations*, 1964.

Blechman's apocalyptical novel is probably too personal, too obscure in its symbolism, to satisfy most readers. It is a tour de force, set, for the major part, in New York's subway toilets, in which the gay protagonist, given only the number 901 for a name, reenacts the stations of the cross. As he cruises each one, he is pursued by a corrupt vice squad officer, known only as D during the pursuit though he is earlier introduced as Dominick Wright. Simultaneously, a character, known as Hero, embarks on a suicide bombing mission, conceived by Our Leader, that may end the world as we know it. (The film *Dr. Strangelove* and the novel appeared in the same year.) The novel flittingly critiques America's cold war mentality. Though neither is mentioned by name, the recent Cuban missile crisis and the escalating war in Vietnam clearly influenced the novel's direction.

It opens with "Fragment of a Manuscript," written by 901, describing the relocation of a colony of ants who are marching to their apparent doom. The first section of the novel is entitled "Dom," short for Dominick but with echoes of *doom*. The radio is carrying news on the war scare, the latest crisis. Dom is planning to put down the family dog. Playing out much in the manner of a blue collar sitcom, wedding plans are underway for a mismatched couple—his daughter, high school graduate Tina Wright, and university student Al Rosso, majoring in physiology—forced into marriage by an unplanned pregnancy. Only Dom seems thrilled by the event, wanting to turn it into a lavish affair. He is restrained mostly by fear that "them reform guys" might find it suspicious if he expends too much money (19). For it turns out that, despite appearances, Dom is quite well off, the results primarily of his shaking down people engaged in the sex industry whom he encounters as a member of the city's vice squad. The section ends with his setting out on his beat of the subway system to fulfill his quota of arrests: "The subway johns will be full of them. Fairies, freaks, hustlers." And so, as "he descends the stairs, Dom enters the *Via Dolorosa*," the street that Jesus walked on the way to his crucifixion (38–39).

The second section of the novel, entitled "901," alternates two sets of chapters. A set of ten, named after sections of the Hebrew Bible (Genesis, Exodus, and on to Apocrypha), recalls the life of the main character from childhood on, mixed with references to the present time. Since 901 is a Christ figure, his mother is called Madonna; his father is just Pop. We learn that 901 dropped out of St. Valentine's College and became a beach boy, using his body to make a little money, before returning to the city and becoming a full-time hustler. He recollects cruising the streets and parks, going after chicken, being arrested but buying off the judge. He suffers "the Sin of Originality, O frightful Original Sin," "the Sin of Being," and "the sin of Desire" (86); he feels godforsaken and desperate: "the need to love; the need to hate; the need to spawn; the need to move on, to rush past the turnstile cross; the need to do it again and again and again till you'd faint with exhaustion, the need, that need, that terrible need to do the stations" (95). The exact significance of the number 901 is never provided: we are told that it represents "a hunched-up nine laboriously peeping through a zero [glory?] hole, your phallus at a full attention."

A set of fourteen chapters reenacts Christ's passion. Undertaking "this the last long journey" in search of "what he hungers and thirsts for: an incredible, a divine, an eye-filling miracle" (46–47), more interested in spying on than actually engaging in sex, he visits eleven subway stations (crossing Grand Central four times), each corresponding to the appropriate station of the cross. Their lavatories become chapels, the urinals and toilets transform into altars, and the glory holes permit peeps at angelic couplings. The layout of the stations themselves forms a cross reproduced at the head of each of the fourteen chapters. The protagonist, "condemned to embark on your dark journey" (43), begins on Line 7 at toilet-less Vernon-Jackson, then progresses across town to Grand Central and on to Times Square. He returns by shuttle to Grand Central, then takes Line 6 uptown to 68th Street. Returning once again to Grand Central, he proceeds downtown all the way to Brooklyn Bridge, before turning back one last time to Grand Central. At each stop he parodicly reenacts that station. For example, leaving the Times Square toilet (Station 3: Jesus falls the first time) he literally tumbles. At the 68th Street toilet (Station 5: Simon helps Jesus to carry the cross) he drops the crucifix that he carries in his pocket, and a man picks it up and runs. In the Lafayette toilet (Station 12: Jesus dies on the cross) he tries but cannot achieve an erection.

All the while, our Hero, an Air Force pilot, is readying himself to carrying out Our Leader's command. Our Leader too is playing out his parody of Holy Week. He has "partaken of His last supper." Now he meets with his Cabinet Disciples. After invoking "the name of the Father, George, and the Son, Your Divine Leader," he asks that "that relic, now known only in laxative advertisements as The Constitution, be laid to rest in the Holy Grail" (45). In Orwellian fashion, he transforms language: it will be a war for peace for trouble requires firmness. He is fully supported by "the Veteran Legion whose motto, Krist, Kuntry and Kunt, is emblazoned on every plowshare" and who are ready for "the holy holocaust" (90). And he places his hand firmly "on the stick now, jacking off as the cabinet leers" (102), waiting impatiently "to come!" The Hero is off on his mission, maneuvering his airplane like a "noble peter" (109).

D meanwhile pursues his prey. He first crosses 901's path at Grand Central and then shows up at almost every station after that, as if he is following 901. At the 14th Street Station, 901 is enjoying watching a "pair of seraphim." Cherub enters, and he and Angel make contact but have to readjust themselves rapidly when D rushes in, catching them innocently "at their stanchions making Holy Water" (124). Ironically, at the Astor Place station, another Angel and Cherub catch 901 peering through the glory hole as they are about to become "partakers of His Divinity" in a "sacred communion"—Angel preparing to drink "the nourishing Sap of the Vine"—and mistake him for a policeman. Instead of retreating, they attack (130). He is assaulted again at the Brooklyn Bridge station by a seraph he cruises. Back at Grand Central, a third time he is betrayed, by another Angel and a perfumed Cherub, who point him out to the relentless D, just as Hero drops the death-delivering bomb. As everything closes in on him, 901 exclaims "in a voice filled with obscenity and obsession: 'Jesus! Jesus! Jesus! Save me!' as illusion plunges to despair" (138).

Burton M. Blechman (1927–1998) was born in New York. He graduated from the University of Vermont and Columbia. The author of five novels, his first was adapted to the stage by Lillian Hellman. He also worked as a librarian at the NYU Medical School. He was an avid collector of Palestinian Jewish silvercraft. His partner was John Marsh. He died in Providence, Rhode Island, of pancreatic cancer.

Blechman, Burt. *Stations.* *New York: Random House, 1964. London: Owen, 1966.

89 Hubert Selby, Jr.: *Last Exit to Brooklyn*, 1964.

One could protest the novel's depiction of homosexuals, were its portrayal of heterosexuals not so much more vicious, in particular the gang rape of a young female prostitute. The contents are repugnant; the writing is powerful (and eccentrically punctuated). A story cycle set in a lower class section of Brooklyn near the Army base, two of the six stories feature gays. "The Queen Is Dead," the first of the stories to be written, describes George Hanson's fixation on a petty criminal named Vincent. A "hip queer" who takes refuge in his Georgette persona, he "took a pride in being a homosexual by feeling intellectually and esthetically superior to those (especially women) who werent gay (look at all the great artists who were fairies!); and with the wearing of womens panties, lipstick, eye makeup [...], long marcelled hair, manicured and polished fingernails, the wearing of womens clothes complete with padded bra, high heels and wig [...]; and the occasional wearing of a menstrual napkin" (23). This pride does not prevent him from abasing herself before Vinnie and his friends, not even complaining when Vinnie and Harry try to frighten him by repeatedly throwing a penknife at him, stabbing him in the leg. Most of the story details a drug and alcohol-fueled party given by guys in drag, attended by Vinnie, Harry, and two other friends. It climaxes with a debauch. Vinnie forces Georgette to service him orally right after he returns from the bedroom where he has had another queen anally. The self-deluded Georgette refuses to accept the evidence of his senses, insisting that Vinnie could not have betrayed him with another: "Vinnie loves me. He loves me. It. Wasn/t. Shit" (79).

Equally self-deluded is the main character in the second, much longer story, "Strike" (which provided the backbone of the 1989 film adaptation). It records the hubris and downfall of Harry Black (seemingly a different Harry from the first one). An incompetent worker who has kept his job only because he is an avid shop steward for his union, he consistently aggrandizes his importance, even more so when a strike is called. He cannot stand sexual relations with his wife. Closeted even to himself, he cannot understand the stirrings he feels when he is strung along by Ginger, one of Georgette's friends whom Vinnie introduces him to. Ginger mentions the existence of Mary's, a drag bar that Harry decides to visit. There he meets Alberta; back in his apartment he has his first sexual experience with another man. Harry, of course, plays "the male." For the first time, "Harry was happy" (196). By now he is padding his expense account as a matter of course, using the money to treat his friends. Often drunk, he becomes a regular at the bar, and "most of the fairies he met liked him" even as they are bored by his constant bragging. Still he leaves them a little uneasy: "There was some little something that they couldnt sense, that they were uncertain about, that eventually made them nervous" (202–03). At a drag ball he hooks up with Regina, and they get along well. But the strike ends, and with it his access to easy money. When he breaks the news to Regina that he can no longer afford the pleasures they have enjoyed, Regina instantly drops him to move on to richer pluckings. Harry beats up his wife. He feels lost. Incomprehensibly, he assaults a ten-year-old and tries to suck him off. The boy breaks and runs for help; Harry's former friends set on Harry, maiming him, perhaps even killing him.

Hubert Selby, Jr. (1928–2004), was born in New York. He dropped out of high school to join the merchant marines. He was not yet twenty when he was diagnosed with advanced tuberculosis. Complications from an experimental treatment and resultant surgery led to drug problems. He alternated between homes in New York and Los Angeles, 1967–85, before settling in L.A. He taught creative writing at the University of Southern California and had a cameo role as a taxi driver in the film adaption of the novel. Married three times, he had four children. He was the subject of the documentary, *Hubert Selby Jr: It/ll Be Better Tomorrow*, 2005.

Selby, Hubert, Jr. *Last Exit to Brooklyn.* *New York: Grove, 1964. London: Calder & Boyars, 1966 (banned until 1968).

90   Edwin Fey: *Summer in Sodom*, 1964.

The novel is a coming out story and a budding gay romance. Ted Randall's boss gives the eighteen-year-old two weeks off his Buffalo, New York, job to recover from his mother's death. He heads to "Silver Beach" on Lake Eire, where they vacationed the previous summer and where Ted had an inconclusive relationship with the owner's daughter, Eileen. On the bus he meets the older and experienced Jerry Sherman. Ted feels a tingle that he does not understand; Jerry falls in love. Trying to size Ted up, Jerry drops all kinds of innuendos. He is forced to concede that the lad is extraordinarily innocent, but he senses that Ted has not understood his true sexuality. Unfortunately for Ted, Jerry has scruples: "I can't start someone into this life even though I think he has all the tendencies toward it. This way of life is all right for me and for a lot of other people, but society looks down on it … condemns it. I just can't do it to you … at least not until you're sure what you are and what you want to be" (85). Equally unfortunate for Ted, Ian Raymond, a decorator staying at the same house, has no such scruples. He introduces Ted to such great sex that the author moves into cosmological metaphors to describe the effect. But Ian also is in debt to a gangster who is blackmailing him. And when Ian discovers that Ted has inherited property worth a good sum of money, he thinks he has a way out. The results are some very incriminating photographs of the two in bed, all showing Ted's face very clearly while Ian's is shadowed. The cost of having the prints and the negatives destroyed is the deed to the property. The cost of the prints getting out is much higher: "'You'll lose your job to start with,' Ian said, 'and you won't be able to get another one that's decent. You won't be able to work for any government office because you couldn't stand a security check. You'll be blackballed from teaching school or working in a bank. You won't even be able to get in the service. In fact, you'll be lucky if you don't end up in prison. Homosexuality is a criminal offense, you know'" (103).

Jerry is willing to fight for Ted. He calls upon the gay network in town to get crucial information about the gangster's operations, including the likely site for developing and storing the incriminating photographs. He destroys them all and arrives in the nick of time to confront Ian and the gangster. The resulting fight culminates in the gangster's death, a disfiguring facial scar for Ian, and a superficial cut on Jerry's arm. Of course, Ted dresses it. And finally they go to bed, with more cosmological fireworks. By now, Ted has also lost his heterosexual virginity with Eileen, so he has something to compare emotionally. The next day Jerry counsels him: "you can only go two ways, Ted. If you chose [sic] my life, you belong to a different society that has entirely different values for its own members, and you live your real life in that society. If you decide against it, it's best to get all the way out. You'll never be happy living just on the fringe, never really accepted by this society, afraid all the time of being found out by the other world. There's a lot of overlapping between the two, of course. There has to be. But you have to figure out which world is the real one for you." Ted listens. He refuses to commit "until he was sure beyond a shadow of a doubt" (152). But on the bus back to Buffalo, he sees Eileen's "figure retreating from him," while he searches for Jerry's face as he passes his house (155). The author's name is a pseudonym.

Fey, Edwin. *Summer in Sodom.* Los Angeles: Argyle, 1964.

91 William Goldman: *Boys and Girls Together*, 1964.

Richard Andersen (28) quotes Goldman about the strong male bonding that appears in much of his work: "What I would like to think is not that I'm a closet queen, but that it has to do with searching for someone of your own sex who will protect you. I am aware of the fact that what I tend to write best are male-to-male relationships, but the only time I've dealt remotely specifically with homosexuality was in *Boys and Girls Together*, and that very gingerly treated." Any number of adverbs more appropriate than *gingerly* come to mind. The novel is brash and clever and dispiriting. All five of the "boys and girls" who come together to put on a play at the end of this sprawling and often clichéd work are in some way damaged. Two of them are gay: Aaron Firestorm and Branch Scudder. Aaron's statement applies to both: "It's really crazy, me being homosexual, because I hate it. I hate it so much. The whole dirty life. Everything. It's just so degrading. It humiliates you so. I hate the life but I lead it. And that's crazy. And I hate them too. All of them. The gay boys that swish; the gray boys too. That's my word. I made it up. The gray boys, the shadowy ones, the ones you can't tell by looking at" (495). Both have nonmaternal mothers. Branch's smothers him to the point of nonsexual incest. Aaron's has no feelings for him at all. Presumably as a result, Branch is a whiny masochist; Aaron is a witty destructor of others and of himself. Both make the Boys in the Band look almost adjusted.

The first time Aaron is with a woman, the only way he can perform is by imagining that he is with his best male friend. He reacts by pulling within himself. But drafted into the Army, he is at once singled out by Sergeant Philip Terry. They become sexual partners, sneaking off to sleazy motels, until Branch shows up in the unit. He has money to lavish on Aaron, and he loves being abused. Terry's days are finished; at least, until Branch's mother pulls strings and obtains a discharge for her son. Back home, Branch is terrified that she will discover the truth about his sexuality, but that does not stop him from cruising. After being almost entrapped by a vice officer, he manipulates her into letting him go to New York, telling her he wants to become a play producer. Meanwhile, Aaron returns to Terry. Discharged "under unusual but 'honorable' (the Army's word) circumstances" (424), he also moves to New York. Now he finds he can recognize other gays. He makes mistakes: he picks up a "jazz dancer from Harlem" who mugs him (483). He sees Branch and faces up to the fact that "when someone offers me something, I take it. I let them use me when I'm really using them, because, see, I have the seeds of the whore in me" (499). He decides to seek psychoanalysis. The clinic turns him down (they are looking for manic-depressives this year instead of homosexuals), but the analyst points out to Aaron, "you're only trying to destroy yourself" (500). He and Branch start up their S/M relationship again.

Branch convinces Aaron to write a play for him to produce. Aaron accepts the challenge. But, as always, his glib tongue hurts him as much as it helps him when it comes to finding backers and then actors. He is also incapable of self-criticism. He has no idea that his play is "wretched" (639); Branch sees how bad it is but cannot bear to tell him the truth. When a man who has been haunting his dreams appears in the flesh, however, he talks Aaron into a major rewrite that will permit casting the young adonis, Rudy Miller. When Aaron predictably reacts to the possibility of Rudy usurping his place in Branch's affections, Branch finally gains courage to throw him out of his apartment. Aaron predictably takes revenge by faking a letter to Branch's mother in which he drops the term "unnatural" as many times as possible. When she turns up to save her son, Branch again surprises by standing up to her. But in the final fiasco, only one of the five, the straight director, gains as a result of the obstacles they face, many of them thrown up by Aaron. Rudy kills himself (his abusive parents are the cause, in this case). Branch's mother recaptures him. And Aaron ends up the kept boy of a sadistic writer who intends to humiliate him until he tires of him. The novel's concluding word is "agony" (751).

William Goldman (1931–) was born in Chicago, younger brother of the playwright James Goldman (*The Lion in Winter*). He has degrees from Oberlin and Columbia. He served in the Army. His first two novels, *The Temple of Gold*, 1957, and *Your Turn to Curtsy, My Turn to Bow*, 1958, have interest for gay readers. He went from novels to plays (he and his brother were friends of

John Kander, with whom they wrote *A Family Affair*) to film scripts, winning Oscars for *Butch Cassidy and the Sundance Kid* and *All the President's Men*. He was married and has two daughters.

Andersen, Richard. *William Goldman.* Boston: Twayne, 1979.
Goldman, William. *Boys and Girls Together.* New York: Atheneum, 1964. London: Michael Joseph, 1965. *New York: Balantine, 2001.

92   R. V. Cassill: *The President*, 1964.

The president is the head of Wellford College in "Buchanan," Illinois. He is gay—though that is something the reader does not learn until late in the novel. He is not the protagonist, however. That is straight Royce Morgan, who turns the job down upon returning from serving in World War II and becomes the dean of studies instead. Preferring order over justice, Morgan is slow to catch on what is happening over the period of more than ten years that the novel covers, but at a pivotal moment he must face the question: "how much of his world had been betrayed with him, through his tolerance?" (203). Somewhere in his thirties, President Winfred Mooney comes to the college from Madison Avenue. His appearance, especially his "pure white hair" ("I'll bet he bleached it for the job"), is remarked upon immediately: "He was simply too perfect—too perfectly the physical stereotype of a college president" (47–48). He begins shaking up the institution in various ways both positive and negative: getting rid of deadwood; seizing on the opportunity to move the school into the national spotlight by cultivating an athletic star, Tommy Barker, and recruiting a football team to support him; inaugurating programs to provide professional training for students, while at the same time augmenting the arts program. He ensures his popularity with students by making himself available to them. He announces democratically, "I'm a disciple of Whitman and the Greeks." He expands on his statement: "I believe in the swarming multitudes within the mind of each person" (158). But it comes out that he is also a discipline of Whitman and the Greeks sexually.

The stereotypical head librarian launches the charges first, accusing Mooney of "entering homosexual relationships with Billy Cox, Lon C. Breckenridge, and F. Milton Santiana (the latter two interior decorators who had refurbished the president's mansion, the former of unknown employment)" (137). But since she has earlier accused young Tommy of trying to rape her, Dean Morgan does not take her allegations seriously. (Her successor as librarian, George Clackfart, whom she also accuses of being "a deviant," does find it expedient to take a position in a Florida university; he is replaced by a married man with five children.) Mooney's dream begins to unravel when Tommy admits to accepting a bribe to throw the final, all-important football match with NYU. Over the years the rumors grow, and finally Morgan must face that he has "'always known' that Mooney was intolerable as president, known that Mooney was homosexual and known the risks that went with such a case" (202). He begins probing and discovers that "a local man named Billy Cox had committed suicide by jumping from a viaduct in front of a train from Chicago. From that instant he knew something that in this world could never be reduced to order" (205). He finds that Mooney met Billy in a lunch wagon and had cultivated the young poet, discharged from the Army probably on some psychiatrist's report. They took a trip to Chicago together, and Billy fell in love. He killed himself after a futile visit with Mooney. Morgan pays a call upon Mooney in high dudgeon. Already one step ahead, Mooney has decided to take a wife as cover and has chosen Morgan's sad, alcoholic former girlfriend. He tries to stop the wedding and messes up once again.

It is left to Morgan's son's puritanical girlfriend to bring Mooney down. The son is indifferent to Mooney's sexuality, but the girl becomes an avenging fury when she discovers him embracing another male at a party. She hastens to Tommy Barker, who rides in to expose his former benefactor and catches the two men "if not actually in *flagrante* then merely fallen back from it into sated dreams" (294). In the ensuing confusion, Mooney decamps to Greenwich Village, where he joins his partner in a shared apartment on Bleecker Street. Mrs. Mooney kills herself. Morgan becomes the new president. As far as the reader can tell, he is still as ineffectual. The sum total of his knowledge seems to be that "Wellford's palmy days came right out of a dung heap of cupidity, hypocrisy, money perversion, perversion of ideals, and (somewhere along the crazy line) simple old sex perversion" (280). From our present perspective it is also clear that Wellford College is symptomatic of that period in American higher education when it was in the act of irreversibly metamorphosing from institutions promoting the liberal arts to ones emphasizing professional training with corporations supporting the costs; it also shows the growing importance of athletics as a recruitment tool for students and funds. Exactly why the mastermind behind this change should be a homosexual of dubious morals is left to the reader to ponder, along withe the question of the author's attitude towards homosexuality.

Ronald Verlin Cassill (1919–2002) was born in Cedar Falls, Iowa. He graduated from the University of Iowa. During World War II he served in the Army. He was a teacher and editor, professor emeritus of Brown University. Married twice, he had three children. He died in Providence, Rhode Island.

Cassill, R. V. *The President*. New York: Simon & Schuster, 1964.

93 K. B. Raul: *Naked to the Night*, 1964; *A Hidden Hunger*, 1968.

In *Naked* nineteen-year-old Rick Talbot, fed up with his weak mother and abusive stepfather and enamored of his own body, leaves his small town in Iowa for New York with dreams of becoming an actor. On the bus he meets Jake and rebuffs his advances. His money runs out and he applies for a job as an usher in a movie theater, to be raped by the manager. Running into Jake again, he accepts his offer to teach him the ins and outs of hustling. When he finds out Jake has been using the money he is making to buy drugs, he moves in with Andy, who runs a clothing store catering to gays. Then Bruce enters his life with tales about a party at which the biggest gay theater and movie directors and producers will show. When he realizes he has once again been gulled, Rick decides to return to Andy, to find that he has killed himself. Completely broke, he makes a porn movie. Then he hooks up with another guy who has Hollywood dreams; they start out in a stolen car. Fearful, Rick ditches him and hitchhikes the rest of the way, having lots of sex with each driver. Arriving in Los Angeles, he is gulled once more: "Dazed, tired, and gnawed at by futility, he began to walk the streets like a lost child, doomed to walk forever naked to the night" (82). Rick now meets Turk, a Santa Monica music store employee, who agrees to subsidize him while he bulks up his body at the gym. There he meets Richard Golden, who enlists him in his callboy service. Closeted movie actor Tom Shane takes him on. Rick simply abandons Turk, not knowing that he has been killed as the result of a bizarre joke. Rick is cast in a movie that becomes a teenage hit and asserts his independence. Now he seduces a younger man at the gym, but Dave turns out to be jealous, possessive, and vindictive. When he catches Rick having sex with a bellhop, he threatens to expose him to his fans. They fight, and Rick is killed with a handy candlestick. Since this is still the early 1960s the language is tame. The novel was revised in 1986 with explicit descriptions of all sexual acts and supplied a happy ending in which Turk is not killed and he and Rick get back together, presumably to live happy forever after.

Hunger is, by spurts, more interesting. In Part I Allen Strider, né Fraticelli, becomes an important New York theater director, marries Julie Taylor, and makes her a star. They have a son, Conrad Strider. The marriage falters, and Allen begins to lose his touch. Fourteen years pass before the beginning of Part II. Now enrolled in a private school he hates, Conrad makes a pass at his roommate and is denounced as a queer. Allen attempts a comeback with a new play and a male ingénue, David. Julie discovers the two men in bed. On his way to see Conrad, Allen is killed in a car wreck. Convinced that he has actually committed suicide and thus ruined his chances to become a star, out of revenge David decides to seduce Conrad. Matters don't go as planned when he is raped by four men and becomes a drowning victim. Julie remarries, and Conrad is packed off to a new school. Four years later, in Part III, he is enrolled in Gratwick College, where the closeted professor Tom Chadwick teaches. He falls for Conrad. Conrad is besotted by a hustler, Tony, who uses him for his own gain, among other things coaxing him into becoming a nude model and making a porn movie. Hooking him up with a sadist frays the relationship to the breaking point. Julie commits suicide. Tony is struck by an automobile and killed. Tom claims Conrad. There are a number of interesting portraits scattered across the novel: the owner of a callboy service, the manager of an apartment complex, a lesbian streetwalker, other college students. The author's name in the Catalogue of Copyright Entries is given as K. B. Rao. A web search of that name elicits a number of interesting possibilities.

Raul, K. B. *A Hidden Hunger*. New York: Paperback Library, 1968.
———. *Naked to the Night*. New York: Paperback Library, 1964.

94   R. McCoy: *Entrapment*, 1965.

A contemporary blurb writer might have written something along the line, "Two men locked in a duel till death—and the woman caught between them." Twenty-eight-year-old California police officer Jimmy Rendon set the plot in motion prior to the opening of the novel. He arrested his old classmate and possible love interest, Rose Ramirez, as a prostitute, a profession she moved into when she was desperate for money. Thereafter, she fell deeper and deeper into hopelessness. Her younger brother, Vince, an unknown to Jimmy, seeks revenge. Jimmy's virginal fiancée, Sylvia Weaver, meets Vince when he applies at the unemployment agency where she works. She immediately feels a spark that she has never felt with Jimmy. The two men are polar opposites: "Jimmy's cold blondness opposed to Vince's passionate darkness" (146–47). Jimmy's piercing blue eyes stare through a person while Vince's dark brooding eyes watch. Jimmy is wary of women; Vince feels at ease with them. Jimmy fears all sex; Vince accepts the body's demands easily. He has worked within the sex trade without hang-ups, ready to bed both men and women. Though it is never made explicit, it is clear that Jimmy is a repressed homosexual: a classic case of a self-hater taking out his feelings on those he identifies with. He is proud of his high arrest record, but an appointment to the vice squad dooms him. He embraces his assignment to patrol a public park frequented by gays so enthusiastically that some officers wonder if "he likes that park detail a little too much" (125). When one of the arrested men claims entrapment, the crack in Jimmy's psyche widens. His fellow cops become concerned. They initially attribute his meltdown to Sylvia's having broken off their engagement. His commanding officer instructs him to take some of his earned time off. But Jimmy cannot let go of his obsession and continues to work undercover.

Returning to a bar where he last encountered Rose, he becomes drunk, vulnerable when Vince appears and invites him to a party hosted by a sexually voracious woman who loves to have threeways with gay men. Jimmy and Vince strip naked, making Jimmy keenly aware of Vince's "superior sex." Just as Vince prepares to enact his revenge and destroy Jimmy's self-image once and for all, "all at once he knew pity, overwhelming pity at his sister's ruin and Jimmy's self-deceiving, aloof and cold existence," and he realizes, "Revenge left nothing but a hollow void." Jimmy reacts: "he saw with fury that [...] his guilt was not to be assuaged" (151–52). He takes refuge in acting like a cop, proclaiming that everyone at the party is under arrest—to be met with derision. Broken, he rushes to Rose's apartment, and there in an altercation with her trick for the evening, he meets his death. Later Rose thinks, "He came to punish and—she knew now—to punish himself. How many others had he entrapped. Poor Jimmy. How he had paid. It had been he who had been entrapped, finally. Entrapped by what he thought of as the world's evils" (159). With Vince's help, Rose starts a healing process. He has already jolted Sylvia out of her benumbed state. The novel ends with the promise that they will form a union. Within the context of the story, the moment does not come across as the usual tacky salvation through the embracement of heterosexuality. And yet a gay reader cannot help wondering if it is not another form of entrapment.

One would like to know more about the genderless pseudonymous author's intentions. How much is the novel trying to be honest to the author's understanding of the complexities of the sex drive, and how much is it simply a response to the accepted fictions of the time? During the course of the park arrests, events at a party, and above all the long flashback detailing Vince's sexual history, the reader is introduced to a fairly wide spectrum of gay types. One of the gays at the party would seem to speak for the author when he says, "I don't like the devious means some police officers feel they have a right to use to catch those people. It's one thing for a uniformed policeman or a detective who first identifies himself with his badge to arrest someone making a public nuisance. But for the police to hide the fact they are police officers so that someone will approach them—and what is worse, in some cases, to entice, to lead on...." Vince interrupts, "To entrap." The most open gay man in the town says, "Still, cruising in a men's room is asking for trouble." But another counters, "You can get awfully desperate in a town like this with no bars to meet in ... no place to go" (84–85). California did not decriminalize homosexuality until 1975, ten years after the novel's publication. *Entrapment* was the last, and arguably the most complex, of five novels that Argyle Books published in hardback, 1964–65, aimed explicitly at gay readers, and the only one not reprinted by Paperback Library.

McCoy, R. *Entrapment*. Los Angeles: Argyle Books, 1965.

95 Ross Hossannah (James H. Ramp): *Gay Vet*, 1965. James H. Ramp: *Wild Strawberry Patch*, 1966; *The Love Smeller*, 1966.

Labeling Ramp's comic fiction "gay fantasies," Hubert Kennedy (*Ideal Gay Man*, 41) remarks, "The characters are often working-class men who don't fit in because they love opera or read Walter Pater [...]. They usually have a large penis and are hungry for sex, but hold out for true love, which they always find at the end of the story, after intervening difficulties." Kennedy does not mention the major fantasy element: by and large, Ramp's characters inhabit a setting in which straights approve of their love. Think of the movie *Big Eden*. The author does not ignore homophobia, but he argues that it is obsolete. In *Gay Vet* his main character, Dur Jeffers contends that "Mosaic law was greatly concerned about raising warriors when the tribes escaped from Egypt to burn a path of rapine and murder through the land that was to become Israel. Fighting men were of prime importance therefore homosexuals were branded criminals and put to death. The quaint custom still pertains in our enlightened democracy where 'Life, Liberty and the pursuit of happiness is the clarion cry.'" When his friend accuses him of being bitter, he asserts, "As long as I do not molest children or minors, and am not lewd or obscene in public, have you the right to deny me happiness with a consenting adult?" (44). Later in the novel the author also critiques race relations in the South. He sums up at one point, "No good American wants to seem different. It makes him suspect" (66). At base, however, Dur is not so much a liberal as a celebrant of a kind of Emersonian self-reliance.

Dur is a thirty-year-old itinerant veterinarian. His former dean at Kansas State asks him to mentor young Terry Sullivan, who excels in academics but fails with his "bedside manner." He loves animals so much that he "is mortally afraid of hurting them," with the result that "they smell that fear" and "shy away from him" (19). The dean is also engaged in a bit of match-making. He is the uncle of Dur's former lover, killed in a car accident, and thinks it is time Dur lets go of his grief. The two men begin a rollicking journey in Dur's "combo truck-trailer" across Missouri to Memphis, and then down to New Orleans. Along the way they tend to horses, dogs, heifers, a lamb, a kitten, a monkey, a Canadian goose, a foul-mouthed parrot, a bullfrog stuffed with buckshot, drunk guppies, a white rat, an opossum, a bobcat, a boa constrictor, an alligator, a brown bear, a pregnant whale, and even a teddy bear and a frightened boy with a splinter. They become friends with a family of black Mississippians and rescue an underage heir held prisoner by his rapacious mother. They comfort many a child. Dur proves to be a wise mentor in all save matters of the heart. Though Terry has obviously fallen in love with him, he shies away from commitment. In part it must be his fear of losing another person he loves. More, he feels older than the seven or so years that divide the two men and does not want to pressure Terry. In matters of the heart the roles of mentor and mentee must therefore reverse.

In a listing of his books Ramp calls the novel *A Walk with Angels*. The book as published opens with a fourteen page "Prelude" followed by a 142-page "A Walk with Angels." It is not clear why it was published under a pseudonym with a changed title (and a confusing one: despite the cover illustration many buyers probably thought they were getting a military romance). Like all of Ramp's writing, the novel is a piece of fluff. But it is entertaining fluff that makes pertinent observations about the nature of relationships and the social contract. If nothing else, it was a welcome antidote to all the stories of sad gays still pouring out of too many presses at the time. It is also remarkable in its choice of profession for its main characters.

This was apparently the only work of his that Ramp thought of as a novel. But both *Wild Strawberry Patch* and *The Love Smeller* are story cycles unified by a common theme, a common setting, and recurring characters. The first is set in Pleasant Valley, Moccasin County, in southeastern Kansas around the time of World War II. The prairie states are still suffering from the vagaries of the weather, and big combines are swallowing up the small farms. Henry Purvis, who has the adjoining farm, hitches up with Lew Driscoll. He argues that the solution they have found works and suggests that they bring other unmarried farmers together to see if they can work out a similar solution. By novel's end eleven couples have been formed. The author's fantasy admits American prejudices—and indirectly exposes why such must be fought openly. One man admonishes another, "This, Brother, is the Bible Belt, remember? Thou shalt not enjoy what the Lord hath given you" (28). Jed Wilkins asks Ned Parker, "You think it should be secretive, something to be ashamed of, queer?" Ned answers, "It isn't what I think, Jed, it's what the world thinks, and we must live in it. Open defiance of sexual mores is both futile and dangerous. We live in the Bible Belt where even married sex is considered nasty and unmentionable. No matter how a neighbor might sympathize, he could never condone. That's why I say love between men is a very private affair" (31). Interestingly, the author has a woman character say, "Sex is not the foundation of marriage, as we like to pretend we believe. Domination is" (86). Ramp also examines other kinds of prejudices that have shamed our nation. One of the men falls in love with an African American; another rescues a Nisei who has escaped the Colorado concentration camp in which he was incarcerated.

There are examples of the loneliness of a rural existence for a gay youth. One teenager comes upon two of the men kissing and exclaims, "I didn't know—except in books, of course. I thought maybe I was the only one who..." (89). But mostly we see warm camaraderie between couples. Monogamy becomes the rule once an agreement is reached, but playing around is permitted beforehand. A father says to his son, "A stiff pecker is a demanding thing and sex should be healthy fun. [...] you are not going to lose your immortal soul because you experimented. A man don't rightly know what he prefers until he tries it" (44). All this is leavened with humor, often of a low kind. The first time that Tag Weaver and Tim Jones, a prominent couple throughout the novel, get together, we have this exchange, beginning with Jones speaking: "'My snake is all coiled, ready to strike. Pure fluff! Really, it's a pet.' 'Could I pet it?' asked Weaver. 'Hummm ... you didn't tell me it was a bull snake.' 'Looks like we've got a pair. Shall we breed them?'" (18). That becomes a running joke, as does the strawberry patch in which two lovers have their first sexual experience and thereafter become known as the Wild Strawberries and the Strawberry Merchants. One also has to put up with a lot of cuteness, as when Lew declares, "Playing Cupid [...] is a strain on my risibilities" (25).

Smeller is set in Possum County, Tennessee, somewhere a hundred miles east of Memphis. It follows the same pattern as *Patch* in recording the formation of twenty male couples—twenty-one if we count two dogs, but it is more mature and more intricate in its development. True, each story follows essentially the same formula. A man, either consciously or unconsciously, is looking to hook up with a partner. Sometimes he knows he wants another man; sometimes he doesn't. The first pairing occurs with the help of Jeth Bleeker's hound dog, Beller, the love smeller. Beller later instructs a bird dog, Fred Frick's Pete, also how to identify suitable partners. Operating separately, the two dogs are responsible for hitching up eight couples as well as exposing an incestuous team of brothers intent on milking the town by preaching against sin while attempting blackmail. The novel concludes with the two canines deciding they also make a good couple. The other twelve couples come together with the help of two "cupids": Bud Hoskins and Tad Hawkins. They swear by swimming holes, which they say "be best, so's you kin see a man's possibles." When pressed to explain "possibles," the definition offered is, "Whut you cotton to most 'bout a man, one thing or t'other" (23), though the definition often seems to focus a bit narrowly on one particular portion of a man's anatomy.

The cast of characters is composed of mountaineers, both stereotypical untutored youths and educated men (who often elect to hide behind feigned naiveté), and outsiders enticed to settle in the pastoral Eden. Professionally they range from a county agent, a university professor, a school teacher, a physician, a banker, a lawyer, and the sheriff to farmers, a sawmill operator, various blue collar workers, and discharged veterans suffering from battle wounds. Most know they are homosexual; some are surprised to discover they must be bisexual; one is a nonsurgical transwoman. They have in common that, as in Ramp's other works, once committed to the relationship, they are monogamous. The county agent says, "In spite of all this light talk, these boys take marrying-up very seriously. It's for life, you know" (35). Some of the townspeople gawk at the obvious ties between the men, but the point is made, whether in word-play or by a happy typo, that "in the mountains we believe in consulting adults" (97). In general masculinity is celebrated, but even that may be modified, as in the case of the transwoman. The men are free of racism, but they are aware of its presence. Age is never an issue. The couples form their own community, responding to the needs of its members, ready to defend anyone against attacks. They help one man, a war veteran, who has been sexually abused by his own father and then committed to keep him from going to the law ("Hillbilly Hobo"). They agree on a plan to expose the hypocritical evangelical team, the ironically named Jonathan and David Muggeridge ("Sinners All"). Both cycles should be read at leisure so as not to tire of their basic formulas. But it is surprising that Ramp has not secured a cult following.

James H. Ramp (1898–1968) was born in Illinois. He was on the English faculty at San Mateo Junior College in the early 1930s and published a book of poetry. Towards the end of his life, living in San Francisco, he began publishing gay fiction. All his stories are humorous, many in dialect. Eight appeared in *Der Kreis* (see Kennedy, 41–48), others in *The Mattachine Review*. Two other collections are *A Far Country*, 1966, and *Consenting Adult*, 1967. One of his stories, "The Prablum" (originally published in *Mattachine Review*, 1964), appeared in *All Shades of Gay* by "Carl Branch," 1968. The others in this collection may also be his; they have similar themes. *Idylls of the Queens*, 1968, is a second Carl Branch collection that may or may not be Ramp's.

Hossannah, Ross. *Gay Vet*. Union City, N.J.: Star News, 1965.
Ramp, James H. *The Love Smeller*. San Francico: FanFare, 1966.
_____. *Wild Strawberry Patch*. San Francisco: FanFare, 1966.

96   James Colton (Joseph Hansen): *Strange Marriage*, 1965; *Known Homosexual*, 1968; *Hang-Up*, 1969. Joseph Hansen: *Fadeout*, 1970.

Hansen did not turn to fiction until he was in his forties. Then he took advantage of the burgeoning pulp industry to write his first novels, all under the pen name James Colton (in one case spelled Coulton), forced upon him by an associate at *ONE* magazine. Throughout his writing career he was attracted to socially transgressive sexual themes: homosexual, bisexual, intergenerational, interracial, and intercultural relationships. These he explored with the fewest constraints in the Colton novels, all set in California. Josh Lanyon has written a detailed appreciation of this body of work, showing how many of the themes Hansen would explore in his later novels were anticipated in this apprenticeship fiction. The least successful of the works are three depicting a gay teenager turning to an adult for help. In *Lost on Twilight Road*, 1964, and, as part of a more complex plot, in *Cocksure*, 1969, Lonny Harms is mentored by the older Gene Styles. *Gard*, 1969 (by James Coulton), describes artist Benson Gard's tragic love for Wylie White, an emotionally troubled teenager. The others are more successful.

Since *Strange Marriage*, the second Colton novel, was published in both hardback and paperback, it remains the most available Colton title. It chronicles a gay man, Randy Hale, on the rebound after his lover leaves him for another man, falling in love and creating a life with a woman, Ruth Anders. George Nelson—older, married himself, in love with him—warns Randy: "It's dishonest, it's a lie. It will wreck your life. [...] it will wreck her life too" (74). For a while, the marriage seems to work. But a miscarriage, Randy's overly charged sex drive, and his need for men buffet the marriage. After he essentially rapes Ruth, she leaves. Randy spills everything to the family doctor. Unexpectedly, he advises Randy to admit he is bisexual and to tell her the truth, in essence proposing he enter some sort of *ménage à trois*. Randy ignores his counsel: he begins a relationship with young Dave Noyes but conceals it from her. All comes to a melodramatic head when George discovers the two men together and kills himself, leaving an incriminating letter behind. George's self-righteous wife tells Ruth; together they tell Dave's mother. Dave is lost (his mother leaves the small town with him in tow), but in a rapid turn of events Randy is given another chance. The doctor tries one more time: "You know what's the matter with you? It's not Ruth's contempt. It's your own. [...] You despise yourself. And it's time you got over that. Suppose your sex life doesn't conform? There's more important things in this world" (176). Hope is held out for some chance of a reconciliation. The autobiographical aspects of the novel grant it interest, but the work is too much a *roman à thèse* to entirely satisfy.

Two Colton mysteries appeared. The teenage

protagonist of *Known Homosexual*, an aspiring African American playwright named Steve Archer, races to discover who has murdered his white boyfriend before the police pin the crime on him. There are six suspects. Sleuthing, however, takes up only four of the novel's twenty-eight chapters. The rest function as a flashback detailing Steve's muddled life as he fails at one relationship after another, the shadow of his powerful father darkening everything, including his roles as playwright, husband to a pregnant white woman, and lover of the amoral hustler, who was yet loyal to Steve. This was the only Colton book that Hansen felt strongly enough about to revise, not once but twice, and publish under his own name, first as *Stranger to Himself*, 1977, and then as *Pretty Boy Dead*, 1984. *Hang-Up* is a much stronger work. Stone Ransom, the narrator, wakes up naked in an alley with no idea who he is. He is rescued by the young and mysterious Matt Evans. Though Stone is certain he has never engaged in a gay relationship before, the two become lovers. Stone realizes that Matt is somehow being controlled by a menacing lesbian, Dublin. She also holds the key to his identity in the form of a Wanted For Questioning poster that indicates Stone was involved in a major embezzlement. He sets out to discover the truth about himself, her mysterious hold over Matt, and the murder of Matt's first lover. The quest uncovers loving and supportive parents and a boyfriend of dubious, perhaps even dangerous, worth. Stone tricks the boyfriend into admitting his guilt. He is in time to save Matt as he hits his lowest point and frees him from Dublin's control. Two more Colton novels appeared in 1971. None of these works has the power of Hansen's subsequent books, in part because he was meeting pulp requirements, in part because he had yet to find his voice.

The Dave Brandstetter mystery series is the gold standard by which all other gay mysteries are judged. Most of them are fine novels in and of themselves regardless of genre labels. Dave makes his debut in *Fadeout*. Forty-four years old, he is an insurance claims investigator working for his father's company. He is grieving, having lost Rod Fleming, his partner of twenty years, to cancer. (His heterosexual father is now ending his ninth or tenth marriage; Dave has lost count.) The case concerns the death claim filed by Fox Olson's beneficiaries. His destroyed car was found in the flooded arroyo into which it plunged, but not his body. His presumed widow argues that it must have been washed to sea, that her husband was finally finding career happiness as an entertainer—reading stories he had written and performing his songs on his own radio program—and had no reason to disappear. Dave discovers, however, that she is having an affair with Hale McNeil, the man who launched Fox's new career. Beginning as a joke, Fox had announced his candidacy for mayor and posed a real threat to the corrupt incumbent. As Dave probes further, he also discovers a coincidence: just before Fox disappeared, a man driving a car with French license plates had shown up. This is Doug Sawyer. Playing a hunch, Dave locates Doug's mother in Los Angeles and then the art school where Doug and Fox met. Back in 1941 the two boys fell in love; they spent one memorable summer at Bell Beach. There they took some indiscrete photographs, which were stolen. When the war came, Fox volunteered he was homosexual; Doug anticipated a heart ailment would keep him out, only to pass the physical without problem. Reported missing in action, Fox married and fathered a daughter but left no trail behind them. Stymied in his search, Doug remained in France, where he fell in love with a race car driver, who was killed at Le Mans. Returning to the States, he by chance saw an article about Fox's improbable run for mayor. The mayor, meanwhile, had gotten hold of the photographs, and Fox had learned of his wife's infidelity. The two lovers staged his disappearance, but after all those years, one night a fight erupted. Doug split. While he was gone, a greedy beneficiary tracked Fox down and, this time, made certain his body would be found.

Dave refuses to abandon his investigation. Someone grills him: "'He's dead. Doesn't that close the case as far as you're concerned? What are you doing here?' Dave didn't know" (65). But it seems fairly obvious that a sense of gay solidarity is part of the reason. Dave displays this sense in a variety of ways. The mayor threatens him; when he is murdered, Dave shields the killer and carefully destroys the photographs. McNeil spits verbal venom whenever gays are mentioned (his son was involved in a homosexual scandal and disowned). Dave generally cares for others' feelings; this time he turns on the adulterous pair. Not that Dave is flawless: despite the fact that Rod was, in Dave's own term, as nelly as could be, he still looks down on effeminate men, such as his contact at the art school. Still, it is important to him to try to be honest. Dishonesty was Fox's downfall. His wife comments about his failure as a writer: "something was missing. [...] It was always as if he was talking about the wrong thing. [...] As if there was something else he ought to be talking about instead" (24). Doug puts it more clearly: "Look at it this way. Suppose Dostoevsky had never mentioned his epilepsy, his compulsive gambling. How far would he have gone?" (78). The novel ends with a new test. Doug, who resembles Rod in many ways, arrives at Dave's home. The reader is left to wonder if the two men, both on the rebound, can make it as a couple.

For twenty-two years gay readers had the pleasure of anticipating the next book in the series. In all, there were twelve novels, one novella, and one short story. Across their span Dave ages, changes, parts from Doug, finds love with a young African American journalist, loses friends, some to AIDS, and himself dies in the last novel. Hansen was awarded the Shamus Lifetime Achievement Award in 1992. He also created another series with a straight investigator, as well as a number of standalones. Joseph Hansen (1923–2004) was born in Aberdeen, South Dakota, but he grew up in Minneapolis and Altadena, California. He was an early gay activist in Los Angeles with the Mattachine Society and was instrumental in setting up the first L.A. Pride Parade. He co-founded the magazine *Tangents*. Although he always self-identified as homosexual (he disliked the word *gay*), he was married for fifty years to Jane Bancroft, a lesbian (to whom he dedicated *Strange Marriage*); they had one child. His 1992 autobiography mentions the dramatist and director Robert Ben Ali (d. 1985) and Wayne F. Placek (d. 1988?) as lovers.

Colton, James. *Hang-Up*. North Hollywood, Calif.: Brandon House, 1969.
_____. *Known Homosexual*. North Hollywood, Calif.: Brandon House, 1968.
_____. *Strange Marriage*. Los Angeles: Argyle, 1965.
Hansen, Joseph. *Fadeout*. New York: Harper & Row, 1970. London: Harrap, 1972. *The Complete Brandstetter: Twelve Novels*. Harpenden, Eng.: No Exit, 2007. 5–93.
Lanyon, Josh. "The Play of Shadows and Light: Hansen before Dave." *The Golden Age of Gay Fiction*. Ed. Drewey Wayne Gunn. Albion, N.Y.: MLR, 2009. 153–66.
White, C. Todd. *Pre-Gay L.A.: A Social History of the Movement for Homosexual Rights*. Urbana: University of Illinois Press, 2009. 106–08, 191–97, 222.

97 James Leo Herlihy: *Midnight Cowboy*, **1965. Richard Miles:** *That Cold Day in the Park*, **1965. Dotson Rader:** *Gov't Inspected Meat and Other Fun Summer Things*, **[1970]**.

Rader's narrator articulates the hustler's dogma: "Hustlers are not queer. [...] Even when I stood with my legs spread, with the meat, my meat, being lapped by a john, I was not gay" (70). "As long as you paid you weren't a fag. Conversely, as long as you were bought, too, you were not one either. It was, psychologically, a safe bet" (88). "When you hustle, the john has an intensity about him, but what is operative in his excitement is not only the sexuality of the encounter—which, I sometimes think, is a minor factor—but the potential for violence. Violence, and the hint of the possibility of sudden death, animate the eroticism in that situation" (191). Many of the same ideas are voiced in Rechy's novels; they also show up in Phil Andros's. And they are implied in Herlihy's and Miles's.

Midnight Cowboy is not truly a gay novel. Yet paradoxically it is an intense love story between two men that goes well beyond the romantic friendships of the nineteenth century. Joe Buck, the title character, leaves Houston to try his luck as a gigolo in New York. So far in his life each "sexual connection with someone" has left him "with the shameful certainty that he was somehow being exploited and made a fool of." He is keenly aware, "The persons, female and male alike, who were so eager to avail themselves of his splendid body never appeared to notice that it was inhabited by Joe Buck" (38–39). His first experiences in New York are no better; he is the one who pays the woman he has thought he was hustling. He realizes, "He had to have some advice" from "someone who knew the ropes and could give him some guidance" (122). As if on cue, Rico (aka Ratso) Rizzo seats himself in a bar beside Joe. Ratso is the opposite of the handsome Texan: an ugly runt with a crippled leg, obviously in poor health. He promises to help Joe by setting him up, for a fee, with a pimp, but the man turns out to be a hypocritical sham, and Ratso has long split. Broke, locked out of his room, his belongings confiscated, Joe turns to Times Square. Typical of his luck, he is picked up by a college student who not only throws up but admits he has no money. At his lowest, he runs into Ratso again. Instead of revenge, Joe seeks friendship: "Too much time alone had done something peculiar to his heart: A confused and unreliable organ at best, it now held something akin to joy" (157). Ratso invites him to share the room he is occupying as a squatter.

The two lost men become "a familiar sight on certain New York streets [...], the little blond runt, laboring like a broken grasshopper to keep pace with the six-foot tarnished cowboy" (164–65). An inept pickpocket, Ratso is marginally better at securing a few dollars for them by arranging "a fast five- or ten-dollar transaction in which little more was required of the cowboy than standing still for a few minutes with his trousers undone" (171). But a bond is established. Ratso's health worsens as winter arrives; he dreams of Florida. Joe does not even have to consider what he should do when he returns—from another failed pickup with a guilt-ridden male from Chicago—to discover that Ratso's condition has become critical. After depositing him at the bus terminal, he returns to the man's hotel room and violently robs him (causing the man to achieve an ejaculation as a result). But on the bus, just before Miami, Ratso dies. The novel concludes: "And then he did something he'd always wanted to do from the very beginning, from the very first night he'd met Ratso at Everett's Bar on Broadway: He put his arm around him to hold him for a while, for these last few miles anyway. He knew this comforting wasn't doing Ratso any good. It was for himself. Because of course he was scared now, scared to death" (254). The 1969 film version gained Oscars and BAFTA awards for both the movie and its gay director, John Schlesinger. James Leo Herlihy (1927–1993) was born in Detroit. He grew up there and in Chillicothe, Ohio. After serving in the Navy, he attended Black Mountain and Pasadena Playhouse Colleges. A novelist, a playwright, and an actor, he moved primarily between New York, Los Angeles, and Key West. He was James Kirwood's friend and sometimes sexual buddy. He died in Los Angeles of an overdose of sleeping pills.

Miles's novel about a pair of hustlers is different, yet similar before it ends. Set in Paris, a sixteen-year-old who goes by the name Mignon is picked up by a mentally unbalanced older woman. She virtually imprisons him, though he secretly slips out to meet Yves, whom he loves but who abides by the hustler's code of never admitting affection for another. Yves is also greedy; even when it becomes apparent that Mignon's life is in danger (the woman kills a prostitute she has brought to the apartment as a present to him), he urges Mignon to remain with her so they can rob her of her jewels. Then Mignon becomes ill—perhaps appendicitis. Yves seems to understand finally what Mignon means to him as he searches desperately for a doctor. The novel comes to an abrupt end with Yves and the doctor heading to the woman's apartment and her returning to the park where she first picked up Mignon. It became the basis for a 1969 film directed by Robert Altman with a script by Gillian Freeman (the author of *The Leather Boys*) in which Yves—and thus any hint of gayness—was omitted altogether. (The Canadian filmmaker Bruce LaBruce used her script as inspiration for his 1991 film *No Skin off My Ass*, which Miles told him he liked better than the Altman film.) Gerald Richard Perreau-Saussine (1938–2002) was born in Tokyo. Under the name Peter Miles, he was a film and television actor as well as a script writer. He wrote novels under the name Richard Miles. He was also a teacher and a curator of art shows. His partners were Errol Jacobs and, at the time of his death, Brian Quarch. He died of cancer in Los Angeles.

Rader's autobiographical novel (copyrighted 1971 but published in 1970) follows the life of the protagonist, nicknamed Angel by his father, from the time his parent dumps him as a child on his aunt in Evanston, Illinois, through his hustling days in New York and on to his relocation, at the end, to San Francisco. During his teens his closest friend is a neighborhood boy named Parker. He sets Angel up with a girl for him to lose his virginity, and he introduces him to Chicago bathhouses, where, Angel says, they "let the faggots go down on us for coins" (43). Parker falls for a married woman; because he is African American, the husband and some of "his off-duty cop friends" drown Parker in Lake Michigan and then castrate him (37). Angel feels guilty. But it is many years before he can admit the full truth: "I loved Parker deeply and without guilt, loved him enough to bend for him" (230). Perhaps in partial atonement, while he is hustling in New York, he pauses long enough to join a "Freedom Ride" to Richmond, Virginia. But he earlier shies away from becoming intimate with another African American, David Cartwright, who "threatens me with his openness, he blurs the lines, destroys distinctions, pulls near" (146). His last act before leaving the city is to visit the St. James Baths for the first time. For him "the place [was] anti-sexual, overstated, ahuman, lacking any semblance of personal interrelationship, except on a highly contrived physical level. It made hustling seem warm and very human in contrast" (193). Dotson Carlyle Rader (1942–) was born, according to most sources, in Evanston, Illinois. He attended Columbia and worked as a male hustler, then became the lover, 1971–77, of actress Ruth Ford (sister of Charles Henri Ford). He wrote for various journals, becoming a prolific interviewer. In 1969 he published his personal account of the 1960s student protests, *I Ain't Marchin' Anymore*; in 1985 he wrote about his association with Williams: *Tennessee: Cry of the Heart*.

Herlihy, James Leo. *Midnight Cowboy*. *New York: Simon & Schuster, 1965. London: Cape, 1966.
Miles, Richard. *The Cold Day in the Park*. *New York: Delacorte, 1965. London: Souvenir, 1966.
Rader, Dotson. *Gov't Inspected Meat and Other Fun Summer Things*. New York: McKay, [1970].

98 Sanford Friedman: *Totempole*, 1965. Bernard Malamud: *Pictures of Fidelman*, 1969.

Both these works explore the problems of an international romance with a Jewish twist. Although the relationship in each ends, it does so on a positive note. A bildungsroman, *Totempole* depicts eight periods in the life of Stephen Wolfe between ages two and twenty-five. These correspond to the different portions of an imaginary totem pole (though a real one, which he helps carve, appears in the forth section). Stephen's early sexual development remains inchoate, confused by bad medical advice and chaotic parenting. All his emotional interests are male-oriented (including the carver of the totem pole), but his only sexual pleasures are solitary and guilt-ridden. Finally, at college he submits to his roommate's overtures. But when he mysteriously contacts crab lice, he reverts to his early indoctrination that sex is sinful and turns to asceticism. Then during the Korean conflict, he ends up assigned to a camp holding North Koreans who refuse repatriation. He agrees to teach them English and, as a result, meets Sun Bo Pak, a medical doctor (whom, Stephen discovers is shielding his own son, another prisoner). Stephen feels a strong, and reciprocated, attraction at once, but is taken aback by the prisoners' easy acceptance of homosexuality. He confronts his own lack of commitment to anyone: "Neither gook nor GI, neither here nor there, fish nor fowl, straight nor queer, prisoner nor free! I'm neither one nor both but in between ... without myself ... partitioned, like Korea" (355). Slowly, under Sun Bo's tutelage, he learns to let go of his inhibitions, of the unhealthy self-consciousness that hampers his acceptance of himself, of his body: "At last he was released—released from his great constricting self, his self-opposing self with all its isolating power and power to negate, its eccentricities and handicaps, willfulness and vainglory—released to join Sun Bo, experience Sun Bo (and, thus, himself) more intimately and fully than he ever had before" (373). The lovers are ultimately separated: Stephen returns to the States; Sun Bo remains behind with his son. But Stephen is liberated from his own prison: "After years and years of reacting to being acted upon, at last Stephen felt he was ready to become an actor" (394). Sanford Friedman (1928–2010) was born and died (of a heart attack) in New York. He graduated from Carnegie Institute of Technology. He served as a military policeman in Korea. In 1975 he published *Still Life*, two novellas that complement each other. For nineteen years he was the partner of poet Richard Howard (1929–), to whom he dedicated the novel.

A story cycle, *Fidelman* exhibits six portraits of "a self-confessed failure as a painter" (3) as he stumbles his way across Italy. Despite bouts of activity, Arthur Fidelman is a passive figure. He ends up finally in Venice, still a failure at all he has attempted, there to have an unexpected adventure of the heart. The womanizing would-be artist becomes the lover of a married woman, then good friends with her husband, Beppo Fassoli, even as he uneasily wonders if Beppo is suspicious. Indeed, Fiddelman and the wife are discovered *flagrante delicto*. But now the author reinvents Boccaccio's tale of Pietro di Vinciolo (*Decameron*, 5.10). It's not the first time low farce enters the novel, but it is the first time the lowness becomes so anatomical: "Don't hurt me, Beppo, please, I have piles," Fidelman begs. "It'll be a cool job, I'm wearing mentholated Vaseline. You'll be surprised at the pleasure," Beppo replies (199). The two men become inseparable, and Beppo arranges to have him hired as an apprentice glassblower at the place he works: "Working with the hot molten glass excited Fidelman sexually" (201). Their bliss is broken by the wife's demand that Fidelman leave Venice: "Beppo may be a homo but he's a good provider and not a bad father when there are no men friends around to divert him from domestic life" (207). So Fidelman returns to the U.S. with widened capabilities: "In America he worked as a craftsman in glass and loved men and women" (208). Bernard Malamud (1914–1986) was born and died in New York. He graduated from CCNY and Columbia. He taught English at Oregon State and Bennington. He was married and had two children.

Friedman, Sanford. *Totempole*. New York: Dutton, 1964. London: Blond, 1966. *San Francisco: North Point, 1984.
Malamud, Bernard. *Pictures of Fidelman: An Exhibition*. *New York: Farrar, Straus, Giroux, 1969. London: Eyre & Spottiswoode, 1969.

99 Casimir Dukahz: *The Asbestos Diary*, 1966.

In the opening chapter "Casimir" announces his purpose: "to put into perspective a relatively unknown area of human activity which has been affrightedly neglected in pornographic and popular literature though not in classical … the necessarily illicit love of a boy by an adult male." He labels the adult male who finds "masculine teenage lads sexually desirable" a "boysexual." He goes on to say, "The true boysexual is a madman—make no mistake about that—but his is a benign uncertifiable madness symptomised by a gullible romanticism and an impractical sentimentality" (1). He ends his prologue averring that he has no desire "to proselytize any man to my way of thinking or mode of life—the competition is too cutthroat fierce as it is!" (3). There follow 134 short chapters, dated from April 1946 through December 1965 (but so shuffled that there is no chronological continuity): paeans to encounters with sixty-six boys, ages twelve to nineteen, along with glimpses of other people he encounters and with musings, often highly satirical in nature, about various topics relevant to his pursuit. Thirty-five of the chapters are devoted to Luc ("Prime T-bone in a hamburger world"), a thirteen-year-old boy he lives with through the whole of 1965, and to whom he dedicates the novel. In response to Luc's question, as recorded in the dedication, he calls the work "an as*bestos* diary" because "it hasn't gone up in smoke and flame" even though he has "written all about you and me, among others" (v). The novel received some degree of attention when it appeared because of its inventive wordplay, its wicked sense of humor ("I have always maintained children should be obscene and not heard"), and its unconventional structure, but its subject matter has caused it to virtually disappear from critical awareness.

The Luc chapters, though interleaved with the others across the stretch of the book, do follow chronological order more or less. They open with the boy's unexpected appearance in January, begging for work, an escapee from a sexually abusive stepfather. From the beginning theirs is a teasing relationship: "He deliberately mangles 'Casimir Dukahz' into disrespectful 'Cashmere Duckass' but addresses me as 'Sir'" (19). Casimir enrolls Luc in school and aids him in his lessons. This effort results in offbeat moments, such as an evening when Luc, during sex, demands the elevation of Mt. Everest. On another occasion they revisit Wilde's argument about W. H. and Shakespeare's sexuality. Casimir takes out life insurance with Luc as beneficiary. They share meals, sometimes seasoned with personal condiments, sometimes accompanied by unexpected actions under the table, sometimes using only one plate and no utensils. They go shopping for clothes. Mostly the chapters describe their sexual life: "It being impossible to be long platonic with a boy like Luc" (231). Casimir remains fearful that the boy will fall in love with a neighborhood girl his age, one Angela. (There is no doubt that the protagonist is a misogynist.) At the end of their year together, it is unclear what direction Luc will take. But the novel ends with the boy's declaration: "I think I love Angela but I *like* you better than I *love* her—isn't that crazy!" (281).

Casimir points out that there are "no entries for the years 1952–3 because I was in prison." He is amused that he "was accepted by embezzlers, forgers, bank-robbers and con-men as still human though possessing odd predilections, but was vilified and rejected by rapists, wife-killers and murderers in general as being beneath contempt" (233). He mentions other near misses, such as the time "I was caught by irate father blowing his son's oboe while the lad practiced on my flute" (185), and the evening he and Luc are in the backseat of his car when a policeman surprises them. (Luc expertly manipulates the cop so that he departs "red-faced, coughing, mopping his brow" [232].) He also mentions being caught by a father, who offers, for a slightly higher fee, to prove that anything his son can do, he can do better. Having "an instinctive objection to undergoing amorous thanatopsis," he escapes being mugged by biting "down hard on that which should never be bitten" (234). In the most bizarre episode, dated February 1964, he confesses to murdering a drug dealer who hooked one of his favorite boys on heroin, leading to the youth's suicide. Unsurprisingly, the novel is laced with withering criticism of the government, the legal system, religion, psychiatry, and Nabokov.

Brian O. Drexel (1909–1988) may have been born in Ohio. He was living in Louisiana when he obtained his Social Security number. He published four other similar novels. It has been suggested he may also have been Brian Lucas, the editor of Coltsfoot Press in Amsterdam. He died in New York.

Dukahz, Casimir. *The Asbestos Diary*. New York: Oliver Layton, 1966.

100 Tennessee Williams: *The Knightly Quest*, 1966.

Williams's novella is a whimsical but deadly satire on the direction he felt the nation was taking during the escalation of the Vietnam conflict, a period also of increasing racial tensions and disregard of civil liberties. Its hero is Gewinner Pearce. His funds being cut off at the death of his father, he returns from abroad (where his family has preferred he live) to their Southern mansion, a pseudo-castle in the town of Gewinner. He finds that the town, under the direction of his younger brother, Braden, has been subverted by The Project. Built on the site formerly occupied by his father's Red Devil Battery Plant, its purpose, as defined by Braden, is to create "a white Christmas" by reasserting the supremacy of whites over "the reds and the blacks and the yellows" who have been "pulling fantastic stunts right out from under our feet" (413, 449). Braden's best friend is Billy Spangler, who holds, "It's all right to talk about tolerance and individual rights and all of that sort of business but you got to draw a line somewhere" (421–22). Gewinner discovers that Braden's wife opposes The Project, is in fact working to undermine it. Significantly, she is named Violet: a color traditionally associated with gays, also the flower evoked by Don Quixote at the end of Williams's play *Camino Real*: "The violets in the mountains have broken the rocks!" Gewinner himself is directly associated with Don Quixote, Williams's symbol of the eternal romantic, and perhaps the ultimate democrat. Gewinner is a searcher for an Other, yet he is narcissistic. He is iconoclastic yet messianic, an idealist who can play underhandedly when he needs to. His nightly quest for sexual partners and his knightly quest to prevent a wrong are opposite sides of the same coin—perhaps the Persian one that he wears around his neck, "carrying a secret" (439). On these (k)nightly excursions he takes an enormous white silk scarf, which he spreads on the ground when he finds the right stranger to take to his favorite spot. Unlike the heterosexual Billy, whom he uncannily mirrors in ways, he feels no shame.

Events rush to a climax. Violet has a friend, Gladys, who takes a job at Billy's drive-in joint. They fake a call that he must deliver a special order to the project. Gladys prepares the sandwiches and a thermos of coffee. The four of them drive to the facility, which instantly goes on high alert. Having "the temperament of the perfect soldier" (453), Billy doggedly proceeds to headquarters, becoming aware too late of an ominous ticking coming from the thermos. Williams indulges in a final whimsy: just before the device goes off taking everything with it, Gewinner, Violet, and Gladys are swooped up into a spaceship. As they zoom along at the speed of light, on one memorable occasion, "the communication system picked up a rhapsodic music, something like what the Good Gray Poet of Paumanok must have had in mind when he shouted, 'Thou Vast Rondure, Swimming in Space'" (454). To Gewinner's satisfaction the ship is piloted by three handsome crew members. He and "the radiant young navigator" swap "stories about the knightly quest as both have known it in their different ways." He promises Gewinner that the "white silk scarf which had made so many festivals of nights on the planet Earth" will gain a place of honor in their galaxy's museum. (Note: the novella and the play *The Red Devil Battery Sign*, 1975–80, share a central conceit but have no characters in common.)

Given the repressive climate at the time Williams was coming into his own in theater, it is not surprising that before "Confessional" (expanded into *Small Craft Warnings*), gays only showed up offstage (Allan Grey in *A Streetcar Named Desire*, Skipper in *Cat on a Hot Tin Roof*, Sebastian Venable in *Suddenly Last Summer*, with a very different Violet) or in small roles (Baron de Charlus in

Camino Real). His short stories, first published in limited editions, dared be more open. In 1975 there appeared his second novel, *Moise and the World of Reason*, with a gay narrator, and his very candid *Memoirs*. Thomas Lanier Williams (1911–1983) was born in Columbus, Mississippi. The family moved to St. Louis in 1918. He attended the University of Missouri, Washington University, and the University of Iowa. He began using the name Tennessee in 1938. He was partners with, briefly, Kip Kiernan (Bernard Dubowsky, 1918–1944), then Francisco Rodriguez y Gonzales (1920–1993), followed by Frank Merlo (1921–1963). His rupture with Merlo marked the beginning of his decline as a writer. Always on the move, he was particularly associated with New Orleans, Key West, and New York. His letters and his notebooks give much insight into the era. Williams died in a New York hotel of a drug overdose.

Spoto, Donald. *The Kindness of Strangers: The Life of Tennessee Williams*. Boston: Little, Brown, 1985.
Williams, Tennessee. *The Knightly Quest: A Novella and Four Short Stories*. New York: New Directions, 1966. *The Knightly Quest: A Novella and Twelve Short Stories*. London: Secker & Warburg, 1968. *Collected Stories. New York: New Directions, 1985. 398–455.

101 Tom Lockwood: *The Ugly Club*, 1966; *Sons of a Beach*, 1966; *Destination Nowhere*, 1966.

Though told from multiple perspectives, *Ugly Club* is essentially the story of Julian Sinclare's grappling with his sexuality in 1964 Atlanta. Straight-appearing, an ex–Navy officer, he knows that he is gay, but he is not sure that he is ready to accept all that means. "I'm always waiting, he thought; waiting for something to happen. Waiting scares me" (76). He has dropped out of Duke law school, affected by a "restlessness" that began "right after he read that book, *City of Night*" (16) and come to the city "to find out what I am" (24). Don Moss, an old classmate from his North Carolina college (apparently Davidson), offers him a place to live. By serendipity he lands a job as the pianist at a nightclub, the curiously named Ugly Club. Through people he meets at his job, he encounters Dirk Lanier, a student at his alma mater and a pot dealer, with whom he falls in love. Unfortunately, Dirk is not ready to commit to a gay relationship, and a girlfriend, Wyckham Newley, offers heterosexual temptation. Don's problems with his family after he was discharged from the army, his former lover's family (the powerfully connected father engineering a threat from the Atlanta vice squad), and his workplace demonstrate, all too vividly, perils a Southern queer may encounter. The novel ends on an upbeat, however; Don secures a job with an interior decorating firm in New York, and the last we hear of him is a postcard from Provincetown, where he is vacationing. It ends on an uncertain note for Dirk; while in New Orleans, fleeing the police (because of his dealing), he meets "a very nice, very rich man" who takes him to Hawaii. And it ends ambiguously for Julian. Still drifting, he tells Wyckham, "I want to try to be an ordinary person" (159). The two become more or less a couple: "But mostly Julian is alone." The last we see of him he is seriously contemplating an offer made by the owner of a cocktail lounge in Palm Beach to work for him (160). The novel offers a fascinating time capsule, reminding us also of the racial tensions, the changing culture, and the music of the period.

Sons of a Beach (a typical pulp title, probably not the author's) also revolves around a nightclub: the Sand Bar at Sea Beach, a village on Burnt Island off the coast of New Jersey (i.e., Ocean Beach, Fire Island, N.Y.). Dandridge Fallston gets a job there as a singer. He is another Southerner, a graduate of an all-male college, this time in Tennessee, and an ex-soldier who first explored his sexuality while stationed at Fort Jackson. He has come to Burnt Island in flight from a failed love affair with a waiter in the Fort Lauderdale nightclub where he previously sang, his having bounced from being "totally absorbed" with the man to "having found things he didn't like about his character" (40). Now Dandridge seems ready to repeat the error with a young waiter here. Jan has taken the job because he is dating Cathy, the proprietress's daughter. They break up, and the two men pair up. Jealousy threatens the relationship, but the two "talk about it" (129). Cathy becomes enamored with the pianist who accompanies Dandridge in the club. An aspiring writer of Broadway musicals, Russ is another man who has experienced both gay and straight sex, but he tell her that he prefers women. Meanwhile, Cathy's mother breaks out of her shell to have an affair with a local fisherman. The waiter Mal busily cruises Oak Grove (i.e., Cherry Grove) on his time off, and the cleaning woman, Anna, picks up tricks to augment her income. At the novel's end, Russ observes that "everybody's paired off [...]. Except Anna and Mal." Cathy counters, "they'll have all the one-night stands they want" (159–60).

Destination Unknown (another misleading title, though in a different way) is a lesser novel than the other two, though it depicts only too well the confusions of being gay in America, particularly in the South, in the mid-60s. (One of the funniest vignettes, which anyone of that generation can identify with, describes how the main character feels he must drive to the next town to buy a tube of K-Y.) The protagonist is Robby Dandridge, "graduate of a southern University [Duke], former naval officer, now of Phillipsville [i.e., Clarksville], Tennessee, in the accounting department of a large corporation" (12). Though knowing he is gay, he earlier became betrothed to a hometown girl; his fiancée, sensing that something was wrong, broke off the engagement; he quit his job at the bank and has taken the new one to get away from her. And now he works at the gateway to "Fort Lafayette" (Fort Campbell, Ky.), training base for sexually tempting paratroopers. Robby, however, falls for David, a gas station attendant whom he obsesses about. Unfortunately, David is married, unwilling to admit that he is homosexual, and sees Robby as a source for easy money. Under the onrush of Robby's passion, David's facade begins to break down, and he determines to leave his wife. Still, he cannot commit to Robby. In a rush of events, David's wife causes Robby to be fired from his job, Robby is beaten up by a paratrooper he picks up, and he falls in love with another soldier: Kevin, an army medic who is far wiser than Robby about humans. Earlier, Robby has thought: *"And now that I've admitted to myself that I'm a queer, that I'm always going to be a queer, now that I've given up hope of a normal life, why shouldn't I make myself as happy as I can?"* (79). The novel ends with the promise that he may, by slightly misquoting a poem by George Herbert ("The Temper," which I suspect the author saw as a source for a better title for his novel): "Sometimes I fly with angels, Sometimes I fall with dust."

Tom Lockwood published these three books, followed by a heterosexual potboiler (*The Schemer*, 1967), and then disappeared. One can deduct a kind of biography from his novels, but I have been unable to find out anything concrete about the author.

Lockwood, Tom. *Destination Nowhere*. New York: Castle, 1966.
_____. *Sons of a Beach*. San Diego: Greenleaf Classics, 1966.
_____. *The Ugly Club*. New York: Award, 1966.

102 Frederic Prokosch: *The Wreck of the Cassandra*, 1966; *The Missolonghi Manuscript*, 1968.

Of the seventeen novels that the author published, bibliographers indicate nearly all have gay interest, beginning with his first, *The Asiatics*, 1935. But not until *Wreck*, his antepenultimate novel, does he finally create a guarded yet indisputably gay protagonist. It is a far more enjoyable read than its critical obscurity would lead one to expect. *Wreck* is set in the second half of 1938. A fire breaks out on a ship bound from Hong Kong to Sydney and quickly destroys it. The novel follows nine survivors who make it to an island. Zeno, "a sexy Japanese boy" (187), is recognizably gay to everyone. He sets his sights on Tony Wagenseller, a closeted, married man from Philadelphia. Tony and his wife bicker nonstop prior to and throughout their ordeal; Laura throws up at him, "You're quite incapable of desiring a woman" (31). Asking him why he is so sad, Zenzo argues that "sadness to like a sickness" and goes on to develop the dangers with an anecdote: "My friend pretty Sado fall in love with American gentleman," but the American "no love Sado. So Sado turn sick with sadness and poor Sado go falling into sea by Yokohama." He informs Laura, "Poor Mr. Wagasala want love but afraid even to touch me!" (89–90). A German baron, a gigolo, writes in his diary, "I've noticed [Tony's] behavior with that Japanese boy. He thinks that he's fooling us all, his shrew of a wife included. It's quite clear what they're up to on those 'fishing expeditions.' The American male would appear to be basically ambidextrous" (71). When Tony decides that they should strike out on their own into the interior, he automatically includes Zenzo in his plan. Laura purrs, "You're fond of Zenzo, aren't you? [...] Kind of cute, wouldn't you say?" (110). While the two men are away from her in the jungle, hunting game for a meal, Tony falls. Zenzo comes to his aid: "Tony reached out his hand and touched Zenzo on the cheek. Then he drew his head nearer and kissed him on the lips." A chapter break precludes our knowing what else happens. But the next day, while they are standing close together,

Tony "placed his hand on Zenzo's shiny black head in a surge of tenderness and Zenzo looked up at him with a sly, coquettish smile" (197). Clearly, Zenzo thinks he has won over Laura. A native spear removes any quandary Tony might encounter when he and his wife are finally rescued. The two of them and another German, back at the beach, are the only ones to survive. The novel has a smattering of other gay references. Even animals are mentioned. A lepidopterist informs the company that one genus in which the male is more beautiful than the female "has so intoxicated certain species that they are driven to homosexuality" (82).

The novel was followed by a historical novel, a recreation of Lord Byron's lost journals from his final days in Greece. Strictly speaking, *Manuscript* is not a gay novel. But it is suffused with homoeroticism—an obsession with the phallus, as well as scatology, and a sprinkling of homosexual activity—to a greater degree than the preceding novel. The entries cover the period from January 25 to April 19, 1824, the day of his death, but in them Byron reviews his entire life. He concludes early on, "The line between love and loathing is as fine as a knife, and just as deadly" (27). When Alexander Mavrocordato asks him about his amatory pursuits, and specifically about any "liaison, copulatory or otherwise, with a man," Bryron responds: "Copulatory, four in number. Noncopulatory, only one." The Greek persists, "Which of these branches of copulatory experience have you found the more pleasurable?" Byron replies that "the answer is simple. Women are constructed more adroitly than men." Still, he admits, "A beautiful man as well as a beautiful woman can make my heart skip a beat" (111–12). He remembers that the poet Thomas Moore has said to him, "You make love to the women but you love, *au fond*, the men" (204). At another point, Byron writes, "There is more poetry in the seam of a scrotum which Archilochus celebrates than in a swarm of Johnny Keats's mellifluous nightingales" (175). But in thinking about Moore's comment, he also says, "There's a twilight quality in pathic love, and wallowing in twilight leads eventually to illusions" (205).

He remembers his masturbatory encounters with schoolmates, his "platonic friends" at Cambridge, his unfulfilled love for John Claire, his encounter with John Edleston—the subject of a poem, "To Thyrza"; surprised one night by a watchman "in a compromising posture with one of the grooms" (44). He mentions a "coquettishness" he senses from Edward Trelawny and the "ambiguous nature of my attitude" (281–82). He records his "strictly scientific experiment" to discover what his friends found so enticing about "the Ottoman posture" through a tryst with Ali Pasha. He notes that when his friend John Cam Hobhouse asked him later whether it hurt, he had replied, "Of course it did. Damnably!" and he goes on to write, "I never was tempted to repeat my Albanian experiment" (61), though it would seem that hygiene looms as large in his decision as does pain. He remembers an encounter with a male prostitute disguised as a woman in Venice; not yet realizing his sex, Byron agrees to *coitus in anum*, "a slovenly substitute," and then is "shocked" when his hands move to "her" thighs and discovers "a blunt and rigid article, the approximate size of a cucumber." He says, "I finished my performance in a state of dejection" (163–64). Mention of various homosexuals he encounters crop up across the pages. In noting the visit of the American George Finlay with a friend, he writes, "They are both *précieux* of the American variety, and alternate between an affected enthusiasm and a spinsterish fastidiousness" (129). He mentions the improvisational actor Tommaso Sgricci, "a celebrated sodomite" (206). Sexually impotent in his final days because of his illness, he is beguiled by a Greek teenager, Loukas Chalandritsanos, but he must acknowledge that his "love will not be reciprocated. He asks, "Is this why men recoil from what Moore calls *Knabenliebe*? Not because of an intrinsic evil, since there is no intrinsic evil, but because this search for beauty brings its own inevitable self-defeat, and paedophilia, like Narcissus, is left to contemplate its own pale countenance?" (261). One cannot escape the feeling that the author is projecting his own sense of futility onto the figure of Byron.

Friedrich Prokosch (1906–1989) was born in Madison, Wisconsin, but spent much of his childhood in Austin, Texas, and Bryn Mawr, Pennsylvania. He graduated from Haverford and had a Ph.D. from Yale. Something of a con artist, he often undercut his own interests. Enamored of Auden, he sent the poet a series of nude photographs of himself, only to be ridiculed in "Letter to Lord Byron" ("notes from perfect strangers" with "sometimes, though I think this rather crude,/The correspondent's photo in the rude"). As his talents fell off after the enthusiastic reception of his first novel, Prokosch became increasingly embittered. In 1952 he met Jack Bady (1926–) in Rome; the two remained together until Prokosch's death. His last work was the wildly inventive *Voices*, 1983, in which he recorded and made up stories about his meetings with most of the century's most outstanding authors.

Greenfield, Robert M. *Dreamer's Journey: The Life and Writings of Frederic Prokosch*. Newark: University of Delaware Press, 2010.
Prokosch, Frederic. *The Missolonghi Manuscript*. *New York: Farrar, Straus & Giroux, 1968. London: Allen, 1968.
———. *The Wreck of the Cassandra*. *New York: Farrar, Straus & Giroux, 1966. London: Allen, 1966.

103 Samuel R. Delany: *Babel-17*, 1966; *Empire Star*, 1966; *The Star Pit*, 1967.

Eric Garber and Lyn Paleo record (viii–x) that a few works with references to homosexuality appeared in the first half of the twentieth century, but they note that then and even later the images that were presented "were fleeting and derogatory." Theodore Sturgeon's 1952 short story "The World Well Lost" is credited as being the first to introduce sympathetic gay characters. Two gay aliens seek refuge on Earth, only to have their repressive native planet demand that Earth return them. It happens that one of the crew of two commissioned to do so is an inarticulate gay man in love with his captain. The latter is a virulent homophobe, who just may be a deeply repressed closet case; at least, he ogles a book with reproductions of Michelangelo's statues, and he covers for his partner when the latter lets the gay prisoners escape (thus protecting his position too, of course). It is worth remembering that the U.S. government's lavender scare is still destroying people's lives at the time of publication.

Delany began pushing sexual boundaries in *Babel* with his analyses of the relationships within triples, "a close, precarious, emotional, and sexual relation" among three people (43). In form a space opera combined with a mystery, the short novel also becomes an extended meditation on the nature of language. The Alliance is being attacked by the Invaders, the users of the eponymous language. The multi-talented poet Rydra Wong is commissioned to crack its grammar. In order to solve the mystery, she proposes "to get a spaceship, get a crew together, and get to the scene of the next accident" (23). Navigators are always a triple. As soon as she meets Calli, Navigator Two, in the act of trying to pick up the customs officer accompanying her, she knows she wants him. Ron is his much younger Navigator Three, but One, the woman in the triple, was killed by the Invaders. Rydra accompanies the men to the Morgue to call back to life a new One for them. In the course of the actual space expedition the three experience troubles forging an emotional relationship. After Ron confides in Rydra, she reveals that she was briefly part of a triple, consisting of herself, Captain Fobo Lombs, and one of Ron's favorite writers, Muels Aranlyde, the author of the Comet Jo series (who named her ship the *Rimbaud*). She successfully counsels Ron the way to "teach each of them how to do what you know already" (97). Other same-sex relationships are less clear. Since they are discorporate souls, the exact nature of the relationship among the three members of her Sensory Detail—Nose, Ear, and Eyes—is unknown. Other crew members could possibly be gay or lesbian. And what is going on with the unmarried and uptight customs officer, Daniel D. Appleby? He is impressed by the pilot Brass's cosmetisurgical enhanced endowment, but he thinks triples are perverts. He has sex with a succubus: "It was a woman…. I think" (45). He sums up: "I saw a bunch of the weirdest, oddest people I had ever met in my life, who thought different, and acted different, and even made love different. And they made me laugh, and get angry, and be happy, and be sad, and excited, and even fall in love a little myself. […] And they didn't seem so weird or strange anymore" (194). Thus he learns to snap his fingers (35, 191). *Empire Star* will be more direct in its depictions.

This novella is identified in *Babel* as one of the stories written by Muels. Delany wrote it with the thought that the two works would make up one of the Ace doubles. A quest story in which people and events curve back upon themselves and repeat in strange, varying patterns, Comet Jo's double charges him to convey the message Jewel to Empire Star. Faithfully accompanied by Di'k, a devil kitten, Jo sets off. Charona, herself accompanied by 3-Dog, provides passage, and he has his first encounter with the Lll, later described as "the shame and tragedy of the multiplex universe" because "no man can be free until they are free" (30). After a brief stay on Earth, he meets Lump ("A linguistic ubiquitous multiplex"), a computer disguised as Oscar Wilde, claiming to have the mind of a Lll (40); the ticket Lump buys Jo for his trip to the Moon is under the alias Alfred A. Douglas. From *Babel* (95) we already know, "In the books [Muels] always disguises himself as a computer," a fact confirmed in *Star*. Later Jo and Lump meet the obviously gay poet Ni Ty Lee, who was mentored by no other than Muels. One of Ni Ty's goals is to write poems so readers will "know that they're not the only ones" (63). Besides Oscar and Bosie, allusions are made to Sturgeon, "Paul V[erlaine] and Arthur R[imbaud]" and "Jean C[octeau] and Raymond R[adiguet]." Certain of Lump's lines resonate for a gay reader: his angry statement "I do *not* intend to pass" (44); his answer to Jo's question ("How did he know you were Lll?"), "Some people can tell right off. That's better than the ones who sit around and talk to you for an hour before they get around to asking" (56–57); his musing, "The only important elements in any society are the artistic and the criminal, because they alone, by questioning the society's values, can force it to change" (75).

Other works from the same time are also relevant. The novella *The Star Pit*, first published in the magazine *World of Tomorrow* (collected in *Driftglass*), concerns the sense of loss (particularly of their children) and the loneliness assailing two men, Vyme and Sandy, exiled from their prokegroups (an extended and more complex triple). In trying to move on, they land at the Star Pit as mechanics working on disabled spaceships. Ratlit, one of the teenage runaways hanging around the shop, was picked up briefly by a stereotypical gay named Vivian, a publisher who brought out a novel Ratlit dictated to him. *Star Pit* is also about goldens, a special group "whose physiological orientation makes life in our interstellar society painful or impossible" for them but gives them the ability to "make the crossing and return" from the limits of intergalactic space (14). Goldens' correspondence with homosexuals, though not exact, is inescapable. Characters in discussing what makes a person a golden postulate various theories: "combination of physiological and psychological"; "some sort of hormonal imbalance"; "environmentally conditioned thalamic/personality response"; "X-chromosome heredity nonsense" (18). On a humorous level, the reader is told that goldens like to wear a little fingernail long (23). Sandy was married to one. Among many things *Star Pit* is about the need to accept limits while paradoxically pushing against them.

Two short stories collected with the novella have gay characters. In "Aye, and Gomorrah...," 1967, spacers have been neutered presumably to prevent their procreating any abnormal mutations as a result of their exposure to radiation. Frelks are sexually attracted to them and become a means for spacers to pick up extra money. With remarkable prescience Delany anticipates "the neo-puritan reaction to the sexual freedom of the twentieth century" (97). "Time Considered as a Helix of Semi-Precious Stones," 1968, is, among other things, Delany's homage to Joyce's *Finnegans Wake*: the name of its hero, a jewel thief and quick change artist, keeps altering but always begins with the same initials: H.C.E., "Here Comes Everybody." H.C.E. was in a relationship at one time with Hawk, a masochistic Singer. Hawk saves him and a potential fence, Arty the Hawk, at a crucial moment. A campy humor runs through all five works, sometimes verging on the ribald: when Jo must hide his Di'k, he posts a sign: "Authorized Entrance for J–O Persons Only" (76).

Samuel Ray Delany, Jr. (1942–), in his autobiography, *The Motion of Light in Water*, 1988 (revised 1993), has a long section on his and his wife's tripling with another man (to whom he dedicates *Babel-17*). It also discusses the significance of being a writer who is gay, black, and dyslexic. Born in New York, he attended the prestigious Bronx High School of Science. He was married to the poet Marilyn Hacker 1961–75; they have a daughter. His wife's job as editor with Ace Books led to his first novel. Garber and Paleo note (63) that *The Ballad of Beta-2*, 1965, and *Nova*, 1968, "contain noticeable elements of sexual variation," but they hold that "these are either too minor or too subjective" to label the novel. In 1974 he published the all-important *Dhalgren*. In addition to science fiction he has published pornography and literary criticism. His works have received four Nebulas (including one for *Babel-17*), two Hugos, and one Stonewall Book Award. In 1993 he was awarded the Bill Whitehead Award for Lifetime Achievement. Despite not having a university degree, he has been a professor at a number of different universities, including Massachusetts and Temple. In

1990 he began a relationship with a homeless man, Dennis Rickett (1954?–). The graphic novel *Bread & Wine*, 1999, describes their relationship.

Delany, Samuel R. *Babel-17*. New York: Ace, 1966. London: Gollancz, 1967. *New York: Vintage, 2001 (bound with *Empire Star*).
_____. *Empire Star*. New York: Ace, 1966. *New York: Vintage, 2001 (bound with *Babel-17*).
_____. *Driftglass: Ten Tales of Speculative Fiction*. New York: New American Library, 1971. *Aye, and Gomorrah: Stories*. New York: Vintage, 2003.

104 George Baxt: *A Queer Kind of Death*, 1966; *Swing Low, Sweet Harriet*, 1967. *Topsy and Evil*, 1968.

The trilogy is a silly, fun read. Its mild irreverence ("even Jesus took time out for Christmas") and political incorrectness ("Why don't I give it all up and retire to Florida? I can't. I'm not Jewish") amuse. Marketed as murder mysteries, they are as much exercises in campiness—with perhaps a few too many excursions into cutesiness. They have misleadingly become known as the Pharoah Love series (and in the 1990s the character was resurrected for a pair of mysteries in which he is indeed the main character), but more accurately they are an ensemble piece and, as such, should be read in order. In the opening salvo, with its in-your-face title, Seth Piro announces that he intends to write a biography of his ex-lover: the New York actor and model Ben Bentley (né Bergheim), a murder victim. Someone dumped a radio, still plugged in, into the bathtub where he was bathing. Seth's wife, Veronica Urquist, whom he dumped when he fell in love with Ben, wants to secure the book for her publishing house, but since she botched up his two novels, he is holding off. She also wants him back physically: "She wanted a man she could handle" (86). He succumbs for a moment to her sexual needs, but he holds off on a marital reconciliation. Pharoah, the detective assigned to the murder investigation, also takes a sexual interest in the thirty-six-year-old Seth. He, of course, is the prime suspect—for good reason since Ben had just dumped him. But the forty-year-old jive-talking African American caricature is not going to allow a little matter like that to bother him. He tells Seth, "I think we'd be good for each other. I need a friend, and you need a lot of what I've got to offer" (192). That includes protection; as he says earlier, "No one harms mine" (23). Seth accepts his offer, but not happily. Other suspects are sixty-year-old Jameson Hurst, Ben's rich lover prior to Seth; Jameson's mysterious sister, Ella; and the Native American Adam Littlestorm, Ben's replacement in Jameson's bed. Since Ben was operating a peyote smuggling business (how innocent the 1960s now seem) and was blackmailing an impressive number of people for impressive sums of money, the list could be longer, but another murder and an accidental death close the case as far as the police are concerned. The novel marked an audacious debut for the author. All the characters, not least Pharoah, leave a reader shaking his head, but Larry Duplechan for one, in an essay in *The Lost Library*, has talked about the impact that encountering a gay black character that he could actually identify with had on him.

In the sequel, set some four years later, the reader learns that Seth's book has been published and did well enough to earn a paperback reprint. He now has a commission to ghostwrite the autobiography of an early film star attempting a comeback via television. As part of his research, he interviews three other actresses from the same period, all of whom worked under the same director and all of whose careers ground to a halt when that director was murdered. Twin brothers, Peter and Robert Moulin, have embarked on their own book project, a compilation about unsolved Hollywood crimes. They have read Seth's book and find his solution to Ben's murder "most unsatisfactory" (20). Seth and Pharoah still "keep house" (41), but Seth is chafing under the detective's possessiveness and has become a full-fledged alcoholic: "Because I have sinned, dear God, he said to himself, must I pay for it the remainder of my life?" (29). Pharoah is stoical: "The best laid plans of mice and men, said Pharoah to himself, often come awry. But I'm not a mouse and he's not a man and the fantasy of making a life with him that caused me to bind myself to his crime is now a nightmare. But he's all I've got. And I'm hanging on to what's rightfully mine, unless somebody jerks the rope and tightens that noose I'm positive is now around his neck" (123). The twins indirectly provide Seth enough backbone to decide he prefers a jail cell to living any longer with Pharoah. With heavy-handed irony, in their ensuing quarrel in the bathroom Pharoah accidentally pushes Seth into the filling tub; Seth tries to catch something to hold onto and pulls the radio in with him.

Pharoah "couldn't remember later how long he stood there sobbing" (171). A few other gays appear in the novel, and the reader is left bemused about what is going on with the seemingly incestuous Moulin twins (they always share a bed) as they dream at the end of finding twin sisters to marry.

All the surviving characters return for the third novel, which takes up the story eighteen months later. Another murder has occurred: that of a wealthy tycoon; a new African American detective, Satan Stagg, has been assigned to the case, and then been told to back off. Satan is not quite so flamboyant as Pharoah, nor is his sexuality firmly established (he thinks of getting married but he does gratuitously kiss another man on the cheek). We learn that in the interim, during a meeting of the Police Review Board, "certain charges against another Negro detective name Pharoah Love were 'dismissed for lack of conclusive evidence' and Love conveniently resigned from the force" and took a job as bartender at his favorite bar. We also find that "a brilliant book on the [Bentley] case [was] published last Christmas, *In Cold Water*, by Peter and Robert Moulin" (12–13). The twins are now set to investigate this latest murder for yet another book. Seth's agent wants the new book, as does Seth's widow. The glutinous agent, by the way, is now happily married to the gay caterer for the party at which Seth's murderer was supposedly unmasked, and he has discovered he is "glad he had come to the decision to rather switch than fight" (111). He still uses his gay contacts, though, to gain an interview with the Transylvania ambassador when a connection between the case and that country becomes evident. We also learn that Jameson Hurst gained his enormous wealth by "organizing the world's underground homosexuals" for a mastermind ready to take over the U.S. economy (134). That mastermind is the great-uncle of the murdered man, to whom the twins' mother has become providentially engaged, thus providing her sons inside access. More, Bentley's sister is acting as nurse to a woman injured in the murder attack. The big mystery is, where is Pharoah? The unlikely answer is that, after sessions with an analyst after Seth's death, he has decided to become a transwoman. The guy who called everyone "cat" transforms into Ocelot, an exotic entertainer. As the novel hurls to a fiery conclusion, another character's repeat of the Burns quotation again becomes apropos: "The best laid plans of mice and men..." (112).

Throughout the three novels the author enjoys dropping names. One gets the sense that in more than a few cases he is also cracking open closet doors. It is not surprising that his next success came with a series of campy "celebrity" mysteries. Then came *A Queer Kind of Love*, 1994, and *A Queer Kind of Umbrella*, 1995. George Leonard Baxt (1923–2003) was born and died in New York. He dropped out of Brooklyn College to pursue a career in theater. He served in the Army during the war. Failing to launch a theatrical career, he turned to radio and then television, working for a number of years in London, before finding his niche as a mystery writer.

Baxt, George. *A Queer Kind of Death*. New York: Simon & Schuster, 1966. London: Cape, 1967. *Los Angeles: Alyson, 1998.
_____. *Swing Low, Sweet Harriet*. New York: Simon & Schuster, 1967. *New York: International Polygonics, 1987.
_____. *Topsy and Evil*. New York: Simon & Schuster, 1968. *New York: International Polygonics, 1987.

105 Victor J. Banis: *The Why Not*, 1966. J. X. Williams (Victor J. Banis): *Good-bye My Lover*, 1966. Don Holliday (Victor J. Banis): *The Man from C.A.M.P.*, 1966. A. Jay: *The Adventures of Harry Chess*, 1966.

A Greenleaf Classics editor (Earl Kemp), has on numerous occasions credited Banis for convincing his firm that there was an important gay market waiting to be tapped. *Why Not* is not only a fine accomplishment, it is also the first gay novel to use what has since become a familiar device: describing the lives of the habitués of a gay bar. (It also seems to have been published pretty much as Banis wrote it; if so, it may be his only work that Greenleaf resisted tampering with in order to make the material more sexual.) Covering some fourteen hours beginning just before noon on Saturday, it is composed of thirty-six vignettes depicting an array of characters. Each, however, is so deftly delineated that one has no problem identifying returning characters and recognizing newcomers. The Why Not is not the only setting; there are also glimpses of apartments, shops, a bathhouse, the streets. There are a few satisfying pickups and a few enthusiastic orgies, but no one seems particularly happy, and a few are downright miserable. Robberies, a gay bashing (in which, ironically, a straight male is mistaken for one of the bar's regulars and killed), a police entrapment, and a series of arrests in which a closeted policeman must seize his own lover occur. Among the more memorable portraits there is Joaquin, who has preserved his dignity by inventing a series of encounters with rich counts and famous actresses, and whose world collapses when a vicious queen exposes his lies. There is Lee Denver, the has-been Western actor who tries to maintain his sense of worth by playing his old movies during sexual encounters in his apartment. There are Ralph and Joe, deeply in love, but beginning to feel confined by monogamy. The author also proves to be a prankster: at the very end we learn that one of the characters with a unisex name is actually a woman whose lover is trying deliberately to impregnate her. Most of the novel is told in the third person, but several of the vignettes are in the first person, including the opening and the closing. The novel ends on a humorous note: the unnamed narrator is approached by, so he thinks, a panhandler—to be offered two dollars for a quickie in the alley.

In yoking a coming out story to a murder mystery in *Good-bye*, the author created the often used template of the sleuth who, in solving the crime, simultaneously solves the mystery of his own sexual difference. Even though it has been extensively rewritten, readers will want to turn to the 2007 reprint; Greenleaf inserted two gross sexual encounters in the original edition, one of which virtually destroys the credibility of the main character. When Dennis Eastman arrives in L.A., he is still debating, at age twenty, whether he is willing to accept his gayness and to create a life with his older friend and lover (a term he still feels squeamish about using) from whom he has voluntarily separated for a year while he attends the Naval Academy. When he learns that Lincoln Gardner has been murdered (as a result, he later discovers, of trying to protect Dennis's reputation in a case of blackmail involving incriminating photographs) supposedly by a trick he picked up at a gay bar, Dennis finds the story unconvincing. Linc hated gay bars in general, and he would have particularly disliked the leather bar in which the supposed assignation took place. He sets out to discover the truth. In order to achieve his goal, he uses his sex appeal to disarm his suspect. As a result of their encounters, he finally embraces his sexuality and finds a new lover. Until this moment, he says, "I didn't think it was possible for two people of the same sex to be really in love with one another." But now he tells his new friend, "I know better" (165).

Perhaps the author's best known work is *The Man from C.A.M.P.*, his satiric takeoff on the television series *The Man from U.N.C.L.E.*, though more people probably know it for its title and its iconic cover than for its contents. C.A.M.P. is "an underground organization dedicated to the protection and advancement of homosexuals" (6). When asked what the acronym stands for, a member says "the C might stand for sucker" (29). In a bow to the television show, one of the entrances to its headquarters is via a secret door in the last stall of the men's restroom at a gay bar in Los Angeles. Interpol and the U.S. Treasury call upon C.A.M.P. for its help to crack a case of diamond counterfeiting. An earlier Interpol agent has been killed, but not before being infected anally with a venereal disease, leading the international organization to conclude that a homosexual ring is running the racket. Straight (and homophobic) agent Ted Summers is assigned to work with C.A.M.P. agent Jackie Holmes. "Small but lethal" (32), he has as many gadgets as James Bond concealed on his figure. He is also quite adept at using "sex as another weapon" (15). Jackie quickly uncovers evidence that an icehouse supplying bars (appropriately enough, since "ice" is slang for diamonds) and a band of hairdressers under the direction of a notorious lesbian, Big Daddy, are integral to the smuggling operation. Summers begins their partnership by announcing, "I don't go your route." But he finds his attitude changing as the two confront danger together. Jackie has already informed him, "That's what they all say [...]. At first" (13). Summers ends up "a freshly cut notch" (114) on "a wood carving" in Jackie's home—"An enormous anatomy portion" (29). There followed eight more novels in the series (plus a tenth written probably by Banis's lover after they split). Again, a reader wants the reedited versions in which the author has tried to return as much as possible to the original manuscripts, before editorial insensitivity interfered with the texts.

Banis wrote too much too fast under too many pseudonyms to make a name for himself outside the pulp industry. Both Williams and Holliday were house names, not even limited to gay books. It also did not help that his best book remains *The*

Why Not, though at least it was published under his true name. In a July 2014 episode of the television show *True Blood*, a character can be spotted reading a copy. Victor Jerome Banis (1937–) was born in central rural Pennsylvania but grew up in Eaton, Ohio. After a brief sojourn in Birmingham, Alabama, he began work in Dayton, Ohio. In 1960 he moved to Los Angeles. He and his then lover, Sam Dodson, became writers, sometimes collaborators. By 1970 he had moved to writing straight romances. In 1980 Banis left the city, eventually settling in San Francisco in 1985. By then he had ceased writing, not to return to publishing until the present century, when he retired to Martinsburg, West Virginia. His 2004 memoirs, *Spine Intact, Some Creases*, is an important historical document; it also lists all his pseudonyms and the books written under each.

The Man from U.N.C.L.E. ran from fall 1964 to the end of winter 1968. A spy spoof responding to the James Bond movie craze, the episodes became progressively campier. Early on it tickled gay literary fancies other than Banis's. Don Rico, the comic book writer and artist, brought out *The Man from Pansy*, 1967. Buzz Cardigan is straight but is called upon to play gay in order to break up a blackmail operation. It was followed by two sequels, *The Daisy Dilemma*, 1967, and *The Passion Flower Puzzle*, 1968. Even earlier the cartoonist calling himself A. Jay had seen the satiric possibilities. When the gay activist Clark Polak advertised for an art editor for his new publication, *Drum*, Allen J. Shapiro applied. Beginning early in 1964, a strip featuring Harry Chess, "That Man from A.U.N.T.I.E.," became a regular feature of the magazine. In 1966 a collection of the strips, with one title on the cover and another inside, was brought out, the graphic novel equivalent of a story cycle. The characters, both heroes and villains, are all super-sexy and frequently unclad. Harry Chess (distinguished by his cleft chin and his hairy chest), sometimes referred to as Agent 0068⅞, is our hero. His sidekick is the naive Mickey Muscle. The stories all begin with outrageous premises. Lewd Leather, head of M.U.C.K., kidnaps "The World's Most Succulently Beautiful Male" to add to Gaygor Dragoff's "private Piece Corps," a case that has "completely baffled" the FBI and the Boy Scouts (7–9). Brownfinger is stealing all the famous collections of pornography, though he bungles the Library of Congress job when he mistakes the Guild Press dirty book room for the library. The Groping Hand steals the "FBI's prized homo-file," which sends the director into a secret retreat with Walter Jenkins, Johnson's aide who had just been arrested for solicitation (19); the theft is somehow tied into the disappearance of the astronaut Hunky Dorie and a rocketship, but by then the cartoonist admits he is having problems following his own story, though he will try to explain how it all fits together for those "who insist on a well-hung plot" (26). Finally, Eggplant Parmesani, the new head of M.U.C.K., schemes to drop ground glass into vats of Cay-Why at the manufacturing plant. The panels are filled with such kinky situations, double-entendres, and up-to-date political and cultural allusions.

The strips unfortunately seem to have fallen victim, like so much, to the myth that gay pride did not exist before Stonewall and have been virtually forgotten; the complete series merits reprinting. Allen J. Shapiro (1932–1987) was born in upstate New York. He served in the Army in Korea. Having attended the Pratt Art Institute in New York, he became an illustrator for children's books. After *Drum*'s demise, the strip moved to *Queen's Quarterly* and later *Drummer*. Shapiro moved to San Francisco, where his partner, Dick Kriegmont, lived. There he created erotic wall art for Cauldron Club and Slot Bathhouse, as well as posters and logos for other gay businesses. He died in San Francisco of AIDS-related illnesses.

[Banis, Victor J.] *Good-bye My Lover*. By J. X. Williams. San Diego, Calif.: Corinth/Greenleaf Classics (Sundown Reader), 1966. *Revised: *Goodbye My Lover*. N.p.: Borgo, 2007.

[_____.] *The Man from C.A.M.P*. By Don Holliday. San Diego, Calif.: Corinth/Greenleaf Classics (Leisure Library), 1966. *Revised: Albion, N.Y.: MLR, 2008. 1–114.

_____. *The Why-Not*. San Diego, Calif.: Greenleaf Classics, 1966. *Revised: N.p.: Borgo, 2007.

Jay, A. *Harry Chess, That Man from A.U.N.T.I.E.* Philadelphia: Trojan Books, 1966. **Meatmen: An Anthology of Gay Male Comics*. Vol. 17. Ed. Winston Leyland. San Francisco: Leyland, 1995. 6–35.

Murphy, Michael J. "The Lives and Times of Harry Chess." *Gay & Lesbian Review*, March–April 2014. Online.

106 Richard Amory: *Song of the Loon*, 1966; *Song of Aaron*, 1967; *Listen, the Loon Sings…*, 1968. Ricardo Armory: *Fruit of the Loon*, 1966.

Though it never appeared on any list of bestsellers, *Song of the Loon* may well have been the first gay novel to achieve that status. Tom Norman reports (3), "It has been estimated that 30% of the gay male population in the U.S. purchased a copy of the first Amory book." It is almost always the work chosen, if any pulp novel is cited in academic surveys (though often mistitled *The Song of the Loon*). It was the first gay novel to become the basis for a film, in 1970. It was the first openly gay western, though its models were pastoral novels from the Spanish Renaissance. Its heroes are mountain men—trappers—and Native Americans in the Pacific Northwest during the late nineteenth century. Why the novel should have attracted such a readership is difficult to say: perhaps its sense of innocence, its ardent appreciation of male beauty, and the way good triumphs over evil all appealed to the turbulent time in which it was published. It was a different kind of call for gay liberation, based on the premise that one must learn to love and to accept oneself. For it is also a novel about a quest to find psychic wholeness: the Way of the Loon. This is the Way into which Ephraim MacIver is to be initiated. He has followed his lover, the manipulative and largely closeted Clarence Montgomery, from California to find that he has taken up with another closeted individual who runs a mission school, the aptly named Mr. Calvin. Sick as a result of what he has discovered, Ephraim is rescued by Ixtlil Cuauhtli. He gives him the loom amulet and sends him to find Bear-who-dreams, "the wise man, the medicine man of the painted cave" (10). Along the way Ephraim meets several Native Americans and a mountain man. From them he learns many lessons, beginning with the futility of jealousy, which is for them nothing more than a wrongful manifestation of fear or cruelty or possessiveness, the desire for power over another. Under the tutelage of Bear-who-dreams he goes on a spirit quest and is accepted into the Loon Society. Ephraim now returns to be with Cyrus Wheelright, the mountain man. But he knows Singing Heron is waiting for both of them, and he knows that it is right for them to share their love. He has learned that gay men do not have to parody straight society: that there need be no distinction between active and passive, no confusion of gender. Ephraim also realizes that there is more for him to learn, so he is willing to separate temporarily from Cyrus. His last words in the novel are sung: "I may be playing games, [...] but, oh! How I will play them! How I will dance, and sing, and love!" (191). Twelve love poems are scattered across the pages of the novel. In this pastoral Eden even Calvin and Montgomery escape their binding confines and set up housekeeping together.

The argument that true love is not possessive continues in *Aaron*. One of the characters sets forth an analogy: "Any man keeps a dawg tied up all the time [...] don't love that dawg. He's a-feared the dawg'll up and run off and won't come back, and more'n likely he's got good reason to be a-feared. And he don't want a dawg in the first place a-tall—he just wants somethin' that'll lick his hand every time he throws 'im a bone. That ain't love, Aaron" (132). Still later, the hero is told, "Lovin' ain't like bronc bustin,' Aaron" (169). This novel is set in the more traditional world of the cowboy, with gunfights and saloons and cattle rustling. Cecil Whitebone, another self-hating homosexual, is the villain, and unlike Calvin, no redemption awaits him. He is the cause of the death of Aaron Buckthorn's lover, Clete Westwick, and Aaron is out for revenge. His search for Cecil brings him to the all male community of Las Nubes (The Clouds, perhaps a never-never land, perhaps heaven). It will also take him to the very different male community of Diablo Flats. In Las Nubes he meets a sentinel, Avispa (Wasp). Avispa warns Aaron, "*I'm* fallin' in love with *you*, Aaron, so watch out." He adds, "Somethin' else you ought to know [...]. You're goin' to love me too, before we're finished" (58). Seven songs become part of their romance. Dreams also play an important part, especially in keeping the novel situated in the Loon mythos: Tsi-Nokha, a Native American introduced in the first novel, returns, first via these visions and finally in the flesh at the end to invite them to the spring meeting of the Loom Society.

All of the characters in the first two volumes assemble for further instruction into the Way of the Loon in the third volume, though Hank, a character introduced in the second volume, to a large extent centers the action, with Tsi-Nokha continuing his role as a wise mentor. There is not a plot so much as a series of tableaus with nine songs. Neil DeWitte, the only critic to have examined the novels as a whole in the context of western pulp fiction, sums up (226) that the "trilogy gives readers a series that celebrates free love, promotes honesty of emotion, and upholds the notion of giving selflessly to others. The books specifically reject self-loathing, thievery and trickery, and using others for selfish gain." Arsenal Pulp Press reissued the first novel in 2005 with a number of valuable appendices that make clear there was no love between the author and his publisher. The author was outraged by the editor's ignorant tampering with his text; the editor has accused Amory of arrogance and self-centeredness, making it clear that the press's goal was to make money, not to nourish literature.

Though Greenleaf Classics published six of the author's eight novels, it took the unprecedented step of issuing a crushing parody of its moneymaker, *Fruit of the Loon*. It seems an underhanded act, though, to be fair, Armory's novel pokes fun at the press itself for the kinds of books it was publishing. There is also the undeniable fact that the parody is not only hilarious but better written than the original. The title plays on the popular underwear brand Fruit of the Loom. Populated with nelly cowboys who work the Circle 69 ranch, an inept trapper who catches ground squirrels and skunks, and leering "redskins," the novel introduces the Wild Goose Club. Dreamed up by the medicine man Squirming Ass, who "read about this Loon Society in a book," the society was concocted with the help of Chief Hot Rocks. Their amulet resembles "a moulting pigeon" more than a wild goose: "Squirming Ass got a cheap deal on them from the traders" (23–24). Happy Down-Hanging has been given the assignment to disperse four of these charms to studs. In a hurry to get rid of them, he slips one around the neck of the sleeping trapper without explaining its significance. It is left up to another member of the tribe, Ixlztxtkzllyxzll (better known as Swinger), with the help of the mute bartender Sam, to initiate Dean into the mysteries of the order. Dean proves to be more than up to meeting the exhausting challenges, perhaps because peanut butter and milk provide the staple of his diet. He is instrumental in averting a showdown between the butch men at Fort Nelly and the swishy cowboys of the Circle 69. They negotiate a swap, with the Fort Nelly guys taking over the ranch and the pseudo-cowboys becoming the new management of the New Marshmallow Pump Room and Afterhours Coffee Shop. Dean is happily reunited with his friend Chad, who discovers that quite a bit has happened since he last lusted after the innocent trapper. Dean assures him that "Sam said he'd get some books from San Diego that would explain anything I still don't understand" (148). There are poems here too, all along the lines of "Barefoot boy with cheeks of tan,/Roll on your belly so I can" (95). The parody ends with Dean's brother showing up at Squirming Ass and Hot Rocks's place. Speaking "the Sacred Language," they observe, "Isthay udstay isay unghay [...]. Iklay ay orsehay" (165), and inquire whether he "would be interested in sharing the company of a couple of more mature gentlemen this winter" (171). The novel offers no moral, no lesson.

Richard Wallace Love (1927–1981) was born in Halway, Oregon, but the family moved to Columbus, Ohio, in the 1930s. He joined the Coast Guard near the end of World War II. Upon graduation from Ohio State, he was drafted by the Army. He moved to California, where he taught high school. He received a master's in Spanish from San Francisco State and began the doctoral program at Berkeley. Married, with three children, he came out in 1970 and became a gay activist. *Frost*, 1971, a murder mystery is one of his finest works. He died suddenly when his liver shut down. Ricardo Armory has been identified as George Davies (dates unknown), who usually wrote under the pseudonym Lance Lester, later as Clay Caldwell or as Thumper Johnson. He is said to have been an illustrator for Walt Disney Studios (the novel contains a fleeting allusion to "Disneyland in June"), but his name as such does not appear in the Disney files.

Amory, Richard. *Listen, the Loon Sings… : Book Three of the Loon Songs Trilogy*. San Diego, Calif.: Greenleaf Classics, 1968.
_____. *Song of Aaron: Book Two, the Loon Songs Trilogy*. San Diego, Calif.: Greenleaf Classics, 1967.
_____. *Song of the Loon: A Gay Pastoral in Five Books and an Interlude*. San Diego, Calif.: Greenleaf Classics, 1966.
Armory, Ricardo. *Fruit of the Loon: A Novel in Several Turgid Books and a Few Frantic Interludes*. San Diego, Calif.: Greenleaf Classics, 1968.
DeWitte, Neil. "The Gay Western: Heroic Trailblazers Stake Their Claim." *The Golden Age of Gay Fiction*. Ed. Drewey Wayne Gunn. Albion, N.Y.: MLR, 2009. 223–34.

107 Kyle Onstott and Lance Horner: *Child of the Sun*, 1966. Frank Yerby: *Goat Song*, 1967.

These historical romances—the first set in Rome, the other in Greece—are alike in being filled with sex and violence. But whereas Yerby's seems passé, Onstott and Horner's remains fresh. It manages simultaneously to evoke the past and to cover issues that remain pertinent. Fairly reveling in the flesh, the novel is an entertaining corrective to the high-mindedness of Yourcenar and Renault, and especially Alfred Duggan, who wrote about the same figure. Horner began exploring Roman themes in *Rogue Roman*, 1956. It tells the story of Nero's unknown half-brother, Cleon, a zealous womanizer from Syria. His faithful companion is Mamax, an Egyptian-born slave who was a prostitute in the service of Apollo. Mamax never lets on that he is in love with Cleon. The nearest they come to sex is a mutual masturbation session that is passed off as a religious ritual. But when Horner teamed up with Onstott for his second excursion into Roman history, same-sex desire permeates the story. They chose as their hero the emperor Elagabalus (203?–222) and at the end of the novel provide thirteen dense pages of notes concerning their sources.

We first meet Varius, as he is then called, on the eve of his fifteenth birthday, when he will become the incarnation of the Syrian god Elah-ga-baal, symbolized by a great black phallic stone. Varius tries to convince his cousin, Alexianus, that "woman, a vile creature governed by the moon, was unclean and not to be desired, whereas man, under the dominion of the Sun was always strong, clean and glorious" (83). His "satyric sexuality and his mystical religion were deeply and inextricably linked together in his character" (187). An insatiable size-queen, Varius becomes enamored of the well endowed and equally insatiable wrestler Zoticus, whom he marries. Upon the assassination of Caracalla, Varius becomes Emperor Antoninus and, despite his youth, is genuinely embraced by his army because of his elan and high spirits. Antoninus shows an unexpected ability not only to command but to delegate responsibly: "Rome under Antoninus reached the peak of glory—a glory she was never to know again," for the men he appoints "proved themselves far more qualified to perform their official duties during Antoninus's reign than the grafting Romans who had purchased the offices by bribes under former régimes" (122). Unfortunately, his mother and his aunt, who have done all they can to make him a weak pawn, now set various intrigues afoot that will plague his brief reign and result in his womanizing cousin supplanting him. On his triumphal entry into Rome, Antoninus sees and falls in love with the charioteer Hierocles. His rival is his slave Gordius, but Antoninus pardons all when he learns that Hierocles returns his love. Martijn Icks writes (190) that *Child of the Sun* "is the first novel to make the relationship of Elagabalus and Hierocles its main theme, and the first to put so much emphasis on the positive aspects of their love." The authors write: "There was a blending between the two of them, each taking from the other the needed qualities he did not possess." Their honeymoon becomes "a week of miracles in which the chariot driver became a little more polished and the Roman Caesar a little roughened" (182). The two find a retreat in the country. At moments of stress Antoninus is ready to throw Rome away and go there with Hierocles.

Various twists and turns ensue. He faces up to the fact that he must destroy Alexianus, or Alexianus will destroy him, and then discovers that his own character is such that he cannot stoop to such heinous acts. He marries a woman and attempts to procreate an heir, but finds he is sexually incapable of the act. Many of his problems are caused by his religion. He agrees to a "lavender marriage" with the Virgin Maxima as an attempt to unite Elah-ga-baal and Vesta, the Sun God and the Sacred Fire. In a moment of infidelity, and despite Hierocles's jealousy, he becomes bewitched by the puritanical tribune Agrippa, a worshiper of the chaste Mithras, and rapes him, saying, "Perhaps I should regret what I have done, and what I have caused you to do. But I do not. We are flesh, Tribune Agrippa, and no god can say that we cannot enjoy this flesh" (303). In the jealous conflict thus provoked with Hierocles, Antoninus cries out, "Oh, Hierocles, what fools we are. Why do we behave so insanely?" He is answered, "Because we love so much" (317–18). The two are killed, offstage, and their bodies gathered by the faithful Gordius to carry safely to the retreat where Zorticus lives. By now, the authors are obviously enamored of their creation, and they bring off a symbolic happy ending that could serve as encouragement to their readers in the changing times during which the novel appeared.

In contrast, Yerby's *Song* is not only a mishmash but a decided letdown. The novel reads as if it were invented as he wrote, then never revised. Characters abruptly change personality and attributes.

The hero proves his improbable prowess as a soldier, a prostitute, an artist's model, an actor, a manufacturer, and a surgeon, but not so much as a lover even by heterosexual standards. Set in Greece in the fifth century BCE, every famous Athenian has his moment in the story, whether he has anything to add to the plot or not. The novel's mixture of Greek terms and modern concepts is disconcerting. For example, the author explains that *sykophantoi* did not mean "fawning, devious flatterers" as it would in Imperial Rome but meant "blackmailer" in classical Athens (327). But rather than use the Greeks' own sexual terminology, he uses *homosexual, bisexual, queer*, and other slang terms. There is no consistency in the author's attitude towards the various kinds of sexuality. At one moment the main character finds it "odd" that anyone could "find physical love between man and man repugnant" (95). For "the Hellenic mind," the authorial voice says, "The gods had made both sexes compellingly beautiful, and for a man to refuse either of them in favor of the other smacked of hubris, if not worse" (179). But increasingly in the novel sexual relationships between men are scorned until the main character comes to say, "the only effect that being kissed or caressed by a member of my own sex has upon me is to make me want to throw up" (267). The nadir is reached when he scornfully says that "it's the coprolitic smell of sodomites that offends my nostrils" (241). The very title seems to shift meaning. The first time it occurs within the story, the author alludes to Pan (13); later he notes that it refers to "tragoidia, the Song of the sacrifical [sic] goat" (109). But it seems to be about rutting much of the time, and the hero asks, "What in our lives is not farce?" (220).

Three men shape the course of the novel. The main character is Ariston. We follow his exploits from the time he is seventeen until his forties, with a brief look ahead to his death. His lifelong problem is to forgive himself so he may learn how to love and respect himself. By birth a Spartan, early on he is in love with a fellow student in his gymnasium. Then he meets a girl who saves his life. Thereafter he is interested only in women. We are told that his putative father "had no patience at all with the growing modern tendency to tolerate homosexual love" and therefore would applaud such "manliness" (34). Captured by the Athenians in battle and sold in slavery, he ends up the star attraction in a male brothel. The experience removes what tolerance he has previously felt for sex as an expression of love between males. His fate is intertwined with that Orchomenus, another Spartan. Early, he falls in love with Ariston's real father. He would like something sexual, but the father rejects such. Under his tutoring, Orchomenus begins to grow. Then, after he too is captured and sold into the mines, he emerges changed: "intelligence and stupidity, good and evil, alternate in him—with no middle ground at all, no place where the warring elements of his being can meet and reconcile themselves" (369). He abuses his wife and squanders money on catamites. From a heroic figure he tumbles to being a despicable fool. The third man is Danaus, an Athenian who falls in love with Ariston. But Ariston tells Sokrates, "He knows and respects my aversion to carnal love between man and man" (274). Danaus is one of the few steady characters across the course of the story and the only reason nowadays for a gay reader to turn to the novel for any kind of entertainment. Women have a strong role, but they are presented as equally inconsistent, vacillating between noble acts and petty reprisals. A strong tinge of misogyny, in fact, runs through the story.

Kyle Onstott (1887–1966) was born in DuQuoin, Illinois. He was a professional dog breeder, writing his first book on the subject in collaboration with his adopted son. Other homoerotic novels include the popular *Mandingo*, 1957, which launched the Falconhurst series (for some of which he collaborated with Horner). Kenric Lancaster Horner (1902–1973) was born in Stateville, New York. He graduated from Boston University and became a commercial art director and antique dealer. He died in St. Petersburg, Florida. Both men were unmarried and likely gay. Frank Garvin Yerby (1916–1991) was born in Augusta, Georgia. He graduated from Paine College and Fisk University. He taught in a number of colleges before beginning his career as a best-selling author of historical romances. Fleeing racial discrimination, he moved to France and in 1955 settled in Spain. He was married twice and had four children. He died in Madrid.

Icks, Martijn. *The Crimes of Elagabalus: The Life and Legacy of Rome's Decadent Boy Emperor*. Cambridge, Mass.: Harvard University Press, 2012.
Onstott, Kyle, and Lance Horner. *Child of the Sun*. *Greenwich, Conn.: Fawcett, 1966. London: Allen, 1966.

Yerby, Frank. *Goat Song: A Novel of Ancient Greece.* *New York: Dial, 1967. London: Heinemann, 1968.

108 Don Carpenter: *Hard Rain Falling*, 1966. Malcolm Braly: *On the Yard*, 1967.

The main character in Carpenter's novel, Jack Levitt, strives for sexual abstinence when he lands in prison. It is difficult, for all around he hears constant talk about sex, and "you could not be in prison long without hearing about the love affairs that were going on right there, between the men themselves" (179). He begins to obsess about his cell-mate, Billy Lancing, whom he knows has been twice raped in prison. He tells himself how ridiculous all sex is when one examines the act. And so they become sexual partners: "It was an arrangement, coldly conceived for sexual satisfaction [...] there was to be no question of emotional involvement, or prying into one another's soul. This, they decided coldly would keep them from going crazy or queer" (184). Then what Jack has been afraid of happens. Billy tells him, "I love you. And I want you to tell me. To say it. In words." Even though Jack now knows that he does love Billy, he cannot bring himself to say the words. Billy begs, "You can't talk; at least, at most, kiss me. You got to. If you love me, kiss me." But Jack refuses. The next day Billy dies in the act of killing an inmate who has sworn to murder Jack: "Jack wept that night, bitterly. He could find no thought to comfort himself. He could not even be enraged, only desolated, and more lonely than he had ever been in his life" (209–11). When he is paroled and married, he names his son Billy. The entire affair, however, takes up only a few pages in the novel. Don Carpenter (1931–1995) was born in Berkeley, California. When he was a teenager, his family moved to Oregon. He served in the USAF, then enrolled in San Francisco State. This was his first novel. He was also a screen writer and lived in Hollywood for much of the rest of his life. Married, he had two daughters. Suffering from a number of debilitating maladies, he committed suicide.

Homosexuality provides an unexpected but pivotal twist quite late in the plot of Braly's novel. The San Quentin, California, prison authorities know that Billy Oberholster, known to all as Chilly Willy, is behind several of the most lucrative rackets operating behind its walls. When he begins to take out inmates who have crossed him, the authorities hatch an unorthodox scheme to neutralize him. It is never clear why they think he is sexually vulnerable, but to this end they assign the very effeminate Martin Cain, aka Candy Cane, to become his cell-mate. The ploy works. The two men become lovers: "A line drawn in Chilly's mind, which he had thought he would never cross, had fallen away like a strand of cobweb the first time he had touched it, and he had pitched into an area of awareness that had either been beyond or forbidden to his imagination. He no longer cared when his hands, or even his mouth betrayed him" (308). Soon for him there ceases to be anything homosexual about their union: "he thought of her excess organs as a biological accident" (319). Then the authorities pounce one night, taking photographs of them having sex. No sooner have the flashbulbs gone off than Chilly realizes that Candy has withdrawn any emotional ties. But it takes his realization that his mother will now be notified to undo him completely. We learn via an overheard conversation that he has tried to take his life and is now in the psychiatric ward. His usefulness ended, Candy has been transferred to the special wing for other queens. Malcolm Braly (1925–1980), a Portland, Oregon, native spent more than sixteen years in three different prisons. He also published a prison memoir, *False Starts*, 1976. He died in a car accident, leaving behind a widow and an infant daughter.

Braly, Malcolm. *On the Yard.* Boston: Little, Brown, 1967. London: Hutchinson, 1968. *New York: New York Review, 2002.
Carpenter, Don. *Hard Rain Falling.* New York: Harcourt, Brace & World, 1966. London: Barker, 1966. *New York: New York Review, 2009.

109 James Purdy: *Eustace Chisholm and the Works*, 1967.

Set in Chicago during the Depression, the novel chronicles the interlinked lives of seven emotionally and (save one) economically destitute individuals, most still in their twenties. The title character functions mostly as an ear, a recording conscious: "Everything in his own life may have been a failure, but he never tired of listening to others or reading their mail" (178). Ace, as he is called, is at work on a long, never described poem, but after the "awful events, ending in the deaths of Amos and Daniel, he never wrote a line again" (249). Before the novel opens, Ace's wife Carla has left him for another man, so Clayton Harms joins Ace in his bed. After Carla infects her new lover with the syphilis she got from Ace, she is thrown out. She returns to Ace; Clayton can put up with a *ménage à trois* only so long before he splits. Nearby lives the homophobic Daniel Haws, who sleepwalks every night to his renter Amos Ratcliffe's bed but is incapable of admitting that he is in love with the boy. Amos, a student of ancient Greek, despairing that anything will develop between him and Daniel, consents to become millionaire Reuben Masterson's kept boy. In order to escape everything, Daniel rejoins the army, from which he "had been separated under obscure circumstances" (87). Posted to a camp in Mississippi, he draws the attention of the sadistic Captain Stadger, who stalks him in a grim dance of death. Finding that Daniel is in love with Amos, Stadger begins physically abusing the private, building to the climatic moment when he inserts a double-edged sword into Daniel's rectum and literally disembowels him before shooting himself. Meanwhile, after taking Amos to his mother's country home, Masterson returns to his nocturnal jaunts. One evening Amos throws himself on the recently widowed gardener. Reuben catches the two, they fight, make up, get drunk—to be interrupted by the mother's untimely appearance. She dies. At her funeral Amos and Reuben are caught, "drunk and necking, Reuben's hand on [Amos's] open fly for the whole world to get the picture" (180). Ace indirectly becomes responsible for Amos's death. Reuben winds up marrying a promiscuous painter, Maureen O'Dell, whom Amos has earlier accompanied to abort Daniel's child, a scene described in graphic detail. At the end Ace accepts Carla back into his bed. The final tally is three dead homos, two converted heteros, and two accepting wives.

James Otis Purdy (1914–2009) was born in Hicksville, Ohio, but grew up in Findlay, Ohio. He graduated from Bowling Green and the University of Chicago. He taught at a military school in West Virginia and served in the Army in World War II. He lived in Mexico and Cuba, before accepting a post at Lawrence College in Wisconsin. He returned to Chicago, where he associated primarily with jazz musicians, and began writing. In the 1960s he moved to New York. His fans seem in agreement that this, his seventh book, was his first truly gay novel. One of the two dedicatees is Edward Albee, who in 1966 dramatized an earlier novel, *Malcolm*. Purdy died in an Englewood, New Jersey, nursing home where he went after fracturing his hip.

Purdy, James. *Eustace Chisholm and the Works*. *New York: Farrar, Straus & Giroux, 1967. London: Cape, 1968.

110 Alfred Chester: *The Exquisite Corpse*, 1967.

Is there another novel containing so many homosexual acts that seems less gay than this one? Various same-sex couples appear: John Doe and James Madison (who kills himself but remains very much alive), Ismael Rosa and Tommy (who exchange a mask), Mary Poorpoor (supposedly based on Susan Sontag) and Emily (Maria Irene Fornés?), John Anthony and briefly Dickie Gold. But their identities and their settings shift and transform. In particular Baby Poorpoor may—or may not—become other characters. In her afterword to the novel, Chester's English editor informs us (252): "The title comes from the game called in England 'Consequences'—it was the Surrealists who gave it the more exotic name." A group of people write a story, each one adding to the previous chapter without knowing what it says. She suggests one read the novel like a fairy tale (traditional fairies show up with a changeling child when Baby Poorpoor is born). For Chester's fans, it is the culmination of his fictional excursions. The closest to a gay moral that one gets is an abortionist's statement to Emily: "Nature is no moralist. She never judges. She merely acts" (171).

Alfred Chester (1928–1971) was born in New York. Scarlet fever left him hairless; the bizarre wig he wore is routinely mentioned in all descriptions of him. He graduated from NYU, then enrolled in Columbia, but dropped out to depart for Paris. There he fell in love with a young bisexual Israeli, Arthur Davis. Encouraged by Alexander Trocchi, he wrote *Chariot of Flesh*, 1955, a pornographic pastiche of Nabokov's *The Real Life of Sebastian Knight*; it was published under the pseudonym Malcolm Nesbit. His second novel, *Jamie Is My Heart's Desire*, 1956, an absurdist affair about different characters' relations with a corpse that may or may not be there, has a gay priest, Father Tulley. Returning to New York, Chester met Sontag, the poet Edward Field, the playwright Jean-Claude Van Itallie. He wrote reviews for various journals, including a scathing putdown of Rechy's *City of Night*. In 1963 he moved to Morocco, met the

Bowleses, and fell in love with a native, Dris. His 1965 collection of short stories, *Behold Goliath*, included "In Praise of Vespasian." He was deported to New York, where he finished *Corpse*. The last years were spent wandering: England, Morocco (from which he was permanently banished in 1968), Israel. His corpse was found days after his death in his Jerusalem apartment.

Chester, Alfred. *The Exquisite Corpse*. New York: Simon & Schuster, 1967. London: Deutsch, 1970. *Afterword Diana Athill. Boston: Godine, 2003.

Field, Edward. *The Man Who Would Marry Susan Sontag and Other Intimate Literary Portraits of the Bohemian Era*. Madison: University of Wisconsin Press, 2005.

111 Robert Somerlott: *The Flamingos*, 1967.

Set in the imaginary coastal town of San Antonio Tlaxtalapan, the novel records the intertwined lives of a number of American expatriates and natives. The fifty-eight-year-old Matthew Selkirk, former professor and translator of the *Satyricon*, is a prominent member of the American colony—an openly gay man who feels his life has "been merely a series of futile experiments from which he had learned absolutely nothing" (109). He picks up twenty-six-year-old Clay McPherson on the beach, not knowing that the young man, going under the alias Touch Crockett, is in flight, mistakenly thinking that he has murdered his horror of a mother. Clay has many of the characteristics of Herlihy's midnight cowboy. Several scenes reveal his compassion for the underdog and his loyalty to those he admires. He self-identifies as straight, but discovers that "he couldn't help liking Matthew" (183). Though deeply mistrustful of "queers," Clay finds himself longing to "tell Matthew the whole story, if he could only count on him" (278). Matthew fully expects Clay to leave him when something better presents itself. To his surprise he realizes, "I'll be sorry to see him go. I'm extraordinarily fond of him" (292). When the opportunity does arise to leave with a friend who shows up, Clay cannot bring himself to do so. What he does not know is that Matthew has just found out from doctors in Mexico City that he has some form of leukemia that gives him at best a year and a half to live. Seeking a second opinion, he flies to New York, taking Clay with him "to give him a chance to escape me." Instead, Clay "harped constantly about coming back here and even used the word 'home.' I found that more than a little touching." But Matthew resists believing that Clay might "really give a damn about me" (383). The assurance that Clay's emotions are genuine comes about as the result of a hurricane that almost destroys the town. Realizing that Matthew, who has stayed at home, is in danger if a dam breaks, Clay risks his own life to rescue him. In amazement but with affection, Matthew reports to an old friend: "He came for me, Stephen. He didn't have to, but he did. [...] There'll never be a moment so beautiful as when he walked in and said, 'Where's your coat? We're getting out of here.' He even seemed surprised I wasn't at the door, expecting him" (416). Clay also, indirectly, saves a new-born baby. Other characters include two pairs of lesbians, three of whom are as unlikable as Clay and Matthew are likeable and all three of whom are killed in the storm.

Robert Somerlott (1928–2001) was born in Huntington, Indiana. He attended Northwestern, Michigan State, and the University of Michigan. For some fifteen years he worked as an actor and stage director. In 1963 he settled in San Miguel de Allende, Mexico. He died in Leon, following bypass surgery.

Somerlott, Robert. *The Flamingos*. *Boston: Little, Brown, 1967. London: Hutchinson, 1968.

112 Bruce King (Avery Willard): *Summer Awakening*, 1967.

Willard published four novels under his King pseudonym. The only reason one would read any of them would be out of interest in the photographer and filmmaker; his narrative skills fall far short of his mastery of the portrait and the excitement of his experimental films. The most interesting is the first for the glimpses it gives us of gay life in the national capital. An autobiographical novel, it recounts the coming out of a Southern youth and his introduction to the gay world in Washington after World War II. It recalls for today's readers the ways a young gay then learned the vocabulary and the signals, as well as the dangers and the pitfalls. It exposes how active gay life actually was in Washington even as the federal government made gay employees' existence miserable. Young Allen visits bars and clubs (revealing incidentally that racial segregation did not exist in some), attends the drag scene, and returns repeatedly to Lafayette Park, reveling in the fact that one of the city's most active cruising spots lay in full view of the White House. He falls in love, has his heart broken, finds an army sergeant with whom he settles down, and comes out to his accepting mother. But he has an itch to try the New York stage. With regret, he and John split, and Allen begins the task of finding his niche in the theater world. He gets a job in summer stock and has a lucky break when the principal actor is unable to go on. Soon he is on his way to success, though his story ends with his being caught in a police raid on an after-play party during tryouts in Boston.

The other three novels appeared in 1969. They are undistinguished pornography. Two involve incest, real or virtual. *Strange Desire*, written with his film actor Paul Ritchards, seems designed solely to incite sexual arousal as a preliminary to masturbation. Steve Williams returns home on leave after six years in the army. He proceeds to rape or seduce every male he encounters with no thought about his partner's interests or desires. The novel concludes with his preparing to take his younger brother to bed. Riddled with clichés and factual errors, *The Triangle* follows the struggles of young Clark to avoid accepting that he is gay although he keeps recalling his teenage crush on a straight friend. He is upset to discover that his "identical" twin, his sister, is getting married, but then is drawn to her very masculine and handsome husband. In a melodramatic finale, he and his brother-in-law have sex while his sister is in the hospital awaiting delivery of her first child. Mother and baby die in childbirth; burdened with guilt, the husband gets drunk, wanders the street, and is hit by a car. At novel's end, the telephone calls awaken Clark (he spends much of the novel asleep). Willard was fascinated by the two extremes of gender play: drag and leather. In *Leather Boy* young Gary learns to associate pleasure with pain as a result of being mugged. He comes to New York, moves into the S/M community, and joins the sex industry. Dale, an agent for models, in the process of finding him jobs, becomes hopelessly besotted with the feckless youth. He forgives Gary time after time after time as he strays, until finally Dale's clinginess drives Gary away. The problem with this novel is not so much its design as its inability to create characters whom one can care about.

Avery Willard Parsons, Jr. (1921–1999), was born in Marion, Virginia. He served in the Veterans Administration during World War II. After the war, he moved to New York and became involved in theater under the name Avery Willard. Tiring of acting, he became renown for his photographs of theater personnel and shows. He also made a number of erotic films under the Avery name and pornographic films as Bruce King. He also used King for *Gay Scene*, the newspaper he published, 1970–92. He died in New York. In 2012 Cary Kehayan produced a film *In Search of Avery Willard*. It was incorporated into Ira Sachs's film *Keep the Lights On*. I can find nothing about Ritchards save that he was the actor in Willard's 1966 avant-garde erotic films *Reflections* and *Dream Boy*.

King, Bruce. *Summer Awakening*. New York: 101 Enterprises, 1967.

113 Nathaniel Burt: *Leopards in the Garden*, 1968.

The title of the novel could easily have been, with a bow to Henry James, "What Howie Knew." The story of what befalls a blended American family living on the Côte d'Azur one summer during the 1920s is told in his prepubescent voice (though with an adult's vocabulary). He is one of seven children, the offspring of four marriages. The tensions of the summer arise from the effect his uncle Dick's visit has on his teenage half-brother, Robbie, and the resulting jealousy felt by Robbie's slightly younger half-brother, Richie—the family outsider, kin to no one else in the family, adopted by them when his parents were killed. Howie is clueless about what is going on, but he leaves the reader enough clues to piece together the probable truth. Dick is the brother of Howie's and Robbie's mother. He is "a myth" to the children, "a famous bachelor," about whom stories circulate concerning "his romantic and dashing service in the war—ambulance driving, aviation, espionage, what not." His first appearance shocks the puritanical Howie: he is "dressed—of all things—like a French sailor, tight white sailor pants and blue-striped, bare-armed sailor's jersey." He moves in a "stagy way," and his voice, though "clear, forceful" is "high-pitched" (12–15). All the young women become agitated in his presence, but his greater interest seems to be in young males: during a motor jaunt, Howie notices how he is "more or less on top" of a boy he is showing his Hispano-Suiza to, his hand "spread out on the boy's sweaty-shirted back" (92). On that same jaunt, however, Howie does see him one night leaving an English divorcée's hotel room—"laughing" (96)—and later Dick moves into her and her daughters' summer house.

The trip is to the "famous ruin" of "Malhaut," a major Catharist site. The father, a Quaker, is a religious scholar. The occasion brings out the opposing views of the brothers-in-law. The father is a puritan; Dick declares himself a follower of Apollo. He argues, "if you really believe in Christianity and love thy neighbor and judge not and turn the other cheek and nonviolence and all that rot, like the Cathars—and look what happened to the Cathars—can you sincerely believe in punishment of anybody for anything? Especially for— well, Catharist tastes?" (113). He concludes, "I'm sorry the Cathars didn't in fact have the courage of those peculiar convictions. The Greeks did, and they were certainly a good deal more civilized all round than the Cathars or the Catholics" (115). Joining in Dick's mock Greek ritual in honor of Apollo, Robbie becomes disoriented and falls off the platform they are on, receiving "a bloody gash on the left side of his forehead" (118). Back home, he undergoes a transformation. Howie has already recorded that girls "did not interest him in the least" (36). He is startled now to see Robbie wearing "a pair of tight filthy white American sailor pants and a loose filthy paint-stained sweatshirt" (124–25), imitating Dick's costumes "as closely as possible" (189). Soon he sheds the demur American bathing suit he has always worn for the more daring French style preferred by Dick. Howie, in searching Richie's secret cache in hopes that he has unearthed something about Dick's alleged spy activities, discovers nude photographs of Dick and Robbie, obviously taken by each other, somehow fallen into Richie's hands. Later he overhears a mysterious exchange between Dick and the divorcée. She says, "I don't care what you call it, *I* think it's rather disgusting," adding, "And don't you dare hurt that child in any way" (249–50). Howie watches as Dick and Robbie stroll across the garden, "arms about each other, toward the fence, out the gate, across the bone-white road, through the sharp edge of darkness into the garage and its cavernous overarch of shadows" (252).

Richie reacts to this intimacy sullenly. Howie wonders, "What was the fight about? Why was Richie so bitter, why was Rob so stern, and yet ... well, frightened? Frightened of whatever secrets Richie thought he possessed, so afraid of Richie's letting something out of its cage" (267). Richie's anger boils over one day as they prepare to go swimming. He screams at the naked Robbie, "All right, you can go to hell! You both can go to hell. That's where you belong and I hope you fry and sizzle" (278). Out on the rocks, Robbie pulls Dick into an embrace: "Richie, standing next to me livid with attention, began slowly, rhythmically to beat the heels of both hands on the parapet, baring his teeth, half crouching, making a low sound like a smothered scream" (280). What happens next, the reader must infer from clues scattered in Howie's account. We know that there is a confrontation between the father and Dick, the father saying, "He *boasted* of it!" (290). Robbie is seen lying full-length on the ground, crying: "with a sound much like the suppressed roar of an animal, he twisted himself face down again and lay beating his head on the ground, clawing at the dirt" (294). He reverts to his American bathing suit. And finally Robbie—the gymnast, always in control of his body—is found on the rocks at the base of a tower, badly injured. Richie is devastated and has "to be dragged from the hospital" (302). The novel ends with a final confrontation between father and uncle: in an echo of Robbie's earlier condition, Dick's face bears "a livid bar of purple black, mark from the blow of a stick," obviously the father's walking cane, and "a bloody patch and bruise on his left eyebrow" (306).

The actual title comes from an escaped zoo animal that Howie fleetingly sees near their home. Significantly it is in the plural. Leopards = panthers. Is there a sly reference to Wilde? We should also wonder what significance his story has for Howie. He says, "Somewhere, in my imaginary worlds, back of the action, was a concealed source of excitement, a magic compartment that contained—what? [...] I could feel it, sense it, almost see it; but it—whatever it was—stayed hidden, a treasure, a mythical beast back of bushes, a grail in a forest. I felt if I just let my mind go, I might get to the magic place; a dark tower, a sacred cave. Then I would know what the secret was, and become a wizard myself perhaps" (159). Nathaniel Burt (1913–2003) was born in Moose, Wyoming. He graduated from NYU and Princeton. During the war he served in the Navy. Another novel, *Scotland's Burning*, 1953, is set in an all-male prep school. Also a music teacher and composer, he was married and had two children. He died in Princeton, New Jersey.

Burt, Nathaniel. *Leopards in the Garden.* *Boston: Little, Brown, 1968. London: John Murray, 1969.

114 John Coriolan: *A Sand Fortress*, 1968.

The first serious novel to depict New York's gay promiscuity, it points the way towards the more famous works ten years later by Andrew Holleran and Larry Kramer. Few of its characters display anything approaching the self-loathing found in earlier glimpses into the world of quick sex and unfaithful unions, but few find the permanence or prolonged happiness that they seek either. The central figure is thirty-year-old Mike Kincade. Actor, poet, and English teacher in a private boys' school, lusted after by many, always on the prowl for sex, he spends much of his time ruing the loss of his lover Carlo Castella, who left him for another man. On an October jaunt to the Riis Park beach with his friend Alex Este (another one in love with Mike), they meet up with Mike's former student, Caswell Green—"the sand-castle boy from Fire Island" (37). Psychologically damaged, the nineteen/twenty-year-old youth spent his mornings the previous summer at the gay getaway making sand structures—fortresses, he calls them—and the rest of his time allowing men to use him as a sexual object. Mike intuits that he is suicidal. He unexpectedly finds himself begging, "Caswell, love me. Please, I'll do anything but it has to be us together because I love you" (151). The two move in together, but it is a setup for disaster. Mike may be a good teacher, but he has none of the qualities required to provide the fortress Caswell needs to keep back the threatening ocean. Mike stupidly, gullibly, falls for a rival's lie, and catastrophe strikes. Shallow, flexible, heartless, self-preserving to the end, Mike embarks on a new relationship. Gay Sunshine reprinted the novel in 1984 with an additional chapter. Set twelve years later, Mike is appearing in a production of Noël Coward's *Design for Living*. The program notes reveal that Mike seems unchanged.

The novel is not just about sex. Because of the characters' social standing and milieu, it includes much discussion of literature (particularly Proust), theater, music, and painting and is studded with allusions that only a broadly educated reader will get. One relishes such lines as, "Hurray for Chandler's Marlowe and Conrad's Marlow and Kit Marlowe and a small lavender raspberry for Miss Madame Marlowe" (116). There is little about politics, though there are some sharp barbs about heterosexual hypocrisy when it comes to sexual matters. In a backhanded slap at himself, Mike says, "I'm as silly as the straights who have never had a homosexual affair but think they have the right to say it's unsatisfying, bad, won't work, can't last" (50). He goes on to muse, "Which is less human in the long run—Caswell obsessed by the pursuit, capture, and subduing of beautiful phalli, or the pleasant man next door trying to do the right things: get a raise, get a newer car, send Harold to college, keep up with the news so he'll have something to gas about at the obligatory coffee break? Neither hurts anyone" (129–30). One wonders what the novel's reception would have been had St. Martin's or Random House published it in hardback rather than its appearing as a paperback original. William J. C. Corington (1915–2011) attended the University of Iowa, where he was classmates with Tennessee Williams. He taught high school English and drama in the New York area and earned a master's from Columbia. For a time he ran a dance studio in the city. He became part of the gay San Francisco circle of writers during the 1960s. Gay Sunshine Press also published a number of his later novels and short story collections. He died in San Francisco.

Coriolan, John. *A Sand Fortress.* New York: Award, 1968.

115 James Kirkwood: *Good Times / Bad Times*, 1968.

Though the work is structured like a conventional novel, its central conceit is that eighteen-year-old Peter Kelburn is writing a letter from his jail cell to his lawyer explaining what led up to his murdering the headmaster of the private school he attended in New England. The creepy Franklyn Hoyt is a closeted and hypocritical pedophile who alternately berates the boy and makes advances upon him. A "lopsided triangle" (243) develops when late in the semester a nontraditional student, the twenty-year-old Jordan Legier, arrives from New Orleans (Peter is from Los Angeles, his father an actor). Both schoolmates are strangely passive for their age. Peter keeps finding excuses for Hoyt's bizarre behavior, telling himself that now the headmaster will back off. The sickly Jordan retreats into camp. Peter insists that there is nothing sexual between the two, but their friendship has a "specialness about it" (25) that clearly moves beyond typical school bonding. Peter says, "I love him," without qualifying how he means the word (174). When they are at a New Year's Eve party in New York, Peter writes, "We threw our arms around one another and we kissed. It was a real kiss." He adds, "That's the only time there was any physical intimacy between us" (259). Peter admits that he has earlier indulged in mutual masturbation with a California friend and that there was "one episode" with a television actor (181). But he makes sure to note that he has had sex with women. Jordan's basic sexuality remains a mystery. In contrast, another student, Dennis Vacarro, is so willing to provide blowjobs to anyone that he earns the nickname "The Vacuum Cleaner" (88). We learn that "Jordan might have had a boy's body, slight and frail, but one part of him was definitely well developed [...]. Dennis Vacarro had checked this out right away and was after him" (148). Apparently he succeeds; at least Dennis spends one night with Jordan, and "the next day Dennis was walking around on a cloud" (218).

At their initial interview Hoyt warns Peter that he does not want him to introduce "any nasty little adolescent practices you might have picked up along the way in Hollywood" (62). But then he begins fawning over the teenager and forces him to recite Hamlet's famous soliloquy as part of a Glee Club program. Never have thirty-three lines of Shakespeare been so intensely rehearsed so many times with one-on-one coaching for a reciter ordered to dress in tights that accentuate his genitals. When Peter pulls a muscle in his back, Hoyt appears in his room to provide a personal rubdown. This involves pulling his pajamas down and sliding his hand between Peter's legs: "he wiggled his fingers and touched my testicles, brushed a finger lightly against them and froze" (229). Peter, to his horror, gets an erection. Hoyt begins stalking him, appearing at odd hours in their dormitory. He is jealous of Peter's friendship with Jordan, advising him to stay away from the "spoiled, decadent weakling" because, "There's nothing to be gained by a relationship with a person of his inclinations" (225–26). One night he surprises the two in bed talking and imagines more. The same scene repeats; this time Peter is "in a semi-erect state" with his penis "angling out of my pajamas" (272). Hoyt gives over the next morning's chapel to a sermon on Sodom and Gomorrah. Jordan's weak heart gives out, and he dies, setting up the final showdown between Peter and Hoyt. Meeting him outside, Hoyt tackles the boy and tries to kiss him. Peter runs. When Hoyt follows him into the boathouse, screaming filthy accusations and trying to grab his genitals, Peter grabs a boat hook and kills him. Ironically, Hoyt was hired in the first place to snuff out any hint of homosexuality after a prominent student killed himself following a breakup with his roommate. Now Hoyt's death creates an even bigger scandal. Peter realizes that "in killing a man, I also killed an entire school" (72).

James Kirkwood (1924–1989) was born in Los Angeles. Both parents were film actors; after their divorce Kirkwood lived mostly in Elyria, Ohio, with his mother. He was also a television actor and a playwright, one of the creators of *A Chorus Line*. Of special interest are the play, novel, and film *P.S. Your Cat Is Dead*, and the nonfiction *American Grotesque*, about his friend Clay Shaw, the gay New Orleans businessman tried on conspiracy charges in Kennedy's assassination. He was close to Herlihy and partners with Arthur Beckenstein (1944–). But he never publicly came out of the closet. Kirwood died in New York of complications from AIDS.

Egan, Sean. *Ponies & Rainbows: The Life of James Kirkwood*. Duncan, Okla.: BearManor, 2012.
Kirkwood, James. *Good Times / Bad Times*. *New York: Simon & Schuster, 1968. London: Deutsch, 1969.

116 Ursula Zilinsky: *Middle Ground*, 1968.

Tyl von Pankow, the teenage narrator recently released from his three-year incarceration in a Nazi labor camp in Heiligendorf, provides a moral for his story near its end: "enemies [...] are the people who draw the lines" (189). Those lines are ideological, political, and religious; they are also, in the context of the story, sexual and linguistic. By their creation they bring into existence a middle ground, "the one place which no one may claim in time of war," because it is the "forbidden" ground "between opposing camps" (98, 131). Yet it is precisely this ground, though Tyl does not realize it at the time, where he manages to survive the camp. It is the last years of the war. Though his mother is Jewish, Tyl's family did manage to save him from a concentration camp, but they were not able to keep him from detention. The proud Prussian resists authority and thus gains the attention of a Communist prisoner, Karel Killian. A master of survival, until typhus strikes him down, Karel argues that one must be flexible in order to achieve the greater cause. When he and his small band of followers suspect that the new camp commander, General Johannes von Svestrom, is gay (a deduction based on the titles of the books Tyl finds at his headquarters) and attracted to the youth, they urge Tyl to accommodate any requests he may make. Survival of the group is more important than an individual. Karel argues, "The idea of the body as private property surrendered at one's will as an act of love was romantic rubbish fit at best for bourgeois reactionaries" (64). A gay guard tries to warn Tyl that Karel is emotionally blackmailing him into perceiving everything as "black and white" when it is not (159), but Tyl is not ready to entertain the idea.

What none of them knows, until Tyl discovers it, is that the general and Tyl's beloved uncle Gabriel, killed during the African campaign, had been lovers. The family resemblance is the reason he signals Tyl out for special attention. When Svestrom takes the boy sexually, he is trying to recapture his relationship with Gabriel. What Karel has not foreseen is that Tyl will fall in love with Svestrom, that caught between the two men, he will enter that middle ground, and admit "Svestrom as father, friend, lover, and beloved" (132). When Karel catches typhus, Svestrom takes him into his headquarters. He explains that he has done so "because Tyl loves you and I love Tyl." Karel admits he loves Tyl, but "not quite the same way." The general replies, "Love is love [...]. The rest is technicalities" (124). But Tyl almost waits too late to say to Svestrom, "I love you" (151), and to start putting to rest the ghosts he is living with. The two are separated by the war's ending. Returned to Vienna, his mother's home, Tyl plays the black market, becomes a scene designer for a theater, goes with a woman as a sexual experiment, and begins to actively explore gay life. He has a liaison with an actor who resembles him in appearance but concludes that Michael is only in love with Michael. He comes under the care of an American officer, Captain William Aspinall. By lucky accident, he finds news about Svestrom. In a moment of inspiration, he fabricates a new biography and claims that Svestrom is his father. The gullible captain immediately takes steps to reunite the two. The novel ends with Tyl planning "to live happily ever after with General von Svestrom" (189).

The novel presents a different slant from the usual on this appalling moment in history. Curiously, it has received little attention from gay critics, even after being reprinted by GMP as a Gay Modern Classic. Ursula Greissemer (1931–2015) was born in Germany. She lived in Munich until she was sixteen. She attended school in Geneva, then traveled in France and England before arriving in New York in 1948 to study at NYU. She was married to poet Pieter Zilinsky and had two children. The couple lived in Seattle.

Zilinsky, Ursula. *Middle Ground*. Philadelphia: Lippincott, 1968. London: Longman, 1970. *London: GMP, 1987.

117   Ronald Tavel: *Street of Stairs*, 1968.

The novel is composed of small episodes recounted by different voices, none directly identified, although it becomes progressively easier to sort out those of the two principal characters and a few of the more important secondary ones. Running through the kif-fueled narrative is a love story between a young American, Mark, and a slightly younger, twenty-one year old, Moroccan, Hamid. Set in Tangier, 1960–61 (the death of the king dates it), that story is interesting enough that one could wish the author had taken Bowles as his model instead of Burroughs, both of whom he mentions (209). Mark is gay. Hamid is a sexual opportunist. He sums up his philosophy: "Why did God make man, but to nik? Why did God make a man with a zib, if it wasn't to niki? That's why a man must only give the niki and never take it, because if he takes it he is not doing what God wants him to do" (191). The person's sex and age is indifferent: "A zook is a zook. What's the difference? I niki it" (53). He values promiscuity: "A man should niki a lot of different zooks, and not just one, because that is really looking for trouble at trouble's house. When a man begins to have love for a woman or a boy he is no longer free. He is full of pain and he wants to always have the other with him" (196). Thus he is uneasy when he finds himself falling in love with Mark. It is possible, of course, since he is a petty thief (even a murderer), that he has actually fallen in love with Mark's generosity, as well as the idea of America that Mark represents. The closest the author comes to a conventional plot is in his depiction of Mark's maneuvers to get Hamid to New York. (Once there, he hates it and begs to return to Morocco.) Most of the novel records the mundane affairs of the two men and their friends and acquaintances, with events sometimes distorted by drugs, alcohol, and sexual jealousy.

A note from the publisher that appears even before the novel's title page insists that "a search after identity and reality" drives the novel: "Who are you?" Understanding the impact that national and ethnic identity has on a person is vital to this quest. Mark, in a mescaline-induced reverie, ponders "deeply where I am, the exact point I have reached [...], how much I really earn about Morocco, and hence America, how much I know about the people and about the truth [...]. How much I earn about myself and the truth" (227). The repetition of *earn* where one would expect *learn* seems significant. Sexual identity poses no problem for Mark, but the significance of his growing emotional attachment to Hamid enters the fabric of his quest: "I forced myself to concentrate on the burning why of any mutual attraction at all between us. There was for one thing, and in the least, the emotional excitement and response to opposite, and for another the associative, the metaphors each conduced for the other of magnetic others and ideals" (202). Hamid is like his distorted mirror image. He too worries over his relationship to his country since he is a Riffian, one of Morocco's many ethnicities. And he is troubled by his changing relationship with Mark: "just before I dropped off to sleep, I reached my hand down below his stomach and touched him and played with him as I had never done with a man before—as I could never, never have even ever dreamt of doing before with a man" (121).

A post-modern work, it is not the easiest of novels to read. Would it be less difficult had we the full work? As the publisher informs us in that same note, the book contains only some forty percent of the manuscript that was submitted to the press. The complete work, minus a few pages, is available online for anyone willing to tackle more than eight hundred double-spaced typed pages. Even a cursory glance at it reveals that, as the publisher suggests, the full novel may be more indebted to Joyce than to Burroughs. Pastiches of Sir Richard Burton, Lord Byron, and others have been eliminated from the printed text, along with almost all the poetry and translations from various sources, particularly classical Greek literature. Dozens of characters have vanished. Would the title and repeated references to "the rose of the sands" take on greater significance? The sections that were retained were not abridged, but whole sections, including an enormous amount of material at the end, were simply cut out altogether. Ronald Tavel (1936–2009) was born in New York. He graduated from Brooklyn College and the University of Wyoming. He worked with underground filmmaker Jack Smith, wrote screenplays for Andy Warhol (including *Chelsea Girls*, 1966), and founded the Theater of the Ridiculous in 1965. He wrote some forty plays. As playwright he was invited to be a guest teacher at several universities. He lived in Southeast Asia during the last decades of his life. He died of a heart attack on the plane taking him from Berlin back to Bangkok. Another novel, *Chain*, was published in 2012.

Marranca, Bonnie, and Gautam Dasgupta, eds. *Theatre of the Ridiculous*. 2nd ed. Baltimore: Johns Hopkins University Press, 1998. 19–35.
Tavel, Ronald. *Street of Stairs*. New York: Olympia, 1968.

118   Peter Menegas: *The Jacklove Affair*, 1968.

Jacklove is a commune located in "Jackpine," Montana, a former coal-mining town close to the Little Bighorn Battleground. The site is owned by a wealthy rancher who has permitted the eighteen or so members, plus eight children, to take up residence, but who then throws up obstacles because her foreman/lover cannot abide "beatniks." In meandering fashion, the novel follows the various dramas of the members during the commune's last year. Most are in heterosexual relationships, including a surprising moment of mother-son incest, but prominent in their midst are Joanne, "an ordinary lesbian" (26); Liverpool Annie, her lover who is ready to go wandering and does when the bisexual Gretchen shows up; and Stephen Wurley, whom Annie calls "a cowboy queen": "He was butch but he loved to sing Ethel Merman songs" (33). His presence in the commune seems mysterious since he trained as a veterinarian and is loved by Hollywood western star, William Frazier, who is eager to share a house (discreetly) with him. Stephen is domestic. He is the tastemaker who has decorated the dining area. He is "the most considerate," the most steady member of the commune, the one who nourishes it: "He would have made a wonderful parent, everybody thought, but they couldn't decide whether it should be mother or father" (13). Only Lois Brown seems bothered by his sexuality: "Stephen shouldn't really be a homosexual" since he would make "some woman a good wife" (65). Only Joanne recognizes the strain he is under when he is around Lois's oblivious but very attractive husband.

Stephen and Joanne bond as friends. He feels sorry for her when she and Liverpool Annie break up. He does get irritated with her on occasion: "One of his biggest complaints about Joanne was that when she got camp, she got bad camp" (99). In a comradely moment, she asks him what is in his homosexual survival kit. Presumably following his idea of good camp, he lists: "Oh, just a little can of gilt, some sequins, an address book, crab-killer, penicillin, Vaseline, a travelling iron, a collapsible vase, a leather belt, some good white plates, not much. Just the ordinary things to make a house a home" (122). Gay allusions pop up across the novel, usually (but not always) in association with him: Montgomery Clift, Morris Graves, Williams, Wilde, Mercedes de Acosta, Capote. When the entire commune dissolves, Joanne is the one who insists he telephone Frazier to come to his rescue. The last we see of Stephen, he is joining Frazier and his beard in his Piper-Cub: "Frazier took big, wide strides and Sylvia Jani bounced along beside him in her silver lamé suit, both looking like the match made in the celestial regions of Filmland. And it was, for the real lover, like a shabby butler or a nanny, jogged behind in the wake with his suitcase. Everybody was hap" (163).

Lawrence Rodney Menegas (1942–1989) was born in eastern Washington, attending prep school in Spokane. He also wrote a very funny novel, *The Service*, 1971, about a callboy whose client turns out to be his father, before turning largely to writing horror stories. He was friends with the painter Morris Graves, the actor Richard Svare, designer Jeremy Railton, and Ricy Soma, John Huston's wife. The "EDH" to whom *Jacklove* is dedicated, she collaborated with him on a proposed musical about Gertrude Stein. Menegas lived for a while in London. The writer Robert Ferro helped him with an immigration request for his lover John Andrews (Yiannakis Eftychiou). He died in Los Angeles.

Menegas, Peter. *The Jacklove Affair.* *New York: Coward-McCann, 1968. *Jacklove*. London: Blond, 1968.

119 Phil Andros (Samuel M. Steward): *Ring-around-the-Rosy*, 1968; *$tud*, [1969].

In his memoirs (107–18) Steward explains Phil Andros's origin. He had begun writing for the Swiss-based journal *Der Kreis*. Feeling increasing constrained by its genteel approach to sex, he sought other outlets and was directed to two Danish gay magazines, *eos* and *amigo*. He had just read Rechy's *City of Night* and felt that his "waffling attitude about his nameless hustler was annoying." In rebuttal he created the character Phil Andros, from *philos*, to love, and *andros*, man. As an added twist he decided to use the same name for the author. In an indirect dig at Rechy, Phil at one point says, "Could be, I'm just another hustler who's writin' a book" (142). In a bit of metafictional play, in Chicago Phil drops by Pete Swallow's tattoo business, where he finds the owner reading Genet's *Querelle de Brest*. (Another Steward pseudonym was Philip Sparrow.) Pete says, "I just read a story about a character named Phil Andros [...]. In one of those little queer magazines they publish in Europe" (223). Phil asks if the author is Ward Stames (yet another Steward pseudonym). The first Andros story appeared in *amigo* in August 1963. Steward arranged eighteen of them to form a picaresque novel, to be published by Guild Press in hardback. Though sex is central to each story, none of the book is hardcore. Phil is a hustler, an admirable character who often becomes involved in his johns' problems. As he says, "A lot is really expected of hustlers, I guess. They are sort of supposed to be like priests or psychiatrists or bartenders. You are supposed not to be able to shock them, and they are supposed never to show any surprise" (42).

In his travels across American cities, Phil meets a spectrum of gay types. Some are as psychologically wounded as those in *City of Night*, but many are well adjusted. One group that Rechy embraces, however, he shies from: drag queens and effeminate men. His is the leather culture. (Rechy's is denim.) As the novel progresses, Phil grows. As he wryly remarks, "all things change. It's a mark of the young to think that any situation as it exists at a given moment is going to endure forever. When we grow older, we see that nothing is permanent" (145). Like Rechy's hustler, he is highly literate, given to quoting a wide array of authors including Blake, Flaubert, Freud, Joyce, Hemingway, Homer, O'Neill, Plato, Swift, Villon, Voltaire, Wilde, and especially Shakespeare. He observes, "I have always said that five minutes in a person's library can tell you more about him than a full course of digging through his itches on a psychiatrist's couch—provided you know your books" (110). He's also knowledgeable about art. When he comments on one client's original paintings, the john notes that "it's a little unusual for a ... hustler to recognize Picasso, to say nothing of Modigliani and Epstein," to which Phil shrugs, "I'm an unusual hustler" (137).

At age twenty-eight, after hustling for four years, Phil confesses, "to tell the truth I didn't yet know whether I was homo, hetero, bi, or a" (24). He gradually acknowledges that he is attracted to men: "Of late I'd found myself having a little flurry once in a while if I saw something that tickled my fancy—a free flurry, that is, without charging the guy anything" (51). After one satisfying evening, he says, "I began to think that perhaps I was really an out-and-out homosexual" (140). He starts to question his profession. Upon encountering Kenny, a naive youth in Chicago, he says, "I felt very dirty, as if my body were coated and covered with the dried accumulations of saliva from all the tongues that had ever been placed on me, and the stiffened and flaking layers to semen that had been spilled on me, and the old and gummy Vaseline" (158). Kenny frightens him: "I was afraid I might fall in love with him. And that mustn't ever happen to a hustler, not even once in a blue moon" (161). Still later he says, "More and more of late I'd been finding myself combining business and pleasure, or even sometimes forgetting about the business end of it. By this time next year, I thought wryly, I'd be a fruit in full flower" (200). One thing he does not want is commitment. In his view, gay marriages "involve everything that hetero marriages involve—debts, backbiting, nagging, and fighting. But there were two things usually missing: fidelity and children" (209). Twice he quotes Kinsey, to the effect that man is a sexual animal, and concludes, "Being promiscuous is part of being queer" (213). He finally sums up courage to say to one man, "I love you" (264), but then flees.

Throughout the novel Phil wrestles with the racial tension in America. As if aware that one day he may be accused of fetishizing African American men, he questions why he is so attracted to them and comes up with no good answer. He enters into a number of short-term relationships with black men, during which he occasionally experiences prejudice against whites. In the last two episodes he meets a Black Muslim, Adam X, and Bennett, his S/M "slave." The novel ends with Phil pushing their doorbell: "I looked through the glass door, up the stairway, and felt my cheeks burn with anger and anguish and desire" (295). Whether he has met his own criteria for a good life is left up to the reader. Earlier he has said, "Know thyself, old fruit. And if thou canst not know thyself, know others. But at least—be well adjusted" (73).

Steward was the first gay American, so far as I can discover, to create the figure that others—Tom of Finland in art and Colt Studios in pornography—would glorify and that pulps would make a plot staple: the super macho, sexy policeman. Phil asks, "why was it that so many homos wanted to make a cop more than anyone else in the world? Their uniforms were often very attractive, but not all that good always. Was it a guilt feeling? Was it the necessity to be dominated or punished? Was it the liking for the idea of being forced to do something, of being psychically raped? Did responsibility disappear under coercion? Was it the search for a Hero in a world of non–Heroes? Or was it just snobbishness? Since cops were generally considered so completely hostile, it would be more than just a single plume in the bonnet to have one—a kind of status symbol in the homo world. A whole gah-damned tailful of feathers" (191). In subsequent novels in the 1970s, Phil would go on to become a policeman himself.

$tud was ready for binding in 1966 but, as Steward explains in his memoir (116), Guild Press, as was its owner's wont, got into financial problems, and the unbound pages languished in a warehouse. J. Brian (James Brian Donahue, 1932?–1985), a San Francisco hustler (in all senses of the word) got a copy and brought out a paperback edition in 1969. At that point Guild published both the hardback and a three-volume paperback edition (with no author's name on the paperback edition), all carrying the 1966 copyright, the erroneous date usually given for its first publication. Brian also directed a pornographic film based on some of the stories: *Four: More than Money*, 1971. A copy escaped the police crackdown that Brian endured and is still available for sale. Brian is one of the characters in the 1975 Phil Andros novel *The Greek Way* (the last of five that continue the story of the Andros character).

Meanwhile, Steward returned to a short story

he had written in 1954 for the photographer George Platt Lyons, about a motorcyclist's encounter with a teenager. Much as the stories in $tud were a response to Rechy's novel, this story was his take on *The Barn*, 1948, by writer/illustrator Blade (Neel Bate, 1916–1989). Even back then Stewart contemplated using it as a starting point for a series modeled after Arthur Schnitzler's play *Reigen* (Spring, 185). He now produced six more stories to complete an interlocking succession of sexual encounters that he entitled *Ring-around-the-Rosy*. Set in rural Kansas and San Francisco one hot August and September, the sequence goes thus: Ed, a Kansas farmboy, and Jack, a motorcyclist; Jack and Joe, a San Francisco masochist; Joe and Mike, a San Francisco patrolman; Mike and Gino, a newspaper boy; Gino and Steve, a cross-country truck driver; Steve and "Don," a Black Muslim stranded in Kansas; "Don" and Ed. Though each of the seven characters stands out as an individual, none of them has the psychological depth or interest of the ones in $tud, with the possible exception of the Black Muslim, and none of the secondary characters is developed at all. The stories are pure pornography, mostly involving domination and scatological humiliation. The writing is sometimes sloppy: for example, Mike goes out of his way to tell the reader that he can't remember Joe's last name (60), then in a twist at the end he reveals that the two men are living together (75). The novel was originally published in a trilingual edition in Copenhagen under its original playful title, to appear the following year in San Francisco with the unimaginative and largely misleading title *The Joy Spot*. In 1972 Brian used the novel as the basis for a hardcore film, *First Time Around*, with Steward providing the script.

Samuel Morris Steward (1909–1993) was born in Woodsfield, Ohio. His description of Dr. Bill Broderick in $tud applies equally to him: "homosexual, eccentric, ex-alcoholic, writer, masochist, professor, artist, dilettante, a lifelong beat, and the farthest-out character" (239). Steward received his doctorate in English from Ohio State. He taught at Loyola and DePaul. He was friends with Stein, Wilder, Julian Green, Fritz Peters, Kinsey, and the Glenway Wescott group. Leaving teaching he became a tattoo artist in Chicago. In his third incarnation, he returned to writing (he had published two books in the 1930s). Under his Andros *nom de plume* he turned out six more novels. As Steward he wrote three novels, 1984–89, in which Stein and Toklas appear as characters. He died in Berkeley of pulmonary problems. In 2010 Justin Spring published Steward's extraordinary series of sexually explicit photographs and designs, including twelve drawings he made to illustrate "The Motorcyclist."

Andros, Phil. *Heksering=Das Tolle Männerkarussell= Ring-around-the-Rosy*. Copenhagen: Eos, 1968. *The Joy Spot. San Rafael, Calif.: Frenchy's Gay Line, 1969.
──. *$tud*. San Francisco: J. Bryan, 1969. *Washington, D.C.: Guild, [1969]. [Washington, D.C.]: Beaumont Classics, 1969.
Blake. *The Barn, 1948, and More Dirty Pictures*. New York: Stompers, 1980.
Spring, Justin. *Secret Historian: The Life and Times of Samuel Steward, Professor, Tattoo Artist, and Sexual Renegade*. New York: Farrar, Straus, & Giroux, 2010.
Steward, Samuel M. *Chapters from an Autobiography*. San Francisco: Grey Fox, 1981.
──. *An Obscene Diary: The Visual World of Sam Steward*. Ed. Justin Spring. N.p.: Elysium, 2010. [48–61.]

120 Frank Newman (Sam Abrams): *Barbara*, 1968. Angelo d'Arcangelo (Josef Bush): *Sookey*, 1969.

Sookey is set in Cherry Grove, Fire Island, "the most famous homosexual resort in the world" (7), during the summer of 1969. Gay revelers at a party watch the manned landing on the moon. The Stonewall Inn uprising is conspicuous by the absence of any mention of it. An unnamed novelist—"Blind Tiersias, nearsighted penpusher and pulp-producing author" (10)—has taken a house for the summer. He begins to meet the people who will intrigue him for the next several weeks and whose lives he will interpret through the Tree of Life spread of the Tarot. Ten cards are revealed. Nine men command his attention. But identity seems to be fluid. The same character may be referred to by as many as three different names within a few sentences, so that the reader must initially scramble to keep up with the fact that Hugh, Hugo, and Joyner all go with the same person. His lover is Mack or McClelland. They are long-time residents, now battling the erosions of time. Sookey is Isaac Athenaeus; his brother Muscles is Constantine Athenaeus. They are sons of a Turkish-Greek immigrant family in the restaurant business. A. J. or Adrian J. Bagley, Princeton professor of Oriental and military history (145), is one of the oldest residents of this part of the Grove.

Then there are Robert (Bob) Bakus and, of lesser interest, Casey (the only man with just one name, one identity), Harold Washington, and Stevie Glick. The last three are younger men. Sexual relationships among them are fluid, or at least casual.

Time is even more fluid. Gradually it becomes apparent that the story of Antonius and Hadrian provides the novel's unifying conceit. Hadrian's one known poem serves as epigraph (in Latin) and coda (in translation). We meet them in a time warp. Later we meet Caravaggio and, via the painting *Bacchus*, his model, Benno, who resembles a carved gem in the painter's possession, a cameo with an unidentified head—presumably that of Antonius. We spend a moment with General Charles Gordon and his servant Issak as they make love while moored on the Nile at "Hermopolis, once great Antinoopolis" (166). They connect to the present via Joyner and McClelland, who during the American occupation of Italy made love in the ruins of Hadrian's palace. Notice the names: Isaac Athenaeus and Issak; his lover Adrian Bagley and Hadrian; Bob Bakus and Caravaggio's painting. The authorial voice says, "Lover's time is elastic. The scythe and the sundial are powerless over lovers" (64). Here the legend has a happy ending. Hugh and Mack renew their vows and accept what time has made them. Forsaken by Sookey/Antonius for another man, the aging Adrian contemplates suicide. He stands razor in hand in his bathroom when Sookey rushes in and they "begin to speak at once in all of the languages they have ever used." The novel concludes: "Their lives will reappear only in fragments, only in dreams. If they make love and sleep today, when they awake even the remains of their suspicions will be gone. Nothing will remain for them but a very ordinary, a very predictable, and a very durable human love. With this, their last life, they are released from the wheel" (187). The novel becomes richer with each rereading.

For all his notoriety in the late 1960s, I can find little about Josef Bush (1933?–). He was a playwright (*De Sade Illustrated*, with Bill Haislip, 1969, among others) and screenwriter for three movies, two directed by Andy Milligan and *Barbara* by Walter Burns. He is often cited for having outed FBI director J. Edgar Hoover, "*Celibataire*," in *The Homosexual Handbook*, 1968, published under his d'Arcangelo pseudonym; under threat, the press removed the entry from the 1969 reprint. He also published *Angelo d'Arcangelo's Love Book*, 1971, and *Angelo d'Arcangelo's Gay Humor Book*, 1972. He joined Jack Nichols as one of the editors of *GAY* and then virtually disappeared.

In adopting Newman's polysexual exercise in pure pornography for the screen, Bush changed the setting from Cape Cod to Fire Island. Though not a gay novel per se, *Barbara* has a high number of homosexual couplings, much in the fashion of Apollinaire's forays into the naughty, and thus has more than a little interest for gay, as well as lesbian, readers. Max is the sexual guru who instructs his protégés in the pleasures of unorthodox sex as interpreted by his brand of Hinduism. Under his tutelage, Tom (who is buggered by him for the first time) hooks up with a Provincetown summer visitor—and his male dog: "Now that he found he could make it with men as well as with women, he couldn't get enough" (39). Tom introduces Barbara's brother Franz to the delights of male-on-male sex, both oral and anal (his twelve-year-old sister has already initiated him to the joys of heterosexuality). In the last scene in the novel the siblings bring their parents into the general orgy; in a final sexual act "his father shot his load of hot sperm ... his own substance ... into [Franz's] mouth, he too came" (177). Samuel Abrams (1935–) was born in New York. He graduated from Brooklyn College and the University of Illinois. He taught at Drew University and retired from the Rochester Institute of Technology. Alongside technical books, he edited *The Neglected Walt Whitman*, 1974. His wife lent her name to the novel, as well as to the title of a poetry chapbook, 1966.

d'Arcangelo, Angelo. *Sookey*. New York: Olympia (Traveller's Companion), 1969.
Newman, Frank. *Barbara*. New York: Olympia (Traveller's Companion), 1968.
Nichols, Jack. "Angelo d'Arcangelo: The World's First Outer." *Gay Today*, 16 Feb. 1998. Online.

121 William Carney: *The Real Thing*, 1968. Dirk Vanden: *The Leather Queens*, 1969; *Leather*, 1969. Larry Townsend: *Leather Ad*, 1970.

In the 1960s visual aspects of gay S/M culture increasingly focused on leather. This outward show was in part a counteraction to visual images of gay men as effeminate. The narrator of Vanden's

Leather says, "I don't want a woman, and I don't want a soft man" (142). Though leather, like the later clone look, is a type of drag itself, former *Drummer* editor Jack Fritscher (196) has complained that "feminism is accepted and masculinism rejected" by the gay establishment. Leather writers are routinely accused of misogyny. Leather grew out of the gay motorcycle clubs that began as early as 1954, inspired by the iconic image of Marlon Brando in *The Wild One*. It was picked up and further inspired by the photographs from Kris Studios, the art of Tom of Finland, and the films of Kenneth Anger. Fritscher in his introduction to a reissue of Townsend's important *Leatherman's Handbook* summed up (*Gay San Francisco*, 193) that leather "arrived linguistically to name a way of being and becoming, of ritualizing and actualizing, of creation and recreation, of politicizing and marketing." It also explores, sometimes graphically, the shifting relationships between *eros* and *thanatos*. Carney, Vanden, and Townsend were in the vanguard of leather novels. Perhaps not coincidentally, they were all in California at the time their books were published.

The Real Thing is a threatening work. An epistolary novel, it consists of twenty-nine letters that an unnamed uncle writes to his likewise unnamed nephew, with a thirtieth to the nephew's mother. The letters serve as a detailed handbook to leather culture. We never see the nephew's answers and can only infer their contents from comments the uncle makes. The reader must draw out what plot exists from hints given and from assumptions possible about the writer's psychology. We are told that the nephew is thirty and was a Marine in Vietnam; he is now interested in exploring S/M culture and has chosen his uncle as mentor. We learn bit by bit that this uncle is a scientist teaching in a West Coast university. He is probably in his forties and served in the Army during the Korean conflict. He hates the nephew's mother, who disapproves of his sexuality. There was also another nephew, in whose death the uncle was somehow implicated. Some sort of power struggle seems to have occurred between the man and woman; only at the end do we realize that one is now occurring between the uncle and the nephew—with grisly results. Though the novel seemingly begins as a celebration of the leather world, it ends as an interrogation of it, if not an outright condemnation. The novel's title takes on an explosive new significance. William Alderman Carney (1922–1987) was born in Florence, Alabama. He served as an aerial gunner during World War II. After the war he attended the University of Missouri School of Journalism and the University of California, Berkeley, receiving a bachelor's in 1955 and a master's in French in 1966. He taught at various colleges in California; during the 1970s he began restoring Victorian homes in San Francisco. He published two other gay novels, *A Year in the Closet*, 1974, and the S/M mystery *The Rose Exterminator*, 1982.

Vanden's two novels have less to do with the leather scene; the titles were the publisher's, not the author's. But the protagonists in both are attracted to the arch-masculinity leather represents. Paul Granger, the narrator of *Leather Queens*, enacts what came to be the archetypal plot for Vanden (the basis for his finest achievement, the *All* trilogy, 1969–71). Paul assumes he is straight until his wife accuses him of having been in love with his best friend (who has just committed suicide). His reaction is to go to a gay bar to prove she is wrong. Saved from a police raid by a mysterious patron, he heads to Los Angeles. There he finds a job in a gay restaurant. After initial denial, he comes to "the startling discovery that the queens were human" but he cannot be comfortable with them "because they were deliberately denying the one thing they should have been above and beyond anything else: Men; males of the species" (36). Fueled by alcohol, he has his first homosexual experience and finds it not only affirming but "just plain fun" (59). But he also realizes that he seeks love, and L.A. seems to be a dead end. He moves to San Francisco and there becomes involved with the leather crowd. The same mysterious figure saves him once more, this time from a raid to bring down his landlord's narcotics and pornographic trafficking. He turns out to be a vice officer, also just emerging from the closet. They exchange leather for a pastoral life together farther down the coast. Though Ron, the narrator of *Leather*, has been out for years, he finds himself in an emotional crisis. Trying to rethink his position in life, he keeps returning to a bar appropriately named The Talisman because it "*seemed* to be the gathering place of men who at least made an effort to retain some of their masculinity" (12). He is attracted by their dress, their stance, their promise of danger. At the same time, he is in an internal war against labels, both verbal and visual. Through the union that intense sex with a series of pickups provides, he explores his past, especially his relationship with his father, his own needs, and the nature of his failures. He moves into S/M sex, seeking out increasingly darker aspects of his desires. But each breakthrough is followed by a retreat. One of the men he goes out with finally says in exasperation, "Ronnie ... you're so damned uptight. Can't you ever relax?" (145). It takes an LSD trip and a near-death encounter for him to open up to another man, at the same time rejecting the leather world. The novel ends on a muted but affirmative note. The author reissued it in 2011 as *Down the Rabbit Hole*.

Richard Dale Fullmer (1933–2014) was born in Myton Beach, Utah. After gaining an MFA from the University of Utah, he moved to California and served as a producer/director for various regional theaters. His discovery of Amory's *Song of the Loon* (which he praises in *Leather Queens*, 152) led to the birth of Dirk Vanden. His disgruntlement with pulp publishers led to his renouncing writing altogether, beginning anew only after the death of his second partner. He was first with actor Winn Strickland (aka Mike Davis, 1945–1986), then with San Francisco chef Irving (Herb) Finger (1936–1987). He published his autobiography, *It Was Too Soon Before...*, the year before his death. He died of cancer in Carmichael, California.

Much of Townsend's prolific production explores the S/M world. His first novel, *Kiss of Death*, 1969—about a gay motorcycle cop who is tapped to infiltrate a motorcycle club, some of whose members have died in a suspicious manner—is a mess, both in plot and in character development. But the authentic Townsend voice is heard in the two-volume work *Leather Ad*. Johnny, the narrator of the first volume, *M*, decides to satisfy his curiosity about the S/M scene by taking out an ad: "inexperienced but curious. [...] Can you show me the ropes?" (3). There follow as escalating series of adventures in which he assumes the masochist's role. These he faithfully recounts to his best friend, Bobby. In the process he becomes aware that he is in love with him. They commit to each other but agree to maintain an open relationship. Bobby moves into the S/M scene and assumes the role of top to Johnny's bottom, to their mutual satisfaction. Bobby becomes the narrator of the second volume, *S*. Johnny's job temporarily reassigns him to Japan. Keeping him abreast via letters of his adventures, Bobby has a series of encounters in which he ends up playing both roles. He becomes worried that he cannot function outside the fetish. But when Johnny returns, he realizes, "I like leather-sex, like being S ... even M, sometimes. But with this guy I love, it doesn't make any difference. It doesn't matter. When sex and love are one, it simply doesn't matter" (195). Michael Lawrence Townsend (Irving Townsend Bernhardt?, 1930–2008) was born and died in Los Angeles. He served with the Air Force in Germany 1950–54. He obtained a degree as a counselor and industrial psychologist from UCLA in 1957. An early gay activist, he had a long publishing career with more than forty books to his credit, including *Run, Little Leather Boy*, 1971, and its sequel, *Run No More*, 1972, in addition to his S/M manual. He was long associated with *Drummer* magazine. His partner of forty-three years was Frederick L. Yerkes (1935–2006). Townsend died of pneumonia.

Carney, William. *The Real Thing*. New York: Putnam's, 1968.
Fritscher, Jack. *Gay San Francisco: Eyewitness* Drummer*: A Memoir of the Sex, Art, Salon, Pop Culture War, and Gay History of* Drummer *Magazine: The Titanic 1970s to 1999*. Ed. Mark Hemry. San Francisco: Palm Drive, 2008.
Townsend, Larry. *Leather Ad*. Volume 1. *M*. San Diego, Calif.: Greenleaf Classics, 1970.
_____. *Leather Ad*. Volume 2. *S*. San Diego, Calif.: Greenleaf Classics, 1970.
Vanden, Dirk. *Leather*. San Diego, Calif.: Greenleaf Classics, 1969.
_____. *The Leather Queens*. San Diego, Calif.: Greenleaf Classics, 1969.

122   Stephen Koch: *Night Watch*, 1969.

Very little happens in this novel; it is an exercise in style. To a degree, it also becomes an arrangement between author and reader to examine the way fiction is constructed. If it has meaning, that is left to the reader. Harriet and David Fontana are teenaged siblings living in Islip, Long Island, with their alcoholic aunt, their mother dead and their equally alcoholic father absent. One night David witnesses his sister having sex with an unknown man on the grounds of their estate. He retires to a garden chalet, where he throws up. The stink awakens Dean, a gardening assistant who is using the site for a quick nap. The presence of the man excites David. He readily consents to let Dean borrow their Lincoln to drive the two of them into

Manhattan. While David waits in the car, Dean meets up with a woman; they take her to her home in New Jersey, before returning to Islip. Remaining in the car when they arrive, Dean coaxes David into giving him a blowjob, promising to reciprocate. In performance David "feels his own groin come alive" (143). The next morning it is Harriet who becomes the spy, watching David alone in the chalet masturbating. Later that day Dean returns. When David brings up the previous evening, he reacts angrily: "Playing around is nothing, it's just playing around." But David will not let go: "I like it. I want more of it. I want it again" (190–91). He unzips Dean's pants, then insists that Dean lower them "until his entire midriff is naked." David takes in the sight, stands, and reasserts their master/servant relationship: "I don't want it. [...] Dress yourself" (193). The same day Harriet terminates her affair. The siblings meet in their childhood nursery, and there they join sexually. The novel ends, leaving the reader to ponder whether it even can be classified as a gay novel.

Stephen Bayard Koch (1941–) was born in St. Paul, Minnesota. He attended the University of Minnesota, CUNY, and Columbia. He taught creative writing at the last. His second novel, *The Bachelor's Bride*, 1986, is much gayer. Koch was friends with Susan Sontag and with the photographers Peter Hujar, David Wojnarowicz, and Robert Mapplethorpe. He wrote *Stargazer*, 1972, about Andy Warhol, and co-edited *Peter Hujar*, 1990. Hujar's will named him executor of his estate. Koch is married and has a daughter.

Koch, Stephen. *Night Watch*. *New York: Harper & Row, 1969. London: Calder & Boyars, 1970.

123 John Donovan: *I'll Get There. It Better Be Worth the Trip*, 1969.

Historically, the novel is important as the first written for young adults to touch on the subject of homosexuality. Since it contains not one positive comment about same-sex attraction, however, it scarcely seems a wise choice as a gift for a gay teenager struggling to understand his sexuality. The protagonist is entering puberty. After living with his Boston grandmother for eight years, ever since his parents' divorce when he was five, David Ross's life undergoes a complete change when she dies of a heart attack. Reunited with his self-dramatizing, alcoholic mother, only Fred, his grandmother's gift of a dachshund for his eighth birthday, accompanies him to the small New York apartment where the "*first Mrs. Ross*" (116) presides. His more sympathetic, but ineffectual, father and stepmother live nearby. Davy meets the more aggressive Douglas Altschuler at the private school his mother selects for him. Within a matter of weeks the latter loses his best friend to leukemia. The two boys grow closer; while playing with Fred, they end up kissing. Davy doesn't know how to react; for a while they avoid each other, then get back together after lying about their experiences with girls. Alone one afternoon the two try out the mother's whiskey and become inebriated, falling asleep on the floor; the mother finds them and turns the moment into high drama. Davy's father says, "She thinks you will end up ... well, I don't know what lengths her imagination will carry her to" (173). The ellipsis, almost certainly, can be filled with "like Jess," her brother, a model who shows up briefly for the grandmother's funeral. While father and son are having their talk, the drunken mother takes Fred for a walk. He escapes and is killed by a car. Davy decides it is all his fault for "messing around with Altschuler" (180). Worried that they will "end up a couple of queers" (185), Davy says, "I guess the important thing is not to do it again." Altschuler replies, "I don't care. If you think it's dirty or something like that, I wouldn't do it again. If I were you" (197). John Donovan (1928–1992) was born in Lynn, Massachusetts. He graduated from William and Mary and earned a law degree from the University of Virginia. He worked for the Library of Congress copyright office before joining St. Martin's Press. He wrote plays and other novels and served as president of the Children's Book Council. Donovan died of cancer in New York.

Cart, Michael, and Christine A. Jenkins. *The Heart Has Its Reasons: Young Adult Literature with Gay/Lesbian/Queer Content, 1969–2004*. Lanham, Md.: Scarecrow, 2006. 8–14.
Donovan, John. *I'll Get There. It Better Be Worth the Trip*. New York: Harper & Row, 1969. London: Macdonald, 1970. *40th Anniversary Edition. Woodbury, Minn.: Flux, 2010.

124 Hunce Voelcker: *Logan*, 1969.

A 2006 reprint of the novella describes it as a "dreamtime narrative." It teases, it puzzles. It shifts focus. Whatever meaning it has must be provided by the reader. Its setting is the imaginary town of

Gosendale, Pennsylvania. It begins by naming six teenage boys. Two of them—Rim Orphney, a budding novelist, and Paul, a poet—enter a sexual relationship. The first description of their lovemaking exemplifies the novel's prose style: "They did know suddenly that they were hard and hungry and almost in love, their bodies moving rhythmically together in the sun in early morning and their mouths and tongues, beginning with the touch beside each other and his hair was falling in his eyes then holding him and kissing him quite slowly with his fingers on his back and hands in hair on back and ass and arms, Rim moving into him and growing slowly building and the climax and ten thousand words (it is impossible to tell the feeling of containing Rim) They climaxed mutually and dressed (blue jeans, white T-shirt and grey sweater over everything Paul wore) and kissed for hours possibly at clearing's edge in forest where Paul's poems were kept" (28). The two earlier have taken a pilgrimage to Pittsburgh and its three rivers, where Rim secretly self-baptizes himself and where the two, in bed, begin the novel that Rim will write about a third boy, John Logan: first in his head, then on paper with "phallic pen" (35). This novel will reflect Rim's own life: "what actually Rim does, then writes, to write Novel of himself and choose John as the subject of his novel making John outside himself and bringing John inside himself as his and Paul's first son nine months since their first love" (43). Or, as earlier he has said, "The novelist becomes the novel finally" (14). Parts of this novel appear in the text, distinguished so subtly by the use of single and double quotation marks that it takes an attentive reader to separate out the fictional levels. Logan has only one eye, having stumbled and accidentally put out the other after discovering that he has killed his own father by mistaking him for a deer; at the end he deliberately puts out the remaining eye with his knife, in an unacknowledged reenactment of the Oedipus story. Rim's name is never explained, but it evokes Rimbaud, who, along with Hart Crane and San Juan, is often mentioned. Religious imagery pervades the narrative. With repeated readings one notices more and more correspondences, though some aspects of the dream remain mysterious, perhaps unknowable to the author himself.

Hunce Voelcker (1940–1990) was born in Danville, Pennsylvania. He graduated from Villanova. He began a graduate thesis on Crane at CUNY; it began the basis for his book *The Voyages of Hart Crane*, 1967. As a hippy, he was caught up in the gay liberation movement. As a poet, he became part of the circle of gay San Francisco poets that included Robert Duncan, Jack Spicer, and Paul Mariah. He wrote a second novel, *Sillycomb*, 1973. His lover Link Martin (Luther T. Cupp, 1947–1973) was one of the dedicatees of *Logan*. In 1972 Voelcker moved to the Russian River area, where he lived until his death from AIDS-related complications.

Voelcker, Hunce. *Logan*. New York: Cowstone, 1969.

125 Hadrian Keene: *Seventh Summer, 1969; Noon and Night, 1969.*

This pair of novels explores the relationship between carnality and love and commitment. In the first, forty-one-year-old Johnny Choate, a New York money manager, describes his affair with seventeen-year-old Allen Gunnery one summer on Cape Cod. Wary of possible legal, social, and emotional consequences, Johnny is also aware of the irony that Allen's father and he were lovers at the same age Allen is now, their sexual relationship terminated when David met Allen's mother. But the tensions of the summer are created by a "fortyish" alcoholic who is almost comically determined to seduce Allen. The teenager comments, "It's something else again when a dirty old woman like Rachel Tate tries to suck you off outside a boathouse. That's queer!" (38). The parents have drifted into becoming socialites, giving too many dinners and parties and drinking too much, and are oblivious to what is happening until Allen finally confronts them. The novel ends on a muted key as Allen leaves for college. The sequel picks up ten years later, just after the deaths of Allen's parents in a plane crash. Allen has not been in touch with Johnny all that time, but now he reappears, a successful photographer. They recognize that, after such a time lapse, they cannot pick up where they left off, but they enter a marriage, albeit an open one. This agreement is tested the first time Allen goes with another man while on a tour of European cities. In a funk, Johnny worries, "Chemistry is the major threat to any dream of a lasting homosexual relationship. We have no legal tie to bind, no children, no place in the community where we can be embarrassed by divorce. We have nothing but things that can be disposed of with little or no trouble, but a lot of heartbreak" (84). The two talk it out and spend the rest of the trip accepting sex as it comes, including threesomes. Through much of the novel, a Japanese fashion model poses a pseudo-threat, which fizzles out when they finally meet up in Rome. The novel ends on *Queen Elizabeth II*, where Johnny yields his anal virginity to Allen. Both novels strive for a rare degree of honesty but somehow do not seem that important. There appears to be no certain information about the author. A novelization of the film *The Laughing Woman*, the story of an S/M relationship between a man and a woman, was published under the name in 1971; the Catalogue of Copyright Entries lists this instance as a pseudonym for Vernon Crame. Bolerium Books has whimsically noted, "A young writer named Hadrian Keene appears as a character in a Judge Dredd graphic novel."

Keene, Hadrian. *Noon and Night*. New York: Award, 1969.
———. *Seventh Summer*. New York: Award, 1969.

126 Dennis Selby: *Sanctity: or, There's No Such Thing as a Naked Sailor*, 1969.

Sanctity is a hallucinogenic romp that is difficult to sum up but great fun to read. Inspired by Symons's *In Quest of Corvo*, the thirty year old, British-born hero, Shelley Skull (aka Swell Wonderass), sets out to track down Guernsey-born writer Rocco Sabine. At the same time, Shelley is "deliberately heading in the direction of sainthood, via Scientology and Aleister Crowley's theory of Magick" (11). To these ends he arrives in New York and checks out the gay milieus that would have attracted the elusive writer. In the baths and at the bars he meets a variety of people, several of whom (so he suspects) may be the same person in disguise. He insists a fat man is pursuing him. Then there is Peter Noble, who may have been Rocco's friend Harry. He too seems to be pursuing Shelley—for sex, Shelley assumes. Peter introduces him to the trucks parked alongside the Hudson River, propositions him at the Cloisters museum, comes onto him during the showing of a porn flick, and acquaints him with the Sloane House YMCA. As a result of one of Shelley's complicated scams, the two end up at Peter's parents' home in Tucson, Arizona. He is kidnapped by Miss B., a Pepsi heiress who, going blind, wants his eyes. Shelley and Peter are crated and loaded onto a plane bound for Tangier, where the operation is to be performed.

Shelley starts a fire inside the crate in an attempt to gain attention; they have to put it out in the same manner Gulliver did whilst among the Lilliputians. Still trapped, they worry about nourishment. Shelley identifies "one sure source of protein available" and counsels "we shouldn't let delicacy get in our way." Peter readily agrees. As they take "sustenance from each other," Shelley records, "Passion unexpectedly entered into the act, to vie with hunger and making its appeasement more fun." As a result, "Our 'naked lunch,' with its unconcealable pleasure, had mated us so well that honesty had become our ally." He sums up: "Mealtimes were now a sacred rite. I approached his body with bestial reverence. He was my life source, and the physical pleasure involved in tapping this source had grown until it was almost unbearably ecstatic. Supper that night, which we deliberately, romantically delayed until the moon had come out, was so overpowering that I passed out from sheer pleasure. Never were two men so needed by each other" (154–57). When they are finally rescued, he worries that he has become "cock crazy since my incarceration with Peter," but assures himself: "Scientology, however, would take care of that" (164). As his final act Shelley determines to evoke the spirit of the now presumably dead Rocco. Demanding Peter's aid and calling upon Crowley's direction, he works out the stages whereby he, in the act of ejaculating, vacates his body and enters a cat's, thus leaving his "available for occupancy" by Rocco (184). After the transfer occurs, the virile Rocco demands Peter arouse Shelley's body orally; once he achieves an erection, he assaults the cat holding Shelley's being. The cat attacks Shelley's genitals, whereupon Rocco, still within Shelley's body, dashes the cat against a mirror. Peter, oblivious to who is where, helps carry Rocco/Shelley to safety—"Such, I thought heavily, is the blindness of love"—while Shelley/cat "were left to die in peace" (189–90). The point of all this? That is left up to the reader.

Dennis Selby (date unknown) was born in Ely, Cardiff, Wales. As a result of a visit to his aunt on Long Island, he became fascinated by American culture and relocated to the U.S. after finishing his national service. He was part of the circle around Chester, Sontag, and Edward Field; in an essay about Chester he mentions that Stephen Snyder, to whom he dedicated *Sanctity*, was his lover. He was also a playwright and later on the editorial staff of *The Nation*. This seems to be his only published novel.

Selby, Dennis. *Sanctity: or, There's No Such Thing as a Naked Sailor*. New York: Simon & Schuster, 1969.

127 Jeff Lawton: *Truck Stop*, 1969; *Screw 22*, 1969; *Callboy*, 1970.

The three novels have perhaps received more attention than that usually accorded pulp fiction because of their innovative layouts. They feature the use of different typefaces, arrangement of text on the page to create attractive visuals, some resembling concrete poetry (including, as one might expect, text in the shape of penises), and the insertion of nude photographs, drawings, and handwritten documents. All three were published in the distinctive, oversized format devised by Greenleaf Classics for a series of novels in which the reader had to flip the book over, from top to bottom, in order to read it. The plot themselves are sex-driven, pornographic in content, but detailing them gives no sense of the experience one has reading them, being forced to construct the novel out of the collage of materials served up. Jeff Lawton (dates unknown) has escaped all my attempts to find out more about him, but it is difficult to believe this was his entire corpus.

A truck diver named Mike is the main character in *Truck Stop*. He is driven by his libido but so crippled by all the social baggage he has inherited as to render him incapable of admitting any emotions for another man or fully reciprocating sexually. As he hooks up for one-way blowjobs on his route, his mind darts between present and past experiences until his psyche so disintegrates that he no longer knows what is real and what he has dreamed. Kenny, the older brother whom he worships, is the source of his hang-ups. A hypocrite, he engaged in sex with others but maintained that only he and Mike could be true buddies. Masking sexual desire as discipline, he created an incestuous S/M relationship between the two, one that still influences Mike's emotional responses even after Kenny has been killed in a car wreck. To some degree Sarge, whom he met in the Marine Corps, substituted for Kenny but could not replace him. Now two men enter Mike's life at age twenty-three and start cracking the facade he has hidden behind. Duke picks him up in a gay bar and introduces him to an orgy in which he is forced to reciprocate. Pete, his fellow truck driver, manages to dispel the dream world into which he constantly retreats, deconstructing the false positions that have ruled him. At novel's end, he meets his mirror image of three years earlier. He is happy with whom he has become.

Michael Perkins (227) calls *Screw 22* "that rarity in homosexual erotic fiction: an amusing novel about being gay—in, of all places, the United States Army. Lawton starts from Joseph Heller's premise that everything is SNAFU in the army, and in a vulgar, boisterous, experimental style, makes fun of both homosexuality and the military." The satiric novel presents the Vietnam conflict as a meaningless war, controlled by a script made for television. Within that script, time, place, and identity are constantly shifting. The soldiers are teenagers who have lost track of their age, are confused about their rank and even their existence (no one can die before the death is shown on television and the Army issues a death certificate), and are doomed to repeat the same actions (the same hill is continually taken and retaken). They prefer sex with each other to fighting, but "the Army doesn't allow homos. It's in the regulations. You're in the Army, so you can't be a homo" (11). That does not prevent the main action being sexual rather than military. A nice moment occurs when one of the soldiers proposes "to put copies of *Song of th' Loon* in th' rooms for th' guys who've already read th' Gideon Bible" (88). The protagonist again is named Mike. In telling his story the novel alternates between conventional narrative, mostly about sexual encounters, across which cut stream of conscious passages; a television script being written by Jeff Lawton; letters between Jeff and his producer; a poorly written piece of gay pornography; a nude male pin-up centerfold and various other images; and letters from the President, Mike's parents (who keep hoping he will be killed so they will gain his insurance and a gold star), and a sixty-two-year-old gay penpal helping out military morale. Towards the end of the novel the television commentator Eric Severveins (i.e., Eric Sevareid) yields to the comic team of Homer and Jethro. Mike and G-2, an Intelligence Officer, discuss the purpose of the war. G-2 states, "Well, we say that the vicious, inhuman enemy is out to enslave the freedom-loving people who are America's allies." Mike asks, "An' what does th' enemy say?" G-2: "That vicious, inhuman America is out to enslave the freedom-loving people who are their allies." Mike: "An' what do th' freedom-loving people say?" G-2: "I don't know. They don't speak English" (66–67).

Callboy plays some of the same visual games, but at base is altogether different. It begins as a conventional story of a hustler, Hunter Maxwell, working on the outskirts of the movie industry in Los Angeles. Interspersed within his story are "retakes" of past events in his life and "flashbacks" into the lives of his uncle Jerry, high school and Navy acquaintances, his handler, and the movie star Brace Butler. But the novel segues into being an account of Hunter's identity crisis and his resulting mental meltdown, which leads to his "murdering" Brace and reawakening as the star, even physically resembling him. It comes out that, though the mental breakdown was real enough, it is Brace who has transformed him into his doppelgänger and then staged his double's suicide for a movie that becomes a smash hit. In the ultimate act of narcissism Hunter's own past has been replaced with Brace's. Then, as we exit the novel, we discover that Brace intends to play a character based on Hunter—his farewell performance before the two men escape to become farmers. The fluidity of identity, the resemblance between the actor and the hustler, the homosexual as narcissist, the impact of the past upon the present, the need sometimes to free oneself from the past's pernicious effect, and the way people use each other—these themes intertwine in the novel, but no conclusions are drawn about their meaning.

Lawton, Jeff. *Callboy*. San Diego, Calif.: Greenleaf Classics, 1970.
———. *Screw 22*. San Diego, Calif.: Greenleaf Classics, 1969.
———. *Truck Stop*. San Diego, Calif.: Greenleaf Classics, 1969.
Perkins, Michael. *The Secret Record: Modern Erotic Literature*. 1976. New York: Rhinoceros, 1992.

128 Bruce Benderson: *Meet Me at the Baths*, 1970.

Benderson's autobiographical first novel is a grab bag, an example of a young author finding his way. Its narrator is the twenty-five-year-old Paul. The opening chapter describes in detail a night spent having sex in the backs of the trucks parked along New York's Hudson River docks off Christopher Street. A few individuals emerge from the tangle of bodies, but the fleeting nature of the encounters disturbs Paul. Concluding that there is "no sense in this whole scene," that "New York was getting me down" (24), he decides to leave for San Francisco. There he promptly ends up in a gay bathhouse, where he remains for the rest of the short novel, engaging in sex. While he is cruising the corridors, he unexpectedly encounters Michael Stanyan, who used to live next door to Paul's family. The two—Michael at age forty, Paul at sixteen—had discovered their sexuality at the same time, and although they never had sex together, their discussions comforted both. Michael, a biology teacher at a military school, was then married. In answer to Paul's question how he ended up in San Francisco, he describes how his life fell apart when he fell for an eleven-year-old student who proceeded to seduce him and then moved on to conquer a newly arrived teacher. Discovering that the boy was not discreet about his relationships, Michael panicked and resigned his post. Paul reflects, "Sometimes the happiness of one summer can be enough to last a lifetime. Some of us aren't even granted that much." He thinks of himself, "walking an endless maze of dimly lit corridors and empty alleyways in search of [a] moment's gratification" (57–58).

The bathhouse takes on symbolic significance with its "endless row of tiny dark cubicles, each one a separate little world of passion-pleasure," with "an endless number of guys like myself, all curled up in their dark little rooms of transient pleasure" (61). One of the men he meets is a watcher, not a voyeur but a seeker of knowledge. Their encounter moves to the sexual. When it is over, Paul flees, determined to escape the maze, only to be waylaid by frantic activity in the orgy room. After another frenetic explosion of sex, he retreats to his cubicle. There he remembers his childhood before Michael: his first awakening to sexuality, his own narcissism, his fantasies gained from muscle magazines, forced sex in the showers with one of the school jocks—a rape that mysteriously became an epiphany consecrated by a "halo of water" as he "knelt before him" (98). The same evening he made his first and only attempt with a girl, which failed, he encountered two brothers, with whom he succeeded: "My path was set and the consequences were inescapable now. But it was what I wanted. I was what I was" (124). Spent, Paul flees the bathhouse, emerging into the light of the next day. The watcher is there, waiting for a bus. They make a date to meet again at the baths. Paul thinks, "I could not imagine myself [e]ver sleeping with him again, but I knew we would be friends" (154).

The various parts of the novel are not integrated. One understands why Benderson has virtually eliminated it from his literary resume. Yet here we see the author beginning to focus on themes that he will develop later. Bruce Benderson (1946–) spent his childhood in Binghamton and Syracuse, New York, where he began his lifelong friendship with Camille Paglia. They attended high school and, briefly, the university together. He moved to New York and then San Francisco. He is a novelist and essayist, at home in English and French. *Kyle*, 1975, was his second pulp novel. His memoir *Autobiographie érotique*, 2004 (*The Romanian*, 2005), won the Prix de Flore. Among many translations from French, he has published works by gay novelist and sexual polemicist Tony Duvert.

Benderson, Bruce. *Meet Me at the Baths*. San Francisco: Gay Parisian, 1970.

129 David Plante: *The Ghost of Henry James*, 1970.

Composed in sixty-seven short chapters, the novel's flow of words sweeps the reader along even though one often has no clear idea what is going on. Presumably talking about James, one of the characters (Julian) could equally be describing the novel in which he appears: "Well, just think of all the stories and novels in which something very big is held back, and never revealed. You wonder if even he knew what he was hiding, because when he does try to reveal it one feels the revelation is a let down, a cheat, hardly equal to all the portent which is evoked and hidden in the midst of all the work. The secret is almost palpable" (89). There are five major characters, four brothers and a sister: the almost asexual Julian, who wants to get away from the family but cannot; the heterosexual Charlotte and Claud, both of whom start affairs they refuse to commit to; the homosexual Charles, who similarly begins and ends a relationship; and the bisexual Henry, who—as is appropriate, given the novel's title—centers the work. He says of his family, "we're ghosts; we float, not from choice, but, somehow, from circumstance." He confesses, "The more I try to break away from them, the more like them I feel I am" (64).

Looked at as a gay novel, it differs in many ways from its contemporaries. Charles feels neither pride nor angst about being gay. Having bought a home in Lucca, Italy, he begins a romance with a young man named Colin. They explore Florence and the countryside and size up the boys they encounter. Charles finds himself bored with Colin and recoils against seeing him again, but while in Henry's company, they run across him in the street. The encounter is followed by one of those strange moments that recur across the novel. That night in their shared bedroom, Charles offers to introduce Colin to his brother. When Henry indicates that he is not interested, Charles suddenly blurts out that Colin is "a filthy little cheat" who is "no different from anybody else. You could have him in any public toilet in Florence." And he bursts out sobbing. At Henry's invitation, Charles comes to his bed: "'What do you want?' Henry asked. Charles wanted to destroy something; Henry did not resist" (164). What happens next, we are never told. In London Charles picks up an Englishman on the bus and takes him back to his room. As they are undressing, Charles asks the youth his name. "Charles" (188). A less happy meeting occurs on Hampstead Heath. Remembering Henry's stories about adventures on "warm moist London nights" (200), Charles cruises a youth sitting on a bench. On the pretext of needing to urinate, they enter the bushes. Charles is mugged, apparently by several assailants. We hear nothing further about the incident.

Henry is mysterious, haunted: "He tried to think of all the cities he had made love in. He tried to think of all the people whom he had had in bed. He tried to recall the names of young men and women whom he could recall only as smooth accommodating bodies" (134). He keeps seeing familiar-looking faces without quite being able to identify who the person is. There is a hint they are his doppelgänger. But it may be his awareness of his impending death. Henry is searching for something, but he does not know what: "He had looked for situations in many cities that would be equal to his imaginings, but something had always got in the way and disappointed—the setting up, the necessary predisposition, the calculated prelude, often no more extraordinary than putting on a condom" (79). Staying at the same hotel in Boston where Wilde had stayed on his American tour, Henry twice seeks diversion in the company of Cuban queens at a bar. He hooks up with an Italian, Signor Baretti, whom he had picked up at the Colosseum in Rome and engaged in a bisexual threesome and who is now in Boston on some unknown business that results in his murder. The event drives him back to Europe and ultimately to his brother's in Italy: "He found himself where he had always resisted being: in the midst of his family" (137). There he dies. Now the family is haunted by him.

Julian idolizes Henry James. Though the author's name is never mentioned even once in the novel, it opens with a pilgrimage Julian, his sister, and two brothers make to the grave site in Cambridge where James's ashes were interred. There Julian hears "a very distant voice" (8). It is significant that the brother Henry is not present. Staying at Charles's, he reads *Italian Hours* and *William Wetmore Story and His Friends*. After Henry's death, the two Henrys become somehow intertwined. Julian, Charles, and Charlotte make a second pilgrimage, this time to Lamb House in Rye: "the magnifying presence of Henry hung in their midst as something heavy and dense, and even their silence referred to it" (175). Now Julian and Claud start seeing figures. The four survivors reunite at the old family home. Charlotte expresses their thought: "I have a feeling Henry will come back." The novel ends with footsteps on the porch just before the door "flew open to them" (219). Which ghost has returned?

David Robert Plante (1940–) was born in Providence, Rhode Island. He graduated from Boston College and the Université Catholique de Louvain. He has taught at a variety of universities in England, Canada, the U.S., and Russia. In 1966 in England he met the Greek-born poet and Penguin editor Nikos Stangos (1936–2004), with whom he lived until Stangos's death from cancer. He has published novels, memoirs, and diaries. He continued to explore gay themes in *Slides*, 1971; *Figures in Bright Air*, 1976; and later novels. Plante holds dual American and British citizenship.

Plante, David. *The Ghost of Henry James*. Boston: Gambit, 1970. *London: Macdonald, 1970.

130   Andrew Blumley: *Twin*, 1970.

The narrator, Mike Price, calls the work his diary (160), but it has all the appearance of a conventional novel weaving the present day with past memories as he tries to understand the nature of his incestuous relationship with his deceased identical twin, Paul Price—"Socratic halves" (124)—and the part played in their common life by Barbara Hickman, the girl that they held at bay as children but whom as adults Paul bedded three times and who now wants a baby from Mike. The reader meets various people whom Mike encounters in New York bars, most notably Tony, who talks him into an S/M game one night (mentored by a third man, by coincidence also named Paul), and Leonard and Harry, both of whom are in love with him but neither of whom attracts Mike. As he writes, the statue of Christ atop a place of worship mysteriously stirs his emotions. The evidence suggests that, as a result of the twins' separation to fulfill their military duty, Paul was beginning to assert his independence of Mike. Mike, a ghost writer by profession, attempts to lay to rest his ghosts. But no epiphany arrives. He bequeaths his "diary" to Barbara, says goodbye to the statue, and leaves. According to the dust jacket Andrew Blumley (1934–) attended the Université de Paris. He worked as an editor, but became a bartender in "southern Florida" while finishing a second, apparently unpublished, novel. He supposedly published two nonfiction books (perhaps under the name Andrew Bluemle?). Otherwise, he evades my searches.

Blumley, Andrew. *Twin*. New York: Stein & Day, 1970.

131   John Weitz: *The Value of Nothing*, 1970.

The reader learns at the beginning that haute couturier Philip Ross is murdered in 1964: "Probably [by] some guy he picked up" (5). The rest of the novel details incidents in his life—and that of his peers, friends, and lovers—from 1945, when he is twenty-two, until his death. While still in the army, he is cruised in a New York nightclub by Captain John Evans-Greene. After their discharges, they live together for two years. Tiring of Philip, John eases him out of his life by getting him a job as an apprentice to a gay dress designer, James Farrow. It turns out that Philip has not only talent but a decent business sense. He is soon moving up in the fashion industry, creating his own name brand line, winning a top award in the field. Ten years after they separate, John reenters his life. He notes that "Philip was someone, now, or close to it. There was sophistication there, and toughness, not just the snot-puss ambition of a kid willing to be kept" (176). This time it is Philip who tires of him, and they part amiably. Philip begins picking up men: "No feelings, no heart, just sex; like masturbating, only better. He used it sparingly, discreetly" (228). An insight occurs when he learns of Farrow's death; he realizes that despite all the acclaim he has received, he was not truly innovative: "Something had driven him, but what? Not creative talent, not burning ambition. [...] It didn't matter much. It simply did not matter any more" (286). He begins to drink too much and to surround himself at parties with gays. Then he propositions the temp who is running the elevator in his apartment house. The burly ex–Marine, interested only in money, threatens Philip with blackmail, then slugs him. The blow causes internal bleeding and death. We learn of the reactions of a few of his former associates. Curiously, we do not hear from Eric Marshall, publisher of a fashion magazine who earlier has turned into his nemesis. Marshall has fled his father when he discovers that he is spending the summer with a "screaming queer" (223). It's a hackneyed ending, serving no clear purpose. Nowhere does the author delve into what part sex, straight or gay, may play in the interpersonal machinations of the fashion industry.

Throughout, homosexuals are routinely referred to as *pansies, queers, fags, queens*, and the like. The novel's anti-Semitism is as rank, and all the more surprising given the author's roots. Hans Werner Weitz (1923–2002) was born in Berlin. The family fled Hitler's rise to power; they settled first in London and then in New York. In 1944 he joined the O.S.S., serving in Germany. In 1954 he founded John Weitz Designs and became a major figure in the world of casual fashion. He was married twice and had four children. He died in Bridgehampton, New York, of cancer.

Weitz, John. *The Value of Nothing.* *New York: Stein & Day, 1970. London: Allen, 1971.

132 William Harrington: *Trial*, 1970.

Cleveland detective Lieutenant Clement Yacobucci is a highly successful and much respected police officer in his thirteenth year on the force. He has been a widower for four years. He is a devout Catholic with a "reverence for life [...] so complete it was an obsession" (47). He is also in a sexual relationship with his supervisor, Captain Paul Chichester, ten years his senior. It began almost casually one day when they were in the shower together and Yacobucci got an erection: "Well, Clem, if that's the way you feel, there's no reason we shouldn't do something about it." Yacobucci concurs, "there was no reason. They were, after all, mature and intelligent men. They were both free—Chichester was divorced. They had been friends for a long time. Besides, they needed what they could give each other." That is, the "relief that his body simply demanded, required," but he also admits that it is more than that, "because the relief was coupled with companionship and sympathy" (68–69). When Clem finds himself becoming aroused by a female stripper, his immediate reaction is to call Chichester: "Paul? Are you in bed? I'd like to come over for a while" (111). Paul is probably homosexual, though he refuses the label. Clem is more complicated. Probably basically heterosexual, perhaps bisexual, he fights with the fact that society, if it knew, would label him a fairy. He finally decides, however, that he must be gay: "If he wasn't, why did he go on doing what he did when he so much feared discovery and the contempt that would follow?" (69).

He is outed to the attorney appointed to defend a killer he has apprehended. Clem immediately informs Lynda, the woman he has begun dating, his former sister-in-law. She shrugs it off, demanding only that he be monogamous: that is, choose her or Paul. When Clem does, Paul reacts with anger and accuses him of lying about the anonymous phone call. Clem hands in his resignation and throws himself into working for a gubernatorial campaign. But by remaining true to his convictions he still brings scandal down on his and Paul's heads. In an interview, Clem speaks out against both capital punishment and police brutality, angering a powerful newspaper editor. When the news breaks, Paul kills himself. Clem sobs. He remembers how gentle and loving Paul had been—"And vulnerable" (307). He lacerates himself for not having been the friend that Paul needed when the time came. He turns to a priest. Full of platitudes, incapable of embodying "God's mercy and His justice" (313)—a "gurgling fountain of vapid homilies," Lynda calls him (325)—all the priest can proffer is his empty offer to help him: "Any time. I'll receive your confession whenever you're ready" (314). Lynda accuses Clem of being ruled by ego, not by conscience, in falling into a funk simply because he "and Paul Chichester frenched each other a few times" (327). For her "it was all a matter of self-control—: subdue your conscience, overcome your shame with brazenness, and do what you want to do—ought to do" (330). The gubernatorial candidate is bothered by the editor's duplicity, not Clem's sexuality. The killer he has apprehended begs him to intercede with the new governor, even though he knows about the scandal. When the appeal fails, he wants Clem to be one of his witnesses when he is electrocuted.

William G. Harrington (1931–2000) was born in Marietta, Ohio. He graduated from Marietta College and Duke and obtained a law degree from Ohio State. He was a practicing lawyer for some twenty years in Columbus, Ohio. He wrote some twenty-five crime novels under his own name, including the Columbo series, and was a ghost writer or a research assistant on a number of others. He was married twice and had an adapted son. He killed himself at his home in Greenwich, Connecticut.

Harrington, William. *Trial.* *New York: McKay, 1970. London: Barrie & Jenkins, 1971.

133 Gerald Walker: *Cruising*, 1970. Tucker Coe (Donald E. Westlake): *A Jade in Aries*, 1970.

These two murder mysteries have in common that the victims are homosexual and the killers are closet cases. Otherwise, they are unalike in every way. *Cruising*, unlike William Friedkin's film version, 1980, has nothing to do with the Greenwich Village leather milieu. Much of the action takes place in the Columbia Circle neighborhood at Central Park, and the gays are mostly fairy stereotypes. Two—Alfred Bronson and Dave Hopper, neighbors of the killers—come across as more complex, quite decent humans. The way the novel is structured, however, we see them only through the killers' eyes. The basic plot of book and film remains the same: up against a sex killer who targets gays, the police department decides to send out decoys resembling the type that attracts the killer. We begin in this killer's mind. Twenty-two-year-old Stuart Richards—nominally a graduate student who is supposed to be working on an English thesis about Rodgers and Hammerstein, a schizophrenic who blames queers for many of his problems, and a son who hates both his parents—kills his fourth victim in the opening chapter. More killings occur during the course of the novel. Richards also beds women (he even fathers a child), but one of his female partners, after commenting on his preferences for fellatio and anal sex, insists that "he actually wanted to go to bed with a boy" (114). Accusing him of being a latent homosexual, Alfred, his gay neighbor, taunts him, "Why don't you go down to the Baths and get it over with? Go ahead, faggot. Once you get started, I'd say you'll take on two dozen guys in an afternoon" (171). Richards ends up killing six bath patrons before being strong-armed by a masseur, who turns his knife upon him.

Twenty-one-year-old John Lynch draws the unwanted assignment to go undercover as "a homosexual on the prowl" (24). NYPD Captain Edelson recognizes that Lynch is a "real hater"—"Commies, queers, Jews" (26)—but he thinks he can be controlled. Lynch is more troubled than he realizes. He has some unresolved problem with his dead uncle Phil, a crooked cop who was killed before he was exposed. And during his military service there had been those "homosexuals he'd picked up and then beaten up at that off-base bar during that one funny period" (189). Lynch recognizes that "he had more in common with the killer, who obviously couldn't stand queers, than he did with the guys he killed" (159). Though he does not know it, he resembles Richards physically, so much so that a homophobic cop mixes the two up. Against orders, Lynch arms himself with a knife. When he mistakes another decoy cop for a suspect and then kills him, he mimics Richards's methods in stabbing the rookie repeatedly and castrating him. When Edelson calls to tell him that Richards has been brought down, the captain mentions that he was the "same physical type as his victims" (188). Lynch processes the information: "First he'd had to get used to the idea of being the same type as the homosexual victims. Now it turned out he was also the same type as the killer" (190). Edelson says, "I'd figured [the killer] for a self-hater, long ago. [...] Doppelgangers, the old double theme. It was the queer in himself he was killing every time he knifed a homosexual. When a self-hater kills, he's killing himself" (188). Lynch's next act is to hunt down Dave, whom he has actually started to like. He accepts a blowjob before knifing him. The murder muddles the whole case against

Richards, but Edelson, now demoted to lieutenant, deduces correctly that a second killer is at work. Friedman based much of his filmscript on a real series of murders that occurred in the Village after the novel's publication. Gerald Robert Walker (1928–2004) was born and died (from complications of a stroke) in New York. He graduated from NYU and Columbia and worked as a magazine editor. He was married twice and had a son.

In Westlake's novel Mitch Tobin, the narrator, and his wife Kate, along with a homophobic (and racist) New York police detective, Aldo Manzoni, are virtually the only straight people. Tobin has hang-ups and misconceptions about gays, but his involvement with them in a murder case leads to a psychotherapeutic breakthrough for him. A former policeman, he was ousted from the job after his partner, whom he should have been backing up, was killed while he, Tobin, "was in bed with a woman other than my wife" (14–15). Burdened with guilt, unable to forgive himself (as his wife has), he works on symbolic projects in his home: erecting a high wall around the yard, digging a subbasement beneath the one they already have. Then Ronald Cornell shows up asking for help to find the murderer of his lover, Jamie Dearborn, since Manzoni has decided he was killed by some guy he picked up and has, for all purposes, closed the case. Because Cornell believes in astrology, he wants Tobin to discover the exact time and the place of birth of six friends—suspects. Tobin wants nothing to do with the case, but is finally persuaded to use a police friend who has access to birth records. Then a newspaper item discloses that Cornell has tried to commit suicide. Tobin already knows enough about the man to deduce it was attempted murder. He is happy that it is none of his business. But the wiser Kate challenges him "to find the killer" (30). With Cornell as a model of someone "pushing himself to be more, because his friend had been killed" (32), Tobin takes the first step in his healing process.

He meets eight gay men and learns more about the victim. They range in age from nineteen to forty and vary widely in appearance. Professionally, there are an owner of a men's clothing store (Cornell), a lawyer, a fashion designer, a model, a composer, two home decorators, and a ticket agent. Six of the men are in a relationship. As he learns more about them, he thinks: "The sexual and emotional ties among these people, which had seemed so simple at first, were starting to complicate themselves. Living in a sub-culture within the normal world, they were more limited for actors from whom to cast the roles in their lives. The same individuals had to play a variety of parts in each other's histories; it became very incestuous after a while" (113–14). Though Tobin does not comment on the fact, their involvements seem as stable as his, or at least no more troubled, despite the added burdens imposed by society on them. The only loner is the killer. Twenty-six, living at home with his mother, terrified she will find out about her son's sexuality, he is a complex mixture of aggressiveness and cowardice. The first murder was triggered by his anger that Jamie had dared call him at his home, contrary to his orders not to, perhaps coupled with fear that he would do so again. He strikes a second time, gratuitously, in order to create a red herring and pull attention away from himself. This time Manzoni closes the case by arresting Leo Ross—to him, another "spade faggot" (140).

Tobin is sometimes free with the pejorative language of the time, but he recoils at Manzoni's use of derogatory terms. At a party he has already observed, "They all seemed so *happy*" (81). There he sees two men kissing and comments, "the only reaction I could dredge up was surprise at never having seen it happen before" (84). Filtering out the narrator's prejudices, the reader can see that the gays, not Tobin, are the heroic ones. Just as Cornell initially pulls him out of the psychic morass he has allowed himself to fall into, his image humorously saves Tobin as he is on the verge of messing up with Manzoni in a confrontation that could turn ugly: "I looked at him, and found myself wondering what Ronald Cornell would think of his clothing, and what this man would think of Ronald Cornell's clothing, and with that thought I managed to regain control of myself and not do anything stupid" (134). Finally, Ross's lover tells Tobin that nailing the killer is his responsibility, for "the only man who can do the job always has the responsibility to do it" (145). At this crucial point, with the lives and happiness of six gay men depending on him, our straight hero has an epiphany: "For the first time in a long while, something outside my own head—other than my wall, or the sub-basement—had distracted me from myself. I became aware of that suddenly, and came to a stop, confused." Now, he understands,

"*I feel I don't have the right to stop punishing myself* [...]. *What a fool*" (151). He does not have to go after the killer alone; three of the gay men are there helping him. This does not mean that Tobin will bond with any of them. But it is worth remembering that, according to a contract drawn up between him and Cornell, he and Kate now own a share of a clothing store catering entirely to trendy gays.

Donald Edwin Westlake (1933–2008) was born in New York but grew up in Albany. He attended Champlain and Harpur Colleges. After service in the Air Force, he settled in New York, where he became a prolific mystery writer under his own name and a variety of pseudonyms, particularly admired for his capers. He was married three times and had four sons. He died of a heart attack in San Pancho, Mexico.

Coe, Tucker. *A Jade in Aries*. New York: Charter, 1970. *New York: Random House, [1971]. By Donald E. Westlake. London: Gollancz, 1973.
Walker, Gerald. *Cruising*. *New York: Stein & Day, 1970. London: Sphere, 1972.

POSTSCRIPT: NOVELS 1971–1981

In his book *Stonewall*, David Carter describes the first march to commemorate the Stonewall Inn uprising. It was called the Christopher Street Liberation Day march and was scheduled for Sunday, June 28, 1970. The organizers had no idea what to expect. Fewer than a thousand showed up at Sheridan Square in the Village. But as the marchers headed up Sixth Avenue, their numbers swelled. Estimates of the total number of people involved range from two to ten thousand; what is certain is that it stretched for blocks. When they arrived at Sheep Meadow in Central Park, many people openly wept from joy. The march ensured Stonewall Inn's place in American history, though no one foresaw a day when a President of the United States, Barack Obama, in his second inaugural address, would say: "We, the people, declare today that the most evident of truths—that all of us are created equal—is the star that guides us still; just as it guided our forebears through Seneca Falls, and Selma, and Stonewall; just as it guided all those men and women, sung and unsung, who left footprints along this great Mall, to hear a preacher say that we cannot walk alone; to hear a King proclaim that our individual freedom is inextricably bound to the freedom of every soul on Earth."

A new spirit entered gay American writing almost immediately. That spirit should be celebrated, but it is also regrettable that, in the headiness of the time, many writers forgot (or were ignorant of the fact) that they were not creating the world anew but were building on a sizable foundation. A group known as the Violet Quill, led by Edmund White, in particular launched a myth that "gay fiction"—"if by that one means unapologetic novels written by gays primarily for gay readers and consequently devoid of the earlier strategy of a let-me-be-your-Virgil-through-this-underworld narrator"—was "invented" by them (*New York Review of Books*, April 14, 2009). Save for a handful of figures, White brushed the pioneers aside.

Eighteen of the authors in earlier entries continued to publish multiple novels in the 1970s. These newcomers joined them. Daniel Curzon's angry *Something You Do in the Dark*, 1971, whose protagonist was entrapped by a vice officer, has been called "the first gay-liberation novel" (though, he said, he had never heard of Stonewall when he wrote it). He followed up with *The Misadventures of Tim McPick*, 1975, and *Among the Carnivores*, 1978. Leo Skir's *Boychick*, 1971, is a bit of fluff about its protagonist's unrequited infatuation with a younger man. Merle Miller came out very publicly in *The New York Times Magazine* in 1971. The next year he published his first novel with a gay protagonist, *What Happened*, the story of a concert pianist and composer. *The Story of Harold*, 1974, published by the children books author George Selden under the pseudonym Terry Andrews, about a children books author undergoing an emotional crisis, is one of the richest novels of the decade. Geoffrey Linden's *Jigsaw*, 1974, tries too hard with too little reason to be postmodern. The earnestness of Laura Hobson's *Consenting Adult*, 1975, seems a throwback to an earlier time, in its plea for tolerance, rather than an outgrowth of the new anger. (It later became a television film.) William Delligan's *Cherry Grove*, 1976, and *Fire Island Pines*, 1977, are poolside reads. Wallace Hamilton's *Coming Out*, 1977, is earnest but fails to engage. He also wrote a historical novel, *David at Olivet*, 1979, and an intergenerational romance, *Kevin*, 1980 (which became the basis for a German film, *Gossenkind*).

The year 1978 was an *anno mirabilis* for gay letters. There had been nothing like it since 1948. In rapid succession there appeared Andrew Holleran's *Dancer from the Dance*, Larry Kramer's *Faggots*, Armistead Maupin's *Tales of the City* (which became the basis for a television miniseries), and White's *Nocturnes for the Kings of Naples*. Less important works are Paul Monette's *Taking Care of Mrs. Carroll* and Joseph Caldwell's *In Such Dark Places*. The next three years saw *The Catch Trap*, 1979, by Marion Zimmer Bradley; *Special Teachers, Special Boys*, 1979, by the activists and partners Peter Fisher and Marc Rubin; *The Confessions of Danny Slocum*, 1980, by George Whitmore; and the campy *A Fairy Tale*, 1980, by S. Steinberg (John Saul). Cliches about married men discovering they are gay, gays hiding that they are gay, gays having a heterosexual fling or even being converted, and the like poured out (and continue with us to this day in films). Then there was the raunchy celebration of sex in Michael Rumaker's *A Day and a Night at the Baths*, 1979, and *My First Satyrnalia*, 1981.

Gay genre fiction flourished. Following Hansen's lead, outstanding mysteries include Robert Bentley's cold war thriller *Here There Be Dragons*, 1971; Carleton Carpenter's *Games Murderers Play* and *Only Her Hairdresser Knew...*, both 1973; Richard Hall's *The Butterscotch Prince*, 1975; John Paul Hudson and Warren Wexler's *Superstar Murder*, 1976 (set in the Club Baths); Frank King's philosophical *Down and Dirty*, 1978; Felice Picano's *The Lure*, 1979 (with similarities to *Cruising*); Nathan Aldyne's *Vermilion*, 1980, the first of a tetralogy; and Richard Stevenson's *Death Trick*, 1981, the first in the still ongoing Don Strachey series. The prison fiction by Frank Hilaire (*Thanatos*, 1971) and John Cheever (*Falconer*, 1977) is more powerful than earlier prison novels; both are genuine love stories in which the couple becomes more important than the individuals' gender or sexuality. Thomas L. P. Swicegood's *Other Side of the Wind*, 1974, is a revenge fantasy aimed against police entrapment.

Science fiction, taking a lead from Delany and the British New Wave, became bolder about exploring gay themes: Robert Silverberg's *The Book of Skulls*, 1972; David Gerrold's *The Man Who Folded Himself*, 1973; Bradley's *The Heritage of Hastur*, 1974; Barry N. Malzberg's *On a Planet Alien* and *The Sodom and Gomorrah Business*, both 1974; Thomas Burnett Swann's *How Are the Mighty Fallen*, 1974; Edgar Pangborn's *The Company of Glory*, 1975; and George Nader's *Crome*, 1978. After a number of important short stories Thomas M. Disch published *On Wings of Song*, 1979. The noted sf editor George H. Scithers continued to turn out pseudo science fiction pornography under the pen name Felix Lance Falkon. Though the novel is a thriller, science fiction writer Thomas N. Scortia and his collaborator Frank M. Robinson wrote a page turner about a skyscraper afire: *The Glass Inferno*, 1974. (The film version omitted the heroic gay character.) Anne Rice launched her career with *Interview with the Vampire*, 1976 (which became a graphic novel and a movie), and Vincent Verga's *Gaywick*, 1980, defined the gay gothic romance for non-pulp readers (the first had appeared in 1968).

The western still floundered, being explored mostly by erotic writers. Richard David's *Ride the Whirlwind*, 1973, and Dan Dakota's *Rezo Strange*, 1981, are more traditional romances. David (Sunset) Carson's *Lament*, 1973, is a comically deranged satire. The military novel practically disappeared. Gay writers seemed unready to take up the Vietnam conflict, the major exception being Charles Nelson's *The Boy Who Picked the Bullets Up*, 1981. Ensan Case returned to World War II for *Wingmen*, 1979. Lucian Truscott's *Dress Gray*, 1979, is an indictment of West Point. (Vidal wrote the screenplay for its television adaptation.) The rare athletic novel returned in the form of a runaway bestseller with Patricia Nell Warren's *The Front Runner*, 1974. The story of a coach and his track star who is gunned down by a homophobic assassin at the Olympics had an enormous impact on a generation of young readers. (During the decade she also wrote *The Fancy Dancer*, 1976, and a *roman à clef* about Anita Bryant, *The Beauty Queen*, 1978.) The historic novel made another fleeting appearance in Carter Wilson's story of the discovery of Machu Picchu, *Treasures on Earth*, 1981; the expedition's photographer is gay.

Children's literature remained nervous: Lynn Hall's *Sticks and Stones*, 1972; Isabelle Holland's *The Man without a Face*, 1972; and Sandra Scoppettone's *Trying Hard to Hear You*, 1974, probably did little to reassure gay youth struggling with their identity. The erotic pulp market poured out novels, but their general quality deteriorated as they tried to compete with the now readily available visual pornography. Midwood Books managed to maintain some degree of literary integrity, and Surree made a last effort at respectability with its short-lived Blueboy Library. Pulp writers of note during the decade included William J. Lambert III (*Valley of the Damned*, 1971, the first gay werewolf novel; as Chad Stuart: *E-Mission*, 1974, a spy thriller); Jerry Murray (as Murray Montague: *Security Risk*, 1976); Roland Graeme, aka Michael Scott (*Private Passions* and *Gay Psycho*, both 1976); and Gordon Hoban (as Tom Hardy: *Adventures of a High School Hunk*, 1976–82, and the very funny caper *Cock Stealers*, 1978). Peter Tuesday Hughes, who published thirty-four novels, 1968–78, merits examination.

It was a rich ten years. For gay baby boomers it probably remains a vital part of their reading experience. Then into their thirties, they joined the eleventh Gay Pride march in New York on June 28, 1981, with much to be proud about. The *New York Times* ran an announcement that morning for them listing the route and the time. Five days later, July 3, the newspaper published an article under the headline "Rare Cancer Seen in Homosexuals," and the world changed.

GENERAL BIBLIOGRAPHY

Bibliographies, Guides and Encyclopedias

Austen, Roger. *Playing the Game: The Homosexual Novel in America.* Indianapolis: Bobbs–Merrill, 1977.

Cory, Donald Webster. "Check List of Novels and Dramas"; "A Check List of Literature." *The Homosexual in America: A Subjective Approach.* 3rd ed. New York: Arno, 1975. 296–315; 296–323 [sic].

Garber, Eric, and Lyn Paleo. *Uranian Worlds: A Guide to Alternative Sexuality in Science Fiction, Fantasy, and Horror.* 2nd ed. Boston: G. K. Hall, 1990.

Garde, Noel I. *The Homosexual in Literature: A Chronological Bibliography c.700 B.C.–1958.* New York: Village, 1959.

Gerstner, David A., ed. *Routledge International Encyclopedia of Queer Culture.* New York: Routledge, 2006.

Gunn, Drewey Wayne. *The Gay Male Sleuth in Print and Film: A History and Annotated Bibliography.* Lanham, Md.: Scarecrow, 2005. 2nd ed., 2013.

Hawley, John C., ed. *LGBTQ America Today: An Encyclopedia.* 3 vols. Westport, Conn.: Greenwood, 2009.

Hogan, Steve, and Lee Hudson. *Completely Queer: The Gay and Lesbian Encyclopedia.* New York: Holt, 1998.

Levin, James. *The Gay Novel: The Male Homosexual Image in America.* New York: Irvington, 1983. Rev. *The Gay Novel in America.* New York: Garland, 1991.

Malinokski, Sharon, ed. *Gay & Lesbian Literature.* Detroit: St. James, 1994.

Nelson, Emmanuel S., ed. *Contemporary Gay American Novelists: A Bio-Bibliographical Critical Sourcebook.* Westport, Conn.: Greenwood, 1993.

Norman, Tom. *American Gay Erotic Paperbacks: A Bibliography.* Burbank, Calif.: Privately printed, 1994.

Pendergast, Tom, and Sara Pendergast, eds. *Gay & Lesbian Literature.* Vol. 2. Detroit: St. James, 1998.

Summers, Claude J., ed. *The Gay and Lesbian Literary Heritage: A Reader's Companion to the Writers and Their Works, from Antiquity to the Present.* New York: Holt, 1995. Rev. Online.

Young, Ian. *The Male Homosexual in Literature: A Bibliography.* 2nd ed. Metuchen, N.J.: Scarecrow, 1982.

Historical and Cultural Overviews

Baim, Tracy, ed. *Out and Proud in Chicago: An Overview of the City's Gay Community.* Chicago: Surrey, 2008.

Berube, Allan. *Coming Out under Fire: The History of Gay Men and Women in World War II.* New York: Free Press, 1990.

Bronski, Michael. *A Queer History of the United States.* Boston: Beacon, 2011.

Büssing, Sabine. *Of Captive Queens and Holy Panthers: Prison Fiction and Male Homoerotic Experience.* Frankfurt am Main: Peter Lang, 1990.

Carter, David. *Stonewall: The Riots That Sparked the Gay Revolution.* New York: St. Martin's, 2004.

Chauncey, George. *Gay New York: Gender, Urban Culture, and the Making of the Gay Male World, 1890–1940.* New York: BasicBooks, 1994.

De la Croix, St. Sukie. *Chicago Whispers: A History of LGBT Chicago before Stonewall.* Madison: University of Wisconsin Press, 2012.

Eaklor, Vicki L. *Queer America: A GLBT History of the 20th Century.* Westport, Conn.: Greenwood, 2008.

Faderman, Lillian, and Stuart Timmons. *Gay L.A.: A History of Sexual Outlaws, Power Politics, and Lipstick Lesbians.* New York: Basic Books, 2006.

Fone, Byrne R. S. *A Road to Stonewall: Male Homosexuality and Homophobia in English and American Literature, 1750–1969.* New York: Twayne, 1995.

Gunn, Drewey Wayne, ed. *The Golden Age of Gay Fiction.* Albion, N.Y.: MLR, 2009.

———, and Jaime Harker, eds. *1960s Gay Pulp Fiction: The Misplaced Heritage.* Amherst: University of Massachusetts Press, 2013.

Hirshman, Linda. *Victory: The Triumphant Gay Revolution.* New York: HarperCollins, 2012.

Kaiser, Charles. *The Gay Metropolis, 1940–1996.* Boston: Houghton Mifflin, 1997.

Katz, Jonathan Ned. *Love Stories: Sex between Men before Homosexuality.* Chicago: University of Chicago, 2001.

Kennedy, Hubert. *The Ideal Gay Man: The Story of Der Kreis.* New York: Harrington Park, 1999.

Sarotte, Georges-Michel. *Like a Brother, like a Lover: Male Homosexuality in the American Novel and Theater from Herman Melville to James Baldwin.* Trans. Richard Miller. Garden City, N.Y.: Anchor, 1978.

Shand-Tucci, Douglas. *The Crimson Letter: Harvard, Homosexuality, and the Shaping of American Culture.* New York: St. Martin's, 2003.

Stryker, Susan, and Jim Van Buskirk. *Gay by the Bay: A History of Queer Culture in the San Francisco Bay Area.* San Francisco: Chronicle Books, 1996.

Woods, Gregory. *A History of Gay Literature: The Male Tradition.* New Haven, Conn.: Yale University Press, 1998.

Further Reading

Baim, Tracy, ed. *Gay Press, Gay Power: The Growth of LGBT Community Newspapers in America.* Chicago: Prairie Avenue, 2012.

Bronski, Michael. *Culture Clash: The Making of Gay Sensibility.* Boston: South End, 1984.

Cole, Shaun. *"Don We Now Our Gay Apparel": Gay Men's Dress in the Twentieth Century.* Oxford: Berg, 2000.

Friedman, Mack. *Strapped for Cash: A History of American Hustler Culture.* Los Angeles: Alyson, 2003.

Gifford, James. *Dayneford's Library: American Homosexual Writing, 1900–1913.* Amherst: University of Mississippi Press, 1995.

Hagius, Hugh, ed. *Swasarnt Nerf's Gay Guides for 1949.* New York: Bibliogay, 2010.

Hunter, John Francis. *The Gay Insider: A Hunter's Guide to New York and a Thesaurus of Phallic Lore.* New York: Olympia (Other Traveller), 1971.

_____. *The Gay Insider USA.* New York: Stonehill, 1972.

Kinsey, Alfred C., et al. *Sexual Behavior in the Human Male.* Philadelphia: Saunders, 1949.

Mayne, Xavier. *The Intersexes: History of Similisexualism as a Problem in Social Life.* 1908. New York: Arno, 1975.

Nissen, Axel. *Manly Love: Romantic Friendship in American Fiction.* Chicago: University of Chicago Press, 2009.

Robb, Graham. *Strangers: Homosexual Love in the Nineteenth Century.* New York: Norton, 2003.

Slide, Anthony. *Lost Gay Novels: A Reference Guide to Fifty Works from the First Half of the Twentieth Century.* New York: Harrington Park, 2003.

Smith, Patricia Juliana, ed. *The Queer Sixties.* New York: Routledge, 1999.

Streitmatter, Rodger. *Unspeakable: The Rise of the Gay and Lesbian Press in America.* Boston: Faber & Faber, 1995.

Stryker, Susan. *Queer Pulp: Perverted Passions from the Golden Age of the Paperback.* San Francisco: Chronicle Books, 2001.

Tippins, Sherill. *February House.* Boston: Houghton Mifflin, 2005.

Wald, Alan M. *American Night: The Literary Left in the Era of the Cold War.* Chapel Hill: University of North Carolina Press, 2012.

_____. *Exiles from a Future Time: The Forging of the Mid-Twentieth Century Literary Left.* Chapel Hill: University of North Carolina Press, 2002.

_____. *Trinity of Passion: The Literary Left and the Antifascist Crusade.* Chapel Hill: University of North Carolina Press, 2007.

Woods, Gregory. *Articulate Flesh: Male Homo-Eroticism and Modern Poetry.* New Haven: Yale University Press, 1987.

Anthologies

Bronski, Michael, ed. *Pulp Friction: Uncovering the Golden Age of Gay Male Pulps.* New York: St. Martin's Griffin, 2003.

Carbado, Devon W., et al., eds. *Black like Us: A Century of Lesbian, Gay, and Bisexual African American Fiction.* San Francisco: Cleis, 2002.

Cory, Donald Webster, ed. *21 Variations on a Theme.* New York: Greenberg, 1953.

Fone, Byrne R. S., ed. *The Columbia Anthology of Gay Literature: Readings from Western Antiquity to the Present Day.* New York: Columbia University Press, 1998.

Gifford, James J., ed. *Glances Backward: An Anthology of American Homosexual Writing, 1830–1920.* Peterborough, Ont.: Broadview, 2007.

Griffith, E. V., ed. *In Homage to Priapus.* San Diego: Greenleaf Classic, 1970.

Mirchell, Mark, and David Leavitt, eds. *Pages Passed from Hand to Hand: The Hidden Tradition of Homosexual Literature in English from 1748 to 1914.* Boston: Houghton Mifflin, 1997.

Nissen, Axel, ed. *The Romantic Friendship Reader: Love Stories between Men in Victorian America.* Boston: Northeastern University Press, 2003.

Wright, Stephen, ed. *Different: An Anthology of Homosexual Short Stories.* New York: Bantam, 1974.

INDEX

References are to entries numbers

adaptations (film, stage, television) 7, 14, 18, 28, 30, 31, 33, 39, 40, 49, 50, 62, 64, 70, 76, 85, 89, 97, 106, 119, 120, Postscript
The Adventures of Harry Chess (Jay) 105
Advise and Consent (Drury) 50
African Americans 7, 11, 15, 16, 37, 48, 49, 67, 83, 85, 86, 95–97, 133
Aldyne, Nathan (Michael McDowell, Dennis Schuetz) Postscript
All Thy Conquests (Hayes) 34
Always Love a Stranger (Davis) 83
American Colony (Brackett) 12
Amory, Richard 106
Anderson, Sherwood 6
Andrews, Terry (George Selden) Postscript
Andros, Phil (Samuel M. Steward) 119
Another Country (Baldwin) 33, 67
Anthony in the Nude (Brinig) 13
Apollo Sleeps (Greenwood) 24
arcadian fiction 1, 3, 106
Arion (Alan Campbell) 26
Armory, Ricardo 106
The Asbestos Diary (Dukahz) 99
Asprey, Robert B. 70
athletics 52, Postscript

Babel-17 (Delany) 103
Baird, Thomas 86
Baldwin, James 33, 67
Ballad of the Sad Café (McCullers) 28
Banis, Victor J. 105
bar and bath culture 7, 9, 11, 15–17, 21, 24, 30, 35–38, 46–49, 63, 65, 67, 71, 82, 83, 87, 89, 101, 105, 112, 119, 121, 128, 130
Barbara (Newman) 120
Barbee, Jim 55
Barnes, Djuana 9, 22
Barr, James (James Barr Fugaté) 48
Baxt, George 104
Beast in View (Millar) 31
Behind These Walls (Teale) 57
Benderson, Bruce 128
The Benefactor (Sontag) 82

Bentley, Robert Postscript
Beresford, Marcus 51
Bertram Cope's Year (Fuller) 6
The Better Angel (Brown) 19
Beyond the Street (Calmer) 23
The Big Clock (Fearing) 33
The Big Nickelodeon (Wolff) 64
The Big Sleep (Chandler) 14
bisexuality 1, 2, 7, 15, 28–31, 33, 41, 45, 51, 53, 58, 62, 64, 83, 96
The Bitterweed Path (Phillips) 41
blackmail 14, 21, 38, 44, 50
Blade (Neel Bate) 119
Blechman, Burt 88
The Blind Bow-Boy (Van Vechten) 7
Blumley, Andrew 130
Bolton, Isabel 46
Bourjaily, Vance 37
Box, Edgar (Gore Vidal) 38
Boyle, Kay 9
Boys and Girls Together (Goldman) 91
Brackett, Charles 12, 30
Bradley, Marion Zimmer Postscript
Braly, Malcolm 108
Break-Up (Schiddel) 63
Brinig, Myron 13
Brooks, Richard Introduction
The Brotherhood of Velvet (Karp) 50
Brown, Charles Brockden Introduction
Brown, Foreman 19
Bruce, Kennilworth 21
Burns, John Horne 37
Burroughs, William S. 39, 76, 117
Burt, Nathaniel 113
Burwell, Basil 68
Butterfly Man (Levenson) 24

Cain, James M. 58
Cain's Book (Trocchi) 76
Caldwell, Joseph Postscript
Callboy (Lawton) 127
Calmer, Edgar 23
camp and satire 9, 11, 13, 22, 25, 62, 63, 69, 71, 100, 104–06, 120, 126
Campbell, Alan 26
Capote, Truman 40, 62
The Captain (Thacher) 55

Carney, William 121
Carpenter, Carleton Postscript
Carpenter, Don 57, 108
Carson, David Sunset Postscript
Case, Ensan Postscript
Cassill, R. V. 92
Cast the First Stone (Himes) 57
Chandler, Raymond 14, 51
Cheever, John Postscript
Chester, Alfred 82, 110
Chicago and vicinity 6, 24, 35, 109
Child of the Sun (Onstott & Horner) 107
Children of Light (Sykes) 50
Chocolates for Breakfast (Moore) 64
A Choice of Passions (Young) 83
The Christmas Tree (Bolton) 46
The City and the Pillar (Vidal) 38
City Crimes (Thompson) 2
City of Night (Rechy) 87, 101, 110, 119
Clifton, Bud (David Stacton) 70
Coe, Tucker (Donald E. Westlake) 133
Cohen, Alfred J. 2
Cole, Jerry 25
Coleman, Lonnie 65
Colton, James (Joseph Hansen) 96
coming out fiction 4, 10, 16, 18, 19, 21, 23, 25, 26, 36, 43, 56, 124, 125
Concert Pitch (Paul) 27
Cooper, James Fenimore Introduction
Coriolan, John 114
Cory, Donald Webster (Edward Sagarin) Introduction, 39, 66
Crane, Clarkson 8
Creekmore, Hubert 41
The Crippled Muse (Wheeler) 38
Cromwell, John 59
Cruising (Walker) 133
Curzon, Daniel Postscript

Dakota, Dan Postscript
Dale, Alan (Alfred J. Cohen) Introduction, 2
d'Arcangelo, Angelo (Josef Bush) Introduction, 120
The Dark Tunnel (Millar/Macdonald) 31

189

David, Richard Postscript
Davis, Fitzroy 18
Davis, Roger 83
De Forrest, Michael 45
Death in the Fifth Position (Box/Vidal) 38
The Deep Six (Dibner) 49
The Deer Park (Mailer) 39
Delany, Samuel R. 103
Delligan, William Postscript
The Demon of Noon (Merrick) 36
Dennis, Patrick 66
Destination Nowhere (Lockwood) 101
The Detective (Thorp) 85
Deutsch, Deborah 58
The Devil in Bucks County (Schiddel) 63
The Devil's Profession (O'Neil) 68
Diamonds in the Sky (Orr) 68
Dibner, Martin 49
Disch, Thomas M. Postscript
Distinguished Air (McAlmon) 9
The Divided Path (Kent) 43
Doliner, Roy 68
Donovan, John 123
Doremus, Thomas 80
Dos Passos, John 15
The Double Door (Keogh) 51
Dowd, Harrison 45
Down There on a Visit (Isherwood) 62
drag 15, 29, 40, 48, 52, 56, 71, 87, 89
Dromgoole, Will Allen 1
The Drowning Pool (Macdonald) 31
Drury, Allen 50
Dukahz, Casimir 99
dysfunctional families 2, 26, 33, 40, 44, 46, 51, 54, 85, 91, 123

Each in His Darkness (Green & Green) 79
Empire Star (Delany) 103
End as a Man (Willingham) 34
The End of My Life (Bourjaily) 37
Entrapment (McCoy) 94
Eustace Chisholm and the Works (Purdy) 109
expatriate fiction 4, 9, 12, 22, 24, 27, 29, 33, 35, 36, 38, 46, 47, 51, 54, 58, 59, 62, 67, 78, 81, 82, 98, 111, 113, 117, 129
The Exquisite Corpse (Chester) 110

Fadeout (Hansen) 96
The Fall of Valor (Jackson) 30
Faulkner, William 14, 41
Fearing, Kenneth 33
Fedoroff, Alexander 77
Fey, Edwin 90
Finistere (Peters) 54
Fisher, Peter Postscript
Flaming Heart (Deutsch) 58
The Flamingos (Somerlott) 111
Flick, Grace 42
Flinders, Karl (Milton Saul) 33
The Flutter of an Eyelid (Brinig) 13
The Folded Leaf (Maxwell) 32
A Fool in the Forest (Burwell) 68
Footsteps on the Stairs (Brinig) 13

For the Pleasure of His Company (Stoddard) 3
Ford, Charles Henri 22, 76
Forest Fire (Stout) 20
42nd Street (Ropes) 18
Fouts, Denham 38, 40, 62
Fraden, Harlow 51, 58
Friedman, Sanford 98
Fruit of the Loon (Armory) 106
Fugaté, James Barr 48
Fuller, Henry Blake 6

The Gallery (Burns) 37
The Gaudy Image (Talsman) 71
The Gay American (Gingerich) 81
The Gay Detective (Rand) 81
The Gay Flesh (Houston) 83
Gay Vet (Hossannah/Ramp) 95
The Gay Year (De Forrest) 45
Gerrold, David Postscript
The Ghost of Henry James (Plante) 129
Gingerich, William 81
Giovanni's Room (Baldwin) 33, 67
The Girl with the Golden Yo-Yo (Schiddel) 63
Goat Song (Yerby) 107
Goldie (Bruce) 21
Goldman, William 91
The Good and Bad Weather (Schiddel) 63
Good Times Coming (Schiddel) 63
Good Times, Bad Times (Kirkwood) 115
Good-bye My Lover (Williams/Banis) 105
Goodman, Alexander (George Haimsohn) 83
Goodman, Paul 53
Goodwin, John 59, 62
gothic 28, 40, Postscript
Gov't Inspected Meat (Rader) 97
A Grain of Sand (Cromwell) 59
graphic novel 105
Green, Anne 79
Green, Julian 79
Greenwood, Daphne 24
The Grotto (Stone) 46
Gysin, Brion 33, 62, 76

Haimsohn, George 83
Hall, Lynn Postscript
Hall, Richard Postscript
Hamilton, Wallace Postscript
Hammett, Dashiell 14
Handsome Is... (Goodman/Haimsohn) 83
Hang-Up (Colton/Hansen) 96
Hansen, Joseph 45, 96
Hard Rain Falling (Carpenter) 108
Hardy, Tom (Gordon Hoban) 62, Postscript
Harrington, William 132
Harvey, Reginald 73
Hawthorne, Nathaniel Introduction
Hayes, Alfred 34
Herlihy, James Leo 97
The Hero Continues (Windham) 78
A Hidden Hunger (Raul) 93

Highsmith, Patricia 14, 51
Hilaire, Frank Postscript
Himes, Chester 57
historical fiction 42, 70, 102, 107, 116
Hobson, Laura Postscript
Hogan, Lou Rand 81
Holland, Isabelle Postscript
Holleran, Andrew Postscript
Home to Harlem (McKay) 11
Horner, Lance 107
Hossannah, Ross (James H. Ramp) 95
The House of the Vampire (Viereck) 5
Houston, Joe Leon 83
Howe, Julia Ward Introduction
Howell, William Dean Introduction
Hudson, John Paul Postscript
Hughes, Peter Tuesday Postscript
hustling 9, 21, 44, 74, 83, 87, 93, 97, 119, 127

I'll Get There. It Better Be Worth the Trip (Donovan) 123
The Idols and the Prey (Goodwin) 59
The Immortal (Ross) 64
Imre (Prime Stevenson) 4
In a Yellow Wood (Vidal) 38
The Incident (Rivette) 55
Infants of the Spring (Thurman) 11
Inside Daisy Clover (Lambert) 64
The Invisible Glass (Wahl) 49
Isherwood, Christopher 40, 42, 62, 87
The Island of Beautiful Things (Dromgoole) 1
The Island of Tranquil Delights (Stoddard) 3

The Jacklove Affair (Menegas) 118
Jackson, Charles 30
Jade in Aries (Coe/Westlake) 133
James, Henry Introduction, 129
Jay, A. 105
Joseph and His Friend (Taylor) 1
The Joy Spot (Andros/Steward) 119
The Judgment of Paris (Vidal) 38

Kahm, Harold S. 25
Karp, David 50
Kastle, Herbert D. 72
Keene, Hadrian 125
Kent, Nial 43
Keogh, Theodora 33, 51
Kerouac, Jack 38, 76
King, Bruce (Avery Willard) 112
King, Frank Postscript
Kirkwood, James 97, 115
The Knightly Quest (Williams) 100
Knock on Any Door (Motley) 35
Known Homosexual (Colton/Hansen) 96
Koch, Stephen 122
Koptic Court (Kastle) 72
Kramer, Larry Postscript

Lambert, Gavin 62, 64, 87
Lamkin, Speed 40
Lanham, Edwin 9
Last Exit to Brooklyn (Selby) 89

Index

The Last of the Southern Winds (Loovis) 82
Latitudes of Love (Doremus) 80
Lawton, Jeff 127
Leather (Vanden) 121
Leather Ad (Townsend) 121
The Leather Queens (Vanden) 121
Leopards in the Garden (Burt) 113
Let Noon Be Fair (Motley) 35
Levenson, Lew 24
Leveridge, Ralph 55
Linden, Geoffrey Postscript
list-making 11, 19, 21, 30, 43, 44, 48, 51, 103
Listen, the Loon Sings... (Amory) 106
Little, Jay 56
Lockwood, Tom 101
Logan (Voelcker) 124
London, Jack Introduction
Lonergan, Wayne 33, 51
Loovis, David 82
Lord Love Us (Statton) 37
The Lord Won't Mind (Merrick) 36
Loring, Frederick Introduction, 1
Los Angeles 13, 14, 15, 29, 38, 58, 62, 87, 93, 105
The Lost Weekend (Jackson) 30
The Love Smeller (Ramp) 95
The Loving Couple (Rowans/Dennis) 66

MacCown, Eugene 47
Macdonald, Ross 31
MacLaren, Mary 58
Madame (Selby) 61
The Mail Boat (Randolph) 58
Mailer, Norman 39
Mainside (Mandel) 85
Making Do (Goodman) 53
The Maltese Falcon (Hammett) 14
Malzberg, Barry N. Postscript
The Man from C.A.M.P. (Holliday/Banis) 105
The Man Who Never Changed (Selby) 61
Mandel, Paul 85
Mann, Klaus 42
March, Joseph M. 7
A Marriage below Zero (Dale) 2
Marvin, Ronn 64
Maupin, Armistead Postscript
Maxwell, William 32
Maybe—Tomorrow (Little) 56
Mayer, Martin 75
Mayne, Xavier 4
McAlmon, Robert 9
McCoy, R. 94
McCullers, Carson 28
McIntosh, Harlan 29
McKay, Claude 11
McKaye, Richard (Richard K. Brunner) 64
Meaker, Marijane 51
Meeker, Richard 19
Meet Me at the Baths (Benderson) 128
A Meeting by the River (Isherwood) 62
Melville, Herman Introduction, 2, 3, 49

Memoirs of Hadrian (Yourcenar & Flick) 42
Menegas, Peter 118
Merrick, Gordon 33, 36
The Messenger (Wright) 83
Middle Ground (Zilinsky) 116
Midnight Cowboy (Herlihy) 97
Miles, Richard 97
military and military school fiction 1, 4, 28, 31, 34, 48, 49, 65, 85, 101, 109, Postscript; *see also* war fiction
Millar, Kenneth 31
Millar, Margaret 31
Miller, Merle Postscript
Mills, Carley 33, 78
The Missolonghi Manuscript (Prokosch) 102
Monette, Paul Postscript
Moore, Pamela 64
Motley, Willard 35
Mr. Ballerina (Marvin) 64
murder 5, 14, 15, 20, 21, 24, 28, 31, 33, 35, 36, 38, 44, 46, 50, 51, 58, 67, 81, 83, 85, 104, 105, 115, 131, 133
Murphy, Dennis 49
music world 7, 19, 27, 57, 67, 75
Musser, Benjamin 10
mystery and crime fiction 14, 31, 33, 50, 51, 81, 85, 96, 104, 132, 133, Postscript

Nabokov, Vladimir 84, 99, 110
Nader, George Postscript
The Naked and the Dead (Mailer) 39
The Naked Heart (Weldon) 60
Naked Lunch (Burroughs) 76
Naked to the Night (Raul) 93
narrative poem 7
A Nearness of Evil (Mills) 33
Nelson, Charles Postscript
Never the Same Again (Tesch) 54
New York 2, 5, 6, 9, 11, 15–18, 21–25, 29, 30, 33, 36, 38, 43, 45, 46, 48, 51, 61, 63, 65–67, 72–76, 79, 83, 86, 88, 89, 91, 97, 101, 104, 114, 126, 130, 131, 133
Newman, Frank (Sam Abrams) 120
The Night Air (Dowd) 45
Night Watch (Koch) 122
Nightwood (Barnes) 22
Niles, Blair 11, 16
Noon and Night (Keene) 125
Nugent, Richard Bruce 11
Numbers (Rechy) 87

The Occasional Man (Barr) 48
O'Connor, Flannery 60
Oh Dear! (Rebow) 69
The Old Masters (Baird) 86
On the Yard (Braly) 108
O'Neil, Russell 68
Onstott, Kyle 107
Orr, Mary 68
The Oscar (Sale) 64
The Other Side of the Night (Schiddel) 63
Other Voices, Other Rooms (Capote) 40

Packer, Vin 51
Pale Fire (Nabokov) 84
The Panther's Feast (Asprey) 70
paperback originals. pulps Introduction, 50, 51, 62, 64, 74, 81, 83, 93, 95, 96, 101, 103, 105–107, 112, 114, 119–121, 124, 125, 127, 127, 128
Parents' Day (Goodman) 53
Park Beat (Harvey) 73
Parties (Van Vechten) 7
Passion Expert (Kahm) 25
Pathetic Symphony (Mann) 42
Paul, Eliot 27
pederasty and ephebism 6, 35, 54, 78, 80, 93, 99, 113, 116, 125, Postscript
Peters, Fritz 54
Phillips, Thomas Hal 41
Picano, Felice Postscript
Pictures of Fidelman (Malamud) 98
Plante, David 129
Portrait of the Damned (McKaye) 64
The President (Cassill) 92
Prezzi, Wilma M. 58
pride and liberation 19, 21, 37, 62, Postscript
Prime Stevenson, Edward 4
prison fiction 57, 98, 107, 116, Postscript
Prokosch, Frederic 102
The Promising Young Men (Sklar) 52
prostitution 21, 38, 44, 74, 83, 87, 93, 97, 119
Purdy, James 109
Pyle, Howard 2

Quatrefoil (Barr) 48
A Queer Kind of Death (Baxt) 104
Quicksilver (Davis) 18

Rader, Dotson 39, 97
Ramp, James H. 95
Rand, Lou (Lou Rand Hogan) 81
Randolph, Alexander 58
Raul, K. B. 93
The Real Thing (Carney) 121
Rebow, Milton 69
Rechy, John 87
Redburn (Melville) 2
Reflections in a Golden Eye (McCullers) 28
Remember Me (Stacton) 70
Rice, Anne Postscript
Rico, Don 105
Ring-around-the-Rosy (Andros/Steward) 119
Rivette, Marc 55
Robinson, Frank M. Postscript
Ronns, Edward (Edward S. Aarons) 50
Ropes, Bradford 18
Rosenthal, Irving 76
Ross, Walter 64
Roth, Samuel 9, 10
Rowans, Virginia (Patrick Dennis) 66
Rubin, Marc Postscript
Rumaker, Michael Postscript
rural life 1, 6, 10, 13, 20, 39, 44, 48, 50, 56, 58, 62, 63, 90, 92, 94, 95, 118, 127, 132

Sale, Richard 64
Sam (Coleman) 65
San Francisco and Bay Area 3, 8, 13, 14, 26, 58, 81, 128
Sanctity (Selby) 126
A Sand Fortress (Coriolan) 114
A Scarlet Pansy (Scully) 9
Schiddel, Edmund 63
school and university fiction 1, 6, 8, 19, 23, 26, 32, 53, 54, 56, 92, 93, 115
science fiction and fantasy 5, 84, 100, 103, Postscript
Scoppettone, Sandra Postscript
Scortia, Thomas N. Postscript
Scott, Michael Postscript
Screw 22 (Lawton) 127
Scully, Robert 9
Secrets of a Society Doctor (Cole/Kahm) 25
Selby, Dennis 126
Selby, Hubert, Jr. 89
Selby, John 61
The Sergeant (Murphy) 49
Seventh Summer (Keene) 125
Sheeper (Rosenthal) 76
Ship's Company (Coleman) 65
The Side of Angels (Fedoroff) 77
The Siege of Innocence (MacCown) 47
Silverberg, Robert Postscript
Singermann (Brinig) 13
The Single Man (Isherwood) 62
Skir, Leo Postscript
Sklar, George 52
Somerlott, Robert 111
Somewhere between the Two (Little) 56
Song of Aaron (Amory) 106
Song of the Loon (Amory) 106, 121, 127
Sons of a Beach (Lockwood) 101
Sontag, Susan 82, 110
Sookey (d'Arcangelo) 120
South 20, 28, 34, 40, 41, 56, 57, 60, 61, 71, 79, 82, 83, 85, 95, 97, 100, 101
South-Sea Idyls (Stoddard) 3
Stacton, David 70
The Star Pit (Delany) 103
Starborn (Arion) 26
The State Department Murders (Ronns) 50
Stations (Blechman) 88
Statton, A. M. P. 37
Steinberg, S. (John Saul) Postscript
Stevenson, Richard Postscript
Steward, Samuel 119
Stoddard, Charles Warren 3
Stone, Grace Zaring 46
Stout, Rex 20
Strange Brother (Niles) 16

The Strange Confession of Monsieur Mountcairn (Musser) 10
Strange Marriage (Colton/Hansen) 96
The Strange Ones (Travis) 74
Stranger in the Land (Thomas) 44
Street of Stairs (Tavel) 117
The Strumpet Wind (Merrick) 36
$tud (Andros/Steward) 119
suicide 2, 16, 49, 50, 66, 85, 91, 92, 96
Summer Awakening (King/Willard) 112
Summer in Sodom (Fey) 90
Swann, Thomas Burnett Postscript
Swicegood, Thomas L. P. Postscript
Swing Low, Sweet Harriet (Baxt) 104
Sykes, Gerald 50

Talsman, William 71
Tavel, Ronald 76, 117
Taylor, Bayard Introduction, 1
Teale, Christopher 57
Tell Me How Long the Train's Been Gone (Baldwin) 67
Tellier, Andrew 17
Tesch, Gerald 54
Thacher, Russell 55
That Cold Day in the Park (Miles) 97
theater and film milieu 3, 15, 18, 24, 38, 39, 45, 63, 64, 67, 68, 74, 78, 91, 92, 112
This Finer Shadow (McIntosh) 29
This Man Is My Brother (Brinig) 13
Thomas, Ward (Edward T. McNamara) 44
Thompson, George 2
Thurman, Wallace 11
Tiger in the Garden (Lamkin) 40
Tony (Dennis) 66
Topsy and Evil (Baxt) 104
Totempole (Friedman) 98
Townsend, Larry 121
Travis, Ben 74
Trial (Harrington) 132
Trocchi, Alexander 76, 110
Truck Stop (Lawton) 127
Truscott, Lucian Postscript
Twain, Mark Introduction
Twilight Men (Tellier) 17
Twin (Blumley) 130
The Twisted Heart (MacLaren) 58
Two College Friends (Loring) 1
Two People (Windham) 78
Tyler, Parker 22

U.S.A. (Dos Passos) 15, 34, 37
The Ugly Club (Lockwood) 101

The Value of Nothing (Weitz) 131
Van Vechten, Carl 7

Vanden, Dirk 121
Verga, Vincent Postscript
Vidal, Gore 9, 22, 37, 38, 43, 62, 82, Postscript
Viereck, George Sylvester 5, 57
A View of Fuji (Goodwin) 59
The Violent Bear It Away (O'Connor) 60
Voelcker, Hunce 124
A Voice That Fills the House (Mayer) 75

Wahl, Loren (Lorenzo Magdalena) 49
Walk on Water (Leveridge 55
Walker, Gerald 133
Wallant, Edward Lewis 67
war fiction 1, 9, 15, 20, 36, 37, 38, 39, 49, 55, 98, 127, Postscript; see also military fiction
Warren, Patricia Nell Postscript
Washington, D.C. 15, 50, 77, 112
Weitz, John 131
The Welcome (Creekmore) 41
Weldon, John Lee 60
western 106, Postscript
The Western Shore (Crane) 8
Westlake, Donald E. 133
Wexler, Warren Postscript
Wheeler, Hugh 38
Whisper His Sin (Packer/Meaker) 51
White, Edmund Postscript
Whitmore, George Postscript
Why Are We in Vietnam? (Mailer) 39
The Why-Not (Banis) 105
The Wild Party (March) 7
Wild Strawberry Patch (Ramp) 95
Willard, Avery 111
Williams, Tennessee 33, 40, 50, 63, 77, 78, 82, 97, 100
Willingham, Calder 34
Wilson, Carter Postscript
Windham, Donald 78
Winesburg, Ohio (Anderson) 6
Wister, Owen Introduction
Wolff, Marietta 64
The World in the Evening (Isherwood) 62
The Wreck of the Cassandra (Prokosch) 102
Wright, Charles 83

Yerby, Frank Introduction, 107
Young and Evil (Ford & Tyler) 22
Young John (Barbee) 55
Young Man Waiting (Doliner) 68
young adult novels 51, 123, Postscript
Young, Seth 83
Yourcenar, Marguerite 42

Zilinsky, Ursula 116

www.ingramcontent.com/pod-product-compliance
Lightning Source LLC
Chambersburg PA
CBHW081558300426
44116CB00015B/2928